RENAISSANCE WOMAN

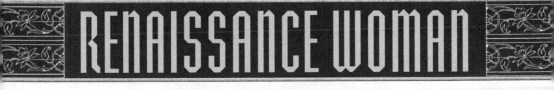

RENAISSANCE WOMAN

THE LIFE OF
VITTORIA COLONNA

RAMIE TARGOFF

FARRAR, STRAUS AND GIROUX
NEW YORK
•

Farrar, Straus and Giroux
175 Varick Street, New York 10014

Published in 2018 by Farrar, Straus and Giroux
First paperback edition, 2019

Owing to limitations of space, illustration credits may be found on pages 341–342.

The Library of Congress has cataloged the hardcover edition as follows:
Names: Targoff, Ramie, author.
Title: Renaissance woman : the life of Vittoria Colonna / Ramie Targoff.
Description: First edition. | New York : Farrar, Straus and Giroux, 2018. | Includes bibliographical
    references and index.
Identifiers: LCCN 2017036978 | ISBN 9780374140946 (hardcover)
Subjects: LCSH: Colonna, Vittoria, 1492–1547. | Poets, Italian—Early modern, 1500–1700—
    Biography.
Classification: LCC PQ4620 .T37 2017 | DDC 851/.3 [B]— dc23
LC record available at https://lccn.loc.gov/2017036978

Paperback ISBN: 978-0-374-53822-4

Designed by Abby Kagan

Our books may be purchased in bulk for promotional, educational, or business use.
Please contact your local bookseller or the Macmillan Corporate and Premium
Sales Department at 1-800-221-7945, extension 5442, or by e-mail
at MacmillanSpecialMarkets@macmillan.com.

www.fsgbooks.com
www.twitter.com/fsgbooks • www.facebook.com/fsgbooks

TO MY MOTHER, CHERI KAMEN TARGOFF

CONTENTS

A PLATE SECTION OF ILLUSTRATIONS FOLLOWS PAGE 150.

RENAISSANCE WOMAN

H IGH IN THE HILLS thirty miles to the east of Rome is the ancient town of Subiaco. Named for the artificial lakes that the emperor Nero created from the upper course of the Aniene River in order to build himself a sumptuous villa—the town's Latin name, Sublaqueum, literally means "under the lakes"—Subiaco was where Saint Benedict spent three years as a hermit in a cave before founding his first monastic community on the site in the early sixth century. Looking as if it had been carved directly into the cliffs, the monastery of San Benedetto lies at the top of a very long, treacherously narrow drive lined with beautiful woods. There are sweeping views of a verdant valley and gentle mountains in the distance.

Just down the hill from the Benedictine monastery on the same winding road is a second monastery, dedicated to Benedict's sister, Saint Scholastica. This was one of the twelve monasteries that Benedict founded in the area before leaving for the town of Cassino to the south. Here he finalized the Benedictine Rule, which laid out the exemplary asceticism that became the standard for the Western monastic tradition. Although less dramatic in its setting, the abbey of Saint Scholastica boasts three magnificent cloisters, the oldest of which dates back to the twelfth century. The monastery was renowned in the Middle Ages for its library, which had a famous scriptorium—a separate room where monks copied manuscripts—and it held ten thousand volumes by the year 1300. It was in the library of Saint Scholastica that Italy entered the world of print: in 1464, two German clerics, Arnold Pannartz and Konrad Sweynheym, crossed the Alps to set up a printing press in Subiaco, where they began to produce books using a technology that soon made the scriptorium obsolete.

It was also in this celebrated library—now located in a different part of the monastery—that I found myself on a sweltering summer day several years ago, facing a Benedictine monk who was handing me a file of precious letters and documents from the early 1500s. I had come to consult the archive of the Colonna family, which has been housed in Subiaco since 1996, when it was moved from Rome. The Colonna archive has almost a hundred thousand items dating from as early as the twelfth century, and the great majority of the holdings are personal letters. From the late Middle Ages through the early twentieth century, the Colonna ruled over much of the territory to the southeast of Rome in the area known as the Castelli Romani, dotted with the castles of the great Roman families. Within Rome, the family owned— and still owns today—a grand palace in the very heart of the city; its magnificent art gallery and selected apartments are open to the public on Saturday mornings.

My interest was in the poetry of one member of the family, Vittoria Colonna, who lived from 1490 to 1547. Among her many accomplishments, Vittoria was the very first woman in all of Italy to have a book of her poems appear in print. I had discovered her work while writing a book on Renaissance love poetry, and had been struck by the hundred or so sonnets that she addressed to her husband after his death. Given their emotional power and complexity, I was surprised to learn that she had subsequently abandoned love poetry altogether, and chosen to write only spiritual verse. In the sixteenth-century Italian books of her poetry that I had read at Harvard's Houghton Library—there are no complete translations of her poems available in English, and the only Italian edition, published in 1982, is out of print—I noticed that in the illustration on the title page of one edition she looked very much like a nun. I also noticed she was consistently called "divine." All of this intrigued me, and when I was in Rome some months later and learned that many of Vittoria's original letters were in a nearby archive, I decided to make the trip.

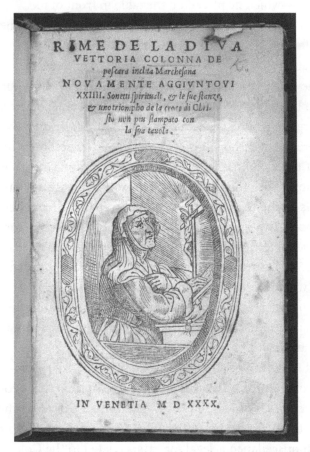

Title page of 1540 edition of Vittoria Colonna's *Rime* (Venice: Zoppino)
(© The British Library Board, May 9, 2017, General Reference Collection
DRT Digital Store 11426.aa.18)

There is no published or digital catalog of the Colonna archive, so I did not know exactly what I was looking for. But there was a rather primitive database on the library's computer, and I was able to do a search for

Vittoria. Two different call numbers came up, which I jotted down on a slip of scrap paper. The monk who had showed me into the room promptly copied the two numbers onto the palm of his hand—I offered to give him my piece of paper, but he said he preferred his method—and he disappeared into the archive. Some fifteen minutes later, he returned with two files—one a very thick set of documents, the other a single, large manuscript—which he placed on the table in front of me.

What I found in those files gave me my first glimpse of the extraordinary life Vittoria had led. I read her scribbled notes to her brother Ascanio about his fight with Pope Paul III over taxes on salt, and to her nephew Fabrizio about Ascanio's difficulties with the princess of Sulmona. I pored over her letter to the *padre generale* of the Capuchin monks urging him to treat the friars well and not serve them a low-quality bread, given how little they ate, and her response to the constables of the Colonna fief of Monte San Giovanni instructing them not to comply with the new system of taxation that the papal commissioner was trying to introduce. I found three pages from her personal account book, listing payments made and monies received for 1543 and 1544. I studied the inventory that her executor drew up the day after her death in 1547, listing the items left behind in her rooms at the nunnery in Rome where she had been living—I was particularly struck by the poignant mention of a single gold spoon. I read an irate letter from the same executor to her brother announcing his horror about the disposition of her wealth.

After I went through the quite substantial stack of letters—carefully taking photographs, with the monk's permission, so that I could study them *con calma*, as the Italians say, later on—I closed up the file and turned to the bound manuscript. Inside this rather grandiose volume filled with miscellaneous legal materials related to the Colonna family was the most elegant document I had seen so far: the wedding contract between Vittoria and her husband, Ferdinando Francesco I d'Avalos, Marquis of Pescara. (A marquis, or *marchese*, was the ruler of lands on the *marche*, the outskirts of territory controlled by the issuing authority, in this case the kingdom of Naples.) The contract was drawn up in Naples on June 13, 1507, when Vittoria and Ferrante (as Ferdinando was known) were both around seventeen years old. Written in a very beautiful hand, it was nearly twenty pages long, and specified, alternately in Latin and Italian, the terms of the dowry. There were many more details than I could possibly take in, and my Latin was very rusty, but I understood that the enormous sum of fourteen thousand ducats—twelve thousand in cash, and the remaining two thousand in portable property—was to be transferred to Ferrante from Vittoria's father, the great military captain Fabrizio Colonna, whom I knew only as the principal speaker in Niccolò Machiavelli's *The Art of War*.

A page from the marriage contract between Vittoria Colonna and Ferrante d'Avalos, signed June 13, 1507 (Reproduced courtesy of Archivio Colonna, Biblioteca del Monastero di Santa Scolastica, Subiaco, Italy)

Toward the end of the wedding contract I found a long list of the witnesses who were present at the signing. There were two princes, three dukes, two counts, one military captain, one bishop, and a number of ordinary citizens; all of them were men. The only woman who seemed to have been included was Ferrante's guardian, Costanza d'Avalos, Duchess of Francavilla, who had raised him since early childhood following the death of his parents. Costanza was one of the three signatories to the contract, along with Ferrante and Fabrizio. From my preliminary glance at the document, Vittoria played no part at all.

I left the archive in Subiaco that day with the desire to know much more about what I had seen—about the marriage between Vittoria and Ferrante, about her relations with her family, about her interactions with the world. I started to seek answers by reading what I could about Vittoria's life. This proved oddly frustrating. For such a celebrated woman— according to the great nineteenth-century historian of the Renaissance Jacob Burckhardt, she was "the most famous woman of Italy"—there was startlingly little written about her. The only respectable biography was by a German diplomat and historian named Alfred von Reumont and dated to 1881, before even an incomplete edition of Vittoria's letters had been published (this volume appeared in 1892, and has not been updated). Reumont's book, which I read in its Italian translation (it has never been translated into English), gave me the basic outline of Vittoria's life, but said very little about her personal thoughts or experience. The handful of other biographies, mostly written in the early decades of the twentieth century and using Reumont as their key source, added very little. I decided to tell her story myself.

The first thing I did was to map out the places Vittoria had lived and to try to visit them all. This proved more demanding than I could possibly have imagined, because she was unusually mobile for a woman of her period and class. Vittoria was born in the town of Marino, one of the Colonna's feudal holdings outside of Rome, where she lived in a heavily fortified castle. When her father became Grand Constable of the Spanish-run kingdom of Naples, the family moved to Naples, where they had a beautiful palace in the heart of the city. Upon marrying, she and her husband took up residence on the island of Ischia in the castle that belonged to his family, and also maintained a palace of their own in Naples. After Vittoria became a widow at the age of thirty-five, she lived for a short time in Rome, then moved back to Marino, and ultimately returned to Ischia, where she stayed for the better part of six years. After this time, she led a very itinerant existence. Vittoria always came and went from Rome but spent long stretches of time in the cities of Ferrara, Orvieto, and Viterbo. In each of these places, she lived as a lay guest in a convent.

Over the course of a few years, which included a sabbatical in Rome, I traveled to every single place that Vittoria had lived. In Ischia, I was able to stay in the castle that belonged to Ferrante's family, which is now a beautiful hotel. In Viterbo, I spent a few days in a convent very similar to the one she lived in, and I tried out the monastic life for myself (it was not for me). I walked through the neighborhood in Naples where she and Ferrante had their home—one of the commercial streets nearby is still called Via Vittoria Colonna—and I saw Ferrante's coffin draped in red velvet in the church of San Domenico Maggiore. I made multiple trips to Marino and the other Colonna properties in the Castelli Romani, and I developed a strong feeling for the isolated, dramatic landscapes that had shaped Vittoria's childhood. These were towns often built high up on rocks or cliffs, strategically positioned in relation to the valleys below. Vittoria never lived in the beautiful Tuscan cities that most of us imagine when we think about the Renaissance—there was nothing remotely comparable to Siena or Florence—nor did she live in elegant courts like Urbino or Mantua. Hers was a rough-and-tumble Italy, filled with feudal lords, mercenaries, and peasants.

Between trips to these often rather remote locations—there is no train service to almost any of Vittoria's homes—I worked in the various archives that held her papers. I spent time in the manuscript room of the Vatican Library with the poems she gave to Michelangelo, and in the Laurentian Library in Florence, wearing thick gloves, with a manuscript copy of the poems given by Vittoria's secretary to Marguerite d'Angoulême, queen of Navarre. I returned on multiple occasions to Subiaco. Most of my time was spent studying the several hundred letters—both in manuscripts and in the printed Italian volume from the late nineteenth century—that have survived of her correspondence. Very few of these letters had ever been translated into English, and a certain number of them had never been transcribed from their original handwritten form.

After all of my traveling around Italy, deciphering Vittoria's manuscripts and translating her letters and poems, a portrait of a fascinating person emerged. Here was a woman graced with all of the privileges the Renaissance had to offer. She came from one of the most powerful families in all of Italy, was extremely well educated, and had many castles. She had made an important marriage with the heir to one of the ruling Spanish families in the kingdom of Naples. She was a very talented poet and wrote beautiful sonnets that brought her great fame. She lived an immensely glamorous life as a young woman, regularly attending parties with royalty from all of Europe. She commissioned paintings from Michelangelo and Titian, and was on a first-name basis with the Holy Roman Emperor.

At the same time, Vittoria was a solitary person, who in her heart eschewed money and fame. She was profoundly religious and, once widowed, wanted to spend as much time as she could living alongside nuns. She was also adventurous in her faith and, despite her strong Catholic roots, became a firm believer in some of the core tenets of Protestantism. She resisted remarriage but developed very deep attachments, sometimes bordering on obsessions, with a number of charismatic men. She loved her family, and was loyal to her brother through his many political struggles at the same time that she avoided living with him or her other relatives whenever possible. She starved and beat herself as part of her religious penance, but also believed in her own election as one of God's chosen few. No sooner did I think I had her pegged than she slipped from my grasp.

There are still holes in Vittoria's archive—letters that have not been found, events that cannot be verified, conversations that left no traces. But enough has remained to conjure her up. As we begin to understand not only her extraordinary accomplishments as a poet and writer, but also her complexity as a person, we see in a new light what made the historical moment in which she lived so remarkable. For Vittoria embodied in a single person—in a single woman—many of the qualities that make this period so different from any other; she captured its simultaneous magic and strangeness. In our learning about Vittoria Colonna, the Renaissance comes to life anew.

THE VIEW FROM THE CLIFF

I N NOVEMBER 1525, a messenger from Milan bearing important news
crossed the Bay of Naples. He was heading for a castle on the island of
Ischia occupied by members of the d'Avalos family, one of the leading
households in the kingdom of Naples, which was ruled at the time by
the Spanish kings of Aragon. Ferdinand II, whose reign lasted only a
year, before his death in 1496, had given the castle to Iñigo II d'Avalos,
Marquis of Vasto, in gratitude for his distinguished military service in
the wars that Naples waged against the French. Following Iñigo's death
in 1503, his sister Costanza d'Avalos had become governor of the island.
It was unusual for a woman to be in such an official position of power—
she was even responsible for several important naval victories fought off
of the island's coast—but Costanza was an unusual woman.

As the boat approached Ischia, the messenger would have glimpsed
his destination, which still produces awe in visitors today. Perched
roughly three hundred feet above the sea on a volcanic rock, the castle
seemed completely inaccessible to the world below. The extremity of the
location was what had made it so desirable: having a castle high on a rock
in the middle of the sea so close to Naples was a significant military

advantage, and since the fifth century B.C.E., when the first fortress was built on the site, it had been occupied in turn by Romans, Visigoths, Arabs, Normans, and Swabians before becoming the property of the Spanish kings in the fifteenth century. The rock itself was rough and scorched, which, according to ancient legend, was a result of Zeus's punishment of the giant monster Typhon, who had threatened the gods by hurling rocks at the sky and breathing out fire. Zeus was said to have crushed Typhon by covering him with nothing less than Ischia itself, but the fires raging from the giant continued to burn and left the island sterile.

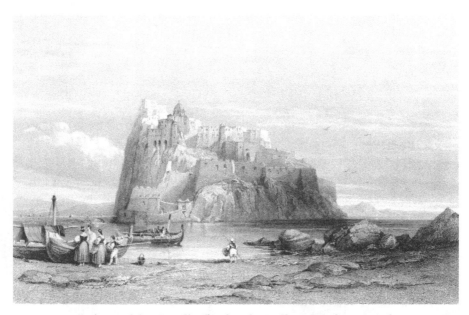

Etching of the Castello d'Ischia, by William Leighton Leitch
(Image courtesy of Libreria Imagaenaria, Ischia)

One does not need to know this myth to see that there was nothing cozy or welcoming about the castle as glimpsed from the sea below. Not only was it treacherously high above the water, but it also sat on its own islet with no obvious connection to the main island, so that the only visible access to the fortress was a terrifying set of broken stairs carved into the side of the cliffs. Scaling a volcanic rock was not normally part of a messenger's mission, but judging from the haste with which he had been dispatched in Milan, the news he was bringing was clearly urgent. What our messenger would not initially have seen was the stone bridge on the western side of the castle that the first Spanish rulers had built in the mid-fifteenth century to connect the islet to the island; he also would not have seen the massive tunnel they had dug out from the rock that leads to the castle gates. The tunnel was both a comfortable means of entry for welcome guests and a form of defense against those who were not: carved into the ceiling along the way were large openings resembling skylights that were designed to allow boiling tar to be poured over intruders' heads.

Luckily, the messenger from Milan was a welcome guest: he was carrying news, most likely in the form of a letter, to Vittoria Colonna, Marchesa of Pescara. Vittoria was living at the castle with Costanza while her husband, Costanza's nephew Ferrante I d'Avalos, was fighting against the French on behalf of the Holy Roman Emperor, Charles V, who was also, as Charles I, the king of Spain (see plate 1). Vittoria had married into the aristocratic Spanish clan, but was herself a Roman noblewoman. Her family's lands in the Castelli Romani were officially part of the Papal States, which spanned out from Rome through Lazio, the Marches, Umbria, and into Emilia-Romagna, although there was nothing that resembled a centralized government in the region. The heads of noble Roman families, known in Italian as *baroni*, governed their own subjects, raised their own troops, tried their own criminals, and controlled their borders and roads. In the early sixteenth century, these feudal lords had very few obligations to the pope: they did not regularly serve in the papal armies—indeed, they were often on the opposing side in battle— and only irregularly paid their taxes. In the words of Ferdinand I, king of Naples from 1458 to 1494, the "Orsini, Colonna, Conti, Caetani, and other barons of the Campagna do not recognize the [rights of the] pope in life or in death." "They are," he concluded, "the true lords of the land."

The Campagna that Ferdinand referred to was the vast and rugged territory surrounding the city of Rome. There is perhaps no other region in Italy that so deeply captures what feudalism looked like: castles and towns sit high on volcanic rocks or steep hills, surrounded by thick walls of stone that seem entirely impregnable from the plain below. The towns were nominally connected by old Roman roads that wove through the valleys, passing along rivers and forests, but travel was perilous. Not only were the roads themselves in poor condition, but they were also famously plagued by robbers and brigands. A papal brief sent in 1516 from Leo X—the Medici pope who ruled from 1513 to 1521—to Vittoria's mother, Agnese da Montefeltro, reproached her for failing to keep order in the woods outside the Colonna castle in Marino. (The fact that the letter was sent to Agnese means that Vittoria's father, Fabrizio, was almost certainly away waging war.) "We are receiving word every day," Leo wrote, "of many criminal acts taking place there, to such a degree that travelers no longer want to pass through; please command your men to capture the brigands and punish the criminals, and leave the roads open and free." Even without the threat of criminal attacks, the overall feeling of the area is of great isolation, with the man-made fortresses perfectly matching the inhospitality of the natural landscape.

Given the strategic position of the Colonna's lands, it is not surprising that over the centuries they were frequently won and lost, bought and sold, by a range of powerful families. Marino had belonged to nearly all of the powerful *baroni* in the Campagna—the Conti di Tuscolo, the Frangipane, and the Orsini—before the Colonna purchased it from the Caetani family in 1419. When Oddone Colonna was elected to the papacy in 1417, becoming Martin V, he granted to his family a number of fiefs that were under papal control, vastly expanding the Colonna's base. In 1426 alone, through a combination of gifts and purchases, the Colonna acquired the territory of Nettuno and the castles of Astuna and Rocca di Papa.

Martin V hailed from the Colonna family based in Genazzano, a feudal town twenty-five miles east of Rome, which was built upon a narrow strip of volcanic tufa with deep ravines on either side. Vittoria's branch of the Colonna came from Paliano, five miles to the east of Genazzano and situated in a similarly dramatic setting: the town sits on top of a high peak dominated by the Colonna fortress, with the beautiful Lepini Mountains looming in the distance. The Genazzano and Paliano branches of the family had very close ties, and fought together in the frequent battles that arose against other baronial families, most notably the Colonna's long-term enemies the Orsini, as well as against the popes. A third branch of the family, based four miles to the west of Genazzano in Palestrina, was estranged from the others, and often sided with their enemies.

Around the time of Vittoria's birth in 1490, the Colonna of Paliano and Genazzano became important allies of the kingdom of Naples. Fabrizio, who was one of the leading *condottieri*, or mercenaries, of his era, formally entered into the service of Ferdinand II in 1495, for which he was compensated with an annual salary of 6,000 ducats, or 6,900 scudi. (As a point of comparison, at the height of his career, Leonardo da Vinci was paid 560 scudi a year by the king of France; Michelangelo was paid somewhere between 300 and 500 scudi per sculpture, and 3,000 ducats for the ceiling of the Sistine Chapel.) Ferdinand also officially invested Fabrizio and his heirs with no fewer than thirty feudal properties in Abruzzo—the mountainous region to the east of the Campagna that stretches to the Adriatic coast—several of which had formerly belonged to the Orsini.

Although the Colonna developed strong ties to the rulers of Naples, they were first and foremost a Roman family. The Palazzo Colonna, located at the foot of the Quirinal Hill just next to the Basilica dei Santi XII Apostoli, was built on a site sacred to the ancient Romans. In the early third century C.E., it was there that the emperor Caracalla chose to erect a magnificent temple to the Greco-Egyptian god Serapis; among the ruins later found on the property was a red granite crocodile from Aswan. Originally built in the 1200s as a fortress, the palace had served over the centuries as both a family home and a refuge. Martin V, who ruled the church from 1417 to 1431, lived in the palace during his papacy—it was his official pontifical seat—and renovated it from its state of decay after years of war and destruction in Rome. The massive structure that we see today reflects a significant expansion of the original building: starting in the seventeenth century, the Colonna began to acquire a number of the neighboring palaces, ultimately incorporating them by the early 1800s into a single, unified complex. Already in Vittoria's time, however, the palace was considered one of the most important residences in Rome.

In early 1525, Vittoria was living far from Rome, on Ischia, when the messenger from Milan arrived on the island and was likely escorted on horseback through the long stone tunnel that led to the castle gates. We have no way of knowing where Vittoria was when his arrival was announced, but it is tempting to imagine her sitting quietly in one of her private rooms. Like most aristocratic women, she would have had the equivalent of a personal apartment inside the castle; the walls were typically hung with beautiful silks and tapestries, the windows draped with heavy satin or velvet, and the spaces filled with an array of wooden chests painted with allegorical scenes, a comfortable daybed for afternoon rest, and several tables, including a *scrivania*, or writing desk. Vittoria might have been reading one of the many books of Italian poetry in Costanza's library—in addition to being a woman warrior, Costanza was also a great lover of literature and ran a salon on the island for several decades, to which she invited the finest writers in Naples. Or she might have been sitting at her desk, keeping up with her very lively correspondence. Unless she was writing to close relatives, she normally drafted her letters and then passed them on to be copied by a secretary, whose handwriting was far better than hers. This was common practice for men and women of her class, and a personally written letter was a sign of great intimacy.

Given how religious she was, when the messenger arrived with news for Vittoria she may well have been praying in one of the castle's chapels. The tiny church of Santa Maria delle Grazie nearly hangs off a dramatic precipice overlooking the sea, and to reach it, she would have walked through a beautiful orchard of lemon trees, and then down a steep stone staircase. Just below the castle was the much grander Romanesque cathedral where she and Ferrante had been married sixteen years earlier. In one of the churches in the castle complex, there was even an altarpiece that included Vittoria's own portrait along with Costanza's at the feet of the Virgin Mary (see plate 3). In this beautiful painting, which was commissioned from a Neapolitan artist, possibly Girolamo Ramarino da Salerno, by a member of the d'Avalos family sometime around 1515, Vittoria is dressed in a rich blue and red gown, with locks of her long reddish-brown hair flowing onto her shoulders from an ornate headdress known as a *balzo* (a wired coif lined with jewels that had a gathered hairnet made from strips of beautiful fabric and lace). She wears a necklace made of enameled gold and pearls with a cross, and holds a small prayer book, possibly an illuminated Book of Hours. The painting, which still hangs today in Ischia at the church of Sant'Antonio di Padova, is the earliest portrait of Vittoria that has survived.

Wherever Vittoria was when the messenger arrived, she would likely have been summoned to meet him in one of the public reception rooms in the castle. The fact that he had come from Milan meant almost certainly that the news was about Ferrante. If Ferrante sent a letter himself, Vittoria would also have recognized his personal seal. In the Renaissance, members of the nobility had their own seals, which they used both as a form of authentication (no one else had their exact design), and to ensure that their letters could not be opened in advance without the recipient knowing. The envelope had not yet been invented—it came into use only in the nineteenth century—so the seal was used to close a letter after an elaborate folding of the sheet of paper into a thick square or rectangle.

Vittoria had been concerned about Ferrante for months, and was anxiously awaiting news that he might be coming home. She had even expressed such a wish in a personal letter to Charles V, in which she suggested that her husband had served in the imperial army long enough. She did this in her characteristically delicate manner, writing that she personally was so dedicated to the emperor's cause as to overcome her desire for Ferrante to return to her: "I hold my name [*vittoria*, or "victory"] in such estimation that I have used it to conquer my own desire that my husband come home and retire with me."

But Ferrante was in no condition to travel, let alone to wage war. The previous February, he had led Charles to one of the most important victories of his reign at the Battle of Pavia in northern Italy, where the imperial troops had definitively defeated the French, and even taken the French king, Francis I, captive. Ferrante had done this in a daring

nocturnal march into the enemy camp, which found the French completely unprepared. But the victory had come at a high cost for Ferrante,
leaving him with grave injuries. His condition had only worsened in
the months following the battle, and he also developed a severe weakness in his lungs, which ultimately became tuberculosis. Whether the
news was delivered by the messenger or in a letter, it was what Vittoria
had most dreaded: Ferrante was dying, and wanted her to come to Milan
as soon as possible.

It is difficult to convey how complicated a political world Ferrante
was living in, and how dangerous a figure he himself was. In the aftermath of the Battle of Pavia, he had earned some formidable enemies,
and not simply among the French. Ferrante's problems were, in fact, more
strictly Italian. In the sixteenth century, Italy was not a unified country—
it became a nation-state only in the 1860s—but was made up of small
kingdoms and city-states that were either self-governed or under the
control of foreign powers. In the north were the duchies of Milan and
Savoy, and the republics of Genoa and Venice; in the middle of the Italian peninsula, the republics of Florence and Siena, and the Papal
States. South of Rome, and occupying the whole of the boot, was the
kingdom of Naples. In 1519, Naples was absorbed into the Holy Roman
Empire when Charles I inherited the imperial title from his Habsburg
grandfather, Maximilian I. Among all these political powers on the
peninsula, there were no obvious or enduring alliances. Treaties were
drawn up between despotic princes and republicans, dukes and popes,
based on the exigencies of the situation. The only abiding principle was
opportunism.

Following the imperial victory at Pavia and the subsequent flight of
the French, Charles seemed poised to extend his power over much of
northern Italy. Given how much land Charles already controlled in the
southern half of the peninsula, Italy seemed on the verge of becoming
a Spanish-Habsburg possession. The urgency of the situation provoked
a group of Italian rulers led by Francesco II Sforza, Duke of Milan, to
form a league. Sforza was in a particularly difficult position, having
been installed in 1521 as ruler of Milan after a six-year period in
which his family had lost control of the duchy to the French. The

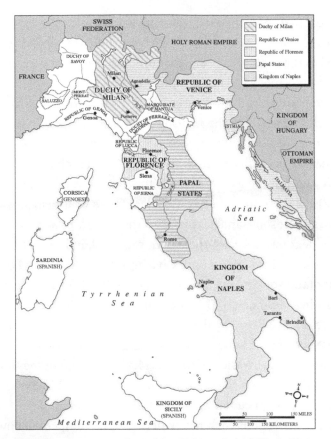

Map of Italy, circa 1494, from Lisa Kaborycha's *A Short History of Renaissance Italy*, 1st ed., © 2011 (Reprinted by permission of Pearson Education, Inc., New York, New York)

Sforza family was relatively new to Milan, and had only a tenuous hold on its power. Francesco II's father, Ludovico, hailed from a family of prosperous farmers in the Romagna—*sforza*, or "force," was a nickname given to his grandfather, a very successful mercenary named Muzio Attendolo—and became duke of Milan in 1494 after usurping the position from his brother's widow, Bona of Savoy. Known as "Il Moro" ("the Moor") due to his dark complexion, Ludovico was a ruthless leader who plotted and schemed his way to power by playing the rival states of Venice, Florence, and Naples against one another. Like so many of his fellow Renaissance princes, Ludovico was both a despotic ruler and a great patron of the arts: it was he who commissioned Leonardo to paint *Il Cenacolo* (known in English as *The Last Supper*), which he intended as the centerpiece for a magnificent family mausoleum in the monastery of Santa Maria delle Grazie in Milan.

The Last Supper can still be seen on the wall of the refectory at Santa Maria delle Grazie, but the mausoleum was never realized. In 1499, roughly one year after the fresco's completion, Ludovico fell from power, having been chased from Milan by the French king, Louis XII. Louis XII was himself a descendant of the first Duke of Milan, Gian Galeazzo Visconti—Louis's father, Charles, Duke of Orleans, was Gian Galeazzo's grandson—and he reasserted the Visconti claim to the duchy. Over the next few decades, the Sforza regained and lost Milan to the French on several occasions, until Charles V finally defeated Louis XII's successor (and son-in-law), Francis I, at the Battle of Bicocca in 1522, and installed Francesco II Sforza as Duke of Milan. Readers of Machiavelli's *The Prince* will recall his analysis of such struggles, and his subtle account of Ludovico as having quietly welcomed the French king Charles VIII's invasion of Italy in 1494, which led in the short term to the French conquest of the kingdom of Naples, and in the long term to decades of foreign battles known as the Italian Wars.

In 1525, with the French newly defeated, the emperor's power unchecked, and imperial troops still occupying Milan and stripping the city of nearly all its resources, Francesco made the decision to rebel. He quickly formed an alliance with the new pope, Clement VII, whose family, the Medici, had ties to the Sforza—Clement's uncle, Lorenzo the Magnificent, was a friend of Ludovico Sforza (Il Moro)—and made plans to raise a new army capable of combating the imperial troops (see plate 2). In search of a formidable commander, he sent his chief lieutenant, Girolamo Morone, to approach Vittoria's husband, Ferrante. In exchange for his service—and assuming, of course, the new league's success—Francesco and his allies offered Ferrante d'Avalos nothing less than the crown of Naples itself.

Under ordinary circumstances, Francesco would never have imagined winning Ferrante over to his side. Not only was Ferrante known to be personally close to the emperor, but, according to his first biographer,

Paolo Giovio, Ferrante's very nature was "*spagnolissimo*," or "very Spanish." Although he had spent nearly all his life in Italy and had married the Italian Vittoria, one of his contemporaries complained that he never even learned to speak decent Italian. Ferrante's natural loyalties, therefore, leaned heavily toward Spain and the Holy Roman Empire, who shared the same ruler, and not toward the league of Italian states. But the offer of the kingdom of Naples would have made him not simply the marquis of a minor principality—Pescara was a fortified city on the east coast of Abruzzo—but the monarch of a major realm. This was no small temptation.

The temptation was stronger due to Charles's failure to reward Ferrante for his truly heroic service at Pavia. If in the 1490s Ferrante's uncle Iñigo II had received the castle on Ischia for helping the Spanish king defend the kingdom of Naples, Ferrante had reason to expect nothing less than a duchy for leading the Holy Roman Empire to its great victory over the French. Indeed, he seems to have had in mind the principality of Carpi in Emilia-Romagna, which was supposed to have been given to Vittoria's cousin Prospero before his untimely death in 1523. But although Charles praised Ferrante lavishly in his letters, and even had elaborate Flemish tapestries made of the battle that depicted Ferrante as one of its heroes, the expected gifts never arrived. Adding further insult, Charles allowed Charles de Lannoy—the viceroy of Naples and one of Ferrante's greatest rivals within the imperial army—to escort the defeated Francis I to Spain, where he was promptly imprisoned, and Lannoy (rather than Ferrante) was presented before the emperor's court as the general responsible for the victorious battle.

There is no obvious explanation for Charles's behavior. On the one hand, he was in rather desperate financial straits: six hundred thousand ducats were already owed to the imperial troops before the Battle of Pavia began, and his agents were having little success raising the money from the defeated states—among them, Florence, Lucca, and Siena—that had been loyal to the French. On the other hand, the withholding of both land and recognition from Ferrante could not simply be explained by a shortage of funds.

Whatever Charles's reasons for largely ignoring Ferrante in the aftermath of Pavia, both Ferrante and Vittoria were bitterly disappointed. In her letter to the emperor in which she quietly expressed her desire for Ferrante to retire, Vittoria referred more boldly to the mysterious lack of compensation, and said that she wanted "the promised accommodation more as testimony of my husband's service, loyalty, and sincerity than out of any strange greediness on my part." "Of course," she hastened to add, "your goodness and generosity have always anticipated every worthy request." As far as we know—and his letters have been much better preserved than hers—Charles did not respond, and no gifts were forthcoming.

Ferrante was in the grip of his frustration with Charles when the Italian league approached him. Torn about what to do, he turned to Vittoria for advice. This is one of the only traces in the historical record of Vittoria and Ferrante actually consulting each other about a major decision: it hints at something like intimacy between them, which is otherwise not much in evidence. According to Giovio, who quoted a letter of Vittoria's in Ferrante's biography (the letter itself has not survived), she was very agitated about the league's offer. However ambitious Vittoria was on Ferrante's behalf, she did not want him to compromise his service to the emperor. And although she came from a Roman family, her father, as we have seen, spent the last decades of his career working directly for the Spanish kings of Naples. She wrote to her husband that "not with the grandeur of kingdoms and states and fine titles but with illustrious faith and renowned virtue is honor acquired," and urged him to reject the offer. In conclusion, she declared that she did not want to be a queen, but preferred to be the wife of an honest captain whose virtue was so strong as to defeat the greatest of kings.

There is no way to know how close Ferrante came to accepting the Italians' offer. Some historians think he was only playing along to curry favor with Charles by ultimately revealing the plot to him, and thereby proving the depth of his loyalty. Sometime during the fall of 1525, however, he turned down the possibility of becoming king of Naples, and reaffirmed his allegiance to the empire. His renewed pledge to Charles was not made quietly: it was the stuff of Renaissance theater. After betraying the Italians' plans to Charles, Ferrante agreed to stage a conversation with Francesco II's agent, Morone, during which one of Charles's advisers was hidden, like Shakespeare's Polonius, behind an arras. Morone was exposed, and subsequently arrested. He never forgave Ferrante. According to the sixteenth-century historian Francesco Guicciardini, Morone remarked that "there was not a man in Italy of greater Malignity, or of less Faith than the Marquis of Pescara." Guicciardini's own estimation of Ferrante was not so very different: he criticized him for "mak[ing] himself great out of the sins of others procured by his own deceits and subtleties." Only a decade or so after Machiavelli's composition of *The Prince*—and it is worth keeping in mind that Guicciardini knew Machiavelli well—Ferrante was recognized as a truly Machiavellian character.

In the weeks between the betrayal of Morone, who was arrested on October 15, and the dispatching of the letter to Vittoria in November, Ferrante had taken new military action against Milan. With an army of several thousand German soldiers and some five hundred Spaniards, his troops besieged the Sforza fortresses in both Milan and Cremona, and forced the Milanese citizens to swear their allegiance to the emperor. It was in the midst of these events that his health took a decisive turn for the worse. Given the number of people he had either deceived or disappointed, there were also rumors that he may have been poisoned.

Ferrante's possible betrayal of Charles followed by his actual betrayal of the Italians, his lack of reward or compensation, the miserable state of his health—all of this would have been in Vittoria's mind when she received the request to come to Milan. The journey before her was in itself a daunting one, and much longer than any other trip she had thus far taken in her life. It would start at the castle gates, from which she and her retinue—she was always accompanied by a number of personal maids as well as valets—would travel by horse, down the long tunnel to the base of the islet's rock, and then cross the bridge to Ischia's port. They would then take a small boat to Naples, where the long passage to the north, probably in a carriage, would begin.

The fastest route to Milan was by sea, and most travelers coming from the south sailed to the northern port of Genoa, whence they made only the final leg of the journey by land; the average time for this trip was around nine days. Perhaps due to stormy seas, or to the risk of encountering pirates, Vittoria's journey was planned entirely on land, which would have taken close to two weeks to complete. Even to get from Naples to Rome, a distance of approximately 140 miles, took an average of two to three days; the distance Vittoria was to travel to Milan was roughly 400 miles. Given that the messenger who brought her the news had just made the same trip that she was taking, and allowing that he would have traveled much more quickly than a noblewoman accompanied by servants and making frequent stops along the way, the time between when Ferrante sent the news and when Vittoria was likely to reach him would have been at least three weeks. The chances of her finding him alive were slight.

There is no record of how Vittoria felt as she embarked on her journey. Our best sources for her private thoughts are her poems and letters, none of which has survived from the fall of 1525. What has survived, however, is a beautiful verse epistle—a letter written in the form of a poem—which she wrote to Ferrante at a similarly difficult moment in 1512, and the feelings she expressed on that occasion give us some sense of how she might have felt thirteen years later. In both cases, Ferrante was away at war and in a position of great danger. In 1512, Ferrante and her father were fighting on behalf of the Spanish in a series of campaigns against the French in the north of Italy; as in 1525, Vittoria had been left behind on Ischia with Costanza. In the verse epistle, she describes both waiting desperately for news—"Never did a pilgrim come from whom / I did not seek to learn news, thing by thing / to make my mind joyous and happy"—and feeling overwhelmed with premonitions from the island: "When, at one point, I saw the rock where I rest / (my body, as my spirit is already with you) / covered with a dark mist / and the air around seemed like a cave / of black fog." "The sirens and dolphins were weeping," she adds, "and the fishes, too."*

---

* A2.1: "*Mai venia peregrin da cui novella / non cercassi saper, cosa per cosa, / per far la mente mia gioiosa e bella, / quando, ad un punto, il scoglio dove posa / il corpo mio, che già lo spirto è teco, / vidi coprir di nebbia tenebrosa, / e l'aria tutta mi pareva un speco / di caligine nera*"; "*piangeano le sirene e li delfini, / i pesci ancor.*"

Just as Vittoria comes to a point of total darkness both in her spirit and in her surroundings, a messenger arrives with news that her husband and her father have been taken captive at the Battle of Ravenna. She reacts, somewhat surprisingly, with more anger than fear. The poem ends with a series of accusations directed at Ferrante, which are far franker than anything we see in her later writings: "If you wanted Victory [*vittoria*], I would have been with you / but you, leaving me behind, also left Her"; "One should follow one's husband both at home and abroad / if he suffers grief, let her suffer too; / if he is happy, so, too, is she, and if he dies, let her die with him"; "You live happily and feel no pain / since you think only of how you might acquire more fame; / you do not care that you leave me starving for your love."* Her only comfort is the presence of "magnanimous" Costanza, who reassures her in the poem that the men will return from this defeat to glory. This turned out to be true in 1512: Ferrante and Fabrizio were both released, and went on to further triumphs. But it is hard to imagine comparable words of comfort being spoken in 1525.

However unhappy Vittoria may have been as she bid farewell to Costanza and set off on her journey, it is tempting to think that a part of her also felt some sense of liberation. Although she clearly loved the isolation and beauty of Ischia, the feelings she had already expressed in 1512 of being trapped by her position as a wife must have been all the stronger thirteen years later. Whether or not she suspected it, her descent from the castle through the dark tunnel out toward the open sea was also a new beginning.

---

* A2.1: "*Se vittoria volevi io t'era a presso, / ma tu, lasciando me, lasciasti lei*"; "*Seguir si deve il sposo dentro e fora, / e s'egli pate affanno ella patisca, / e lieto lieta, e se vi more mora*"; "*Tu vivi lieto, e non hai doglia alcuna, / ché, pensando di fama il novo acquisto, / non curi farmi del tuo amor digiuna.*"

DONNING WIDOW'S WEEDS

ITERBO IS A WALLED CITY, with many gates. There is no record of exactly where Vittoria arrived in early December 1525 when she and her entourage stopped in Viterbo, roughly fifty miles north of Rome, on their way to Milan—it was most likely Porta San Sisto, now known as Porta Romana, the most common entrance for visitors from the south— but it is certain that she traveled no farther. Awaiting her was a messenger bearing the tragic news that Ferrante had died (the date of his death is not certain but was sometime between November 25 and December 3, 1525). How it was known that she would be arriving at Viterbo that day, or whether the messenger had been waiting for her for some time, is not clear. Perhaps there was an available itinerary of sorts, or perhaps there were simply networks of servants who knew the comings and goings of their masters. Legend has it that upon hearing the news, Vittoria promptly swooned and fell off her horse.

It's hard to believe that Vittoria was actually making the journey from Naples to Milan on horseback. Women of her class did regularly ride horses—one of the grandest of all Renaissance women, Isabella d'Este, Marchesa of Mantua, described many trips on horseback in her personal letters—but for a trip of this length, Vittoria was more likely to have been traveling either by mule or by carriage. Carriages had only recently come into vogue as a mode of transportation, and were specifically used by aristocratic women; they spread next to clergymen, and finally to noblemen in the latter half of the sixteenth century. The detail of Vittoria's falling from her horse may simply have been invented to enhance the story: falling from a mule, or fainting inside a carriage, has a less dramatic ring. Legend also tells us that it took her two hours to revive.

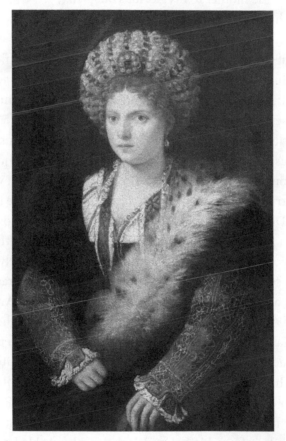

Portrait of Isabella d'Este, Marchesa of Mantua, by Titian
(Kunsthistorisches Museum, Vienna)

When Vittoria recovered from her state of shock, she found herself confronted with a set of difficult decisions. She was thirty-five years old, a widow, and childless. This last detail—her childlessness—was perhaps her greatest source of sadness. She wrote about her infertility on several occasions in her surviving letters and poems, and tried to cheer herself up with the idea that although she had not given birth to Ferrante's child, she had at least borne his fame. In one sonnet, she declares:

> Our bodies were sterile, our souls fecund,
> and his valor combined with my name
> makes me mother to his glorious offspring,
> which lives immortal.*

It is difficult not to hear in these lines a note of self-justification: the principal aim of marriage within the Italian aristocracy was to produce an heir. Her match with Ferrante had been, in the most fundamental sense, a failure.

The terrible burden of having failed to provide her husband with children was compounded by Vittoria's feelings of inadequacy, given Ferrante's long history of infidelity. Already within the first year or two of their marriage, he fell in love with the beautiful Isabel de Requesens, the wife of Don Ramón de Cardona, viceroy of Naples, whose splendid portrait can be seen today at the Louvre (see plate 4). Although Ferrante's passion seems to have been unrequited, it was widely known in Neapolitan society and became a source of great embarrassment for Vittoria. At a grand party in Naples thrown by Isabella d'Aragona, the daughter of Alfonso II, king of Naples, and the widow of the would-be duke of Milan, Gian Galeazzo Sforza (whose title had been usurped by his uncle Ludovico), Ferrante had embarrassed himself with behavior worthy of a besotted teenager. According to a sixteenth-century chronicler known as Filonico Alicarnasso, whose source was Paolone, the music tutor for both Isabella d'Aragona and Isabel de Requesens, Ferrante stole a kiss from his beloved Isabel, and scribbled a short love poem to her—in the form of a Spanish song—on the surface of the tam-

---

* A1.30: "*Sterili i corpi fur, l'alme feconde; / il suo valor qui col mio nome unito / mi fan pur madre di sua chiara prole, / la qual vive immortal.*"

bourine that Paolone was playing. The chronicler also reported that Ferrante had been so bold as to give Isabel one of Vittoria's necklaces, a beautiful string of pearls and precious gems. Isabel supposedly returned the necklace directly to Vittoria with a note advising her to keep better watch over her jewelry.

Several years later, Ferrante fell madly in love with a noblewoman from Mantua named Delia, one of the ladies-in-waiting to Isabella d'Este. (There is at least one account that she was also Vittoria's *damigella*, or lady servant, at some point.) This time there seems to have been a full-blown affair. We know a little bit about it, or at least about Ferrante's feelings, from the letters he exchanged with one of Isabella's courtiers, the humanist Mario Equicola, who served as his go-between. Ferrante mentioned enclosing secret letters for Delia inside his letters to Equicola, and confessed to his friend that she was the source of "all my well-being, my every lofty thought and every grace." In the last letter exchanged between the two men, Ferrante also expressed his fervent hope that he would see Delia again before he died.

There are no similar letters from Ferrante declaring his love or desire for Vittoria, and judging from everything we know about their marriage, they were not well suited. Ferrante was at heart a soldier, who thrived on military conquest. There are few signs of his having much of an intellectual life, and his moral compass was, at best, mutable. Vittoria was a quiet and strict young woman whose favorite activities seem to have been reading and praying. At the time of their marriage, Ferrante spoke mostly Spanish—according to his biographer Giovio, "his clothes were always in the Spanish manner, and he always took great delight in that language"—and Vittoria knew only Italian, although Giovio claimed the couple adopted Spanish habits, and that Ferrante spoke Spanish with her.

Ferrante was dashing and passionate: Giovio described him as "handsome to look at in the flower of his age, with a beard that stood out for its reddish tint, his aquiline nose, his eyes large and full of fire" (see plate 5). Vittoria's appearance was much less fiery, and by all accounts more severe. According to Giovio, she had raven black hair with gold highlights, arched brows, and a wide forehead. He praised her "mouth smoothed out in accordance with good manners, in a rather fleshy chin," and her nose as having "a very slight bridge," which, he conceded, "could convey a manly aspect, [but] does not deprive her of any of her feminine beauty, even though it gives her a stern look" (see plate 6). Another contemporary described her more frankly as "not being a great beauty," but distinguished instead by the virtues of her soul. The most striking portrait of her, by Sebastiano del Piombo and dated sometime around 1525, confirms these impressions (see plate 7). Vittoria is depicted as a serious young woman, with a rather large frame that looks as if it was carved from a block of stone. Although she meets the viewer's eye, she seems to do so with some reluctance, and there is nothing remotely seductive or coy about her.

As with other members of their class, the match between Ferrante and Vittoria had not been their choice. Indeed, to make a marriage between two noble families in sixteenth-century Italy was closer to negotiating a treaty between nations than to forging a domestic union. The engagement had initially been agreed upon sometime between 1495 and 1497, when Ferrante was between six and eight years old and Vittoria one year younger. The union formed part of the new alliance between the Colonna family and the kingdom of Naples, following Vittoria's father, Fabrizio, and his cousin Prospero's entering the service of Ferdinand II. The d'Avalos family, as we have seen, arrived in Italy with the first Spanish kings in the mid-fifteenth century, and rose to be one of the most powerful households in the reign.

Vittoria's dowry of fourteen thousand ducats was an enormous sum at the time. In Renaissance Italy, dowries had actually become so extravagant that many cities imposed ceilings on their maximum value in order to prevent families' expending their entire fortunes to marry off their daughters. In 1471, Rome passed a statute making it illegal for a dowry to exceed eight hundred florins—roughly the equivalent of eight hundred ducats—a sum that was raised to two thousand ducats in 1532. (In Florence, by contrast, the city actually created a public dowry fund for parents to invest in beginning around their daughter's fifth birthday, a development that apparently led to further inflation in the average dowry's value.) Vittoria's dowry, then, was nearly twenty times the maximum amount set by Roman law in 1471. There is no record, however, of any penalties exacted for this violation, and the Colonna family may have been given an exemption, since the marriage was to a foreigner. Of the fourteen thousand ducats, twelve thousand were dispersed in separate cash distributions to be made during the first year of marriage; the remaining two thousand ducats were distributed as personal property listed in a separate document that has not survived.

In addition to the dowry, there were also expensive gifts given to Ferrante that were not to be returned to Vittoria if he predeceased her, but would remain with the groom's family or heirs. This was a varied list, which was valued at approximately two thousand ducats and included: a French-style bed with curtains, bedding, three mattresses, and four pillows (all adorned with ornaments in gold thread and indigo taffeta stitching); a mule bridle of gold thread; precious stones; several *gamurra* gowns (a style of dress fashionable at the time) brocaded in rich silks as part of Vittoria's trousseau; and sheets of damask, which, according to the contract, must be of the "brightest colors." Ferrante's family in turn made expensive gifts to Vittoria: a diamond cross on a gold chain; brocaded gowns adorned with velvet or silk fringes; bodices of crimson and indigo silk; a cape of yellow silk adorned with black velvet; a mantle of crimson velvet and another of white silk stitched with jacquard brocade; twelve gold bracelets with inlaid gems in three colors; and other precious jewelry (possibly including the necklace Ferrante subsequently gave to Isabel de Requesens). These gifts were valued at 4,666 ducats.

There is no way to know what Vittoria's life was like between the announcement of her engagement in 1495 and the signing of the nuptial contract in 1507—no traces from this period survive. She may well have spent her entire childhood, however, from age five to seventeen, without ever meeting her future husband. The preliminary signing of the wedding contract took place on June 6, 1507, at the Colonna castle in Marino, although Ferrante was not present. The first known encounter between the engaged couple was one week later, on June 13, when the contract was officially executed by a notary in Naples, with all parties in attendance. Following the signing of the contract, Vittoria's family held an extravagant party in their beautiful palace on Via Mezzocannone, a home that had belonged to their enemies the Orsini, until it was given to Fabrizio by Ferdinand II.

The reason for celebrating the engagement in Naples rather than in Marino was no doubt largely practical: Naples was the capital of the Spanish kingdom, and Marino quite remote. This was a match made for political reasons, and its political capital was to be fully reaped. One of the major social events of that year, the party brought together both the Italian and the Spanish aristocracy living in the city. Most people today think of Florence and Rome as the centers of the Italian Renaissance, and in many respects this characterization is true. But Naples, which was at the time one of the largest metropolises in Europe— its population was almost three times that of London, and five times that of Rome—was also the most cosmopolitan, and reached an extraordinary height of cultural achievement. The guest list for the Colonna fete reflected the great diversity of the city, and included cardinals, bishops, poets, scholars, princes, dukes, military generals, ambassadors, and members of both Vittoria's and Ferrante's extended families.

The celebration of Vittoria and Ferrante's marital contract was followed by another period of waiting: more than two years passed before the couple took their vows on December 27, 1509, at the castle on Ischia. Why the wedding was not held sooner is not clear, but certainly the number of events to be held required a great deal of planning— aristocratic weddings in the Renaissance were not one-day affairs, but typically lasted close to a week. Every detail of the festivities would have been choreographed, beginning with Vittoria's departure from her castle in Marino.

To get from Marino to Naples—a distance of 105 miles—took an average of three days, and the trip was probably broken up by stops at the various Colonna castles that lined the way. In these feudal towns, the wedding party would have been hosted, and celebrated, with great ceremony: crowds of citizens and local nobility awaited the future bride and her family's arrival, and provided them with a festive meal within the castle walls. According to one eyewitness, "the bride was conducted by the most stately and grandiose procession, as was fitting for the magnificence of the two families." In addition to the carriages and coaches drawn by horses that transported the family, there were less noble animals in the rear of the convoy, bearing the bride's possessions and all of the baggage: yoked oxen hauled trunks filled with clothes and precious gifts, and mules trudged along wearing heavily stuffed saddles. At some point en route, the Colonna entourage was met by members of the d'Avalos family, all of whom were heading to the port at Naples to board boats for Ischia.

It is surprising that such a long-awaited wedding in so remote a location was planned for late December, one of the least pleasant times of year, and with the shortest days. But however gloomy the natural landscape may have been on a volcanic island in winter, this gloominess would have been more than compensated for by elaborate artifice. For a wedding of this grandeur, there was no limit to the ornamentation that enhanced the event. We might imagine bowers of beautiful foliage lining Vittoria's path as she walked to the cathedral, children dressed in white throwing petals, bells and cannons pealing through the air, and performers wearing elaborate costumes and reciting verses such as these, from the late fifteenth-century wedding of a comparably aristocratic bride and groom, Costanzo Sforza and Camilla Marzano d'Aragona:

> I come from heaven just to welcome you
> here into your realm, O glorious lady,
> everyone rejoices, everyone comes to shake
> your hand, to say be welcome, my lady,
> the streets, the castle, and the town cheer
> *Long live Costanzo and his Camilla.*

According to one of the guests at Vittoria and Ferrante's wedding who left behind a written description, Vittoria was a splendid bride, dressed in white silk brocade interwoven with gold, with a rich blue cloak lined with white fur covering her shoulders. (Ferrante's clothes were not mentioned, but we can safely assume they were equally luxurious.) The ceremony likely began in one of the halls of the castle, where the couple exchanged their vows with a notary presiding. It was not until the 1560s, after the end of the Council of Trent—an event we will return to later on—that jurisdiction over marriage was given to the church; until that time, oaths or vows were always taken in a secular setting. During this ceremony, there was no blessing from a priest or promise of God's love and protection—it was simply a business transaction. Religion entered the picture only after the contract had been signed, when there was a nuptial Mass celebrated in church. And then the festivities began.

There is no record of the wedding feast served for Vittoria and Ferrante. But banquets of this sort were extraordinary affairs that might last six or seven hours and include forty or fifty different courses. The menu from the Sforza and d'Aragona wedding gives us a sense of the kind of meal that would have been served, which combined theatrical pageantry with the most artful display of food imaginable. Costanzo and Camilla's banquet was divided into two parts, dedicated respectively to the sun and the moon; each part was then further divided into six courses identified with a single god or goddess who either "appeared" in person or sent another mythological figure as his or her messenger to present the food (the servants must have been kept very busy changing their costumes from one course to the next). From the first half of the banquet, here are the dishes presented by Iris, and delivered by Juno, which made up the fourth course:

> An enormous quantity of roast meat: loins of veal, roast kid, roast capons, pullets, pigeons; cameline sauce [made from raisins, nuts, and breadcrumbs]; oranges, citrons, and lemons; a veal pie for each person; peacocks for all tables dressed in their feathers standing on golden plates [these were a common feature at banquets, and were dressed so that when cooked, the bird still appeared to be alive, and even spewed fire from its beak]; roast peacocks with gilded beaks and feet for everyone; peacock sauce [made of hard-boiled eggs, pullet livers, and toasted almonds]; and young peacocks cooked pheasant-style.

After this very heavy set of dishes revolving around different preparations of peacock, another set of delicacies appeared. This time the food was presented by Orpheus on behalf of his father, Apollo, and included "various types of pies with crusts made with eggs, sugar, and rose water, in which were quails and other live birds that flew around the hall; and very large, sculpted Parmesan cheeses, gilded and painted in Costanzo's armorial colors; three for the high table and two each for the other tables." According to a 1549 Italian cookbook, the birds that flew out of the pies were a popular mid-meal entertainment, designed to delight—if not startle—the guests.

When the guests recovered from the feast prepared for Vittoria and Ferrante, there were likely several days of festivities that followed, which might have included pageants and parades with elaborate floats; daylong hunts; musical concerts and dances; jousts; and theatrical plays. The cost of these events was, needless to say, mind-boggling. In the words of the great humanist Leonardo Bruni, who paid for his own festivities: "I have not just spent money on my marriage, but almost entirely used up my patrimony on one wedding. It is unbelievable how much is spent on these new weddings; habits have become so disgusting."

Following their wedding, Vittoria and Ferrante had as their primary residence a palace in Naples on the slope of the hill of Sant'Elmo, with the ruins of the great medieval castle hovering above (the castle had been damaged by an earthquake in 1456, and was not refortified until the 1540s). Thanks to the status of both families, they moved in the highest echelons of Neapolitan society. Ferrante took part in jousting tournaments, which Vittoria attended as a spectator. They went to see plays (usually in Spanish) performed in the palaces of their friends and relatives. They attended the kingdom's most extravagant parties.

One such occasion stands out in the record, and gives us a glimpse of Vittoria that is hard to reconcile with her much more reserved persona of later years. On December 6, 1517, a party was held in the twelfth-century Castel Capuano to celebrate the engagement of Bona Sforza, the daughter of Isabella d'Aragona and Gian Galeazzo Sforza, to Sigismund I of Poland. Oddly, Sigismund himself did not attend the party—he sent a proxy, a Polish nobleman named Stanislaw Ostoróg, to represent him. Ferrante was also not present, but Vittoria was there in full splendor.

Dressed in a gown of crimson velvet embroidered with gold, a beautiful golden bonnet, and a crimson sash in satin with the same golden embroidery as the dress, she was accompanied by a group of her ladies-in-waiting, wearing blue damask, and her male valets, dressed in blue and yellow satin. Even the horse she arrived on was an accessory to her appearance: it had a luxurious saddle with fringes of gold and silver.

Vittoria stood out at this party not simply for her sumptuous attire—many of the women were no doubt dressed with equal magnificence—but for her striking performance of a solo Hungarian dance. She must have learned it for the occasion, in order to honor the ties between Poland and Hungary, which had been forged through Sigismund's first marriage, to the Hungarian princess Barbara Zápolya, who had died in 1515. Vittoria was not the only one to emphasize the Hungarian connections of the groom: the menu for the banquet included a dish of "boiled wild meat with Hungarian potage," not typical fare for the Neapolitans. But she seems to have been the only guest who performed a Hungarian dance.

We know about Vittoria's dance because Ferrante's cousin Alfonso d'Avalos, Marquis of Vasto, was present at the party and described her performance in great detail in a conversation he had with Giovio some ten years later (see plate 8). Alfonso had been orphaned as a young child and raised by Costanza at the castle in Ischia; Vittoria and he were very close, and she considered him almost like a son (he was twelve years her junior). Vittoria, he recounted, had been the center of attention at the engagement party, drawing praise from everyone present. "From what woman," he asked,

> even the most skilled, did she not snatch away first prize in performing the dance? She wanted to perform a Hungarian dance, which is a type of solo ritual dance accompanied by foreign-style music; the other women, being untrained in it, were dumbstruck at her performance. She carried it out knowledgeably, and with such charm and dignity, that when she performed alone with no young man accompanying her in the spacious yet crowded room, everyone formed a circle around her and gazed with admiration.

In the middle of the grand hall of Castel Capuano, with hundreds of elegant Polish, Spanish, Italian, and possibly Hungarian guests watching in silence, Vittoria danced alone, to the tune of a single flute. "Nothing was more attractive," Alfonso concluded, "than when, with the most pleasing gestures, she matched all her movements to the rhythms of the dance, whether she was pretending to wave her feathery fan to stir the air or was gathering up her long flowering sleeves, or when she swept the floor with her wide skirts tracing delicate circles." This enchanting vision captures Vittoria's self-composure and confidence at the time. It is also the most sensual account of her that has survived.

All of this must have seemed like the very distant past as Vittoria reconciled herself to her new status as a widow on that late autumn day in Viterbo eight years later. She was not only now a childless widow, but also a very wealthy one. Given that both of her parents had recently died—Fabrizio in 1520, and Agnese in 1523—her sizable dowry would be returned directly to her. She found herself, therefore, in an extremely unusual position of independence. Although her brother Ascanio had taken her father's place as the head of the family (another brother, Federico, also younger than Vittoria, had died in 1516), and although Alfonso d'Avalos would be named Ferrante's heir, neither man was officially authorized to make decisions on her behalf. For the first time ever, Vittoria's life was hers to shape.

The most obvious choice to make was to remarry. Her age, admittedly, was not ideal: according to a census done of fifteenth-century Florence, only one in ten widows between thirty and thirty-nine remarried. But Vittoria was no ordinary widow, and from the perspective of the marriage market, she must have feared, like Odysseus's Penelope, having many suitors to ward off. To get some idea of the prospects that awaited her, we might consider the story of her contemporary Lucrezia Borgia, the daughter of Rodrigo Borgia, who became Pope Alexander VI. Lucrezia was subjected to one marriage after another by her scheming father and her brother Cesare, whose ruthless and vengeful character supplied Machiavelli with one of his prime examples of the Renaissance prince. After her first marriage, to Giovanni Sforza, Lord of Pesaro and Count of Cotignola, was annulled on dubious grounds—

Alexander VI (her father) claimed the union had not been consummated so as to break the family's ties with the Sforza, who had fallen from power—Lucrezia was married to Alfonso d'Aragona, Duke of Bisceglie, an illegitimate son of Alfonso II of Naples. After Alfonso was mysteriously murdered, she was married a third time, to Alfonso I d'Este, son of Ercole I, Duke of Ferrara, who upon his father's death in 1505 became duke himself. This match, made two years before Alexander VI's death in 1503, seems finally to have satisfied both her father's and Cesare's ambitions, and Lucrezia remained at the court of Ferrara until her own death in 1519.

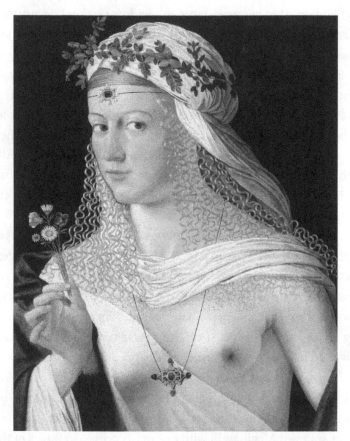

Portrait of an idealized woman often identified as Lucrezia Borgia,
by the early sixteenth-century painter Bartolomeo Veneto
(Städelsches Kunstinstitut, Frankfurt)

Vittoria, however, did not want to remarry, and there was no one to force her to do anything against her will. Although she left behind no explanation for her decision, there are three very different but equally compelling ways to understand her resistance. First, she was still passionately tied to Ferrante. Despite how ill-suited he was for her temperamentally, and his frustratingly long absences and infidelities, everything she ever wrote in her letters and poems suggests that she was deeply devoted to him. In a letter from August 1524 to her friend the papal datary Gian Matteo Giberti, who was nominated bishop of Verona that month, she described how angry she was about gossip that had reached her about both Ferrante and her marriage. She was ill at the time, but explained that her illness was not due entirely to her poor physical health. "What they blame me for, maddeningly," she wrote, "and what needs to be cut out at its cause [in order for me to be well], is the idea that the Marquis was not worth what he is worth, that we were not two in one flesh, and that I was not so obligated to him as I am."

This is the only instance in Vittoria's surviving correspondence in which she spoke frankly about what people thought of her marriage, and she affirmed in the strongest terms the depth of her and Ferrante's bond. Despite rumors to the contrary, she insisted that they were "one flesh" (the Italian phrase, "*due in carne una*," is similar to the language used in the marriage ceremony, where the spouses are declared to be "*una carne sola*"). To be Ferrante's widow, then, was a way for her to keep their marriage alive, and preserve its memory in the best possible terms. This is what we might call the romantic explanation for her decision not to remarry, and the best proof for it comes in the sonnets she wrote to him after his death, which we will turn to later on.

The second possible explanation for her decision not to remarry pulls in the opposite direction (we might call it the antiromantic, or feminist, position): namely, that the very last thing she wanted was to be tied down by another man. After years of feeling that she was not free to move around as she liked—we will remember her bitterness at being left behind on Ischia while Ferrante was fighting alongside her father in the north—the idea of being unbeholden to anyone had a strong appeal. Why would she want to submit to the will of another husband when she could finally live on her own? This may sound like a projection of a modern sensibility onto someone from a very different world, but there were certainly expressions of such feelings in the Renaissance. The most famous example comes from a literary text. In Shakespeare's *Much Ado About Nothing*, Beatrice responds to her uncle's remark "Well, niece, I hope to see you one day fitted with a husband" with these fighting words: "Not till God make men of some other metal than earth. Would it not grieve a woman to be overmastered with a piece of valiant dust?"

Vittoria certainly was never so outspoken about her choices, but there is ample evidence that she came to treasure her freedom. She never settled down in a single place—she moved, in fact, almost every two or three years—and her own interests dictated where she went, and with whom. There were a few occasions when conflicts involving her family compelled her to take refuge at Marino or another family home, but these were exceptions to her normal pattern, and she typically left as soon as she could. Otherwise, when she wanted to visit a particular friend, or follow her favorite preacher from one city to the next, there was no one to stop her. In her 1512 verse epistle, she complained about being restricted by the roles of both daughter and wife. In 1525, Vittoria was about as free as any Renaissance woman could be.

The third reason (and ultimately perhaps the strongest) for Vittoria's not wanting to remarry was her desire to lead a predominantly religious life. It was by no means unusual for someone like Vittoria to be very devout—indeed, Renaissance Italy was saturated with religion to a degree difficult to imagine today. But Vittoria was unusually focused on her faith, and in the aftermath of Ferrante's death, she wanted to put her religious practice at the very center of her existence. In a conversation I had a few years ago about Vittoria with a very worldly nun, I commented that Vittoria was an extremely pious woman, and she replied, "All women were pious at that time." I demurred, and asked about Lucrezia Borgia, for example—surely she wasn't pious?—to which she gave me the wonderful response: "Lucrezia Borgia was not moral, but she was pious. There's an important difference." Vittoria, needless to say, was both moral and pious: on this front, we quickly agreed.

The clearest evidence for Vittoria's desire to lead a life shaped at its core by religion lies in the choices she made over the next few decades about the company she kept, the places she lived, and the way she spent her days—these are, in effect, the stories at the heart of this book. But in the immediate moment of confronting Ferrante's death and pondering what to do next, Vittoria's first decision already revealed the path she most wanted to take. She did not go to the funeral service for Ferrante in Milan, where his corpse was laid out at the Gothic church of San Pietro in Gessate with *real pompa*, or royal ceremony—in fairness, even had she wanted to attend, she may well have arrived too late. Instead, she returned to Rome, where she promptly took up residence as a guest in the convent of San Silvestro in Capite.

San Silvestro in Capite was a beautiful church established in the eighth century, possibly on the ruins of a pagan temple dedicated to Sol Invictus, the god of the sun. Christians loved to build churches on the ruins of pagan temples—it was a gesture of aggression on the one hand, and superstition on the other. We might understand it as a version of Pascal's wager—the idea put forward in Pascal's *Pensées* that either God exists or he does not exist, so we're best off to wager on God. "Let us weigh the gain and the loss," Pascal writes, "in wagering that God exists. Let us estimate these two probabilities; if you win you win all; if you lose, you lost nothing. Wager then, without hesitation, that He does exist." The convent's name, "*in capite*," literally "in (or with) the head," most likely refers to the church's most famous relic—a piece of a skull claimed to be St. John the Baptist's, which is kept in a splendid shrine from the fourteenth century in the Chapel of Our Lady of Sorrows. Although the church still stands today, the convent is no longer there. Far from its original purpose of sheltering women from the world outside, the building was transformed in the late nineteenth century to house the Central Post Office, a bustling space overflowing with Romans sending letters and paying bills.

The decision for Vittoria to go to San Silvestro in Capite—a decision that seems to have been made, as we shall see, by none other than Pope Clement VII—was not accidental. The church had been tied to the Colonna family since the late thirteenth century, when Vittoria's celebrated ancestor known today as the Blessed Margherita was buried there (Margherita was beatified—hence the title "Blessed"—in the nineteenth century). By all accounts an extremely beautiful and intelligent girl, Margherita had angered her family by refusing to marry, and had instead become a nun, taking the veil at the Convent of Santa Chiara in Assisi.

After her death in 1284 in the Colonna fief of Palestrina, Margherita's tomb became a popular pilgrimage site. In 1285, Pope Honorius IV, who was a close friend of Margherita's brother, Giacomo, decided to transfer her corpse to San Silvestro in Capite, and to honor her memory by bestowing the convent on the nuns of Santa Chiara, known in English as the Poor Clares. The order was founded in 1212 by a woman a few generations older than Margherita, Chiara di Favarone di Offreduccio, who was born in Assisi to noble parents but turned away from her family to follow the man known to history as Saint Francis, who had similarly rejected the wealth of his father, a cloth merchant named Pietro Bernardone, also from Assisi. Chiara made a vow to live a life of total poverty, refusing all personal possessions and inheritance. It is easy to imagine that Vittoria saw both Margherita and Chiara as models for the chaste and simple life she wanted to live.

Vittoria's decision to stay in a convent during her initial period of mourning was not uncommon—the nunnery was the Renaissance equivalent of a retreat—and there were at San Silvestro in Capite, as in nearly all monasteries, special quarters reserved for guests. She would have been welcome to pray with the nuns in their daily services, but also free to come and go as she pleased. The choice also meant that she avoided returning home with her brother Ascanio. Ascanio was a notoriously difficult man—many thought he was completely mad—and although Vittoria remained connected to him throughout her life, she saw his weaknesses very clearly. Ascanio's marriage in 1518 to Giovanna d'Aragona, one of the most beautiful and accomplished women of the era, was notoriously unhappy. Despite their having six children together, Giovanna abandoned him in 1535 to live alone with the children on Ischia, and Vittoria quietly supported her sister-in-law's decision. In a letter dated tentatively to 1536, Vittoria wrote to Eleonora Gonzaga della Rovere, Duchess of Urbino, that she was sure that "there has never from [Giovanna] been any defect whatsoever, in fact only the highest discretion and patience."

Ascanio, for his part, showed no resistance to leaving Vittoria at least for the time at the convent—who knows if he wanted to live with his pious sister any more than she wanted to live with him—and all would perhaps have been fine if Vittoria had not done something shocking. After she settled into her rooms at the convent, to the great astonishment of just about everyone, she evidently asked permission to remain there permanently. Vittoria wanted to become a nun.

LONGING FOR THE NUNNERY

FEW WOMEN IN RENAISSANCE ITALY chose on their own to become nuns. The decision was usually made by parents, who either could not afford to pay for their daughter's expensive dowry—they may have had older daughters whose marriages they had already arranged, or sons for whom they wanted to ensure an inheritance—or considered their daughter somehow ill-suited for marriage. Entering a convent was not free of charge: when the girl (or woman) took her vows, the family had to pay a "conventual dowry," which was reserved, at least in theory, to pay for her individual needs over the years. In practice, the convent often used these dowries as loans to subsidize its expenses, and when the nun died, the sisters kept the capital. There were also additional fees known as *vitilazi*, which could be paid annually or in a single lump sum. Some nuns also had private servants accompany them to the convent, for whom families provided separate dowries. But all of these costs were relatively low compared with the exorbitant sums being paid for marriage dowries, weddings, and trousseaux. The convent remained the most affordable alternative to marrying off one's daughter.

For those who were forced to take the veil against their will, life in the convent often felt like a form of punishment. In the words of one very bitter nun from Venice, Arcangela Tarabotti, who wrote a treatise in the mid-seventeenth century entitled *Tirannia paterna*, or *Paternal Tyranny*: "Over the gate of Hell, Dante says, are inscribed the words, 'Abandon every hope, who enter here.' The same could be inscribed over the portals of convents." Arcangela took her vows of poverty, chastity, obedience, and stability in a Benedictine convent when she was sixteen. In her treatise, she lashed out against fathers like her own who "do not offer as brides of Jesus their most beautiful and virtuous daughters, but the most repulsive and deformed: lame, hunchbacked, crippled, or simple-minded. They are blamed for whatever natural defect they are born with and condemned to lifelong prison." Such fathers were no better than murderous Cain, slaying their own kin: their long-suffering daughters, Arcangela railed, were "overwhelmed by despair at not finding some spiritual escape from the intricate labyrinth enclosing them." Men like this were driven, she continued, solely by greed: "Ponder my words, judicious Reader, for I have undertaken to describe only in part the sacrilege of these inhumane men who mass together wealth, titles, and prestige for their male offspring . . . but who cast away as wretches their own flesh and blood that happen to be born female."

To someone like Arcangela, who had also authored a book with the uncompromising title *Monastic Hell* (*L'Inferno monacale*), Vittoria's desire to become a nun would have been incomprehensible. No one had forced Vittoria to dedicate her life to serving God, and she had plenty of money to provide a dowry for a second marriage. She wanted not merely to become a nun, moreover, but also to join one of the traditionally strictest and poorest of orders. There were very fancy convents, usually either Dominican or Benedictine, with reputations for being filled with aristocratic nuns; their chapels were covered with jewels and gold, their dormitories adorned with the most sumptuous furnishings. Ferrante's cousin Costanza d'Avalos Piccolomini took up residence as a long-term guest in such a nunnery in Naples, where there were not only splendid decorations, but also social entertainments, and certainly such a choice was available to Vittoria. In fact, she would have been highly sought after by the nuns at the luxurious convents: her income would have helped to support annual costs, and her name would have added prestige.

But Vittoria wanted to be a Poor Clare. The Poor Clares, as we have seen, were a branch of the Franciscans founded by the noblewoman Chiara di Offreduccio, to whom Francis gave permission to establish her own order, only three years after he himself established the Friars Minor, the first order of the Franciscans (the Poor Clares were the second). Francis had been inspired by a sermon on the ninth and tenth verses of chapter ten in the Gospel of Matthew, in which Christ instructs his twelve apostles to go out with "neither gold, nor silver, nor brass in your purses, / Nor scrip for your journey, neither two coats, neither shoes, nor yet staves." After hearing this sermon, Francis made the decision to dedicate himself to a life of poverty and itinerant preaching. Clare fully embraced Francis's commitment to poverty, but made certain adjustments appropriate for women's monasticism. The Poor Clares did not share the Franciscan mission of preaching, but lived in enclosure, devoting their days to prayer and labor (thus their motto "ora et labora"). Once Vittoria had taken her vows, she would never have left the cloister.

Daily life in a convent like San Silvestro in Capite began with the tolling of bells around 4:00 a.m. for morning chores—sweeping, dusting, opening windows, preparing for breakfast, and so on. The nuns then proceeded to the chapel for morning prayer, called Lauds, during which, as the sun began to rise, they praised God for creation. This was the first of eight liturgical hours, which consisted of reciting particular psalms and hymns, and made up the so-called Divine Office. Following Lauds, there was the office known as Prime, usually said at the first hour of full daylight, before the most important service of the day, the Holy Sacrifice of the Mass, which was celebrated by a priest. This was the only service in which a priest was necessary, since, according to canon law, the nuns were not allowed to consecrate the Eucharist.

After nourishing their souls, the nuns at San Silvestro in Capite had a very simple breakfast at around 8:30 a.m. The day continued in a combination of prayers and chores, with Terce, or midmorning prayers, at 9:00 a.m., and Sext at noon; this office was then followed by dinner, which was the only substantial meal of the day, served around 12:30. After the meal, there was a period of rest before returning again to the chapel for None, or midday prayers, at 3:00 p.m. Then there was more work either in the garden or in the cloisters until Vespers, or evening prayer, when it became dark. A light meal was served after this service, followed by one hour of daily recreation at around 6:30 p.m. The nuns returned to the chapel for Compline, or night prayer, sometime before 9:00 p.m., and then retired to their rooms for several hours of rest before being awakened at 12:30 a.m. for Matins, also known as Vigils.

Meals in the convent were taken in silence, and officially complied with the rules of fasting. Fasting did not mean what it does today—a total abstinence from food—but instead referred to a diet in which very frugal fare was served at both breakfast and the evening meal. Sometimes this was "dry eating," which consisted of bread, salt, and water; sometimes fruits and vegetables were also permitted, but there was permanent abstinence from meat. Saint Clare took the fasting one step further and urged the nuns to eat only once a day. She also practiced a special form of food deprivation during the forty days of Lent, in which she ate nothing at all on Mondays, Wednesdays, and Fridays.

The extremity of this diet turned out, not surprisingly, to be harmful to Clare's health, and Francis finally had to intervene to force her to take an ounce and a half of bread per day. (As we shall see, Vittoria found herself in a similar situation in the 1540s, when she was forced to eat against her will, for fear that she was starving.) There was a long history in medieval and Renaissance convents of what has been described as "holy anorexia," where nuns believed the sustenance of the Eucharist wafer ought to provide sufficient nourishment for their bodies. As Jacques of Vitry, a thirteenth-century cardinal and historian, described it, some nuns "in receiving the bread of him who came down from heaven obtained not only refreshment in their hearts but a palpable consolation in their mouths sweeter than honey and the honeycomb . . . [They] languished with such desire for the sacrament that they could not be sustained . . . unless their souls were frequently refreshed by the sweetness of this food."

In addition to following this strict program of prayer and diet,

Vittoria would also have adopted the dress of the nuns. Gone forever were the days of the crimson velvet gown and golden bonnet that she wore to Bona Sforza's party; even her much more somber widow's robes would have had no place in the convent. The Poor Clares wore loose-fitting gowns in gray, and tied a cord of thick rope around their waist. The belts had four knots, which represented the four vows of their order: poverty, chastity, obedience, and enclosure. In addition to giving up her wardrobe, Vittoria would also not have been allowed to keep any personal property. The lands and estates, the jewelry and art—everything, in short, she had inherited from both her family and Ferrante—would have been given away. Outside of the nuns' collective ownership of the convent and its gardens, their only possession was meant to be Jesus Christ himself.

As a lay resident in San Silvestro in Capite, Vittoria would have had the freedom to come and go as she pleased, to dress as she liked, and to supplement the ordinary food of the nuns with delicacies of her own. She would have had the choice, in other words, to dedicate herself to religious devotion while also maintaining her independence. This made sense as something she might have chosen for herself. Indeed, it was common at the time for women to use convents, in effect, as residential hotels—it was not considered either safe or appropriate for women to lodge in public inns.

It is much harder to believe that someone as sophisticated and wealthy as Vittoria, with so many friends and connections, wanted to turn away from it all and spend the rest of her days in the cloister. Perhaps her marriage to Ferrante had been even more traumatic than it seemed. Or perhaps her years spent in grand castles and palaces had not pleased her in the least. Above all, however, the desire must have reflected a religious vocation so strong that giving up everything in the secular world was not a renunciation, but a positive gain.

Vittoria never got to find out whether life as a Poor Clare would have suited her, as the fates were against her fulfilling her dream. More accurately, the opposition came from the pope. When Clement found out that Vittoria wanted to take the veil—and the news apparently went straight to the pontiff himself—he explicitly forbade it. On

December 7, 1525, less than two weeks after Ferrante's death and presumably within days of Vittoria's having heard the news, the pope sent a rather extraordinary brief to the nuns of San Silvestro. He began gently, declaring his profound sympathy for Vittoria's loss and indicating his personal preference for her to recover in their convent:

> Knowing that the very honorable daughter in Christ, Vittoria Colonna, Marchesa of Pescara, recently deprived of her most illustrious husband, is struggling in her pain and in her tears, day after day, and that she desires to rest in a pious place, where she can serve God more freely and pray for the soul of her husband . . . to these ends we have chosen your monastery, which we know is also held in particular veneration by the entire Colonna family.

Given the help and companionship Vittoria might require, he also kindly requested the nuns to allow her to bring three honest young ladies with her, and specified that "even if these women do not embrace your religion or enter into your order or change their worldly clothes," they should be welcomed with true affection and given every form of comfort possible.

So far, so good. At this point, however, the letter took a less friendly turn. Vittoria should be welcomed to the nunnery, of course, but under no circumstances should she be permitted to change her "widow's costume to a monastic one." Any desire she had to take holy vows, he wrote, owed more to an "impulsiveness in her grief than a mature conviction." Therefore, he concluded, "we prohibit, under pain of immediate excommunication, that she be allowed admittance to your order without my express permission."

It may seem incredible that Clement took the time to worry about whether an individual woman, however prominent, should become a nun. Clement was a relatively new pope—he had been elected in late November 1523—and in 1525, his papacy was far from stable. First, there was the growing threat posed to the church by Protestantism. During the papacy of a predecessor—and Clement's cousin—Leo X (Giovanni di Lorenzo de' Medici), Martin Luther had posted his revolutionary

Ninety-Five Theses. Despite Leo's efforts to stop him, the German monk's message of reform was spreading like wildfire throughout Europe, and Italy was not immune. Second, in the ongoing war between France and the Holy Roman Empire, Clement had switched his allegiance multiple times without ever choosing the winning side, and found himself in a political muddle. Most recently, he had participated enthusiastically in the Italian league's efforts to fight Charles V—an effort that had failed, of course, due in part to Ferrante's manipulations. Vittoria was therefore the widow of someone who had betrayed him, and the daughter of someone who had fought for decades on the side of the Spanish enemy. Given all of this, why would he not have been happy for her to be shut away behind the walls of San Silvestro in Capite?

The only plausible answer to this question is that Pope Clement recognized Vittoria's value to him as a sane and intelligent member of the Colonna family. To understand why this was so important, we need to remember that Vittoria's brother Ascanio, who had inherited his father Fabrizio's land and titles upon his death in 1520, was a volatile and difficult man. In addition to problems in his character, his loyalties were strongly with the emperor: he had served in Charles V's army during the wars against the French in the north of Italy, and he had no sympathy for the pope. Indeed, there was no one Ascanio instinctively disliked more than Clement, and he challenged the pope's authority over his lands at every step.

For Clement, having someone in the Colonna family to serve as an intermediary between him and Ascanio was no small matter, and he had the utmost respect for Vittoria. Vittoria had shown herself to be a canny diplomat in the months before Ferrante's death—she had been in regular contact with both Charles V and Pope Clement—and had managed to retain her loyalty to the church despite her ties to the emperor. It is altogether possible that the pope simply could not afford to let her disappear from the scene.

From our perspective today, Clement's interference in Vittoria's life turned out to be a blessing in disguise. Had she become a nun, she may never have written her rich and complex body of poetry, which in turn paved the way for hundreds of other women to publish their own verse.

She would not have met Michelangelo, and therefore would not have inspired him to make the magnificent works of art and poetry that he gave as gifts to her. She would not have become so involved with the Italian reform movement, or played so important a role in efforts to reconcile crucial tenets of Lutheranism with Catholic doctrine before the irreparable break of the Counter-Reformation. She would not, in short, have led such a rich and fascinating life that touched so many of those around her, and made her, to recall Jacob Burckhardt's phrase, "the most famous woman of Italy." We should be grateful to Pope Clement for forcing her back into the world.

For Vittoria, however, Clement's refusal to allow her to consider life as a nun seems to have come as a horrible blow. It threw her into an even deeper state of despair over Ferrante's death, and left her without hope for her future. She stayed in the convent's guest quarters for several more months before a new political crisis emerged involving her family, and Ascanio insisted that she take refuge at the Colonna castle in Marino. The crisis returned Vittoria to the nightmare that had swept Ferrante up in its midst the previous summer. For in spite of the treaty signed in January 1526 between Charles V and Francis I, who was still pining away in a gloomy tower in Madrid, the peace did not last. Francis was freed from prison in March, but only after surrendering a great deal of property and handing over two of his sons to Charles as hostages. By late May, he was ready to return to combat, and entered into a new agreement with his Italian allies, known as the League of Cognac, which included Pope Clement and Francesco II Sforza, the beleaguered duke of Milan. As loyal supporters of Charles V, the Colonna men found themselves once again preparing for war, this time much closer to home.

Vittoria moved from San Silvestro in Capite to Marino sometime in the spring of 1526. While she was there, she missed the very grand funeral held for Ferrante in Naples that May. As we may recall, Ferrante's corpse had first been entombed in a ceremony in Milan, but this was only a temporary step before its transfer to its final resting place. The coffin was transported from Milan in a formal procession that included a large number of friends, family members, and servants, all dressed in mourning clothes. When the group reached the outskirts of Naples—a trip that would have taken nine or ten days—they were met by an additional twenty soldiers and gentlemen, along with two bishops, who entered the city by Porta Capuana; this large entourage was joined by forty horse-drawn wagons, forty Carmelite monks, and nearly all the members of Ferrante's confraternity, who were carrying torches. The coffin was then enclosed in a second coffin richly decorated in gold, and covered in black velvet. Directly behind the funeral litter, which was drawn by two mules, a group of Neapolitan barons and members of the royal court also wearing mourning clothes accompanied the cortege as it made its way to the cathedral church of San Domenico Maggiore. There, a very short distance from the Colonna palace on Via Mezzocannone, Ferrante was laid to rest alongside the sarcophagi of the Aragonese kings Alfonso, Ferdinand I, and Ferdinand II, as well as other members of the Spanish ruling class. A monument for Ferrante was planned, for which the great poet Ludovico Ariosto wrote an epitaph in Latin, praising Ferrante for having conquered Mars, mortality, and envy ("*Mortem et Martem vincit et Invidiam*") with his glorious fame.

Neither monument nor epitaph was ever erected, however, and in the eighteenth century the Spanish tombs were relocated within San Domenico Maggiore from the main chapel to the new sacristy, where they still can be seen today. The sacristy is a haunting space, largely empty save for the walnut benches and cabinets along the walls to keep the clerical vestments. But the gallery above, which can be accessed only by a small staircase at the far end of the room, is densely packed with Aragonese tombs. There are forty-two coffins in all, each of which is covered in beautiful velvets and silks, in hues of red, pink, and gold. The coffins lie side by side on two different levels of the gallery, with small but dignified gaps between them, so that no two touch. Gracing almost all of the tombs are framed portraits of the dead, which meet your eye as you gaze upward from the stone floors of the sacristy below. Ferrante's tomb not only bears his portrait, which was done in profile (his eyes are therefore harder to meet), but also a painted epitaph and a sword nailed at a diagonal. The sword is not the original—this is kept in Naples's

Capodimonte Museum—but its presence serves as a reminder of Ferrante's fame as a soldier.

In the very detailed description of the funeral that has survived, there is no mention of Vittoria's presence. Her absence was not surprising: starting in the thirteenth century, women were prohibited from attending funerals in many Italian cities. This came about in response to the perception, which had developed over the course of the Middle Ages, that women were too loud and wild in their grieving. They were said to wail, tear their clothes and hair, and make an enormous racket, all of which violated basic funerary decorum. In Bologna, a law was passed in 1276 decreeing that female mourners were not allowed to leave the house until the corpse was actually buried, and similar statutes were passed in a number of other cities. Women's grieving, the church ruled, should be conducted within the home, where the corpse was typically brought to rest in the days preceding the funeral. Outside the public gaze, widows, mothers, and daughters could touch, kiss, and weep over their dead as much as they liked.

It is certainly possible that Vittoria would have been permitted to attend Ferrante's funeral—aristocrats routinely broke all sorts of rules—but it seems she remained in Marino. Indeed, at just about the same time that Ferrante was being buried in Naples, Vittoria was planning her own move back to that city. Sometime in the spring of 1526, she sent a letter to Pope Clement with a very unusual request. Her letter has not survived, but his response—written on May 5, just three weeks before he signed the new treaty with France and became once again the Colonna's enemy—was found in the late nineteenth century inside the Secret Archive of the Vatican (Archivio Segreto Vaticano). The term "Secret" officially means that this is the personal archive of matters related to the pope, as opposed to other departments of the Roman Curia, and does not carry the connotation it does in English of something hidden. But in this case it may just as well mean secret, since the letter was unknown to the world until its discovery in the late 1880s.

To the best of my knowledge, the translation I am providing here marks the first time Clement's letter to Vittoria, which was written in a very formal and difficult Latin, has ever been published in either Italian or English. Although it is quite long, I am reproducing it in its entirety in order fully to convey just how peculiar the circumstances it describes actually were:

> Beloved daughter in Christ, our greetings and our apostolic blessing.
>
> You have informed us that, being bereft of your husband (a man of distinguished memory), in order to give rest and recovery to your mind and for a retreat free from human concerns, you intend to inhabit a certain house in the city of Naples, which was left to you by said husband, together with four or six honorable women of chaste life and there to serve God the highest more in mind and heart than with the profession of any Rule; and that you would like to be able to have Mass and the Divine Office celebrated, in accordance with the inward fervor of your devotion, in a certain shrine or chapel, which you intend to have built in said house, and to be able, for the sake of your devotion, to keep the Sacrament of the Eucharist in a marble tabernacle gilded and under lock and key, with lamps burning day and night, something which you are not permitted to do without the special permission of the Apostolic See, and for this reason you humbly implored us to deign to assent, out of apostolic kindness, to your pious and honorable desire of this sort.
>
> What your Nobility seeks from us is something we have so far granted to no other, and something that has customarily been granted by the Holy See only rarely, since the home of the Sacrament (which wisdom has built for itself) ought to be the church alone. Nevertheless, in our opinion, since your devotion and piety and manifold virtues (which you, surpassing your womanly sex, have added to the nobility of your family) are as formidable as our own fatherly benevolence toward you and all your people would demand, we have judged that we should not deny this very thing [i.e., your request] for your spiritual consolation, since we hope (and hold as certain) that you, mindful of the dignity and glory of your heavenly Bridegroom and Lord (whom you will be hosting), will take care of and venerate such a great sacrament with that purity of spirit and feeling of devotion that is proper

for you, being born from such a family and being distinguished by so many virtues.

Therefore giving assent to your humble and devoted prayers, [we grant and allow] you so long as you can and are able to: have in said tabernacle, adorned as is fitting, the Sacrament of the Eucharist, kept by a suitable priest to be chosen by you with due honor and reverence, in your domestic shrine or chapel of this kind, which you will have blessed by some bishop who has the favor and fellowship of the Apostolic See, in such manner that it never hereafter be turned to any profane use, due to this kind of placement of the Sacrament; keep it there continuously in due veneration; and retain it there with the lamps continually lit; and have Mass and other Divine Offices celebrated as often as you shall wish; and receive the Sacrament of the Eucharist, for yourself as well as the aforesaid women, from the same priest, even on Easter Day (without the prior clearance of a parish priest); that you can and are able to [do these things] without anyone's permission being required, we grant and allow by Apostolic authority, by the intent and meaning of the matters contained here, with no opposing Apostolic or synodal or provincial dispositions or regulations or any other contrary issue whatsoever.

The letter was signed at Saint Peter's at Rome "under the ring of the fisherman"—this was the signet ring that the pope used until the mid-nineteenth century to seal official documents—on "the fifth day of May, 1526, in the third year of our pontificate."

Clement's letter is dense and theologically fussy, but it sheds important light both on Vittoria's plans for her widowhood and on her status in the world. Above all, it reveals that she had absolutely no intention of giving up on her desire to live like a nun. The pope may have forbidden her from taking the veil in December, but she had come back to him the following spring with a bold new proposal to create, in effect, a nunnery of her own.

At its core, Vittoria's request can be reduced to three central points: she wanted to live alone with a small group of women in Naples; to build a private chapel within her house; and to have her own priest at her disposal so that she could celebrate Communion whenever she liked. This last detail was certainly the most radical of the three. Because Catholic doctrine holds that once consecrated, the Host, or Eucharist, is the real body of Christ, keeping it from contamination or harm was an absolutely central concern of the church. Indeed, there was great anxiety among theologians as to what might happen to the crumbs that could fall from the priest's hands after breaking a piece of the bread or wafer to give to the celebrant. Priests were instructed to keep their fingers close, and the celebrant, for his or her part, was not supposed to cough or spit immediately after receiving Communion. If any crumbs escaped and were picked up by a mouse, for example, the consequences were very unpleasant. According to Peter Paludanus (Pierre de la Palu), a Dominican monk active in the early fourteenth century, the priest was required to reserve and sort through the mouse's entrails, in order to recover the portion of the wafer that the mouse had eaten. This remainder of the wafer, whatever its condition, "must reverently be laid up in the tabernacle, until it may naturally be consumed."

Given this level of anxiety and precaution, for Clement to give a laywoman the right to keep the Host within her own home—requiring her, of course, to secure it "in a marble tabernacle gilded and under lock and key, with lamps burning day and night"—was truly exceptional. Was he feeling guilty for having prevented her from taking the veil at San Silvestro? Or did he think this might be a way of keeping her as his ally while tensions with her brother were escalating? Why Vittoria would have asked for these arrangements, by contrast, is much easier to understand. She wanted to live a completely religious life, worship whenever she pleased, and have no need to leave her home even on Easter Day. She also wanted the exclusive company of women. Far from accepting the fate that had been dealt her, she was fighting to control her own future. In Clement's response to her lost letter, Vittoria's innermost hopes and desires were laid bare.

There is no trace of this exchange anywhere in Vittoria's surviving correspondence, and therefore no way of knowing why her plan never came to fruition. Without Clement's letter, the whole episode would have been absent from the historical record, and it would have seemed that Vittoria had simply accepted her fate to live with Ascanio and his family. Most likely, however, her desire to create her own religious house in Naples was thwarted by the unfortunate timing of events later in May. Within several weeks of having granted her permission, Clement had signed the treaty with France, and therefore had committed himself to going to war against the Colonna and their allies. The idea that Vittoria would at that very moment set up the equivalent of a private convent with his blessing must have been out of the question. She was stuck, for the time, in Marino.

Glancing back in June 1526 at the events of the previous year, Vittoria had reason to be overwhelmed with despair. Not only had she lost her husband, but she had also been refused the right to become a nun, forced to move home with her brother, and then prevented from embarking on a new religious life designed to suit her every need. She was back where her life had begun, in the family castle, with Ascanio waging war against the pope. What was she to do? Having run out of options for formally withdrawing from the world, she found a new medium for her grief. Following in the footsteps of the great fourteenth-century poet Francesco Petrarca, Vittoria transformed her sorrows into verse.

BECOMING A POET

I T IS TEMPTING TO THINK that Vittoria felt liberated by her widow-hood, but all the evidence suggests this was not the case. Whatever her disappointments with Ferrante may have been during their marriage—and they certainly were very real—they seem to have disap-peared with his death. When Giovio spent time with Vittoria on Ischia in the fall of 1527, he described her as having finally "tempered and assuaged her incredible anguish." "Although the abiding reason for her bitter lamentation lies heavily on her mind," Giovio wrote, "it seems to have been limited and brought under control, as if her tears had been dried." Whether Vittoria genuinely missed Ferrante, or felt overwhelmed with regret for all the things that had not gone well between them, or was simply struggling to imagine her future as a widow, it was clear to Giovio that she had spent several years consumed by grief.

None of this was necessarily surprising. Italian widows were expected to mourn their husbands, and pray on behalf of their souls, for most of their waking hours. Being a widow was considered, in effect, a full-time job. Everything about the widow's personal appearance was supposed to communicate her new status: she was to wear all black, eschew any ornaments or jewels, and cover her hair with a long veil. The use of the veil was a relatively recent innovation in Vittoria's period: before the fifteenth century, widows let their hair fall wildly about their bodies as a symbol of their own undoing after the priest had administered their husbands' last rites, and then began their often very loud lamentations. We might think of the many paintings done of Mary Magdalene at the foot of the cross, for example, in which she is weeping extravagantly, with her hair loosely falling onto her dress or the legs of Christ himself.

The idea of taming the female mourner's hair was part of the general trend in the Renaissance to quiet women down, if not to repress their grief altogether. This is consistent with the laws that prohibited women from attending funerals: the widow's mourning was officially moved, as we have seen, from the public to the private sphere. When widows did appear in public, they were supposed to keep a very low profile. According to the Venetian author and engraver Cesare Vecellio, who wrote a book in the late sixteenth century on habits of dress that included several hundred woodcuts modeling female costume, if widows need to appear in public, they "wear their *cappa* [mantle] low on their foreheads, and go through the streets sadly, and with lowered heads." "As long as they want to remain widowed," Vecellio added—using the verb *vedovare*, from the noun for "widow," *vedova*—"they wear a train and put on no colored clothing." The fact that Italian has a special verb for the state of being a widow suggests how important a role this was, and how carefully the widow's boundaries were patrolled.

On the whole, Vittoria seems to have adhered to the standard widow's protocol. As Giovio and others attested, she dressed in black, covered her hair with a veil, stayed largely indoors, and prayed regularly for her husband's soul. But in other respects Vittoria was unconventional, or at least her mourning did not take the standard form of lamentation. For unlike any of the recommended behavior described in Renaissance advice manuals for women, she chose not simply to pray, but also to write. In poetry, Vittoria found a more complex outlet for her grief than anything the prayer books had in mind.

When Vittoria started to write her poems to Ferrante in the mid-1520s—in the end, she composed more than 130 sonnets—she broke entirely new ground for women's poetry. There was a tradition in Italy of male poets writing sonnet cycles—long series of sonnets linked to one another to form a kind of narrative—which dated back to the thirteenth-century poet Guittone d'Arezzo, but was associated primarily with Petrarca (known in English as Petrarch). Petrarch's *Canzoniere*, consisting of 366 poems, became the most imitated book of poetry ever written, and launched a sonnet vogue across all of Europe. Very little of this poetry was written by women, however, before Vittoria took up her pen, and no Italian woman had ever published a book of her own poems before Vittoria's *Rime* appeared in 1538. Thus Vittoria was a pioneer both in reversing the usual gender roles of the sonnet series—for the first time, a woman was writing poems to her husband, and not a husband (or more often, a lover) to his wife or mistress—and in having her sonnets to Ferrante circulate in print.

One of the most striking features of Petrarch's *Canzoniere* was that his beloved, Laura—whom he probably never spoke to at any length in real life and certainly did not know well—died two-thirds of the way through his series. Despite her death, Petrarch did not miss a beat: he talked to Laura's spirit in heaven on a regular basis, and even received reassurances from her that she was waiting for him there. Laura's death, in fact, turned out to be something of a vindication. After decades of loving her without any real contact between them—"Love held me," Petrarch exclaims in one of the last poems in the series, for "twenty-one years gladly burning in the fire and full of hope amid sorrow," and then for "ten more years of weeping"—the celestial Laura confides to him that she expects them to spend eternity together.* "Peace be with you," she tells him, "here never again, no, but we shall meet again elsewhere."†

Vittoria read the *Canzoniere* carefully—there are many echoes of

---

* *Canzoniere* 364: "*Tennemi Amor anni ventuno ardendo, / lieto nel foco, et nel duol: pien di speme; / poi che madonna e 'l mio cor seco inseme / saliro al ciel, dieci altri anni piangendo.*"
† *Canzoniere* 328: "*Rimanetevi in pace, o cari amici. / Qui mai più no, ma rivedremne altrove.*"

Petrarch's poems in her own—and the final sequence of 103 poems that many Renaissance editions labeled "*in morte di Madonna Laura*" ("upon the death of my lady Laura") resonated powerfully with her feelings as a widow. Yet however much she both admired and imitated Petrarch, her own *in morte* poetry assumed a very different emotional tone. For Petrarch, the transition from loving Laura while she was alive to loving her when she was dead was relatively seamless (it helped, of course, that they did not have a real relationship). Vittoria's poems, by contrast, reflect her active struggle to maintain a connection with her deceased husband. She was not nearly so gifted a poet—he was one of the greatest lyric poets ever to have lived—but her sonnets reveal much more of her lived experience than we ever glean about Petrarch from the *Canzoniere*. Vittoria's sonnets are compelling less as poetic artifacts than as personal confessions.

The idea that writing sonnets liberated Vittoria to express her grief might at first seem counterintuitive. After all, the sonnet was a highly restricted and inflexible form: its rhyme scheme and meter had to follow certain patterns, its length of fourteen lines was nonnegotiable. But it is entirely possible that Vittoria was attracted to the sonnet because, not in spite, of its formal limits. For someone who had hoped to spend her life in a nunnery performing ritualized cycles of prayer and worship, the discipline of the sonnet may well have been its chief attraction. Like the cloister, it was a completely enclosed form. Indeed, Vittoria seems to have thrived on creative constraints, which heightened rather than hindered her self-expression. Within the confines of the sonnet, she found her poetic voice.

Vittoria had already written poetry before she began the posthumous sonnets to Ferrante. How much she had written is not clear, since only one poem from earlier in her life has survived: the long verse epistle she composed for Ferrante in 1512 after his capture at the Battle of Ravenna. But the fact that several of her contemporaries referred to her as a poet in the decade before Ferrante's death confirms that she was both composing and sharing poems at the time. Some of the praise she received in that period was quite extravagant. The first time her name appeared in print was in a 1519 collection of poems, *La gelosia del Sole*

(*The Sun's Jealousy*), by the Neapolitan poet Girolamo Britonio, who met Vittoria at Costanza's salon in Ischia in 1512 and became one of her great admirers; he dedicated the first book of his poems to her. Britonio writes that the god Apollo—patron of music and poetry—became jealous of Vittoria's gifts after hearing her poetry, and grudgingly named her "this gentle new Phoenix in the world." Sometime around 1520, a second Neapolitan poet, Iacopo Campanile (known as Capanio), also a member of Costanza's literary circle, declared Vittoria "a new Apollo."

In a similar spirit, an anonymous artist made a portrait medal of Vittoria, just under two inches in diameter, that seems to be modeled after the image of Sappho that Raphael had recently painted in his Parnassus fresco for the Stanza della Segnatura in the papal apartments of the Vatican Palace. It is not clear when the medal was struck, but the fact that there is an image of Ferrante on the reverse side suggests it was done during their marriage, and Vittoria is certainly not portrayed as a widow, as she is on other medals made later in her life. She is shown in profile wearing a draped classical garment, her hair loosely tied back and knotted on the top of her head; several locks drop onto her neck, and her left breast is bare. We do not know who commissioned the medal, but these portraits were a popular way for the Italian elite to share their images with friends and admirers, and they were steadily exchanged within Vittoria's social circle. If she commissioned the medal, it is worth registering that she may have already been imagining herself—in the years before Ferrante's death—as a poet.

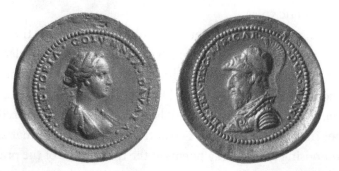

Unattributed medal of Vittoria Colonna and Ferrante d'Avalos
(Kunsthistorisches Museum, Vienna)

There is no question that Vittoria wrote poems during her marriage, and she may even have come to identify herself as a Renaissance Sappho. But it was only after her widowhood that she embarked on a major poetic project. Whether she actually made the decision to write a series, modeling herself after Petrarch and the scores of male poets who had imitated him, or simply wrote the sonnets one at a time until they ultimately achieved a critical mass, remains unclear. But she left several clues about her purpose behind.

First, Vittoria never bothered to put the sonnets in any particular order, nor did she establish which of the multiple versions she wrote for many of the sonnets was her final version. This has made editing her poetry a complex task, and helps to explain why there is still no authoritative edition, even in Italian. Given the fact that the poems were published many times during her lifetime—we will discuss these publications later on—she could easily have made sure that they were printed in the order and form that she preferred. The fact that she never did so makes it difficult to believe that she was particularly concerned about how they would be read.

Second, on the few occasions when Vittoria commented on her reasons for writing the sonnets, she described something more like psychotherapy than literary ambition. The very first line that most readers would have seen when they opened one of the early printed editions of the sonnets was this: "I write only to vent my inward pain" ("*Scrivo sol per sfogar l'interna doglia*"). This very personal sense of what she was doing is worlds away from how Petrarch, for example, begins the *Canzoniere*, which opens with a very self-conscious gesture toward his audience: "You who hear in scattered rhymes the sound / of those sighs with which I nourished my heart / in my first, youthful error."* Vittoria is speaking to herself, Petrarch to his public.

The rest of Vittoria's first sonnet intensifies this sense of privacy:

---

* "*Voi ch'ascoltate in rime sparse il suono / di quei sospiri ond'io nudriva 'l core / in sul mio primo giovenile errore.*"

I write only to vent my inward pain
sent to my heart by his eyes without peer,
and not to add more light to my fair Sun,
to his distinguished spirit and honored flesh.
I have good reason to express my fear
that I reduce his glory through my rhymes,
he who merits greater voices, wiser words
to spare his name from the reach of death.
May the purity of my faith, the depth
of my passion serve to justify me
since neither time nor reason relieves my grief.
Tears born of bitterness, and not sweet song,
sighs draped in darkness, and not voice serene,
will redeem not my style, but my sorrow.*

Perhaps in her mourning she has forgotten or at least put aside all memories of Ferrante's flaws—she refers to him not only here, but throughout the sonnets, as her "Sun," and imagines his glory to have no equal. And yet, she understands her own task not as one of enhancing his fame—this she claims she would leave to "greater voices, wiser words"—but simply as expressing her sadness. This theme of her weakness as a poet surfaces repeatedly: she declares in a later sonnet, for example, that she resists using a file (*lima*) to polish her poems, and does not like to "adorn or erase my rough, unsophisticated verse."[†] Perhaps this was a useful strategy for her to adopt as a woman working in a genre so entirely dominated by men, or perhaps she truly felt inadequate in the face of what she perceived as Ferrante's great heroism.

* A1.1: "*Scrivo sol per sfogar l'interna doglia / ch'al cor mandar le luci al mondo sole, / e non per giunger lume al mio bel Sole, / al chiaro spirto e a l'onorata spoglia. / Giusta cagion a lamentar m'invoglia; / ch'io scemi la sua gloria assai mi dole; / per altra tromba e più sagge parole / convien ch'a morte il gran nome si toglia. / La pura fe', l'ardor, l'intensa pena / mi scusi appo ciascun; ché 'l grave pianto / è tal che tempo né ragion l'affrena. / Amaro lacrimar, non dolce canto, / foschi sospiri e non voce serena, / di stil no ma di duol mi danno vanto.*"
[†] S1.4: "*S'in man prender non soglio unqua la lima . . . Io non adorno / Né tergo la mia rozza incolta rima.*"

The claim to substitute weeping for style is in tension, however, with the sonnets' technical perfection. Vittoria does not usually deviate from the traditional Petrarchan model, in which the fourteen lines divide into an octave, made up of two groups of four lines each known as a *quartina*, or quatrain, with a rhyme scheme of *abba abba*, followed by a sestet, which introduces either two or three new rhyming words, forming two groups of three lines, known as *terzine*, or tercets (*cdc cdc, cde cde*, or a variant on this pattern). Not only does she follow this formula carefully, but she also tends to use a limited number of metaphors so that the images she introduces early in the poem are almost always carried through, without great variation, to the end. In this sense, Vittoria was not a great exploiter of the *volta*, or turn, at line 9, which is where the drama of the Italian sonnet occurs: in leaving behind the first set of rhymes, the poet often makes a significant change in position, so that both form and content shift. (In the Shakespearean sonnet, which features three quatrains, the most striking transition is usually in the final couplet.) Vittoria's sonnets, by contrast, usually reflect a single mood, or explore a particular problem, without radical changes in positions. This somewhat static use of the genre, combined with her rigorous adherence to rhyme and meter, can make the poems feel less compelling; Michelangelo, for example, with whom she exchanged many poems later in her life, was a more idiosyncratic, and therefore often more original, sonneteer.

It is also the case that Vittoria's declaration in the first sonnet that she is writing only for herself is belied by many subsequent poems in which she makes clear that she anticipates an audience, whom she is eager to impress. It is the intensity of her grief, however, and not the quality of her verse, that she wants to convey. These sonnets seem driven by two central motivations: to bestow more praise on Ferrante, and to receive more recognition for the gravity of her loss. So she begins one sonnet with a reference to her "great immortal wound that assures me / of fresh pain as the long years go by," and then declares: "I take pleasure in making known to the world / what I have always known."* This mention of

---

* A1.82: "*L'alta piaga immortal, che m'assicura / di novo stral con lungo volger d'anni . . . / Godo tanto in veder che 'l mondo intende / quel ch'io pria vidi.*"

"the world" ("*il mondo*") suggests she had in mind a large and presumably anonymous group of readers who would come to appreciate Ferrante's heroic virtue through her poems. It is for this reason, she declares, that she pursues her poetic project, even if the writing itself is a daily reminder of his glory, which prevents her from moving past her mourning. The recognition she brings to her husband, she concludes, transforms her sorrow into a *soave offesa*, an injury that nonetheless brings pleasure.

This is the most positive account that Vittoria gives of her poems, and it is by no means a position she maintains. On another occasion, she worries precisely that the quality of her verse is so poor as to intensify her pain, and annoy those around her:

> My grief pushed me to write, and yet I found
> no style worthy of my noble cause,
> so that I carry hidden in me the pain
> of my error, so much that it hurts my heart.
> My sad song, which grows only sadder with time,
> annoys others more than it comforts me;
> I fear in truth it has so little merit
> that it would be for the best to be quiet.

Perhaps, she concludes, she should simply keep her suffering to herself:

> It helps neither me, nor my luminous saint;
> since his valor and suffering surpass
> even what Mount Helicon might express.
> The time has come for me to hide the fire
> that burns within, and dry my outward tears,
> only those in my heart will live and die.*

---

* A1.74: "*Spinse il dolor la voce e poi non ebbe / per sì bella cagion lo stile accorto, / ma del palese error nascosta porto / la pena, tanto al cor poscia n'increbbe. / Il tristo canto, che col tempo crebbe, / più noia altrui, ch'a me stessa conforto / temo che porga, e al ver tanto vien corto / che per il suo miglior tacer devrebbe. / Né giova a me, né a quel mio lume santo; / ch'al suo valor ed ul tormento è poco / quanto può dir chi più Elicona*

On the one hand, she wanted to give voice to her grief as part of her private process of mourning. On the other hand, she wanted her mourning to be admired by others, and feared their disapproval so much that she claimed to consider putting an end to her poetry altogether. She was clearly torn.

Whatever Vittoria's hopes for her readership, her poems succeeded in giving voice to her personal experience in a manner that surpassed all but a handful of her letters. In this respect, her aim of venting her pain—the verb *sfogare*, which she uses in the first line of the first sonnet, means literally to allow liquids or gases to flow openly—seems to have been achieved. To work through the full collection of her sonnets to Ferrante is to come to understand not only her sadness about her widowhood, but also her reluctance to remarry, her regret over not having children, her feelings of despair, her expectations for her afterlife. It is to glimpse Vittoria as intimately as possible.

What do we learn about Vittoria's inner life from reading her sonnets? We already knew that she wanted to be a nun, and this meant that she was imagining a future without men. But in her sonnets, she explains her certainty that she is incapable of ever loving again. "Love wrapped me in so noble a flame," she begins one poem,

> that even once out it continues to burn.
> Nor do I fear new fire, since the first
> is so strong it extinguishes all others.
> So rich a bond ties me to that fine yoke,
> that my heart disdains all lesser chains.
> It feels no longer either hope or fear,
> Since one fire inflames it, one knot binds it tight.

---

onora. / *Tempo è ch'ardendo dentro ascoso il foco / mai sempre sé di fuor rasciughi 'l pianto, / e sol d'intorno al cor rinasca e mora."*

"A single pungent arrow afflicts my breast," she continues,

> so that it keeps alive the immortal wound,
> it shields all other love from entering.
> Love consumed the passion where once he lit it,
> he broke the bow with his enduring shot,
> he melted his knots in tying this one.*

This is a good example of how Vittoria uses the sonnet to express a single idea. The metaphors may shift from fire to arrow to knot, but there is no *volta* at line 9, no rethinking or reversing her position. Instead, the accumulation of images is meant to strengthen her point: that her love for Ferrante, however unreciprocated, affected her so deeply that she considered herself finished with romantic love. As we shall see, this did not prevent her from forming profound attachments to several men over the next decades. But it was her strong conviction in the sonnets that Cupid "broke his bow," and was done with her forever.

We knew that Vittoria was in deep mourning after Ferrante's death. But only in her sonnets do we learn that she had contemplated taking her own life. Given how religious she was, this is truly surprising, and it shows that grief brought her to what might today be diagnosed as severe depression. What stopped her from taking her own life was not her awareness of the church's prohibition against suicide, and her fear of the punishment that would follow. Her primary concern was more romantic, and less pious. In one of the only long poems—a *canzone* of seventy-six lines—that she wrote in her widowhood, she compares herself to Brutus's wife, Portia, who killed herself in despair following her husband's absence and change in fortune after his murder of Julius

---

* A1.7: "*Di così nobil fiamma Amor mi cinse / ch'essendo morta, in me vive l'ardore; / né temo nuovo caldo, ché 'l vigore / del primo foco mio tutt'altri estinse. / Ricco legame al bel giogo m'avinse / sì che disdegna umil catena il core; / non più speranza vuol, non più timore; / un solo incendio l'arse, un nodo il strinse. / Scelto dardo pungente il petto offese, / ond'ei riserba la piaga immortale / per schermo contra ogni amoroso impaccio. / Per me la face spense ove l'accese; / l'arco spezzò ne l'aventar d'un strale; / sciolse i suo' nodi in l'annodar d'un laccio.*"

Caesar. As the ancient Greek biographer Plutarch related in his *Life of Marcus Brutus*, a text Vittoria may well have known in its Latin translation (it did not appear in Italian until 1543), Portia "snatched some burning charcoal out of the fire, and shutting it close in her mouth, stifled herself, and died."

For Vittoria, what differentiates her own situation from that of the Roman matron is that Portia did not have expectations for a better life after death: "with little hope / of another better life, she gave herself other wings." As Vittoria imagines it, Portia thought her suicide would bring her to a complete, annihilating end—what Portia's contemporary the great Roman poet Catullus famously described as an eternal sleep ("*nox est perpetua una dormienda*") without any subsequent consequences. But in a Christian universe, death was followed by judgment, and Vittoria was concerned about the life to come:

> In my heart a quick and mortal sorrow
> grips me without end, and only the hope
> of my serene soul for immortal life
> restrains me from my burning desire.
> Not only the fear of eternal pain
> but the longing for my Sun holds me back.*

She worries, in short, that by committing suicide she will be sent to hell, and hence will never have the chance to meet Ferrante again. This is a fear she repeats in a second poem:

> So heavy are the thoughts that afflict me,
> and dominate my mind, my heart, my soul,
> that life is to me pure bitterness,
> and my body a tedious weight . . .
> The time will come when either my sorrow

* A1.89: "*con poca speme / d'altra vita miglior le diede altr'ale; / e nel mio cor dolor vivo e mortale / siede mai sempre, e de l'alma serena / vita immortal questa speranza toglie / forza a l'ardite voglie; / né pur sol il timor d'eterna pena, / ma 'l gir lungi al mio Sol la man raffrena.*"

defeats me, or by his help I am called
to Heaven, ending these long, painful days.
My own hand, encouraged so often by grief,
would have done it, but then my burning zeal
to find him again keeps holding me back.*

As in Petrarch's fantasies about Laura, Vittoria was clearly imagining a posthumous reunion with her husband in heaven. (She may have over-estimated Ferrante's whereabouts—purgatory at best seems a more realistic bet.)

We knew that Vittoria spent much of her day fulfilling her duties as a widow. But nowhere outside the sonnets did she express frustration with her mourning or the desire to put it behind her. Indeed, in a few of the poems that typically appeared late in the series, she makes a startling confession: she is tired of mourning and wants to embark on a new path. So she begins one sonnet:

Why endlessly implore the deaf ears of Death
and cry to the Heavens with my sad plaint
if I might defeat my strong desire
myself and bring a quick end to my grief?
Why beat on the closed doors of others
if I can open within me a door to forget
and close the window to my thoughts,
so that I deceive my ill-fated star?

The notion of bringing "a quick end to my grief" or "open[ing] within me a door to forget" sounds as if it will lead to another consideration of suicide. But at the *volta* in line 9—in this instance, she uses the opportunity to shift gears afforded by the rhyme scheme to

---

* A1.47: "*Di gravosi pensier la turba infesta / domina sì la mente, il cor e l'alma, / che l'aspra vita e la noiosa salma / l'una m'è grave omai, l'altra molesta . . . / Tempo ben fòra ch'o del martir vinta / o dal soccorso suo chiamata al Cielo / avesser fin sì lunghi e amari giorni! / La propria man dal duol più volte spinta / fatto l'avria, ma quell'ardente zelo / di trovar lui fa pur ch'a dietro torni.*"

great effect—it becomes clear that she has something very different in mind:

> How many defenses have I tried in vain,
> How many ways have I sought to free
> my soul from this blind prison of grief.
> I am left only to see if I have
> reason enough within me that I might
> turn my unsound desires to better works.*

To describe her widowhood as a "blind prison of grief" ("*carcer cieco del mio grave dolor*") and her mourning for Ferrante as sick or unsound desire (the Italian is *insano*, which was used in the period more often to indicate poor judgment rather than actual insanity) takes us far from anything we might expect a devout Catholic woman to say. But the sonnet is not, in the end, impious or irreverent—on the contrary. It is a quiet declaration of her intention to shift from mourning her husband's death to serving God. Vittoria wants to perform "better works" ("*miglior opre*"), a phrase that picks up on the Catholic Church's commitment to works alongside faith as the means to salvation. In this sonnet, we glimpse the earliest hints of her preparing to lead an exclusively religious life.

We knew that Vittoria was devoted to both Ferrante and God. But nowhere outside the sonnets did she express her fear that her two loves were potentially incompatible. In one sonnet, she compares the influence of Ferrante's heavenly spirit to the burning heat of the sun dissolving ice, or the north wind scattering clouds. "So my beloved Sun forbids," she declares, "all base thoughts from polluting my heart." If Ferrante's influence is so strong while she is on earth, how can she even

---

* A1.64: "*A che sempre chiamar la sorda morte / e far pietoso il Ciel col pianger mio / se vincer meco istessa il gran desio / sarà in por fine al duol per vie più corte? / A che picchiar l'altrui sì chiuse porte / se in me con aprirne una al proprio oblio / e chiuder l'altra al mio pensier poss'io / spreggiar l'aversa stella e l'empia sorte? / Quante difese, quante vie discopre / l'anima per uscir del carcer cieco / del mio grave dolor, tentato ho invano; / riman sol a provar se vive meco / tanta ragion ch'io volga quest'insano / desir fuor di speranza a miglior opre.*"

imagine what it will be like to "perceive his splendor unimpeded?" Her joyous anticipation of seeing Ferrante in heaven provokes, however, one of the most interesting conflicts raised in the sonnets:

> As the burning heat of the sun dissolves
> the ice, and the northern wind scatters
> the clouds, so my beloved Sun forbids
> all base thoughts from polluting my heart.
> My lord enters his dominion and clears
> my mind of its enemies, so that he
> illuminates my spirit with his blessed light,
> and extinguishes all other concerns.
> Now if this is my fate on earth, what then
> will await me when I lose my mortal flesh
> and perceive his splendor unimpeded?
> I fear only that my joy in his rays
> will block from my view Heaven's greater light
> and no other fire will ignite me.*

Perhaps, she worries, her great love for Ferrante will actually impede her from being "ignite[d]" by God's love (the Italian verb is *accendere*, which is what one does with a candle). In a moment of profound honesty, she asks whether her love for her husband, however chaste and pious, might not prove an obstacle in her heavenly future.

Given the religious and intellectual world in which Vittoria lived, the question she raises in this sonnet is quite radical. For it runs directly counter to the central tenets of Florentine Neoplatonism, the school of philosophy that dominated Italian ideas about love in the late fifteenth

---

* A1.86: "*Come il calor del gran pianeta ardente / dissolve il ghiaccio, o ver borea tur-bato / fuga le nubi, così il Sole amato / nïun basso pensier nel cor consente. / Vien donno nel suo albergo e la mia mente / di suo' nimici sgombra, ond'è illustrato / mio spirto alor dal suo lume beato; / l'altre cure men degne ha in tutto spente. / Or, se ciò è in terra, che fia dunque poi / che sarà tolto il grave mortal velo, / sì che tanto splendor non mi contende? / Temo sol che sì lieta i raggi suoi / vedrò ch'altro maggior lume nel Cielo / non mi fia noto, n'altro ardor m'accende.*"

and sixteenth centuries. Neoplatonism came into fashion in Renaissance Italy largely due to the work of a single man, Marsilio Ficino, who was born near Florence in 1433. The son of the personal physician of Cosimo il Vecchio de' Medici—the founder of the Medici dynasty—Ficino was educated in a city newly inspired by Platonism, thanks to a visit to Cosimo's court in the 1430s by a passionate Platonist from Constantinople, George Gemistos Plethon. In the 1460s, Ficino took on the enormous task of translating the complete works of Plato (he also translated, along the way, all of Plotinus). By making Plato available to such a wide readership—nearly all educated Europeans in the fifteenth century read Latin—he dramatically transformed the philosophical landscape.

For Renaissance poets interested in love, Ficino's greatest contribution was his commentary on Plato's *Symposium*. More an original dialogue than a straightforward translation, Ficino's work was written in Latin, but he translated it almost immediately into Italian, thereby reaching an even greater audience. The popularity of his book, written in the late 1460s, centered on his treatment of a single speech of the female philosopher Diotima in the *Symposium*, which introduced the idea of the so-called ladder of love. At the end of the long, drunken banquet attended by Socrates and his friends, Diotima explains that there need be no incompatibility between loving the beauty of a single person and loving the abstract idea of beauty—these are merely stages on a continuum. Love leads, she affirms, from the earthly to the heavenly spheres without interruption or conflict:

> The correct way for [someone] to go, or be led by another, to the things of love, is to begin from the beautiful things in this world, and using these as steps, to climb ever upwards for the sake of that other beauty, going from one to two and from two to all beautiful bodies, and from beautiful bodies to beautiful practices, and from beautiful practices to beautiful kinds of knowledge, and from beautiful kinds of knowledge finally to that particular knowledge which is knowledge solely of the beautiful itself, so that at last [he or she] may know what the beautiful itself really is.

In the hands of Ficino, Diotima's ladder of love was adapted to a Christian model, whereby love of a single person could ultimately lead to love of the divine. This was an immensely useful concept for Italian poets, who found in Diotima's words a justification for their adoration of their earthly beloveds. It also represented an important change from what Petrarch had done in his *Canzoniere*, written a century before Ficino's translation of the *Symposium*—a text that Petrarch likely knew about, but probably never read (despite his great learning, he did not know Greek). At the very end of the *Canzoniere*, Petrarch officially renounces his love for Laura and turns his devotion to the Virgin Mary. "Escort me to the better path," he implores, "and accept my changed desires."* How sincere Petrarch was in making such a renunciation is a matter of debate, but what is important is his sense that he needed to do so.

One hundred years later, however, and equipped with Ficino's commentary, Italian poets no longer needed to fear—as Petrarch evidently had—that their love of a woman was inherently idolatrous. Located somewhere along Diotima's ladder, earthly love could be justified as a means to a spiritual end. Ficino made possible, that is, a completely harmonious transition from human to divine love, and his ideas spread throughout Italian courtly and poetic circles. The strongest example of this diffusion came in a book written by one of Vittoria's friends, Baldassarre Castiglione, entitled *Il Cortegiano*, known in English as *The Courtier* (see plate 9). In a speech at the end of *The Courtier*, which became one of the most popular books in all of Europe, the great poet and humanist Pietro Bembo (who was also Vittoria's friend) summarized the Christian interpretation of Diotima's speech (see plate 10). "The lover," Bembo declared, "will make use of this love as a step by which to mount to a love far more sublime . . . By the ladder that bears the image of sensual beauty at its lowest rung, let us ascend to the lofty mansion where heavenly, lovely, and true beauty dwells, which lies hidden in the inmost secret recesses of God."

Vittoria may well have read Ficino's commentary on Plato's

---

* *Canzoniere* 366, "*prego che sia mia scorta, / et la mia tòrta | via drizzi a buon fine.*"

Symposium—she was an avid reader—and she certainly knew the Neo-platonic poetry, Bembo's included, that had been written in the fifty years since Ficino's book first appeared in print. But all signs suggest she was no Neoplatonist, and she actively resisted the very idea that she might reconcile her earthly and divine love. The fact that after finishing the sonnets to Ferrante Vittoria abandoned the project of love poetry altogether is the strongest possible proof of her misgivings about climbing the Platonic ladder.

Vittoria began writing her sonnets to Ferrante sometime in 1526, when her grief was fresh. She was still working on the poems—and working through her mourning—seven years later, as she announces in one of the sonnets:

> I hoped that with time my ardent desire
> would cool down some, or that my mortal grief
> would so overwhelm my heart that by now,
> this seventh year, my sighs would be heard no more.*

This long period of mourning—and writing—was also described in an ode addressed to Vittoria by her friend Bernardo Tasso (father of the more famous poet Torquato, author of the great epic *Gerusalemme liberata*):

> But you in the seventh year
> weep as much as in the first,
> and with heavy grief,
> call to your great d'Avalos,
> now with your voice, now with your ink.†

We will return to the way in which Vittoria's poems circulated during this period, as well as to the praise she received from Tasso and other

---

* A2.29: "*Sperai che 'l tempo i caldi alti desiri / temprasse alquanto, o dal mortale af-fanno / fosse il cor vinto sì che 'l settimo anno / non s'udisser sì lungi i miei sospiri.*"
† "*Ma voi nel settim'anno / Qual nel primo piangete, / E con gravoso affanno / Il gran Davalo vostro / Chiamate or con la voce, or con l'inchiostro.*"

poets. But there is ample evidence that during the seven-year period Vittoria and Tasso described—roughly between 1526 and 1533—the sonnets she wrote after Ferrante's death were being widely read within literary circles, if not also by a larger public audience. By the end of those seven years, as we shall see, her mourning was behind her, and she had begun to dedicate herself to spiritual verse. Yet however much she may have wanted to distance herself from her poems to Ferrante later in her life, they played a crucial role in her self-understanding both as a poet and as a woman. It was through these sonnets that she was able to say things that had no place in the official language of Renaissance widowhood—things that were meant to be repressed, along with loud wailing and loose hair—and came to recognize her desire to forge her own path, outside her obligations to the dead. Through her sonnets to Ferrante, Vittoria became a powerful artist, with a vocation of her own.

THE SACK OF ROME

VITTORIA BEGAN THE PROJECT of writing her sonnets to Ferrante around the time of her move to Marino during the spring of 1526. Marino, which despite its name was far from the sea, occupied a strategically important location as one of the first elevations in the lands above the surrounding plain in the area to the east of Rome. (The town's Latin name, Castrimoenium, from *castrum*, or castle, and *moenium*, fortification, was a better fit.) Located directly on the postal route that led from Rome to Naples, it had also become something of a commercial hub, and was much more lively than many of the neighboring Colonna towns. Today Marino is far from the A1 *autostrada* that leads from Rome to Naples. Apart from several partially ruined towers, the castle has left few traces, and the town feels worlds away from either the metropolis or the battlefield. There is no reason, frankly, for tourists to go to Marino, and the people I have met on my multiple visits there seemed incredulous that I had come on purpose. It's a perfectly pleasant city, but there are no wonderful churches or squares, and no monuments of note.

How Vittoria felt about her birthplace is not clear. Unlike Ischia, whose landscape she praised on multiple occasions, she never mentioned Marino in any detail. There were certainly things in Marino that would have appealed to her, especially its religious sites. At the Sanctuary of Santa Maria dell'Orto, a cult site dedicated to the Virgin, there was a beautiful altarpiece of the Madonna dating to the eighth or ninth century; the lovely Gothic church, Santa Lucia da Siracusa, had as its prize possession a Byzantine icon known as the Madonna del Popolo, which a member of Vittoria's family, Cardinal Giacomo Colonna, had brought home from Constantinople around 1280. Given how many of Vittoria's religious poems and meditations later in her life were dedicated to the Virgin, it is tempting to think some of her inspiration may have come from her early encounters with these works of art.

Even if Marino were full of places and objects that Vittoria loved, it was not where she had wanted to live following Ferrante's death. Although she had been prevented from taking vows as a nun, she did not intend to spend her years as a widow residing in a family castle. What she wanted most of all, as Pope Clement's letter from the spring of 1526 made clear, was to be left to mourn in peace. We will recall Clement's explanation for why he was granting her the special permission to set up a private religious house in Naples: "in order," he wrote, "to give rest and recovery to your mind and for a retreat free from human concerns." Perhaps in some respects the castle in Marino provided this kind of retreat: Vittoria could hide away in her rooms to pray or write as she liked, while her brother and his allies busied themselves with planning their latest attacks.

By May 1526, Ascanio and his cousin Pompeo Colonna were actively preparing their armies to join Charles V's troops in battle against the pope. On the surface of things, Pompeo was an odd partner in this enterprise, having been named a cardinal by Leo X in 1517. This choice of profession, however, was not his own: when his uncle, Cardinal Giovanni Colonna, was dying, Pompeo was the only relative eligible to take over Giovanni's office, as his three older brothers were already married (the church tried to keep benefices within the family if at all possible). In his heart, Pompeo remained a soldier, and he spent most of his career serving the kings of Naples. Indeed, his loyalties leaned so heavily toward the Spanish that he was twice excommunicated from the church: first, in 1501, when he fought on behalf of the Spanish against the French allies of Pope Alexander VI; and again following the events of 1526.

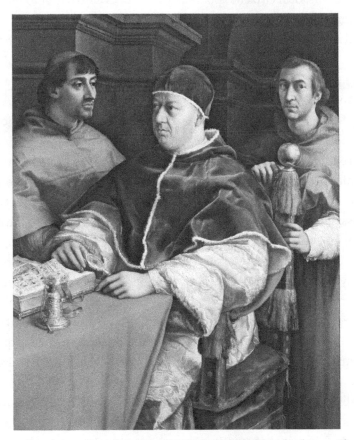

Portrait of Pope Leo X with Cardinals Giulio de' Medici (the future Clement VII) and Luigi de' Rossi, by Raphael (Gallerie degli Uffizi, Florence)

Ascanio and Pompeo were directly involved with Charles's plan to attack Clement on his own terrain and raid the city of Rome. The combined forces of the Colonna's armies and the available troops of the emperor, led by the Spanish general Hugo of Moncada, were approximately five thousand infantry and more than three hundred horsemen. By contrast, Clement had sent much of his army to Lombardy, in the north of the peninsula, where he was also fighting against imperial troops, and was left in Rome with roughly two hundred infantry and a hundred horsemen.

When the Colonna troops entered the gates of Rome in September 1526, the local citizens apparently did not even attempt to interfere: the family enjoyed great popularity among the people, many of whom shared their hostility toward the pope. The citizens were therefore shocked by the heavy looting and destruction that followed as the soldiers, joined by the Spanish troops led by Moncada, made their way toward the Vatican. Pope Clement fled to the papal fortress of Castel Sant'Angelo along the banks of the Tiber to take refuge, and there was almost no resistance to the troops' advance.

Around this time, Ascanio seems to have decided that Vittoria was not safe in Marino, where the pope's army was likely to strike back. This would not have been the first time in Vittoria's life that papal troops had assaulted the family castle. In 1501, Alexander VI ordered the castle in Marino, along with several other Colonna castles in the area, to be razed to the ground in retaliation for Vittoria's father Fabrizio's having destroyed the harvest of several of the pope's allies in the region. This was part of a much larger conflict between Alexander and the Neapolitan king Ferdinand IV, in which the Spanish and the Colonna troops were ultimately defeated. Fabrizio was taken prisoner and subsequently excommunicated, along with his cousin Pompeo; Alexander also deprived them of their feuds and all of their temporal goods.

Fabrizio and Pompeo's losses lasted only until Pope Alexander's death in 1503, when they made peace with his son Cesare Borgia, captain general of the papal army. The new pope, Julius II, born Giuliano della Rovere, was on much better terms with the Colonna than Alexander had been—his family had close ties both to the Colonna and to the family of Vittoria's mother, the Montefeltro of Urbino. Julius not only welcomed Fabrizio and his relatives back into the church, but also returned to them their properties, several of which had actually been refortified at great expense by Pope Alexander.

Ascanio may not have been old enough to register what was happening when the family fled from Marino in 1501—his birthdate is not

certain but is estimated to be a few years before 1500. Vittoria, however, was eleven, and would no doubt have remembered the flight from
home, if not the conflagration itself (there are no records of the family's
movements at this moment, but it is likely they left Marino before the
attack on the castle). In the fall of 1526, history repeated itself: the papal
troops once again attacked the Colonna estates, and destroyed Marino
along with fourteen of their other feudal territories. The destruction was
carried out by papal soldiers from the nearby city of Velletri, who, in
addition to burning down as much as they could of the Marino castle,
also stole the celebrated icon of the Madonna del Popolo and the bells
in the campanile from the church of Santa Lucia. This gave rise to a famous chant among the Marinesi about their neighbors the Velletrani:
"*Velletrani, rubba Madonne, rubba campane*" ("the Velletrani, they steal
Madonnas, they steal church bells"—it has more of a ring in Italian).

Vittoria left Marino before the castle was attacked, and traveled to
Aquino, some sixty miles to the southeast of Marino. Aquino had recently been restored to the d'Avalos family after a tumultuous period
in which control over the town changed hands multiple times. There,
in the birthplace and namesake of the great thirteenth-century philosopher Tommaso d'Aquino, or Thomas Aquinas (a distant relative of
Ferrante's grandmother Antonella d'Aquino), Vittoria spent several
months far removed from the destruction sweeping the Colonna lands.
Whether she saw much of Aquino's beautiful medieval quarter with its
imposing rectangular tower, the remains of its Roman aqueduct and the
stunning first-century arch, or ever prayed in the town's splendid Romanesque church, the Chiesa della Madonna della Libera, graced with
mosaics from the twelfth century, cannot be said. Her letters from this
period were entirely consumed with the events taking place in Rome.

Soon after her arrival in Aquino, Vittoria received a long letter from
Charles V. Perhaps he was finally registering how inadequately he had
recognized Ferrante's service to him, or perhaps he was making sure of
her continued support in the escalating conflict with the pope. The letter,
dated November 9, 1526, and written from Granada, rehearsed once
again both Charles's grief in the loss of Ferrante—nearly equal, he
imagined, to Vittoria's—and the joy he felt, and urged her to feel, in

celebrating Ferrante's posthumous glory. He concluded by suggesting that the rewards owed to Ferrante might now be passed along to his heir and cousin, Alfonso d'Avalos, Marquis of Vasto: "We certainly will always honor [Ferrante] with the most pleasant memories of his outstanding service, both from the more remote past as in more recent days, and the heartfelt gratitude that we have shown for him, we now feel for the illustrious Marquis of Vasto, who has succeeded him not only in his skills but also in his virtues." We do not know what Vittoria made of this letter—no response of hers has survived—but it is striking that Charles was thinking about her, and concerned about her state of mind.

At roughly the same time that she received the emperor's letter, Vittoria wrote to her friend (and Charles's adversary) Gian Matteo Giberti, the papal secretary and bishop of Verona. This was not the first or last time that Vittoria managed to maintain relations with both sides during an active conflict, and Giberti himself recognized the sacrifice she was making in writing to a member of the pope's inner circle. Vittoria's letter to Giberti is lost, but we can reconstruct at least some of its contents from his response, which was dated December 9, 1526. He began by expressing his deep regret about the devastation of the Colonna lands, and the expulsion of Vittoria's cousin Pompeo from the Sacred College of Cardinals. "Your excellence may rest assured," he wrote, "that it was most bitter to me to see our Lord [Clement] forced by the serious offense to turn and destroy that house which I have always desired to see most great."

Vittoria had no doubt shared her deep dismay over the razing of the Marino castle, but she must have done so without calling into question her continued affection for Giberti. He thanked her, in any case, for not subjecting him to the "hatred of the others, which has been the reward of my service [to the pope]," and indicated his willingness to do absolutely anything that she might ask of him. "Nor can you do me a more singular favor than to command me," he wrote, "for you will find me always most ready to obey you."

The year 1526 came to an end with a truce between the warring parties, which lasted several months. During that time, Vittoria moved from Aquino to Ischia, where she stayed for most of the next five years. From this safe distance, she learned about the gruesome siege on the part of the imperial troops, known to history as the Sack of Rome. News of the sack took two to three days to reach Florence; it must have taken twice that time to arrive at the remote island castle in the Bay of Naples. Thus sometime in the middle of May 1527, Vittoria got word of what had befallen her beloved city.

On the evening of May 5, the emperor's commander Charles III, Duke of Bourbon, reached Rome with an army of roughly eight thousand men. Having begun his career as one of the finest soldiers in the French army, which led to his appointment as constable of France in 1515, Bourbon fell out of Francis I's favor in the early 1520s, and in 1524 joined Charles V's service as, among other charges, commander of an army of German mercenaries. He was the last of the French lords to fight against his own king. After his heroic service leading the cavalry at the Battle of Pavia (Ferrante was in charge of the infantry), Bourbon was appointed governor of Milan. It was from this northern city that he made his way to Rome, accompanied by his underpaid and already pillaging troops. The men were mostly German and Spanish, with a smaller number of Italians and Frenchmen.

The pope's army in Rome, led by an Italian mercenary from the Orsini family, Renzo da Ceri, was once again inadequate in both numbers and skill. However talented a commander Renzo was, his chances of success against Charles's soldiers were very low: he was given only three thousand infantry to defend the entire city, some of whom were men who had been dragged out from the households of the papal curia. We might recall Falstaff's piercing description of his soldiers in Shakespeare's *Henry IV*: "Tut, tut, good enough to toss; food for powder, food for powder. They'll fill a pit as well as better."

Bourbon arrived beneath the walls of the Borgo—the area of Rome bordered by the Vatican to the west and the Tiber to the east—and demanded that his troops be admitted to the city. Not surprisingly, the pope refused them entry. At this point, early in the morning of May 6, the soldiers began to scale the Borgo's stone walls, aided by a dense fog, which made it difficult for the artillerymen inside Castel

Sant'Angelo, where Clement was once again sequestered, to fire their cannon—they simply could not see their targets. The fog was later interpreted by Charles V's followers as a sign of divine support for their cause.

Bourbon himself was positioned with a group of Spanish troops outside one of the lowest points in the wall, not far from Saint Peter's Basilica. After making a rousing speech in which he compared the Spaniards' imminent attack on Rome to their recent conquests in the New World—"When I begin to imagine this," he reportedly said, "I seem to see all of you shining in golden armor, all lords and princes of conquered lands"—he was killed scaling the wall, shot by a ball fired from an arquebus (a type of rifle invented in the fifteenth century). Bourbon's death did not, however, deter his soldiers: it only increased their rage. Once they had successfully knocked down part of the wall, they poured into the city. In the three days that followed, Rome was subjected to the worst violence it had seen in more than a thousand years. As the Florentine statesman Luigi Guicciardini—brother of the famous historian Francesco—recounted in his book *The Sack of Rome*: "If anyone had been walking through the streets of Rome by day or night, he would have heard not sighs and tearful laments, but the pitiful cries and screams of hapless prisoners coming from every house and building." If we think of the fantasy captured by Raphael in his painting *Incendio di Borgo*, or *Fire in the Borgo*, which depicts the ninth-century pope Leo IV miraculously extinguishing a fire that was raging in front of Saint Peter's, we see how far the image of the pope had fallen. Raphael's painting, commissioned by Leo X and begun in 1514 for his private dining room in the Vatican, shows the medieval pontiff standing proudly in Saint Peter's Loggia delle Benedizioni, saving both the church and the people of Rome with a simple sign of the cross. Clement, hiding away in Castel Sant'Angelo while the imperial army burned and looted his city, cut a very poor figure indeed.

Rome turned out to be so easy to conquer, in fact, due to a series of miscalculations that Clement had made in the months immediately preceding the sack. In March, he had signed a truce with one of the emperor's chief generals, Charles de Lannoy, viceroy of Naples from

1522 to 1527. Mistakenly imagining that this agreement carried with it the consent of all of Charles V's commanders—the army was made up of many different factions, each with its own ax to grind—Clement had prematurely dismissed the so-called *Bande Nere*, or Black Bands, the hugely effective group of Italian mercenaries formed originally in 1516 to protect Leo X. (The Black Bands were constituted by Pope Leo's cousin, Ludovico di Giovanni de' Medici, known as Giovanni delle Bande Nere.) Clement made this decision for purely economic reasons: he was already in bad financial straits and desperately needed to reduce his expenditures. What he had not anticipated, of course, was that Lannoy had failed to convince Bourbon to accept the peace treaty.

Apart from the local militia, there were very few soldiers left in Rome to defend the city, and among them were several cowards, including, as it turned out, the papal commander Renzo da Ceri. Seeing that the battle was lost, Renzo was said to have screamed out, "The enemy are within! Save yourselves, retreat to the strongest and safest places!" and then run to Castel Sant'Angelo to escape from the fighting. According to Guicciardini, who described the events as vividly as if they unfolded before his eyes, Renzo "was immediately followed by everyone who was around him in a state of confusion and terror . . . He reached the bridge at the same time as many other soldiers and Roman civilians who had abandoned the ramparts when they heard he had fled."

Having managed to kill or scare off nearly all the papal troops within a day's time, the attackers began the robbing and pillaging of Rome. One palace after another was seized from its owners, and churches were systematically plundered. The destruction visited upon the churches was generally blamed on the German mercenaries known as the Landsknechts, who were Lutherans and despised the Catholic sanctuaries. In truth, the Italian and Spanish Catholics did not behave much better than their Protestant counterparts. There were men from the Colonna estates who flooded into the city on May 10 to profit from the looting; Pompeo tried to stop them, but to little avail.

Charles's soldiers not only plundered riches from Roman palaces and churches, but also committed countless acts of violence against

Roman citizens, who were kidnapped, raped, and murdered. One of the pope's followers, Pietro Corsi, described seeing fathers forced to buy back, "at the cost of robes, gold, houses, [and] estates," the corpses of their children, who had died from tortures "of the kind that all antiquity did not see." He also reported with horror the soldiers' cruel persecution of victims of the plague, which was already raging and only intensified as the living conditions in the city continued to worsen: "Men dragging with difficulty their infected limbs were summoned into foul torments and hung from a beam either by the feet or by that one part of the body which public decency covers (but always with the miserable one's hands bound behind his back), compelled by fire or by the sword, amidst a hastened death, to [produce] gems and precious vases and gold that they had never possessed."

Guicciardini similarly recounted perverse and inhuman acts of violence meant to reveal the soldiers' depravity. A priest was "shamelessly and cruelly killed because he refused to administer the most holy sacrament to a mule." The mule, he added, had been dressed in clerical vestments. Young girls were torn away from their mothers' breasts, and violated inside churches. "I will not describe what happened to the noble and beautiful young matrons, to virgins and nuns," he exclaimed, "in order not to shame anyone. The majority were ransomed, and anyone can easily imagine for himself what must have happened when these women found themselves in the hands of such lustful people as the Spaniards."

Because it was nearly impossible to flee the city—the gates had all been barred—the only hope for the desperate Roman populace was to take refuge inside the city walls. The pope remained in Castel Sant'Angelo, where he was joined by several thousand churchmen and friends. Others retreated to the homes of the emperor's allies, which they mistakenly thought would be spared. Nearly four hundred people, for example, including Pietro Corsi, moved into Cardinal Andrea della Valle's palace, and a group of comparable size crowded into the home of Cardinal Giovanni Piccolomini. Within a week or two, however, and after exorbitant sums had been extorted from the inhabitants to keep themselves safe—an Italian captain in the imperial army managed to collect more than thirty-five thousand ducats to protect those hiding away in della Valle's home—the palaces were attacked by the Landsknechts. The only residence in Rome that seems to have escaped harm was the Palazzo Colonna in Piazza Santi Apostoli, which Pompeo Colonna had personally secured, with more than two thousand Roman citizens lodged within.

Although Vittoria was on Ischia, far away from these events, she kept herself well informed. She also worked hard to intervene on behalf of her friends implicated in the conflict, especially Giberti, who was one of seven hostages whom the pope had handed over to the imperial troops. After Vittoria sent a letter to Pompeo begging for Giberti's release, Pompeo moved him to the Palazzo Colonna. The letter Vittoria sent to Pompeo is lost, but a letter from Giberti to Vittoria, written on November 26, 1527, reveals how instrumental she had been in securing his safety. His language was almost absurdly mannered, although such exquisiteness, bordering on aggression, was not unusual for formal letters of the period. "I would wish," Giberti declared, "not to have been as certain as I have already been of 'your love and goodness for me,' so that these demonstrations of it that you have made and make more effectively every day, were they new and unexpected, would fill me with so much pleasure that they would make every travail I experience delightful." Vittoria must have included a copy of her letter to Pompeo inside the letter she sent to Giberti, since he mentioned that he had seen what she had written, and was more grateful to her than ever: "I would thank you for the collateral you offered from your estate, on my behalf, but how can I thank you, or what do I have that I can promise to you again, being as I am completely obliged and indebted to you now more than ever."

Pompeo turned out to be one of the only imperial commanders who helped to rescue some of the papal supporters, and to restore order in Rome. When the German and Spanish troops who had left the city over the summer of 1527 due to the onset of plague tried to resume their looting and plundering that fall, it was Pompeo who kept them at bay. According to the humanist Pietro Alcionio, who had taken refuge with the pope in Castel Sant'Angelo but successfully defected to the

Colonna side in the siege's immediate aftermath, Pompeo was almost single-handedly responsible for rescuing the city from ruin. Alcionio died sometime in early 1528, but he wrote four Latin orations on the events in the months preceding his death. The last of these, addressed to Pompeo and entitled "On the Deliverance of the City," praised his new patron for having "dashed to pieces the audacity and ruthlessness of those who returned by force of arms into Rome, from which they had gone out by force of law." Alcionio described the Machiavellian tactics Pompeo used to persuade the invading soldiers to put an end to their destruction—he bribed, threatened, and did whatever was necessary. In one instance, Alcionio reported that Pompeo helped the hostages inside Palazzo Colonna get the guards sufficiently drunk so that they could escape; the liberated citizens then rode through Rome dressed as German soldiers. For all of Pompeo's service to the city, Alcionio declared, the citizens planned to erect a statue in honor of him (no trace of such a monument has survived).

None of Pompeo's heroic gestures, however, were of use to the pope. Bankrupted by the combination of military costs and ransom money that he was forced to pay the emperor, Clement was held as a prisoner in his very own fortress. After long negotiations with the emperor's agents, on December 6, 1527, he was finally given permission to leave Rome. He slipped out at dawn in disguise, out of fear for his safety at the hands of the Landsknechts, and traveled to Orvieto. Perched high on top of a volcanic rock, this town of Etruscan origins had served as a refuge for no fewer than six popes in the thirteenth century, and was particularly favored by Clement, who referred to it as "our city" in 1525.

Despite his physical safety in Orvieto, Clement was hardly a free man: nearly all his territories were occupied by imperial troops, five of his cardinals were being held hostage in Rome and Naples, and those members of his curia who had moved with him to Orvieto were under close surveillance by Charles V's agents. When the English king Henry VIII sent ambassadors to meet with Clement in Orvieto in hopes of obtaining support for his divorce from Catherine of Aragon, Charles made clear that Clement would face serious consequences should he abandon the cause of his beloved aunt (Catherine was the sister of Charles's mother, Joanna of Castille). In addition to his lack of freedom, Clement was also stripped of his usual splendor. According to the cleric Luigi Lippomano, the court in Orvieto was "more or less in ruins, and penniless." "The bishops go about on foot," he remarked, "with skullcaps and threadbare cloaks, and the courtiers blaspheme against God, as though they have lost all hope. The cardinals go about with four menservants and riding mules, the way they did in the primitive church, but with their accustomed dishonorable attitudes, and they would sell Christ for a farthing." Orvieto's papal palace was itself in a state of neglect, and its furnishings regarded as inadequate. In the words of the English ambassador, Stephen Gardiner, bishop of Winchester, the pope's chambers were "all naked and unhanged, the roofs fallen down, and as we can guess, 30 persons, riff raff and other, standing in the chamber for a garnishment."

Clement was finally able to return to Rome in October 1528, but the city he found was severely broken. To observers both in Italy and abroad, Rome's second Golden Age seemed to have come to an end—and with it, the end of an era more broadly. As the great Dutch humanist Desiderius Erasmus put it in a letter to the Italian reformer Iacopo Sadoleto, bishop of Carpentras: "Assuredly this was more truly the destruction of the world than of a city." Many of the most talented artists and poets who had enjoyed the extravagant patronage of the Medici popes, Leo X and Clement VII, fled from Rome, seeking refuge in courts and palaces elsewhere. One of the most sought-after destinations was the d'Avalos castle in Ischia. There, Costanza d'Avalos opened her doors to an extraordinary group of individuals who came together on the beautiful island in the middle of the sea to form a civilized world of their own. Once again, Vittoria was thwarted in her desire for a quiet retreat. And yet, what looked at first like the very last thing she wanted turned out to have its rewards.

LIFE AT COURT

W HEN VITTORIA LEFT ISCHIA for her ill-fated trip to Milan at the
end of 1525, the d'Avalos castle had few inhabitants, and even
fewer guests. Two years later, in the aftermath of the Sack of Rome,
the castle was transformed from a sleepy fortress to a bustling world of
its own. For the first time since the Aragonese kings of Naples had used
the castle as a playground at the end of the fifteenth century—they would
travel across the Bay of Naples with visiting dignitaries and statesmen,
friends and relatives, to enjoy the pleasures of the island—life on Ischia
rivaled that of the liveliest Renaissance courts.

There is no comparable environment in our modern world to a Renaissance court. An elegant country house filled with talented guests is
probably the closest equivalent, but the comparison works only super-
ficially. Even if Renaissance courts looked from the outside like fancy
homes filled with impressive people, they were also the equivalent of
small kingdoms. Each court had its own ruler—a duke or marquis, or
sometimes a duchess or marchioness—who was officially the vassal of a
larger entity, such as the Holy Roman Empire or the Papal States, but
in practice exercised nearly complete control over his or her dominion.

The servants at court included ambassadors, political advisers, military officers, lawyers, masters of revenue, soldiers, secretaries, architects, musicians, artists, and entertainers, as well as the domestic staff typical of any great household: stewards, chamberlains, grooms, paymasters, dispensers, muleteers, coachmen, falconers, butlers, cantineers, carvers, cooks, under-cooks, bakers, keepers of the poultry, stable assistants, charwomen, and personal maids and valets for each member of the family.

Vittoria did not grow up in such a world: her childhood was largely spent, as we have seen, in the feudal castle of Marino and the busy metropolises of Rome and Naples. She would have known all about court life, however, from her mother, Agnese, who was the daughter of Federico da Montefeltro, Duke of Urbino. The illegitimate son of Guidantonio da Montefeltro, whose long marriage to Rengarda Malatesta had produced no heir, Federico was officially recognized by the church as legitimate in 1424, following Guidantonio's remarriage to Caterina Colonna, whose uncle was Pope Martin V. After the very brief reign of his half brother, Oddantonio, who was assassinated under suspicious circumstances, Federico became Urbino's ruler and transformed this small hill city in the Marches into one of the most cultivated courts in all of Europe. He did this through his terrific success as a *condottiere*, using the vast wealth he acquired by waging war to support art, architecture, literature, music, astronomy, philosophy, and medicine at a level unparalleled in all of Italy.

Agnese's mother was Battista Sforza, daughter of Alessandro, Lord of Pesaro, the illegitimate son of the great Sforza *condottiere* Muzio Attendolo. (Alessandro's brother Francesco was the first Sforza duke of Milan.) Battista was thirteen years old at the time of her marriage to the thirty-eight-year-old Federico, whom she had previously considered her uncle—Federico's sister Sveva da Montefeltro had married Battista's father, Alessandro, after the death of Battista's mother, Costanza da Varano. Despite the age difference and the complexity in family relations, the marriage was known to be a happy one and yielded many children: Battista bore Federico at least six daughters before dying after giving birth to a son, Guidobaldo, when she was twenty-five years old.

For lovers of Renaissance art, the marriage of Federico and Battista has been preserved through the magnificent double portrait painted by Piero della Francesca (see plate 12). Piero was the most significant artist of the period to enjoy Federico's patronage, and his paintings for the duke rank among his finest work. The portraits, which can be seen today in the Uffizi Gallery in Florence, are both in profile, a decision shaped in part by Federico's having lost one of his eyes in a jousting tournament, but which lends to the paintings a formal quality typical of ancient medals. Indeed, the portrait of Federico, who is perhaps best remembered for his crooked nose, conjures up the solemnity of a Roman statesman: his expression is simultaneously benevolent and impassive; his gaze does not meet our eyes. Battista's portrait is perhaps most striking for the eerie whiteness of her skin, which has led some art historians to think it was painted after her death in 1472 (the Uffizi dates the panels to sometime between 1465 and 1470). She wears an extravagant headdress, and her forehead is extremely high, which was considered a sign of great beauty. In the background, there is a landscape of infinite gentleness and serenity, which adds to the sense of the exquisite world Federico created for himself and those around him.

There is no record of Vittoria visiting Urbino as a child, when her uncle Guidobaldo and his wife, Elisabetta, the daughter of Federico I Gonzaga, Marquis of Mantua, had replaced her grandparents as duke and duchess. She also had no cousins from that union. As nearly everyone in Italy seems to have known, Guidobaldo was impotent, and his marriage to Elisabetta had never been consummated. Elisabetta was said to have appeared before the court visibly filled with shame the morning after the consummation of the marriage had been "scheduled"—the date was carefully selected by astrologers—and over the coming years, Guidobaldo was rumored to have tried every possible remedy, including magic, but all in vain. Notwithstanding his physical limitations, Elisabetta remained by his side and was regarded by all as a model of wifely virtue and patience.

Vittoria may not have been to Urbino as a child, but she was able to read all about the glories of its court in Castiglione's *The Courtier*. Born in 1478 into a noble family from outside of Mantua—his father, Cristo-

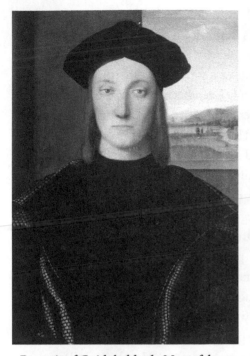

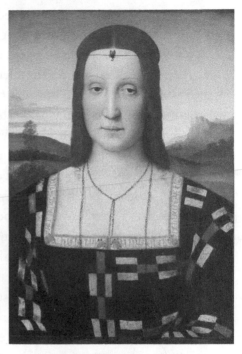

Portrait of Guidobaldo da Montefeltro,
Duke of Urbino, Vittoria's uncle, by
Raphael (Gallerie degli Uffizi, Florence)

Portrait of Elisabetta Gonzaga,
Duchess of Urbino, Vittoria's aunt,
attributed to Raphael
(Gallerie degli Uffizi, Florence)

foro, was one of the leading soldiers in the service of Francesco II Gonzaga, Marquis of Mantua, and his mother, Luigia, was herself a member
of the Nobili branch of the Gonzaga family—Castiglione received a very
fine humanist education at Milan before becoming, in effect, a profes-
sional courtier. He served first at the courts of Ludovico Sforza in Milan
and Francesco II and Isabella d'Este in Mantua before coming to
Urbino in 1504, where he served Guidobaldo and Elisabetta until
Guidobaldo's nephew and heir, Francesco della Rovere, sent him to
Rome as his diplomat in 1513.

When Castiglione arrived in Urbino, Guidobaldo had only recently resumed power after the city had been seized—twice—by Cesare
Borgia. It was only after Cesare's father Alexander VI's death in 1503 and
the subsequent release of fervent anti-Borgia sentiment in Rome that

Guidobaldo's duchy was reinstalled, although his hold on the city remained far from secure. Castiglione's initial appointment at Urbino was as a soldier: he was put in charge of a squad of fifty of Guidobaldo's men to defend the ducal palace. His talents as a statesman quickly emerged, however, and in 1506 he was sent on a diplomatic mission to London, where he received, on Guidobaldo's behalf, the Order of the Garter. While in London, he met with Henry VII, who showered him with gifts, including a thoroughbred horse and several pedigree dogs.

In addition to his military and diplomatic skills, Castiglione was a brilliant observer of the world around him, and a very gifted writer. After leaving Urbino in 1513, he began work on *The Courtier*. On the surface of things, *The Courtier* recounted a series of conversations that supposedly took place at the ducal palace in 1506 (the conversations were almost certainly altered or enhanced). But the experience of *The Courtier*, as its enormous success suggests, was something far greater. Castiglione gave his readers, many of whom were members of the middle or gentry class, an intimate glimpse into the rarefied world of the Italian elite. Aspiring gentlemen in Madrid or Hamburg or Paris could learn about elegant people they never knew, and watch them talk to one another. They could enjoy, in effect, the pleasure of being voyeurs.

Gathered at the ducal palace in Castiglione's book were some of the most celebrated figures of the era. Among them were Giuliano di Lorenzo de' Medici, the son of Lorenzo the Magnificent, who settled in Urbino in 1502 after staying in various other Italian and French courts following the Medici exile from Florence in 1494 (he returned to Florence as ruler of the city in 1512); Count Lodovico Canossa, a nobleman from Verona who became bishop of Tricarico in 1511; Bembo, perhaps the most famous man of letters in all of Italy; Ottaviano Fregoso, who became doge of Genoa in 1513, and his brother Federico, who was made archbishop of Salerno in 1507; and Francesco Maria della Rovere, Guidobaldo's nephew and heir. In all, there were roughly fifteen men mentioned by name, and four women, the most famous of whom was the duchess herself. A great patroness of music and the arts, Elisabetta was celebrated throughout Italy for her exquisite taste and sound judgment, and when Guidobaldo was away from the palace, she ruled the court with great skill.

The conversations that Castiglione recounts took place in the Hall of the Vigils, which lay on the far side of the magnificent Throne Room, and represented the transition between the public and private spaces of the palace's *piano nobile* (literally the "noble level," or main floor). As the Irish poet William Butler Yeats described it some four hundred years later in his poem "The People," it was in the Hall of the Vigils that

> . . . the duchess and her people talked
> The stately midnight through until they stood
> In their great window looking at the dawn.

The "great window" Yeats describes opens onto Urbino's principal piazza and its beautiful cathedral, which was erected in the eleventh century, but was rebuilt by Federico as part of his ambitious renovations to the city. On the other side of the spacious but also somewhat intimate hall where the guests would gather was the duchess's private apartment— her bedchamber, dressing room, and prayer room—which was elaborately decorated with magnificent stucco ribbons, garlands, wreaths, cupids, spirals, and medallions gracing the ceilings; the large wooden doors were carved with symbols of the Montefeltro family and exquisite architectural perspectives. Today the duchess's rooms are open to the public, along with the rest of the palace. But in the sixteenth century, Castiglione's book was the only way in.

The reason for *The Courtier*'s success, however, was not simply the vicarious pleasure of observing famous aristocrats talking to one another in their private chambers. It was the particular topic of their conversation. Every evening after supper, the guests chose a different game or entertainment to occupy them. On the occasion Castiglione described, the evening's activity was to discuss the qualities of the ideal courtier. The group found the conversation so engaging that it was resumed on three consecutive evenings, over the course of which they discussed all of the qualities that young men—and, less centrally, young women— needed to possess in order to become perfect courtiers.

It is not surprising that for educated and ambitious Europeans interested in climbing the social ladder, *The Courtier* became an immensely powerful tool. As Roger Ascham, the tutor to the English princess Elizabeth, described it in his own book *The Schoolmaster*: "Advisedly read, and diligently followed, [*The Courtier*] would do a young gentleman more good than three years travel abroad in Italy." A mixed compliment, to be sure—Englishmen were on the whole fearful of being corrupted by worldly Italians, so the opportunity to stay at home and learn from a book was compelling indeed. But Ascham's observation gets at the allure of Castiglione's book. It handed over a secret code for becoming something you were not.

What did an attentive reader of Castiglione's book learn? The list is nearly endless, but here is a small sampling. The ideal courtier should play the lute or the *viola da mano* (the Spanish *vihuela*, similar to a modern guitar). He should dance without "those quick movements of foot and those double steps" that hardly befit a gentleman. He should play tennis, and also know how to swim, jump, run, and throw stones. He should dress neither as the French, who are sometimes "over-ample," nor as the Germans, who are often "over-scanty," but instead adopt the style of the Italians. He should also wear mostly black. He can play at cards and dice, so long as he is not distracted from more important obligations, but should not spend too much time on chess, which requires too much study and hence deserves the ironic praise of Alexander the Great for "the fellow who at a good distance could impale chickpeas on a needle." He should not be the bearer of bad news, nor be "obstinate and contentious, as are some who seem to delight only in being troublesome and obnoxious like flies." He should not have any "peasant ways that bespeak the hoe and the plow a thousand miles away." He should under no circumstances practice tumbling.

The single most important quality that the courtier needed to have was the most difficult to acquire. The perfect courtier, Castiglione wrote, should "practice in all things a certain *sprezzatura*, so as to conceal all art and make whatever is done or said appear to be without effort and almost without any thought about it." At its core, the idea of *sprezza-*

tura, for which there is no adequate English translation—the closest is "nonchalance," which is actually French—licensed deception. Nobility and grace were not qualities you needed to be born with: they were roles, Castiglione implied, that you could put on. Doing this, of course, was no easy task, but the sheer possibility of becoming a gentleman not by blood but through skill ran counter to everything the world of the Colonna and the Montefeltro stood for. Almost certainly without intending it, Castiglione had launched a revolution.

It is not obvious what a supreme aristocrat like Vittoria gained from reading *The Courtier*. Even if she was not raised at court, she had been surrounded by courtiers her entire life, and the ideal world that Castiglione described was that of her family. The pleasures for her of Castiglione's book must have come in part from seeing that world so beautifully represented. It is a deeply human delight—even if it is often mixed, of course, with some level of discomfort—to have one's own life captured as a form of art. Vittoria may also have felt a kind of nostalgia, as Castiglione himself clearly did, for the milieu of her parents and grandparents, which seemed, however fictitiously, to have been more refined and civilized than her immediate surroundings.

What Vittoria described taking pleasure in when she read Castiglione's book, however, was of a more writerly sort. Put simply, she loved the elegance of his prose. "Beyond its most beautiful and novel subject," she wrote to him in September 1524, "the excellence of its style is such that with a delicateness never felt before it leads you to a lovely and fertile hill, rising so slowly and carefully that you never even realize you are no longer on the level where you began; and it is a path so well cultivated and ornate, that only with difficulty can you discern who had worked harder to make it so beautiful: nature or art."

This is a gorgeous piece of literary criticism, and it shows a very subtle appreciation for what Castiglione had achieved. Indeed, the comparison of reading *The Courtier* to climbing a hill without realizing the effort involved, or struggling to discern whether the path itself is natural or man-made, transformed the book into its own example of *sprezzatura*. At moments like this, Vittoria shows us why writers and artists of the very highest quality—Castiglione, Bembo, and Michelangelo—would seek her opinion of their work in the decades to come. She was a true intellectual peer.

Vittoria wrote these words to Castiglione in response to a request she had received from him to return her copy of his manuscript. In her letter, she politely refused:

> I haven't forgotten to keep my promise to you; on the contrary, it grieves me that my memory [of it] is so fresh that it has continually impeded the delight I take in reading your book, reminding me that I have to return it to you without rereading it as many times as I'd like. And now that you have done me such a disservice of soliciting it from me, and because I am already halfway through my second reading of it, I beg Your Excellency to allow me to finish it.

The combination of compliment (she is reading the book for the second time through) and complaint (he is ruining her reading experience by making his demand for the manuscript) suggests a level of familiarity between the two friends that is otherwise not much in evidence in the surviving letters. It also shows Vittoria at her most playful, or even cheeky: we rarely witness her assuming such a tone of mock grief.

Not only did Vittoria hold on to Castiglione's manuscript, but she also seems to have shared it with some friends, who shared it with other friends—this was the way that manuscripts circulated in the period, often with new copies made along the way. In September 1527, when Castiglione was serving as papal ambassador to Spain, he got word that everyone in Naples was reading his unpublished book. Vittoria had promised him not to show the manuscript to anyone, but apparently she had not kept her word. In fact, she was by no means the only person with a copy: Castiglione had shared the book with many others, but he singled Vittoria out for blame. Having learned of what he regarded as the promiscuous circulation of his manuscript, he claimed that he felt compelled to take matters into his own hands, and decided to allow *The Courtier* to be printed. This was more than a decade after he had finished his first draft—he revised the book rather obsessively over the course of many years. Indeed, it is almost certainly the case that the manuscript Vittoria had was not up-to-date, which may explain why he was so nervous about its falling into the wrong hands, and ending up in print in the earlier version.

In his dedicatory letter to the first edition, which appeared in 1528, Castiglione named Vittoria as responsible for having rushed him to publish the book prematurely:

> Being informed from Italy that signora Vittoria della Colonna, [Marchesa] of Pescara, to whom I had already given a copy of the book, had, contrary to her promise, caused a large part of it to be transcribed, I could not but feel a certain annoyance, fearing the considerable mischief that can arise in such cases . . . Wherefore, alarmed at this danger, I decided to revise at once such small part of the book as time would permit, with the intention of publishing it, thinking it better to let it be seen even slightly corrected by my own hand than much mutilated by the hands of others.

No doubt he was using Vittoria's name to his advantage—she was a famous noblewoman, who added prestige to the book—and there is evidence that he had already made arrangements to print *The Courtier* regardless of whether Vittoria returned the manuscript to him. But in the dedicatory letter, he wanted to stage his resistance to print, for all of his readers to see.

In a private letter to Vittoria, meanwhile, from late September 1527, Castiglione claimed to forgive her for what he called her theft. "I remain in fact more indebted to you," he wrote, "because the necessity of having the book printed immediately has relieved me from the chore of adding many things to it." And yet, his bitterness lingered. He compared himself to a "father who saw his son maltreated, as if he were abandoned in the street to the whims of nature" (he was the father of three children), and then complained that whatever was good about the book had been ruined, because it had been deprived of its only virtue: novelty.

As it turns out, Castiglione was both overestimating the number of people in Vittoria's circle who read the book, and greatly underestimating the number of people across Europe who would soon be his readers. By the early 1600s, there were at least 110 editions of *The Courtier* in print—60 of those in Italian and 50 in other languages, including French, Spanish, German, English, and Latin. The book traveled far and wide, even beyond European borders: in 1586, a Florentine merchant found a copy of *The Courtier* in a match-seller's shop in India. It was, in short, one of the bestselling books of the era, and its success reveals how strong an appeal the elite world of Renaissance Italy had for the rest of the globe.

Vittoria certainly would have had *The Courtier* in mind when she got to Ischia in the summer of 1527. Not only was she in the middle of her exchange with Castiglione about the book's publication, but she found herself for the first time in her life in the position of its female protagonist as the hostess of a lively social world. Ferrante's aunt Costanza was still living in Ischia, but she was by then in her late sixties, and seems to have handed many of the responsibilities of entertaining the guests to her niece. How consciously Vittoria imagined the parallels between her own circumstances and those of her aunt Elisabetta is not clear, but it is telling that within months of her arrival, she had asked one of her guests, Paolo Giovio, to write a version of *The Courtier* situated at the Aragonese castle.

Giovio was the perfect choice to write such a book. Born into a patrician family in the north of Italy in 1483, he had studied both philosophy and medicine, but his real passion was contemporary history (it was he who later wrote Ferrante's biography, also commissioned by Vittoria). The notion that his own world deserved to be recorded reflects an unusual awareness that some Italians had during this period of living at an extraordinary time. The more traditional subject for historical inquiry was the ancient past, which Renaissance humanists had both studied and emulated. But starting in the sixteenth century, there was also a sense of the present moment as remarkable in itself. Hence books such as Castiglione's *Courtier*, or Giorgio Vasari's *Lives of the Artists*, which told the history of Italian art from the late thirteenth-century Tuscan artist Cimabue to Michelangelo, began to appear;

contemporary figures were treated as equivalent in their talents and accomplishments to the great ancient Romans.

Giovio had entered the service of Clement VII as one of his personal physicians, while also fulfilling various humanistic roles, and remained at his side during the Sack of Rome. While they were holed up in Castel Sant'Angelo during the summer of 1527, the pope rewarded him for his loyal service by naming him the bishop of Nocera dei Pagani, a region south of Naples. Shortly after conferring this honor upon him, however, Clement was forced to dismiss Giovio from the fortress due to the enemy's demands that he reduce the number of his retainers. Giovio remained in Rome, which was overwhelmed with plague, before accepting an invitation from Vittoria to come to Ischia. He stayed for a little more than a year. During this time, he began writing *De viris et feminis aetate nostra florentibus*, or *Notable Men and Women of Our Time*.

Giovio's book, like Castiglione's, purported to record a series of conversations that took place in a single location over the course of a few days—in Castiglione's case, there were four dialogues, and in Giovio's, three. The conversations on Ischia were limited to three of the guests: Alfonso d'Avalos, Marquis of Vasto, who at twenty-five was a rising star in Charles's army—he had become commander of the emperor's infantry in Italy; a Neapolitan statesman and humanist, Giovanni Muscettola, who had been sent to the island to urge Alfonso to return to his military duties (it seems he was taking too long of a vacation); and Giovio himself. There were many other interesting figures at the castle, including the young Latin poet Antonio Sebastiani, known as Minturno; the learned and beautiful Princess of Salerno, Isabella Villamarino; Alfonso Piccolomini, Duke of Amalfi, and his wife, Costanza d'Avalos (who was Alfonso's sister and a close friend of Vittoria's); and the very talented wives of Alfonso and Ascanio, the sisters Maria and Giovanna d'Aragona.

Each of the three days that Giovio recorded was dedicated to a single topic of conversation. On the first day, the three men discussed the most outstanding soldiers; on the second, the finest men of letters; and on the third, the most excellent noblewomen. In this respect, *Notable Men and*

Women was more like a lofty gossip column than a handbook that might be useful to its readers: it rehearsed the virtues, and sometimes the flaws, of particular people living at the time. Over the course of describing his contemporaries, Giovio also narrated the activities of the other guests with whom he was living. The events surrounding the first of the three dialogues were the most richly recorded, and give us a good sense of what life at the castle was like during this extraordinary period. The weather that day was fine, and a large group of men and women assembled early in the morning to embark on an ambitious outing. They traveled from the isolated cliffs of the castle to the mainland of the island, where above the scorched rocks was a lake surrounded by "a very beautiful amphitheater, which the leafy hills on all sides, as if drawn in a circle by a compass, display to the singular delight of observers." In this natural theater, the men were to hunt waterfowl. Hunting was one of the central activities on Ischia—in addition to waterfowl, there were regular hunts for deer, partridge, and other game—and the women accompanied the men as spectators.

Giovio described the day's hunt with great ethnographic detail, as if he imagined an audience for whom the events would be both unfamiliar and of great interest. "Young men armed with poles and dogs trained in swamp hunting formed a blockade along the shores," he wrote, while others with bows boarded boats from which they shot clay missiles. Once the hunt began, the birds "were scattered and attacked on every side by a constant rain of missiles, accompanied by applause and mutual congratulations." After those birds that survived retreated from the shoreline into the reeds—"they were too fat, sluggish, and timid to dare to fly out either into the hills or to the adjacent sea"—the battle was resumed in a gorier form on land, with the dogs, wading into the reeds, catching the birds directly in their mouths, and the men killing them with stones and clubs. By the end, there were more than three hundred birds either captured or dead, which were indecorously placed inside the ladies' boats for transport back to the castle.

When the hunt came to an end, the entire group prepared to leave. The women were apparently unwilling to get back on their boats—they were no doubt rightly concerned about becoming nauseated due to the piles of dead birds they would have been sitting with—and the chief magistrate of the island managed at the last minute to arrange for a group of horses to transport the women back to the castle. Giovio lamented, however, that his conversation with Alfonso and Muscettola was brought to an abrupt end. In the modern edition of Giovio's text, this dialogue alone is roughly one hundred pages of small print, so it had in fact been a rather long day.

Giovio's account of the events became even more interesting for our purposes when the group returned to the castle. It was at this point that he first mentioned the fact that Vittoria had not been with them. "Once we had entered the fortress," he wrote, "we offered the entire catch to Vittoria Colonna—because she, having imposed constant mourning upon herself owing to her grief at the loss of her illustrious husband, was not only keeping herself from the public light, but, enclosed in darkened bedchambers, allowed nothing into her grief-stricken mind except for solemn readings and holy sermons." Two years after Ferrante's death, and notwithstanding the company of so many friends, Vittoria's grief had not yet abated. On the contrary: while her guests were out hunting—or swimming, as the Neapolitan queens used to do by the little islands that were subsequently known as the Queens' Rocks; or visiting the ancient temple of Neptune; or relaxing at the beach on benches carved out of mossy tufa—she remained in her dark chambers, reading prayers and sermons. "Such is her lofty and incredible piety," Giovio declared, "that she subdues the flower of her youth by fasting; she covers her delicate flanks not with a silken but rather a woolen vest as her tunic, she wears out her back and knees with daily supplications before statues of the saints; and she even lashes private parts of her body [*pudicas corporis partes*] with the stinging blows of a whip, a punishment undeserved."

How Giovio learned these intimate details about what Vittoria wore under her garments, or in what fashion she whipped her "private parts," was not revealed—perhaps one of her maids was particularly indiscreet. Yet whatever his source, he judged her religious fervor to be excessive: "But why may perpetual divine services be heard at almost every hour? Why are there holy readings from the Old and the New

Testament, why the pious meditations, when even she herself would acknowledge in a lofty preamble that chastity does not reside in great and difficult labor, but in a certain steadfast and firm application of the mind and in a good and zealous will?" From this account, it seems that Vittoria had arranged for a full schedule of liturgical hours and scriptural readings at the castle, possibly within a private chapel of her own. Perhaps she wanted to realize at least partially the dream she had the previous year of creating her own religious house in Naples before the horrors of the Sack of Rome.

At the same time that Vittoria was absorbed by her mourning, she was also successfully playing the role of worldly chatelaine. In Giovio's portrait of her, two very different images emerged. On the one hand, Vittoria was the would-be nun, overdoing her penance, arranging for extra services, and refusing to come outdoors. On the other hand, she was the elegant and gracious hostess, who not only took care of her guests, but also genuinely enjoyed their company. According to Giovio, though she herself was "abstemious," she "brings enthusiasm to choosing the wines, lest the guests find anything lacking. Moreover, she measures the delight of the feast in accordance with desire rather than satiety, and she gauges its splendor, not in terms of recherché, elaborate, and extravagant dishes, but in healthful and delicate provisions as well as elegant and consistently immaculate service."

In addition to choosing the meals and managing the staff with "a hand that is so very generous as almost to be prodigal," Vittoria also strove to create a sophisticated, convivial atmosphere. She had always been accustomed, Giovio remarked, "to receive those calling upon her in a friendly, pleasant and dignified fashion; and if elegant men are present, and especially those renowned in literature, she converses beautifully about matters of the heart and about the entire range of cultivated pleasures. And since she has ears that are neither gloomy nor severe, she takes pleasure in her own wit and in the jokes of others." This is the first instance in the historical record where Vittoria is described as having a good sense of humor, although there is certainly some evidence of this in her letters. But what Giovio especially wanted to emphasize was her commitment to literary conversation. For Vittoria, he

added, there was "nothing finer than to rescue those cast out by shipwreck and by the savage waves of a hostile storm," especially those "who
have derived some commendation and praise from the excellent study
of literature."

It is not a coincidence that many of Vittoria's guests at the time of
Giovio's visit were interested in discussing literature. Indeed, the 1520s
were a very rich decade for Italian poetry, which was having a Renaissance all its own. Although Dante and Petrarch had written the most
famous of all Italian verse centuries earlier, it was only in the early sixteenth century that Italian achieved real parity with Latin. The Italian
that the poets chose was not always their mother tongue: there were
many different dialects spoken at the time (as there still are today), and
the dominant literary language was that of Dante and Petrarch, namely
Tuscan. Giovio, in fact, referred to Vittoria's sonnets as her "Tuscan
poems," which shows that she was well aware of current trends and had
adjusted her own language accordingly.

The second day of Giovio's conversation on Ischia was dedicated to
the most distinguished men of letters, and began with Alfonso's asking
Muscettola why "most of those schooled in Latin and Greek literature
have in this age turned their attention entirely to the vernacular tongue,
departing from the usage of their predecessors?" The question arose
during their discussion of Bembo, who in 1525 had published a treatise
on the Italian language, entitled *Prose della volgar lingua*, or *Discussions of the Vernacular Language*. It is hard fully to capture the cultural
authority that Bembo enjoyed at this time. After leaving Urbino, where
he had been at the very center of Duke Guidobaldo's court, he took up
a position in Rome as secretary to Leo X, who was the brother of his
friend Giuliano di Lorenzo de' Medici (il Magnifico). Already famous
throughout the peninsula for his elegant writings in both Latin and
Italian—he was often compared to Cicero—that circulated during his
nearly ten-year stay in Rome, Bembo became one of the most influential
cultural figures of the era.

Bembo had begun writing *Discussions of the Vernacular Language*
in his final years in Urbino, but he did not finish it until roughly twelve
years later, and it subsequently appeared in print with a dedication to

Pope Clement himself. Thus his book carried with it not only the prestige of Bembo's own name, but also, in effect, a papal imprimatur. His
argument, meanwhile, was a polemical one: he wanted to defend the
vernacular, and specifically Tuscan, as equal to Latin in literary value.
Along the way, he also established a set of grammatical and ortho-
graphic norms that he thought all writers in Italy should follow. The fact
that Giovio and his friends were already debating the virtues of Bembo's
work and the extent of its influence within two years of its publication
gives us some sense of its success. Another sure indication was the fact
that many of the most important Italian authors, including Ariosto and
Castiglione, revised their own works to make sure they conformed to
Bembo's new norms.

One of the unforeseen consequences of Italian replacing Latin as
the standard language for composing poetry was that many more women
entered the literary field. Although many aristocratic girls studied Latin
as children, they were not typically educated at the same level as their
male counterparts, and generally lacked the formal humanist training
that would have enabled them to feel comfortable writing Latin verse.
When Vittoria began composing her sonnets in the 1520s, more women
than ever before—albeit mostly from the upper classes—were writing poems in Italian, and circulating them among their friends. As we
saw with Castiglione's *Courtier*, sharing literary manuscripts did not
necessarily involve publication, but it also did not mean that readership was strictly limited to the author's immediate circle: poems were
routinely copied out, and passed along, without the author's permission. Someone entirely unconnected to Vittoria could have had access to
her sonnets without her knowing anything about it.

Vittoria's sonnets first traveled far from the shores of Ischia through
Giovio himself. During his stay at the castle, Vittoria had given him
her sonnets to read, and he must have had a copy of them made before
he left the island in the fall of 1528. One year later, he attended the
congress held in Bologna to finalize the settlement reached between
Clement VII and Charles V—the occasion when the pope finally recognized Charles as Holy Roman Emperor. Among the many papers that
Giovio brought with him to the congress were Vittoria's poems.

It is worth pausing to think about what it meant for Vittoria's sonnets to have circulated at this great event, which was attended by diplomats and statesmen from all across Europe. Charles arrived in November 1529 with hundreds of courtiers and literally thousands of soldiers; the Italians accompanying the pope were comparably represented. It was during this congress that Bembo, who was there as part of Clement's entourage, first read Vittoria's poems. Vittoria was not altogether a stranger to Bembo. The two may have met roughly a decade earlier in Rome, when the festivities were held to celebrate her cousin Pompeo's cardinalship, and they certainly had dealings with each other in 1525 in relation to the small papal city of Benevento, which was under Ferrante's rule. Benevento had a *commenda*, or ecclesiastical benefice, belonging to the religious order of the Knights of St. John of Jerusalem, which Pope Julius II had given to Bembo in 1508, and which he had fully taken possession of in 1517. The appointment turned out to be much more problematic than Bembo had ever imagined, however, due largely to the town's conflicted loyalties between Rome and Naples. In 1525, when Ferrante was away at war and Vittoria was acting as governor in his place, Bembo appealed to her for help. She managed to have some success, largely through the intervention of Pompeo, although the resolution was short-lived: once Ferrante was dead and Vittoria was no longer ruling Benevento, the benefice met with even more serious trouble, especially in the aftermath of the Sack of Rome.

Whatever their earlier interactions, it was only at the congress begun in late 1529 that Bembo came to know Vittoria as a poet. In January 1530, one month after his arrival in Bologna, he sent her a letter in which he exclaimed, "Among the women in this art form you are more excellent than it seems possible for nature to concede to your sex." "I have taken infinite pleasure [in your poems]," he added, "mixed with great marvel." That this was not merely a compliment paid to a lovely and important woman is proved by a letter Bembo sent to his friend Vettor Soranzo several months later, in which he affirmed that Vittoria's poetry was "truly fine and ingenious and serious, more than one would expect from a woman."

It would be easy today to respond to these comments with some annoyance—why was it so astonishing for a woman to be writing good poems? But in a culture in which women had very rarely been recognized as authors, Bembo's words represented a radical shift. Indeed, he was so impressed with Vittoria's poetry that he sought her opinion of his own poems, and was dazzled by the sensitivity and intelligence of her response. In a letter that Vittoria sent to Giovio, but that was immediately passed on to Bembo, she declared:

> No sonnet I read by anyone, contemporaries or ancients alike, can equal his . . . It seems the endings of his rhymes arrive so often when necessitated by his well-arranged syntax that their beautiful and gentle harmony is heard sooner in the soul than in the ear, and the more they get reread and the more often they are considered, the more they provoke admiration—in fact, I would say [they provoke] envy, if it were not such that my intellect feels so out of proportion to that light . . . I end up feeling totally in love with him, a love beyond any sensual desire.

Bembo was thrilled with Vittoria's words, and wrote to Giovio that "she seems to have far more solid and well-founded a judgment, and can do a more detailed and thorough treatment of my poems, than what I see these days held and executed by the better part of the most knowledgeable men and the greatest teachers of these very things." He also told Giovio to let Vittoria know that he was very eager to meet her but thought he was too old to travel to Ischia (twenty years her senior, he was sixty at the time). This was the beginning of a long and warm friendship—without, as she made clear in this letter, "any sensual desire" ("*ogni sensuale appetito*")—in which the two exchanged not only sonnets but also portraits of each other as tokens of their affection. He sent to Vittoria a medal; she seems to have sent him a small painting.

The most visible proof of Bembo's admiration for Vittoria was his decision to include a sonnet that she had written to him in the appendix to the 1535 edition of his poems. In Vittoria's sonnet, she bemoans the inadequacy of her verse to do justice to Ferrante, and suggests that if a poet of Bembo's stature had praised him instead, both he and her husband would have increased their earthly fame:

Alas, how cruel Fate was to my dear Sun
that with the noble virtue of his rays
he did not find you sooner, so that for thousands of years
you would be more famous, and he more praised.
His name, adorned with your style, would fill
the ancient poets with shame, our own
with envy, and in spite of time would save him
forever from the grip of a second death.*

In Bembo's response, he praises Vittoria's poetry, and demands that Apollo bestow upon her the poet's laurel:

Crown the temples of this woman with the plant
beloved by you when it bore a human face,
since in her rare and elevated verse
she soars above even your finest poets.†

The "plant"—or, more literally, "sapling" ("*arboscello*")—that Bembo refers to was the maiden Daphne, who was transformed into a laurel tree as she ran from Apollo's pursuit. In an elegant twist of this myth, Bembo celebrates Vittoria's more triumphant run, as she "with great strides ascends to true glory."

By the time Bembo published this sonnet exchange in 1535, Vittoria had left Ischia to live once again in Rome. Later in her life, she could look back at these years at the castle as having both launched her poetic career and brought her mourning to a close. The two developments were, in fact, entirely linked. Writing the poems to Ferrante was in the deepest sense, as we have seen, an act of working through her grief, and the island itself seems to have helped her to heal. In one of the son-

---

* A1.71: "*Ahi quanto fu al mio Sol contrario il fato, / che con l'alta virtù dei raggi suoi / pria non v'accese, che mill'anni e poi / voi sareste più chiaro, ei più lodato. / Il nome suo col vostro stile ornato, / che dà scorno agli antichi, invidia a noi, / a mal grado del tempo avreste voi / dal secondo morir sempre guardato.*"

† "*Cingi le costei tempie de l'amato / da te già in volto umano arboscel, poi / ch'ella sorvola i più leggiadri tuoi / poeti col suo verso alto e purgato.*"

nets she wrote at the castle, she movingly describes the way the Ischian landscape lightens her heart:

> When I look out from my beloved rock
> at the earth and sky in the rosy dawn,
> whatever clouds were born in my heart are
> chased away by the clearness of the day.
> Then my own thoughts rise with the sun so that
> I return to my Sun, whom God honors
> with more light, and from this height my soul
> seems to be recalled to its sweet home.*

Vittoria clearly loved the wildness of Ischia's cliffs, the splendid colors of its sea, and the beautiful skies that surrounded her. And yet, by 1534, she was ready to move on. Being in the castle with so many learned and literary people had been very good for her as a poet, but it had not provided her with comparable nourishment for her spirit. She was far away, moreover, from the exciting new world of religious reform that was spreading on the mainland. Word almost certainly had reached her of a group of Spanish and Italian reformers known as the *spirituali*, whose central focus on the individual's relationship to God—without the intervention of priests or even of the church—very much appealed to her own sensibility. After seven years of living more or less continually in the social and largely secular world of the castle, Vittoria left Ischia to pursue a life more fully focused on her faith. She never returned.

---

* A2.13: "*Quando io dal caro scoglio guardo intorno / la terra e 'l mar, ne la vermiglia aurora, / quante nebbie nel ciel son nate alora / scaccia la vaga vista, il chiaro giorno. / S'erge il pensier col sol, ond'io ritorno / al mio, che 'l Ciel di maggior luce onora; / e da questo alto par che ad or ad ora / richiami l'alma al suo dolce soggiorno.*"

AMONG PREACHERS AND PILGRIMS

I N THE CHURCH OF SAN LORENZO in Damaso, adjacent to the Palazzo della Cancelleria in the very heart of Rome, Vittoria sat spellbound. It was Lent, 1535, and she was living once again in the guest quarters at San Silvestro in Capite. Perhaps her favorite outing from the convent was to hear sermons, and on the pulpit that day in San Lorenzo was her favorite new preacher: a charismatic friar from Siena named Bernardino Ochino, who had recently become a Capuchin monk. Named for the pointed hood, or *cappuccino*, they wore on their heads—the modern term *cappuccino* comes from the hood of frothy milk sitting on top of the coffee—the Capuchins were a new order, founded in the 1520s by a Franciscan friar who felt his fellow monks had strayed too far from the strict observance of Saint Francis. This kind of internal strife among the Franciscans had been going on already for several centuries: the absolute poverty that Francis demanded was very difficult to reconcile with the needs of a more established community. By the early 1500s, the Franciscan order had been formally divided between the more moderate Conventuals and the more extreme Observants.

The Capuchins were originally members of the Observants, but had decided that even this stricter way of life was not adequately severe. In 1525, they became an independent branch of the order—the equivalent, in effect, of Franciscan fundamentalists. The Capuchins' monastic houses were not to contain any valuable possessions, and their supplies were not to exceed provisions for a few days. Everything they had to eat or drink was to be obtained through begging, although the friars could not ask for meat, eggs, or cheese—these could be accepted when offered spontaneously—and food was to be gathered each day (and not stored). They were not allowed to touch money. Fasts were to be frequent, and intense. At least two hours a day were to be spent in private prayer. Above all, the order was passionately committed to ministering and preaching to the poor.

When Ochino joined the Capuchins in 1534, he quickly emerged as their most powerful spokesman, delivering sermons that moved his listeners in ways they had never been moved before. Ochino was himself of very humble origins: he was born in 1487 in Siena, where his father, Domenico Tommasini, was a barber. It is not clear where Ochino got his name: some think he was named for a district of Siena known as the Oca; others think the name was given to him due to his small eyes (*occhio* is the Italian for "eye," *occhino* is the diminutive). In 1503 or 1504, he joined the Observant Franciscans, and he remained with them for a number of years before deciding to study medicine at the University of Perugia. He returned to the Franciscans sometime in the early 1520s. The move to the Capuchins a decade later required, as he described it, a very strong act of will: "When I beheld the severity of [the Capuchin] life, I put on their garb, yet not without a severe struggle with my carnal wisdom and my sensuousness. I now deemed to have found what I sought, and I well remember that I turned to Christ with 'Lord, if I do not now save my soul, I know not what more I can do.'"

At the pulpit of San Lorenzo in 1535, Ochino conveyed all of his ambition to reform himself and his fellow Christians. Listeners old enough to have heard Giralomo Savonarola compared Ochino's oratorical gifts to those of the famous late fifteenth-century Dominican, whose thundering sermons about the Apocalypse had drawn nearly all of Florence to hear him. Savonarola was on fire with the zeal to reform the church, and was prepared to risk everything to combat the wickedness he saw around him. It was he who famously burned thousands of objects—cosmetics, mirrors, clothes, books, manuscripts, paintings—in what came to be known as the Bonfire of the Vanities in 1497 during *Carnevale*, or Carnival (in Latin, it means "a farewell to meat," which is why it is celebrated just before the Lenten fast). It is even believed that Botticelli willingly destroyed several works that he had come, thanks to Savonarola, to regard as sinful. Needless to say, the fierce Dominican earned many enemies, including the Borgia pope, Alexander VI, against whom he had preached on many occasions and even organized a council. Alexander excommunicated Savonarola in May 1497, and in 1498 the pope's lawyers and the Florentine government ordered him to be hanged and burned at the stake in the Piazza della Signoria.

Ochino's sermons were of a different emotional order from Savonarola's: his message was focused on love, not fear, and his words reached into the hearts of seemingly everyone who heard him. Bembo, who had invited Ochino to preach in Venice, sent Vittoria this assessment: "He expresses himself quite differently, and in a more Christian way, than any others who have climbed up to the pulpit in my days, and with vibrant compassion, about love and more elevating things." In a second letter to Vittoria following another of Ochino's sermons, Bembo's enthusiasm was even greater: "Our brother Bernardino (from whom now on I want to call mine with you) is adored in this city these days. There is no man or woman who does not raise him to the heavens with their praise. O how worthy he is, o how he delights, o how much help he is!"

Ochino's words may have been filled with "vibrant compassion" ("*viva carità*"), but his underlying message was in fact far from gentle. Like many of his Capuchin brethren, he was very critical of the Roman church—its extravagant riches, its lax discipline, its overwhelming hierarchy and distance from the common people—and wanted to see it reformed. At least at this point in his life, Ochino did not identify directly with Luther, whose reforming zeal had been menacing Rome since he posted his Ninety-Five Theses in Wittenberg in 1517. But Protestantism was only one of a number of evangelical movements popular at this time, and by the early 1530s, groups across the continent were

calling for serious ecclesiastical change. For many, the extravagant ambition and expenditure of the early sixteenth-century popes, Julius II
and Leo X, both of whom behaved more like Roman emperors than
like men of the cloth, had pushed their patience over the edge. For some
in Spain, it was the horror of the Inquisition, which began in the 1470s
and had developed into a veritable reign of terror. Whatever the reasons—
and there were certainly many sources of discontent—the urge to reform
was sweeping Europe, including the Italian peninsula. Even a pious
Catholic such as Vittoria, who had wanted to be a nun, found herself
powerfully drawn to a message of change.

Ochino's evangelism was itself inspired by a charismatic reformer
from Spain, Juan de Valdés, who had arrived in Italy sometime between December 1529 and August 1531 in flight from the Inquisition.
Valdés was a brilliant theologian who came from a family descended
in part from knights in La Mancha, the land of Don Quixote, and in
part from *conversos*, or converted Jews, who may not have left their
Judaism completely behind. In 1512, when Valdés was a small child, a
witness for the Inquisition claimed he saw Valdés's father praying in
Hebrew with several of his older sons.

In Spain, Valdés had become involved with a religious group known
as the *alumbrados*, or "enlightened ones." The *alumbrados*, who often
came from *converso* families, were frequently likened to the Lutherans,
but their emphasis was less on changing the institution of the church,
as Luther and his followers passionately wanted to do, than on fostering
spirituality. These Spanish evangelicals believed the human soul was
capable of seeing the divine and communicating directly with the Holy
Spirit. Many of their preachers were women—this alone got the movement into plenty of trouble—and they encouraged their followers, both
male and female, to pursue their relationships with Christ independent of priests and liturgy. Because they believed in personal forms of
spiritual healing that were often conducted through private encounters, they also made themselves vulnerable to charges of sexual miscon-
duct. Indeed, one of the women leaders, Francisca Hernández, claimed
she had discovered a cure to prevent students of the clergy from mastur-
bating; the cure may have involved some fondling of her own, although

other reports suggest she merely lent a sash or scarf to the afflicted. The group also espoused the idea that human lovemaking was a valid means to achieve union with God.

Valdés's troubles in Spain came less from his involvement with the *alumbrados*, however, than from his 1529 publication of the *Diálogo de doctrina Cristiana*, or *Dialogue on Christian Doctrine*, which was immediately censored by the Spanish Inquisition due to its harsh criticism of the church. In this short book of roughly one hundred pages, which included several long excerpts from Lutheran works, Valdés advocated for the primacy of the "glory of God" as opposed to the elevation of church officers, and challenged the idea that papal authority should extend beyond the function of the bishop of Rome. He believed, in other words, that the pope should not have a universal claim over the church. The core of his message, here and elsewhere in his works, was to stress the individual's spiritual life as the foundation of his or her religious experience. He argued against what he regarded as the institutionalization of belief: the idea that people needed a priest to hear their confessions, help them with their prayers, and interpret for them the words of God. Although Valdés maintained the importance of two of the sacraments, Baptism and the Eucharist, he otherwise envisioned little need for the clergy. All of this spoke deeply to someone like Vittoria—it coincided, for example, with her request in 1526 to live in her own religious house where there would be a priest to conduct Mass, but where she and her female companions would otherwise be on their own. Religion, Valdés argued, could be practiced almost entirely in the home.

One implication of Valdés's emphasis on the individual's direct relationship to God was that everyone had the right to read the Bible in his or her mother tongue. (This was also a key tenet of Lutheranism.) Reading the Bible in Spanish—or Italian or German or Portuguese— might seem innocuous enough, but it was not encouraged by the church, and certain vernacular translations were expressly forbidden. Laypeople were taught to read Scripture ideally under the supervision of a priest, as ordinary individuals could not be trusted to understand the Bible properly. The same principle applied to the layperson's access to liturgy, which the church insisted remain in Latin. In one of the religious debates between Catholics and Protestants raging in England during this period, the Catholic priest Thomas Harding, prebendary of Winchester, made the argument that it was *better* for the congregation not to understand the priest's prayers: if the service is conducted in the vernacular, he declared, "the people will frame lewd and perverse meanings of their own lewd senses." He recommended instead that they perform simple and rote acts of prayer, enhanced by rosary beads or other devotional aids. It was not until Vatican II in the 1960s that the Catholic Church moved away from the Latin Mass, more than four hundred years after the Protestant Reformation.

All of the beliefs that Valdés espoused make it very surprising that when he arrived in Rome in flight from Spain, he was received by none other than Clement VII. Clement had given him a "safe-conduct"—an official document rather like a visa—not for his religious beliefs, but as a political favor to Charles V. This was a moment in which the pope was desperately trying to maintain peaceful relations with the emperor, who employed two of Valdés's brothers. Valdés not only was admitted to Rome, but also became one of Charles's secretaries, and served in this capacity at the papal court. It is worth fully registering how little collaboration there was at the time between the office of the Spanish Inquisition and the pope—the fact that Valdés was a wanted heretic in Madrid had no effect on his reception in Rome, as if there were two entirely different churches involved. Some twelve years later, when Pope Paul III reinstituted the office of the Inquisition in Rome and shortly thereafter called the Council of Trent, this would never have happened. But in the early 1530s, it was still possible for a man accused of heresy in Catholic Spain to find a warm welcome in the papal city.

After several years in Rome, Valdés settled in Naples, where he quickly attracted a group of religious followers around him. This was the group Vittoria had most likely heard about on Ischia: the so-called *spirituali*. The *spirituali* were more Lutheran in their orientation than the Spanish *alumbrados*. In particular, they had come to embrace Luther's idea of *sola fide*: that faith alone—without good works—can save you. The nineteenth-century American poet Henry Wadsworth Longfellow dramatized Valdés's position on the subject in his unfinished poem *Michael Angelo*, in which his character Valdesso exchanges these words with his loyal disciple, Julia:

> Valdesso: . . . With the human soul
> There is no compromise. By faith alone
> Can man be justified.
>
> Julia: Hush, dear Valdesso:
> That is a heresy. Do not, I pray you,
> Proclaim it from the house-top, but preserve it
> As something precious, hidden in your heart,
> As I, who half believe and tremble at it.

Julia's assessment was correct: the Catholic Church hated the idea of *sola fide*, which not only removed the most obvious incentive to perform charitable deeds, but also threatened to take away an immensely profitable revenue flow (the pope was still trying to raise funds to complete the massive building project of Saint Peter's Basilica).

Longfellow's Julia was none other than the famously beautiful Giulia Gonzaga, Countess of Fondi, the widow of Vittoria's cousin Vespasiano. Vespasiano was the son of the famous *condottiere* Prospero Colonna, who had fought alongside Vittoria's father on many occasions and had amassed a great deal of wealth. Vespasiano married Giulia in 1526 when she was only thirteen and he was forty; he died less than two years later. Although Vespasiano's will stipulated that Giulia would inherit all of his lands and titles only under the condition that she did not remarry, she was nonetheless courted by many powerful figures in the years to come, including Ippolito de' Medici, a cousin of Pope Clement. Ippolito was in fact supposed to marry Giulia's stepdaughter, Isabella, but instead became a cardinal—and, almost certainly, Giulia's lover. Ippolito commissioned the painter Sebastiano del Piombo to paint Giulia's portrait for him in 1532, several copies of which have survived. One of these is a small painting in the Palazzo Ducale in Mantua that appears to have been a portable version for Ippolito to carry before the final portrait was completed. In 1535, Ippolito died under mysterious circumstances; many believed he was poisoned by members of his own family, who were deeply opposed to his love affair with Giulia.

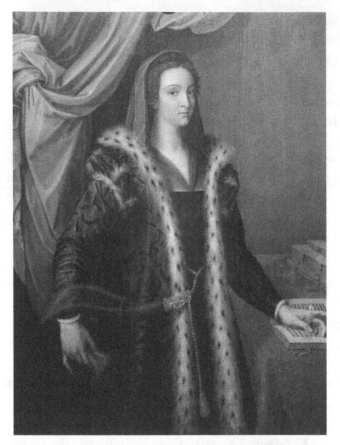

Portrait of Giulia Gonzaga, Vittoria's cousin by marriage, after Sebastiano del Piombo and attributed to the sixteenth-century painter known as Cristofano dell'Altissimo (Gallerie degli Uffizi, Florence)

Giulia's great beauty had also reached the ears of the African corsair Khair ad-dīn, known as il Barbarossa, who tried to kidnap her in 1534 from the Colonna fortress in Fondi in order to offer her as a gift to the Turkish sultan, Suleiman the Magnificent. The castle was sacked, but Giulia managed to escape in the night, thanks to the quickness of one of her servants. It was after both the attempted kidnapping and the death of Ippolito that she met Valdés, who clearly represented a purer, simpler life. Following a visit he made to Fondi in 1535, Giulia decided to move to Naples in order to dedicate herself to his religious teaching, and took up residence in the monastery of San Francesco alle Monache, where she lived on and off for the rest of her days. Not only did Valdés become her spiritual guide, but he also became completely devoted to her. It was, he wrote, "the greatest sin that she is not lord over the whole world."

The relationship between Valdés and Giulia was recorded for posterity in a dialogue Valdés wrote, entitled *The Christian Alphabet*, in which Giulia served—as was in fact the case—as the hostess of his religious circle. The occasion for the conversation that Valdés chronicled was a sermon that he and Giulia heard Ochino preach at San Giovanni Maggiore in Naples during Lent in 1536. By that time, Ochino himself had become a devoted follower of Valdés—it was said that the Spaniard even prepared the topics and outlines for some of Ochino's sermons. The Lenten sermons in Naples were an extraordinary success, and counted among their listeners none other than Charles V, who had stopped in the city as part of his official "triumph" following his military victory in Tunisia the previous year (the emperor's ceremonious procession, modeled on the triumphs of ancient Roman commanders, began in Sicily and progressed up the peninsula to Rome). Charles was reported to have said that Ochino "preached with such Spirit, and so much Devotion, that he made the very stones weep."

Let us return now to Vittoria's experience of Ochino's preaching at San Lorenzo in Damaso during Lent in 1535. There is no record of what he preached that day, but a typical sermon might have addressed one of his favorite topics, the practice of confession. Ochino's message was, as always, a simple one. Confession, he preached, was not fulfilled either by going through the motions—by responding to the priest's questions and uttering formulas given to you in a book—or by pretending to be anything but what you were. A true confession was an act of serious self-inquiry, which required digging deep into the heart. To convey these ideas, Ochino did not expound the relevant doctrines in the way a theologian might do. Instead, he told a story.

There was once a nun, Ochino began, who wanted to impress her confessor with her humility. "Oh Father Confessor," this nun declared, "I acknowledge that of all others in the convent I am the most haughty, the most careless, and most ungodly." The priest responded: "My daughter, I knew that before; they have told me that thou wast the haughtiest, most careless, ungodly of all in the convent, and therefore surely thou art not worthy to bear the dress of thy order." The nun was shocked, and turned to the priest in anger: "Father, you are too credulous, it is not so bad." And yet, Ochino remarked, "she had just told him the same thing in her confession." "That was wrong," he continued, "for we should tell the truth, neither more nor less." When you come to confess, he concluded, "act like the woman that lost a penny and sought through the whole house until she found it. If thou dost ransack thy conscience well, so wilt thou find all therein that accuses thee."

Hearing Ochino preach sermons like this stirred Vittoria's soul in a way that no one had ever done before. The ruthless interrogation that he advocated was not altogether different from the scrutiny she applied to herself in her prayers and poems, but she had never before heard anyone articulate so vividly the ideas that lay behind her beliefs. Vittoria's commitment to Ochino was not limited to him personally, but extended to the Capuchins as a whole, who were struggling for their very survival. The much more powerful Franciscans, from whom they had broken away less than a decade earlier, were determined to bring them to their ruin—they obviously did not like to be cast in the position of corrupted monks—and already in 1534 one of their generals had sent a letter to Clement begging him to bring the Capuchins to a quick end. "It would be better to dissolve this petty and barely newborn congregation," he warned the pope, "than permit it to threaten the tranquility of the greater, time-honored Order."

The pope, for his part, had become concerned about both the Capuchins' anti-ecclesiastical message and their enormous popularity, which was principally centered on the figure of Ochino. In early April 1534, Clement decided to take matters into his own hands and summoned all of the Capuchins—there were roughly seven hundred of them at the time—to Rome. The monks came to the papal city, where, at daybreak, they visited the seven churches considered sacred to pilgrims, but this show of piety did nothing to soften the pope's resolve. It is recorded that on April 25, Clement issued a decree ordering the Capuchins to depart from the city before a single candle that he kindled had burned down.

The papal message reached the monks while they were gathered together for a meal. They left their house immediately, taking with them only their prayer books, and proceeded two by two to Porta Tiburtina, later known as Porta San Lorenzo, on the eastern side of the city. Something about this spectacle—the long procession of hooded monks being forced out of the ancient Aurelian walls—won the hearts of the Romans, and protests against the monks' expulsion broke out in the streets. Leading the large crowd was an old hermit with a long gray beard, who shouted with all his might: "Woe for thee, O Rome! You love to harbor harlots and drunkards, you nourished dogs, and you would banish the Capuchins."

Vittoria may well have seen the monks proceeding through the city, and heard the hermit's chant denouncing the church's hypocrisy. Whether she witnessed this or not, she certainly knew about the pope's decision to expel the Capuchins from Rome, and was determined to fight it as forcefully as she could. Joining forces with another noblewoman, Caterina Cibo, Duchess of Camerino, who had been the Capuchins' earliest benefactor—she had given them a house on her land in the Marches, and also helped them acquire their first settlement in Rome, at the hospital of San Giacomo degli Incurabili—Vittoria began a fierce letter-writing campaign to put pressure on Clement to reverse his decision. Thanks in no small degree to the tenacity of the two women, Clement ultimately relented and agreed to readmit the monks to Rome, although he specified that they could not return to the city as they had exited, in procession (he must have feared the sympathy they would garner once again from the Roman citizens). This was one of Clement's final acts. He died on September 25, 1534, exactly five months after his original decree expelling the monks.

For Vittoria, however, the fight for the Capuchins was far from over. Ochino and his fellow monks were still actively struggling to maintain their independence from the Franciscans, and were facing a range of new accusations that they were espousing Protestant beliefs. They also desperately needed a larger home in Rome. Defending Ochino and his order was the first significant cause outside the domain of her family that Vittoria had embraced, and it is striking how far she was willing to go in drawing upon her circle of friends and relations to help her to convince the new pope, Paul III, to come to the Capuchins' aid.

Paul III, born Alessandro Farnese, was a member of a wealthy family of obscure origins, with lands in the area around Orvieto (see plate 11). The Farnese rose to power in the late fifteenth century when Alessandro's sister Giulia, a famously beautiful woman—she was known as Giulia la Bella—became the lover of Pope Alexander VI. It was thanks to her that Alexander named her brother Alessandro a cardinal in 1493, but it was Alessandro's own political skill and intelligence that explained his subsequent success. Before becoming pope, Alessandro oversaw the building of a splendid palazzo, now known as Palazzo Farnese, a short distance from the banks of the Tiber in the very heart of the city. Originally in the hands of the architect Antonio da Sangallo the Younger, the project passed upon Sangallo's death in 1546 to Michelangelo. A man of great culture and taste, Alessandro kept some three hundred servants in his palazzo, including an organist, carpenter, butler, gamekeeper, barber, upholsterer, embroiderer, saddler, silk weaver, apothecary, stable-master, bookkeeper, chief cook, under-cook, pastry cook, amanuensis, master of page boys, master of *contrabasso*, master mason, and soprano.

Alessandro's election to the papacy in 1534 was celebrated with great pomp throughout the city. Vittoria's brother Ascanio led the group of noblemen who carried the pope on their shoulders through the streets; he also served as one of the hosts of a tournament held in Piazza di San Pietro, in which fifty young gentlemen hurled balls of baked clay at one another while protecting themselves with shields. Paul generated enthusiasm not only among the Roman aristocrats, but also among the religious reformers, who were encouraged by his decision to admit a number of reform-minded men to the cardinalship during the first years of his papacy. This group included Bembo; the Englishman Reginald Pole, to whom we shall return at length later on; and the Venetian diplomat Gasparo Contarini, with whom Vittoria had become friendly since she returned to Rome. Before becoming a cardinal, Contarini had served as ambassador to Charles V both in Germany and in Spain. Paul relied upon Contarini for his cautious but sympathetic attitude toward the reform movement, and put him at the helm of the Reform Commission he created in the curia in 1536.

Vittoria seems to have understood Contarini's influence with Paul almost immediately, and hence when she set out to write a defense of the Capuchins, she addressed it to Contarini directly. Her letter is the longest of all her surviving missives—at more than three thousand words, it was, in effect, a short treatise —and she used the opportunity not only to lay out her arguments in favor of the Capuchins, but also to defend her right as a woman to speak on their behalf. "However much my feminine ignorance and excessive ardor might seem to detract from my credibility," she began, "so much more my reason and the exclusively Christian interests that drive me lend me as much authority."

On page after page Vittoria answered the charges leveled against the monks, sometimes revealing her own exasperation. "Only if Saint Francis himself was a heretic are his followers Lutherans," she quipped, "and only if preaching the freedom of the spirit over vice but subjection to every order of the Holy Church can be called an error would it also be an error to follow the Gospel, which in many places says 'It is the spirit that quickeneth.'" Throughout the letter, she never wavered from her strong conviction that the Capuchins should be allowed to live according to their own rules, choose their own habit, and exercise their spiritual freedom. She closed with a combination of plea and threat: "May the cardinal protectors leave these poor people in peace, and [may] you as well, you who know best that it will not be pardoned before God if human concerns intimidate you, given that Christ had no concern over dying for us."

There is no way of knowing for certain to what extent Vittoria's letter to Contarini played a role in Paul's decision later that year to issue a bull protecting the Capuchin order. She was without doubt instrumental, however, in Paul's appointing Ochino as one of the four generals of the order, and she thanked Contarini later that year for having "held the rudder of Peter's little ship that is safe from shipwreck" ("Peter's little ship," or "*la navicella di Pietro*," is a common metaphor for the Roman church).

Vittoria also saw to it that Ochino was invited to preach in important places—it was through her recommendation, for example, that Bembo brought him to Venice—and she also worked to obtain better property for the Capuchins within the city of Rome. In a letter dated November 8, 1536, to the clerk of Saint Peter's, Iacopo Ercolani, Vittoria pledged to do everything necessary to help the monks restore their church of San Nicola, and also to assist with their building a new convent on land attached to the gardens of the Palazzo Colonna. This was made possible by Ascanio, over whom she had great influence, and who had come to embrace the Capuchin cause himself. The following year, she convinced her friend Ercole II d'Este, Duke of Ferrara, to create a home in his city for the Capuchins. He was, it seems, easily persuaded, and obtained land and a house along the Po River for Ochino to establish a new monastery.

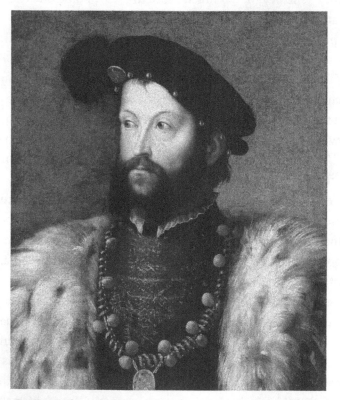

Portrait of Ercole II d'Este by the sixteenth-century artist
Nicolò dell'Abate (Private collection)

At the same time that Vittoria was occupied with Ochino and the Capuchin cause, she was also pursuing two different projects of her own. The first was yet another attempt to live a more monastic life and establish a private house in which she could worship exactly as she pleased. She had made such a proposal in 1526, after Clement forbade the nuns at San Silvestro to allow Vittoria to take holy vows as a Poor Clare. Several months later, we will recall, she had asked his permission to form her own religious house in Naples, with a number of chaste women as her companions, a request that he granted. In 1536, Vittoria made a similar request, which we know about from two surviving letters of Paul III granting her a new set of extraordinary privileges.

In the first of the two letters, which spelled things out in great detail, Paul declared that he was giving Vittoria permission to live in a home with a portable altar to be used in "places suitable and decent although not sacred"; to hear "Masses and other Divine Offices celebrated or sung" by a suitable priest; to keep the Eucharist in a tabernacle "observed continuously with lamps and other kindled lights"; to choose her own confessor, even a member of the mendicant orders; and finally (and most mysteriously) to enter freely, with "ten other honest women chosen by you to visit any monastery of any order of monks, even Saint Clare's, with the consent of the people presiding there, and converse with these same monks, provided that you not lodge there overnight." There is no trace of this last request elsewhere, and we are left simply to guess at what it could possibly mean. It seems she was hoping to enter into the cloistered space of the monasteries, where visitors and lay residents were not typically allowed. Nothing further about her plans in this case can be verified, but it is striking that the pope sent two letters conveying the same message, one in April 1536, and another simply reaffirming his position in December of the same year. Nothing, he repeated in the second epistle, should stand in her way. We have no way of knowing if her wish was ever fulfilled, but it is clear she had not lost her determination.

Vittoria's other project during this time pulled in a very different direction: she wanted to make a pilgrimage to the Holy Land. Her plan was to travel to Jerusalem, where she would, according to the itinerary of most pilgrims, have been led by friars down the Via Dolorosa; visited the Stations of the Cross; spent three days and nights in the Church of the Holy Sepulchre, where Christ was crucified, buried, and resurrected; and sung Mass with the monks and other pilgrims before his tomb. She most likely would also have visited Bethlehem and seen the place of Christ's birth. Nowhere in her letters did she explain her desire to do any of this, but the plan corresponded to her deep religiosity and her special interest at this time of her life in developing an ever more personal relationship to Christ. It also reminds us of how absolutely unencumbered she was: without husband or children, and with money of her own, she was free to pursue her own interests, whether to follow her favorite preacher or to take a long journey across the seas.

What is surprising, however, about Vittoria's wish in this instance was how far away a pilgrimage was from anything Ochino or Valdés might have recommended. Indeed, making a pilgrimage to the Holy Land was a quintessentially traditional (and not reformed) thing to do. Luther included attacks on the cult of saints and the granting of indulgences, both important features of pilgrimage, in his Ninety-Five Theses, and reformers decried the idea of pilgrimage as expensive, corrupt, and superstitious. At the very moment Vittoria was becoming increasingly involved with the *spirituali*, she wanted nonetheless to intensify the nature of her own spirituality in a manner deeply associated with those practices of the Catholic Church—granting indulgences and the worship of saints and relics—specifically targeted for reform. Once again, her life seemed full of contradictions.

In early 1537, Vittoria sent Pope Paul another letter, this time requesting permission for her pilgrimage. Her letter is lost, but Paul's response has survived. As in his brief to her from the previous year, he seems simply to have reiterated, and granted, her requests, which makes it possible for us to reconstruct exactly what she had in mind. Paul's letter began by praising Vittoria for her great piety and commitment to her faith, qualities that have convinced him to allow her to make the journey. "After having been relayed to us," he declared, "the desire of your nobility to set out abroad and visit, in addition to the churches of

Saint James in Compostella and of Saint Maximinus in Provence, in which the body of the Blessed Mary Magdalene is believed to have been laid, the sacred tomb of our Lord Jesus Christ, has greatly enlarged our opinion of your probity, your devotion, and your piety towards God the Highest."

"Because you have put this pilgrimage, laborious indeed and dangerous, before your rest, your wealth, and your many comforts," Paul continued,

> and because you have not been able to be shaken from it by the prayers of your close and extended family, and because you have set the love of Jesus Christ before all human emotions, you have shown most clearly a manly spirit in a woman's body, for which we, who desire to kindle your fervor rather than to extinguish it in any way, bless you, daughter in Christ, and we ask God that he favor your pilgrimage and that he deem it worthy that you be accompanied on your journey.

This was all an elaborate prelude for the privileges he then extended to her:

> Having listened to your requests, we therefore concede and grant to you by apostolic authority in the spirit of the circumstances, that you be able to visit the tomb, and that you lead with you on this pious effort up to fifteen people including our beloved son Girolamo of Montepulciano of the order of the congregation of the minor Capuchins, your confessor, and two other of his companions at the discretion of their superior.

Outside this letter, there is no mention of Vittoria's plan to visit the two European sites, but perhaps she had in mind a future occasion when she might make a second pilgrimage without crossing the seas. From a reformed point of view, both of these sites were linked to the worst forms of Catholic superstition. At Santiago de Compostela, Vittoria would have seen the relics of the apostle Saint James the Greater, whose body was said to have been removed by angels from the Holy Land following his death and made its own way, by boat, to the coast of Spain. Legend had it that an enormous rock closed around James's relics, miraculously protecting them, until they were safely enshrined at the cathedral in Compostela. At Saint Maximin in France, Vittoria would have visited the site believed to be the burial place of Mary Magdalene. Once again, a miraculous journey over seas was involved: Mary Magdalene was said to have fled the Holy Land in a boat without rudder or sail and made it all the way to the southeast of France, where she hid in a cave at the foot of the Sainte Baume mountains for the last thirty years of her life. In 1279, it was claimed that her sarcophagus was found in the cave with most of her body intact; shortly thereafter, a Gothic basilica was built nearby in the town of Saint Maximin, where her remains, including her skull, encased in gold, can still be seen today.

In addition to its marked departure from the more reformed practice of religion she had recently become so engaged with, for Vittoria to make a pilgrimage to the Holy Land was also a potentially dangerous undertaking. Of course, pilgrims both male and female had gone on such journeys for more than a millennium—readers of English literature will recall Chaucer's famous widow, the Wife of Bath, who boasted of having been to Jerusalem three times. But however freely Vittoria moved around as a widow, she had never even left the Italian peninsula, let alone traveled on the pirate-ridden seas. All of her other trips, moreover—from Rome to Naples, or Ischia to Viterbo—had always been particularly catered to her needs and comfort. For the trip to the Holy Land, she would have participated in the Renaissance equivalent of mass tourism.

By the early sixteenth century, pilgrimage to the Holy Land had become a major industry. The trips ranged widely in both length and destinations: the shortest pilgrimages were around four months long, and the longest could be more than a year. Just to make the journey from Venice, where most Italian pilgrimages began, to the port of Jaffa took an average of five weeks, and was considered the most difficult part of the trip. In addition to the risks associated with the rough seas, the food and wine were generally horrible, the water spoiled, fights between pilgrims frequent, and crews often dishonest. Sometimes the ships were also carrying horses, whose constant scraping of their hooves on the planks of the galleys exacerbated the already unpleasant atmosphere.

Manuals giving advice as to how best to survive all aspects of the trips, from seasickness to fleas to pirates, were widely available in both manuscript and print, and the cost of the trips varied sufficiently so that people from a wide range of social classes could choose according to their means (there were both luxury and low-frill options). A popular French guide by Anthoine Regnaut published in 1573 included an eleven-point list for the average pilgrim to follow on his or her journey. Among the highlights were these pieces of advice:

1. Take two purses on the journey: one full of the virtue of patience, the other with two hundred gold Venetian ducats.
2. Find a place on board the pilgrim galley to put your belongings in the part of the ship nearest the entry; this way you'll have the maximum amount of fresh air.
3. Buy eggs, chicken, preserves, and fruit each time you stop at port. You'll need the extra food for when captain and crew are too busy resisting storms to cook.
4. Dress poorly, so as to avoid having to pay endless tips.
5. Once in the Holy Land, carry your bedding with you. Don't, ever, leave the caravan, and don't argue with the locals, for there is great danger.
6. Take letters of permission to travel from your bishop, and the safe-conduct from the king, and, before leaving Jerusalem, get a certificate from the pope's commissary to say you have been there.

It is hard to imagine Vittoria reading such a book—she did not generally concern herself with the details of travel, and certainly all of the arrangements would have been made for her. Once in Jerusalem, however, her experience probably would not have been different from that of other Christian pilgrims, since nearly all visits to the holy sites were organized by the Franciscan friars who lived there, and pilgrims were lodged in Franciscan monasteries. Unfortunately, none of the details of the trip that was planned has survived; we know only that she left Rome in the spring of 1537 immensely excited, with the pope's letter of permission in hand.

Shortly after arriving in the northern city of Ferrara, where she had been invited by Ercole II d'Este to stay at the ducal palace on her way to Venice, the pilgrimage was canceled. There is no explanation for this anywhere in the archive, but the most likely reason was her health. She referred in multiple letters from this period to suffering from a serious case of catarrh—a condition in which her nose and air passages filled with mucus and made it difficult at times to breathe—and the long and demanding journey may have seemed more than she could safely bear. Her only direct acknowledgment of the canceled trip took the form of asides in two different letters. First, in a letter written from Ferrara on June 12, 1537, to Cardinal Ercole Gonzaga, the son of Isabella d'Este and Francesco II Gonzaga, Vittoria said that she had thought about coming to visit him, "not being able for the moment to go to Jerusalem," but then changed her mind because she feared that Mantua—roughly forty-five miles from Ferrara—would be too crowded due to the papal council being held there at the time.

Second, in a letter Vittoria sent in September 1538 to Pietro Aretino— a very surprising acquaintance, given his reputation as a writer of both literary pornography and caustic satire—she explained that she was in Lucca, not in Pisa, as Aretino had somehow imagined. "Not being able to go to Jerusalem," she wrote, "I have taken consolation here, but now I am constrained by His Holiness to return to Rome, instigated by my and your Marquis of Vasto [Alfonso d'Avalos]." Alfonso had been Aretino's patron for a short time in the early 1530s, although the relationship ultimately disintegrated, as did Aretino's relationships with other patrons, including Alessandro di Lorenzo de' Medici, Duke of Florence, and Federico II Gonzaga (Aretino was too irreverent, if not openly unpleasant, to maintain courtly ties, which earned him the epithet "the scourge of princes" from the far more diplomatic poet Ariosto). In Vittoria's account to Aretino of her whereabouts, we find a subtle hint of the regret she felt about missing the opportunity for the pilgrimage: some eighteen months after she would have embarked, she was still searching for "consolation."

It is hard not to feel that whatever the reason for Vittoria's not making her trip—the phrase she used to both Gonzaga and Aretino was "*non possendo passer in Jerusalem*," not being able to get to Jerusalem— it was yet another instance in which she had been thwarted from satisfying her deepest desires: to be a nun; to live with other chaste women in a religious house of her own; to visit the Holy Land. But once again, what looked like a pure loss turned out to have surprising gains. The time she ended up spending in Ferrara not only was richly productive for her as a poet, but also deepened her understanding of the current mood of religious reform. It was in the ducal palace of Ferrara that Vittoria was introduced to the work of the most radical reformer in Europe: John Calvin. Calvin had been a guest of Duke Ercole's wife, the French princess Renée, a year before Vittoria herself arrived in Ferrara, and had profoundly influenced Renée and her court. Without forewarning, our devout Catholic heroine found herself in the den of Protestantism.

HIDDEN HERETICS

VITTORIA ARRIVED IN FERRARA in April 1537, accompanied by six female companions and an unspecified number of male servants. The city was unlike anywhere she had been before. Ferrara was part of the Holy Roman Empire from the late twelfth century until 1471, when it was officially transferred to the Papal States. But the real rulers of Ferrara were the powerful Este lords, who had first emerged as leaders of the Guelphs—the faction to which Dante's family belonged—in the famous wars between the Guelphs and Ghibellines fought in Italy in the Middle Ages. By the end of the thirteenth century, the Este family gained dominion over Ferrara, Modena, and Reggio in Emilia. Ercole I d'Este, the grandfather of Vittoria's friend Ercole II, was one of the Renaissance's most important patrons of the arts, rivaling only Vittoria's grandfather Federico da Montefeltro in Urbino and the Medici lords in Florence. In his thirty-four-year reign as duke of Ferrara (1471–1505), Ercole I brought to his city some of the most outstanding painters, musicians, and poets in all of Europe.

What made Ercole I so distinctive, however, was his commitment to urban design and planning. His greatest innovation, known as the

Herculean Addition, was one of the first architectural plans based on the idea of perspective, and involved a dramatic reshaping of Ferrara's boundaries by pushing back the walls on its northern border, introducing a network of waterways and streets, and constructing new palaces for the nobility that were in harmony with the environment around them. Ercole also made important changes to the ducal palace, including the creation of an exquisite outdoor garden in the court facing the castle. Known as the Garden of the Duchesses, it spanned an area of more than thirty thousand square feet, and was graced with beautiful hedges and flowers, trees of all variety, graceful porticoes, and a gilded fountain.

Although Vittoria was arriving from the south, and hence would not immediately have seen the glorious northern walls and their surroundings, her introduction to Ferrara would have been equally grand. Her exact route is not known, but let us imagine that she passed in front of the city's cathedral with its splendid combination of Gothic and Romanesque façade, and then through the beautiful archway known as the Volto del Cavallo, named for the equestrian statue of Ercole I's father, Niccolò III d'Este, atop the column to the right of the arch. To the left of the Volto del Cavallo was a second column with a statue of Borso d'Este, Niccolò III's illegitimate son and duke of Ferrara from 1450 until his death in 1471. This column had a disturbing subsequent history: after having been destroyed by a fire in 1716, it was reconstructed using gravestones removed from the nearby Jewish cemetery. (The Este rulers had been welcoming to the Jews as part of their efforts to strengthen the economic conditions of the city, and had even protected them against Pope Sixtus IV's request for their expulsion in 1473.) The early eighteenth-century authorities claimed that there was a shortage of marble in the city and that they were forced to take what they could find. If you look carefully at the column today, you can still see Hebrew inscriptions literally supporting the Este duke.

Once she passed through the arch with Borso on one side and Niccolò III on the other, Vittoria would then have had her first glimpse of the ducal court—the grand public space in front of the castle where the Este family staged their lavish entertainments. This was where, for example, some of the first Renaissance performances of the ancient Roman playwright Plautus took place. Plautus, who was born in the mid-third century B.C.E. to the south of Ferrara in present-day Emilia-Romagna, had a risqué sense of humor well suited for the Este, a family well known for its love of pleasure. (A century later, Shakespeare would transform one of Plautus's most celebrated plays, *The Menaechmi*, into *The Comedy of Errors*.)

After crossing the grand piazza, Vittoria would have been led to the magnificent staircase known as the *scalone monumentale*, which was built by one of Ercole I's court architects to create an impressive entrance to the palace. Lined with marble columns and covered with a vaulted ceiling, it featured at its halfway point a small dome in the Venetian style that fused Byzantine and Moorish elements. At the top of the stairs, she would finally have found herself within the ducal palace. Beautiful public rooms, such as the Golden Hall, shimmered from the diamond panels and golden stucco rosettes lining the ceilings, and frescoes featuring tritons—the sons of Poseidon—were set against a deep crimson background. There were also exquisite private chambers, like the *studiolo*, or private study, designed by Ercole II's father, Alfonso I, which was filled with paintings by Bellini, Titian, and Raphael; or the apartment of Ercole II's mother, Lucrezia Borgia, who renovated two different sets of rooms for herself during her seventeen years in the castle, each with sumptuous tapestries, luxurious silks, and painted friezes. Alfonso was Lucrezia's third, and final, husband, and the match, arranged by Lucrezia's brother Cesare, had been made against Alfonso's will—just months before they were wed, she had appeared in public with a three-year-old boy believed to be fathered either by her brother or by her father, Alexander VI. But the marriage was relatively peaceful.

Given her preference for spiritual works of art, Vittoria may well have been taken aback by the overwhelmingly pagan decorations in Ferrara's palace. There were many depictions of Greek and Roman gods—Aurora and Apollo were especially dear to the Este family—as well as elaborate frescoes of mythological and allegorical figures known as "grotesques." In this, as in everything else, the palace was at the height of contemporary fashion. The grotesque style of painting was very much in vogue following the discovery around 1480 of Nero's imperial residence in Rome. In one of the most fortunate accidents of the Renaissance, a young Roman walking on the Esquiline Hill literally fell through a cleft. He found himself in what looked like a lavishly painted grotto, with images of fanciful and sometimes frightening creatures, interwoven with elaborate foliage and geometric designs. Thus the particular decorative schemes found there came to be known as *grottesche*, or grotesques (had the figures been beautiful cherubs and not unattractive creatures, the term "grotesque" would now mean something altogether different).

The cave-like space that the man fell into was only the smallest part of Nero's Domus Aurea, or Golden House—a massive palace complex covering hundreds of acres and stretching across much of the city. According to the ancient historian Suetonius, there was "a colossal statue of the emperor a hundred and twenty feet high" in the courtyard, and a triple portico extended a full mile in length. The villa had been dismantled and stripped of its riches following Nero's suicide in 68 C.E.; the Romans then began to build new structures on top of its ruins, burying what remained of the imperial residence. Even more than its nearly unfathomable size, the Domus Aurea became famous for its sumptuous interiors, covered with precious marble, gold, ivory, and jewels. This was a level of luxury that even Renaissance princes and popes may not have imagined. What could most easily be imitated were the grotesques they found on the walls.

The figures that Vittoria encountered on the surfaces of the ducal palace in Ferrara were in fact part of a much larger trend in the Este family of adorning their homes with secular, if not pagan, art. The most extravagant example was the Palazzo Schifanoia built by Niccolò III's father, Alberto V d'Este, in the late fourteenth century as a banqueting house and hunting lodge less than a mile from the ducal place. *Schifanoia* literally translates as "escape from boredom," and the Palazzo Schifanoia was designed to amuse its inhabitants and visitors as much as possible. If Vittoria visited this palace during her long stay in Ferrara, she would have seen the stunning fresco cycle commissioned by Borso d'Este in the 1460s for its central hall, whose theme was the calendar:

each of the twelve months was figured with a pagan god riding on his or her triumphal cart, the appropriate signs of the zodiac, and portraits of Borso and his courtiers involved in activities related to the time of year. The effect was—and is still today—truly overwhelming, and showed off both the brilliance of Ferrarese painting and the fantastic inventiveness of its designs.

As in Ferrara's ducal palace, the Palazzo Schifanoia was striking for its total lack of engagement with Christianity. The Este family's aesthetic commitment to paganism was by no means unusual: it was at the very heart of the period's interest in recovering the artistic and literary glories of antiquity. But it was terribly at odds with the dominant religious mood of the Ferrara court at the time of Vittoria's visit. In Ferrara, perhaps more than anywhere else in her life, Vittoria was confronted with the incompatibility of two cultures: on the one hand, a seemingly unrestrained and often wild embrace of paganism; on the other hand, a serious and unrelenting engagement with Protestantism. The exuberance of the Italian Renaissance was clashing before her eyes with the demands of the Reformation.

This clash of cultures was the result of Ercole II's marriage to Renée of France, the daughter of King Louis XII and Anne of Brittany, who had embraced Protestant beliefs at a very early age. When Ercole married Renée in 1528, he could hardly have imagined how much trouble she would cause him. Like her childhood friend Anne Boleyn, who became a member of the French royal court in 1514 when Renée's sister Claude married their second cousin Francis I, Renée was hardly the demure Catholic princess Ercole had hoped she would be. Orphaned at the age of four, she had been raised by tutors and governesses strongly influenced by Luther's program for reform. A visitor to France during this period reported that Anne Boleyn was reading the Bible in French and studying St. Paul's Epistles—it was Paul who ultimately inspired Luther's doctrine of justification by faith—and it is likely that Renée was doing the same.

By the time the seventeen-year-old Renée married Ercole, she was a fully committed Protestant, and she filled the ducal palace with French courtiers and servants who shared her beliefs. When Vittoria arrived

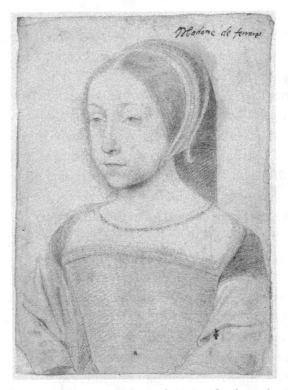

Portrait of Renée of France, Duchess of Ferrara, by the early sixteenth-century French artist Jean Clouet (Musée Conde, Chantilly)

on her visit nine years later, the duchess had earned a reputation throughout Italy as a radical reformer. French Protestants fleeing from persecution in their native land came straight to Ferrara, where, much to Ercole's dismay, Renée offered them shelter. In the company of Renée, Vittoria found herself surrounded by people whose tastes for reform went far beyond anything she had found in Naples or Rome.

Among the most impressive of Renée's guests was her secretary Clément Marot, who was one of the great French poets of the period. Among his many accomplishments, he gained fame in particular for popularizing the *blason*, a poetic form that praised the female body, usually from head to toe, in great detail. He also introduced a range of classical genres into French (the elegy, the eclogue, the epigram) and translated many of the great Latin poets, including Ovid and Virgil. In

addition to his literary innovations, Marot was a staunch religious reformer. After authoring several fiercely anti-Catholic pamphlets, and
having been arrested for eating meat during Lent—a sure sign of Protestant sympathies—Marot fled to Ferrara.

No sooner had Marot arrived than Ercole received a warning from
a papal legate in Venice, informing him that his new houseguest was a
Lutheran, "who would bring with him that plague that God does not
want" to his court. Although Marot returned to France for several
years in 1537, he ultimately came back to Ferrara after being condemned
for his translations of the Psalms, which were the first poetic render-
ings into French (Marot claimed he translated the Psalms directly from
the Hebrew, but it is generally believed that he used Jerome's Latin Bible
as his primary source). According to the university authorities at the
Sorbonne, who were actively fighting Francis I's relative tolerance toward
the Lutherans, Marot's texts smacked of Protestantism, and he was forced
into exile again.

Marot was a mild heretic, however, compared with Calvin, who
stayed at the palace for roughly a month in the spring of 1536. The twenty-
six-year-old Calvin arrived in flight from authorities in France dressed
in disguise, and traveling under the pseudonym Charles d'Espeville. None
of this fooled anyone, of course: the papal authorities in Ferrara immediately took note of his presence, and Ercole received another letter
informing him that his wife was harboring "Lutheran outlaws from
France." Little did they know that "Lutheran" was an inadequate tag for
Renée's new guest, who was carrying with him the first edition of his
revolutionary book of theology, *The Institutes of the Christian Religion*.
Published in Latin in Basel, Switzerland, around the time of Calvin's
arrival in Ferrara, the *Institutes* forever changed—and hardened—the
face of Protestantism.

The book that Calvin brought to the ducal palace in 1536 went
through many elaborate revisions and expansions over the next twenty
years (the first edition had only six chapters; the final edition, published
in 1559, boasted eighty), but it already contained the key doctrines that
came to be known as Calvinism. Although Calvin's theology was based
at its core on the teachings of Luther, the young Frenchman pushed

Luther's ideas—on the sacraments, on salvation, on predestination—further than the German reformer had ever intended, and in ways that were not to his liking. The two men never met in person, and Calvin was spared the terrific venom that Luther released on some of his fellow Swiss Protestants, most notably Ulrich Zwingli and Heinrich Bullinger, who understood the Eucharist as "memorial"—that is, as an act done in memory of Christ's sacrifice, but not containing any traces of Christ's presence. Luther was on the whole, as his modern biographer Lyndal Roper puts it, "a grand hater," and viciously attacked anyone who crossed him. Calvin nonetheless maintained respect for the great German reformer, and claimed that "even though he were to call me a devil, I would nevertheless hold him in such honor that I would acknowledge him to be a distinguished servant of God."

There is no way to know if Vittoria read through the dense Latin pages of Calvin's *Institutes* when she was in Ferrara. But she would have heard a great deal about it, and probably found some of it quite shocking. For at its core, the *Institutes* challenged many of the rituals and practices Vittoria had grown up with and had been taught to consider absolutely essential for Christian salvation. Calvin not only regarded most of the sacraments as unnecessary, but also dismissed all but Baptism and the Eucharist as vain creations of man: Penance; Extreme Unction (the anointing of the sick or dying); Holy Orders (the bestowing of the office of the priesthood); Confirmation; and even Matrimony were each individually denounced. In the 1559 edition of the *Institutes*, Calvin declared, for example, that the "holy oil" of Confirmation was not "worth one piece of dung," and defined Extreme Unction as the spreading of grease on "half-dead corpses."

This attack on the sacraments was part of a much larger assault on the corruption of the Roman church, and especially on ecclesiastical hierarchy. The papists, he exclaimed, "think only of gold and silver, and are so dazzled . . . that they cannot raise their minds to heaven"; the bishops are often so ignorant that "many peasants and artisans who have never tasted letters" had more knowledge of the "principles of their faith." As for the monks, many of whom Vittoria greatly admired, Calvin had nothing but disdain: "They are all completely unlearned asses, though because of their long robes they have a reputation for learning."

Calvin's vitriol against the church was certainly more aggressive than what Vittoria had heard from Valdés or Ochino, but in its larger aims, it was not entirely dissimilar. Where Calvin departed entirely from the Italian reformers was in his notion of "double predestination." Luther had already argued that God predestined certain individuals to salvation, but he allowed for the possibility that the fate of the rest of the world was not yet fully decided. Calvin, however, took the Lutheran position one very drastic step further. Not only did God choose who would be saved; he also chose who would be damned. According to this severe theology, a man who was not born "elect" had no chance of improving his fate, however pious a life he led. There was no flexibility in the system.

Vittoria and the other guests at Ferrara in 1537 did not read the full-blown, terrifying expression of Calvin's doctrine of double predestination—it grew stronger over the course of his lifetime. Already in the 1536 *Institutes*, however, he defined the true church as "the number of the elect," and affirmed that some souls were "condemned" by God's "eternal plan." In theory, Calvinism was supposed to be comforting to those who felt they were among the chosen. But how anyone knew whether he or she would be saved is a question that kept generations up at night. According to the early twentieth-century German sociologist Max Weber, it also gave birth to the Protestant work ethic.

Vittoria herself never warmed to Calvin's idea, and may in fact never have fully abandoned the Catholic doctrine that salvation could be earned. According to her friend Pietro Carnesecchi, "she came to observe and follow the advice that she said was given to her by [Reginald Pole], whom she believed like an oracle, namely that she should act as though on the one hand she had faith alone to save her, and on the other hand as though her salvation consisted in works [alone]." From our perspective, Vittoria's position may appear nothing more than a useful strategy for staying out of trouble with the church. But in the 1530s—a decade before the Council of Trent convened and initiated the Counter-Reformation—Vittoria's straddling of the line between Catholicism and Protestantism was surprisingly common. Indeed, many of the Italian reformers with whom she was in contact made demands for change, but stopped far short of Luther, let alone Calvin. In 1537, Vittoria would have had no reason to see the differences between the evangelical project of Valdés and the more moderate group of cardinals advising Pope Paul as irreconcilable.

It was precisely Vittoria's more cautious approach to reform that made her attractive to Ercole, who encouraged her to stay in Ferrara for as long as possible. Ercole was hostile to Protestantism, and horrified by the negative attention that Renée was visiting upon him; he seems to have hoped Vittoria might be a calming or conservative influence on his wife. In the months preceding Vittoria's arrival, Ercole had seen to it that several members of Renée's circle were arrested for their heretical behavior, which was embarrassing him before his own court. One of the singers in his choir, Jeannet de Bouchefort, had hurled insults at the Eucharist during the celebration of Mass, and then refused to bow before the cross during the traditional Good Friday service. Even closer to home, Renée's trusted secretary and treasurer Jean Cornillau was accused of both denouncing the pope and rejecting the idea of free will.

As a sign of how bad relations were between the duke and duchess, Ercole not only forbade the two men to return to France, but also requested papal permission to keep them locked up in Ferrara. It was only when Francis I intervened on behalf of his former sister-in-law (and cousin) Renée that Ercole relented, and obtained permission from Rome to release the prisoners. In an effort to cleanse the palace of the taint of heresy, Ercole had also seen fit to dismiss Renée's childhood governess and companion Michelle de Saubonne, known as Madame de Soubise, who was one of the people first responsible for introducing the French princess to Protestantism. In the words of the great writer François Rabelais, who visited Renée on his way to Rome with Cardinal Jean du Bellay, "The said duke has already taken from [the duchess] her governess Madame de Soubise and had her served by Italian women, which is not a good sign." Du Bellay himself wrote to Francis to suggest that if he cared about Renée, he should consider taking her under his protection.

Unfortunately, the situation between Renée and Ercole only worsened in the years to come. In the early 1540s, the duchess stopped celebrating the Catholic Mass and chose instead to worship in the manner prescribed by Calvin, along with other members of her household. Ercole finally became so exasperated that in 1554 he himself denounced Renée before the inquisitorial court that had been established in Ferrara some nine years earlier as part of the church's newly expanded efforts to root out heresy. Due to his incriminating testimony, Renée was condemned as a heretic and detained as a prisoner in the city's old castle. Before she was freed and allowed to return to her former position at court, she was forced to dismiss from her service all of her fellow Protestants (her preacher, her children's tutor, and her almoner—the distributor of her alms, or charity—were specifically named); attend Mass every day; recite the Divine Office of the Virgin and the Rosary; hear only sermons approved by the duke; and convert to Catholicism.

Although Renée officially agreed to all of these conditions, she never altered her beliefs, and longed above all to return to her native France. In 1560, following Ercole's death the previous year, she finally realized her dream and spent the final fifteen years of her life at her estate at Montargis, roughly sixty miles south of Paris. Now free to follow her own beliefs unencumbered, she maintained the castle as an asylum for French Protestants, known as Huguenots, who were routinely persecuted during the religious wars that culminated in the horrendous massacre on Saint Bartholomew's Day in 1572 (Renée was herself in Paris on the day of the massacre but managed to return, unharmed, to Montargis, where she offered protection to the survivors in the region). Throughout all of the turmoil of her time in Ferrara and her first years back in France, Renée never gave up her close correspondence with Calvin. One of his final letters, sent from his deathbed in 1564, was addressed to her.

It is not clear how much Renée shared her religious beliefs with Vittoria during the time of her visit, or how familiar Vittoria was with the state of her hosts' marriage. Although she came to Ferrara as their guest, Vittoria had chosen not to stay in the palace, but seems to have resided in the nearby convent of Santa Caterina di Siena. This was the kind of choice she made repeatedly over the course of her widowhood: she preferred living with nuns to living at court. At Santa Caterina, Vittoria would have been surrounded by frescoes depicting the extraordinary life of the fourteenth-century female saint to whom the convent was dedicated, and who was a great source of inspiration to her. Born in Siena in 1347, Catherine began to have visions and ecstatic experiences as a very young girl. After joining the Dominican order as a "tertiary"— a member of a monastic order who does not take religious vows and lives outside of the monastery—she divided her life between on the one hand deepening her own personal spirituality, and on the other hand bringing peace to the world around her. Both Catherine's celebrated mystical dialogue, *Libro della divina dottrina* (*The Book of Divine Doctrine*), which was published in 1475—one of the very first books written by a woman to see print—and the hundreds of letters she wrote in her beautiful Italian (or, more precisely, Tuscan) echoed throughout Vittoria's own works. It is tempting to think she may have had these volumes by her side during her time at the convent in Ferrara.

During the months in Ferrara, Vittoria also found inspiration in a contemporary woman: Marguerite d'Angoulême, queen of Navarre (a small, independent kingdom) and sister of Francis I (see plate 13). Marguerite and Vittoria, who were introduced through Renée, never met in person: their friendship, which lasted until Vittoria's death in 1547, was conducted entirely through letters. But once they began their correspondence, they wrote to each other in such intimate and familiar terms that their physical distance counted for very little. Part of their closeness was due to the fact that they were nearly exact contemporaries (Vittoria was two years Marguerite's senior) and had led oddly parallel lives. Both were born into the most elite circles imaginable and received extremely good educations. Marguerite, who was raised alongside her brother, was taught a wide range of Latin literature and philosophy, several foreign languages (especially Italian and Spanish), and deep familiarity with the Bible. Details of Vittoria's childhood education are not known, but her earliest writings already display a fluency in both classical and Italian literature, and it is likely that the Colonna chose their children's tutors from the many impressive humanist scholars in Naples and Rome at the time.

Both Marguerite and Vittoria were married in their teens to important noblemen. King Louis, who became Marguerite's guardian following the death of her father in 1496, when she was not yet four years old, had offered her hand early on to a number of different foreign nobles, including Arthur, Prince of Wales, in 1500, and his brother, Henry, Duke of York (the future Henry VIII), in 1502, but these offers were not accepted. Several years later, Louis rejected marriage proposals for Marguerite from the same English family—indeed, Henry VII generously offered either to marry Marguerite himself or to wed her to his son Henry, on whose behalf the match had been rejected several years earlier. But this time the French king did not want an English match: his ambitions had shifted toward obtaining more territory within France, and he saw Marguerite as a useful pawn for his expansion. Thus he chose for her husband Charles, Duke d'Alençon, who owned much of Normandy and had inherited a claim to the county of Armagnac; Louis made the deal irresistible by giving her a dowry of sixty thousand crowns (roughly the equivalent of Vittoria's fourteen thousand ducats).

Both Vittoria's and Marguerite's husbands had fought in the Battle of Pavia, although on opposite sides—Charles, in fact, earned the dubious honor of being the only French officer not captured by the imperial army, which led to his being widely blamed for abandoning his king. Both women were widowed in 1525 by deaths related to the battle. Ferrante died nine months later, as we have already seen, having never fully recovered from his wounds; Charles died of mysterious causes within two months of returning to France (it was rumored that he had died of shame). At this point, the obvious parallels end. Marguerite was remarried in 1526 to the king of Navarre, Henry II, and bore him two children; Vittoria remained a widow.

More important than the biographical similarities was the fact that Vittoria and Marguerite were both poets who used their verse to express their newly reformed faith. Although Marguerite was not so radical as Renée, she had been drawn to Lutheranism since its very beginnings: she was reading Luther's works already in the early 1520s, and even arranged to have his writings translated for her into French. She sympathized above all with Luther's idea of humanity's innate sinfulness, and his related belief that only our complete dependence on God's grace (rather than a combination of faith and works) would lead to salvation. She also agreed with his understanding of the Bible as the only source of true learning about God, and his conviction that all people should be able to read the Bible in their own tongue. Luther remarked that "a simple layman armed with Scripture is greater than the mightiest pope without it." Although Marguerite was no simple layman, she took comfort in this sentiment and pored over her French Bible.

In 1524, when Vittoria was still living on Ischia waiting for Ferrante to come home, and certainly had little or no knowledge of Lutheranism, Marguerite was writing poetry with a strong Lutheran bent. In that year, following the death of her beloved niece Charlotte (the daughter of Francis I and Renée's sister, Claude), Marguerite wrote the *Dialogue en forme de vision nocturne* (*Dialogue in the Form of a Night Vision*), a twelve-hundred-line poem in which she expounds a clear set of Lutheran ideas on salvation. She counsels her niece not to shed tears over her death, since tears would only offend God, who has liberated her soul in order that she might join Christ in heaven. She also assures Charlotte, who died at age seven, that she will be saved not on the merit of her good works, but through Christ's grace alone.

In 1531, Marguerite published a more polemical spiritual poem, *Le miroir de l'âme pécheresse* (*The Mirror of the Sinful Soul*), which quickly became her most famous, and most controversial, work. On the surface of things, *The Mirror* did not seem particularly radical: assuming the voice of a female soul, Marguerite held up a mirror to her readers in order to reveal their (and her own) inner sinfulness. The underlying message, however—that she was *"trop moins que rien"* ("so much less than nothing"), and that in spite of, or even because of, this complete abjection, Christ showered her soul with love—showed signs of Lutheranism, and the poem earned Marguerite the strong censure of the theological faculty at the Sorbonne. Francis ultimately came to her defense, but from this moment on, many French Catholics considered her a heretic.

Confirming the Sorbonne's worst suspicions, *The Mirror* found many enthusiastic readers in Protestant lands, including Henry VIII's daughter the future Elizabeth I. Elizabeth translated the poem into English in 1545, when she was eleven years old, and gave a copy—written out in her own hand—as a gift to her new stepmother, Katherine Parr, Henry's sixth (and final) wife. This small, precious book is today one of the treasures of the Bodleian Library at Oxford; it still has its original binding of blue silk, and the gold and silver embroidery on its cover is credited to Elizabeth herself. Another small book in the Bodleian Library that the young princess also translated—this time from Italian into Latin—and copied out in her own hand is a sermon of Ochino's. It is extraordinary to think of this circle of aristocratic women—Marguerite, Elizabeth, and Vittoria—who never met in person but were connected through their shared interests in both poetry and religious reform.

There is no way to know when or how Marguerite's poems first reached Vittoria. But we know that she was both deeply impressed by Marguerite's skills as a poet, and struck by how much the French queen's beliefs resonated with her own. To be sure, there were differences of degree in their reformist zeal—Marguerite was several crucial steps ahead. But Vittoria found in Marguerite the finest model for her own spiritual project. In what was probably the first letter Vittoria sent to her new friend, dated February 15, 1540, she explained that "in this long and difficult path of our lives we all need to have a guide," and that for her, models from her own sex seemed more fitting than the examples of men. "I turned," she therefore explained, "to the great ladies of Italy to learn from them and to imitate them," but although they were certainly virtuous, she did not find anyone fully worthy of her adulation.

And then, Vittoria recounted, she found Marguerite. "In only one woman," she declared, "who was outside Italy, could I find the perfection of both the will and the intellect conjoined." At first, Marguerite's virtue and accomplishments left Vittoria only more desperate, more wanting: "and thus were generated in me," she confessed, "that sadness and fear that the Hebrews had seeing the fire and the glory of God on the top of the mountain, where they, still too imperfect, did not dare to climb." This was how she had felt until she received a letter from Marguerite, which, she declared, quenched her spiritual thirst and poured onto her manna from heaven. At a certain level, of course, Vittoria was simply crafting an elegant compliment, something she knew how to do well. But her words also revealed feelings of isolation or loneliness—as a woman, as an Italian, as a spiritual creature seeking guidance— which she did not often express.

Vittoria may have already been actively imitating Marguerite in the year or so before she came to Ferrara, for in 1536 she had embarked on a new poetic path. In a letter written that summer to Cosimo Gheri, bishop of Fano, Vittoria's secretary Carlo Gualteruzzi reported: "Her ladyship, the Marchesa di Pescara, has turned her pen to God and writes of nothing else, as you will see by the sonnet that I have included here. I send you this as an illustration of her newly changed style. I would very much like that you make sure Monsignor Bembo sees this, and that you write back to me with his opinion." Having at this point finished her poems to Ferrante and put her mourning behind her, Vittoria had begun writing spiritual sonnets. As Gualteruzzi represented it, the decision to shift from secular to spiritual poetry was a conscious one, and it went along with Vittoria's desire at this point in her life to present herself less as a widow than as a religious woman. In the poem that appears first in the only surviving manuscript dedicated to the spiritual sonnets, she explains her self-transformation:

> Since my chaste love long kept my soul inflamed
> with hope of fame, and nourished a serpent
> in my breast, so that now I turn in pain
> to our Lord, who is my only remedy,
> may the holy nails now be my quills,
> and may his precious blood now be my ink,
> may my paper be his lifeless sacred flesh
> so that I may record what he suffered.
> I will not call upon Parnassus or Delos

since I aspire to cross other waters,
and climb mountains, where human feet do not tread.
That sun, which illuminates the earth and sky,
I pray will open to me his source of light
and give me a draught equal to my thirst.*

I am replacing, she declares, my quills with the nails of the cross, my ink with Christ's own blood, my paper with his corpse. And I am doing this, she continues, in order to make a spiritual, not earthly, journey, on which I will be guided by Christ alone. In this last detail, Vittoria seems to renounce not only the heights of Parnassus, the home of the Greek Muses, and the pagan sanctuary of Delos, known as the birth-place of Apollo, but also perhaps the earthly pilgrimage she herself had planned to the Holy Land. She was embarking on an inner pilgrimage.

Vittoria's religious sonnets alternate between personal poems de-scribing her own experience of her faith and the challenges it posed, and more generic poems in which she speaks on behalf of Christians more broadly. The sonnets alternate, that is, between poems that re-semble confessions and poems that resemble liturgy. For readers today, at least, the sonnets in the first category tend to be more interesting, in that they show us the challenges she personally faced. In the sonnet that begins, for example, "If with heavenly arms I had overcome / myself, my senses, and my human reason," she describes her difficulty in ar-riving at the point of "true light":

Already have I fixed my eye toward
the desired end, but I cannot yet fly
with firm and steady wings on the right path;

---

* S1.1: "*Poi che 'l mio casto amor gran tempo tenne / L'alma di fama accesa, ed ella un angue / In sen nudriò per cui dolente or langue / Volta al Signor, onde 'l rimedio venne, / I santi chiodi omai sian le mie penne, / E puro inchiostro il prezioso sangue, / Vergata carta il sacro corpo exangue, / Sì ch'io scriva ad altrui quel ch'ei sostenne. / Chiamar qui non convien Parnaso o Delo, / Ch'ad altra aqua s'aspira, ad altro monte / Si poggia, u' piede uman per sé non sale. / Quel sol, che alluma gli elementi e 'l cielo, / Prego ch'aprendo il suo lucido fonte / Mi porga umor a la gran sete eguale.*"

I see the rays of the sun, I glimpse the dawn,
but I don't yet enter into the true light
that fills the divine rooms of the heavens.*

Here we witness Vittoria actively struggling: she is near, but has not arrived at, her spiritual destination; she sees where she ought to be, but does not yet know how to get there.

In a sonnet that opens with Vittoria's longing to meet her new spouse, Christ, she describes her fear of falling short of what she should be:

The time is near when I with my robes
tightly wound, and my eyes and ears alert,
with my torch held firm in my hand, burning,
await my dear Spouse, joyful and ready
to honor him chastely with reverence,
all other desire in my heart quenched,
and I long for his love, fear his anger,
that he might find me at the vigil, ready.
Not only for his infinite gifts
nor even for his words sweet and divine,
with which he offered immortal life,
but so his holy hand may not point at me,
"Here is the blind woman who failed to choose
her true Sun despite his many bright rays."†

Vittoria burns with a spiritual desire—the Italian verb she uses in line

* S1.58: "*Se con l'armi celesti avessi'io vinto / Me stessa, i sensi, e la ragione umana / . . . / Ben ho già fermo l'occhio al miglior fine / Del nostro corso, ma non volo ancora / Per lo destro sentier salda e leggiera; / Veggio i segni del sol, scorgo l'aurora, / Ma per li sacri giri a le divine / Stanze non entro in quella luce vera.*"

† S1.8: "*Tempo è pur ch'io, con la precinta vesta, / Con l'orecchie e con gli occhi avidi intenti / E con le faci in man vive e ardenti, / Aspetti il caro sposo ardita e presta / Per onorarlo riverente, onesta, / Avendo al cor gli altri desiri spenti, / E brami l'amor suo, l'ira paventi, / Sì ch'ei mi trovi a la vigilia desta. / Non per li ricchi suoi doni infiniti / Ne men per le soavi alte parole, / Onde vita immortal lieto m'offerse, / Ma perché la man santa non m'additi, / 'Ecco la cieca, a cui non si scoverse / Con tanti chiari raggi il suo bel sole.'*"

seven, *bramare*, is much stronger than *desiderare*—that seems to surpass in its intensity the love she expressed for her husband. And yet she worries that she will not make the right choice, or that her devotion will somehow be found lacking. Conjuring up the Parable of the Ten Virgins as related in the Gospel of Matthew, Vittoria both imagines herself in the position of one of the wise virgins, ready with extra oil for her torch when the bridegroom, Christ, appears, and worries that she may find herself among the five false virgins, without redeeming faith.

The other category of her spiritual sonnets—the ones I have termed "liturgical"—tends to rehearse basic tenets of the Christian faith, or to resemble hymns of praise or thanksgiving that we might imagine being sung in church. One such poem begins:

> The Lord on high, as he languished, burning
> for our love, saw how poor were our hopes
> if he did not descend and make himself
> a man, and give up his blood on the cross.*

In a more joyful poem to the Virgin, she celebrates Mary's feeding her son:

> I see the Son of God nursing at the breast
> of one both virgin and mother, and glimpse
> their mortal bodies shine together in heaven.†

This celestial vision, she exclaims, fills Christ's "faithful servant with precious hope" ("*fedel servo qui la cara speme*").

In her multiple sonnets to the Virgin, as well as in those celebrating particular saints, Vittoria seems to be working firmly within Catholic devotional norms (Protestants do not worship the Virgin, and they are forbidden from praying to saints). Taken as a whole, however, her hun-

---

*S1.30: "*Vedea l'alto Signor, ch'ardendo langue / Del nostro amor, tutti i rimedi scarsi / Per noi s'ei non scendea qui in terra a farsi / Uomo e donarci in croce il proprio sangue.*"
†S1.101: "*Veggio il figliuol di Dio nudrirsi al seno / D'una vergine e madre, ed ora insieme / Risplender con la veste umana in cielo.*"

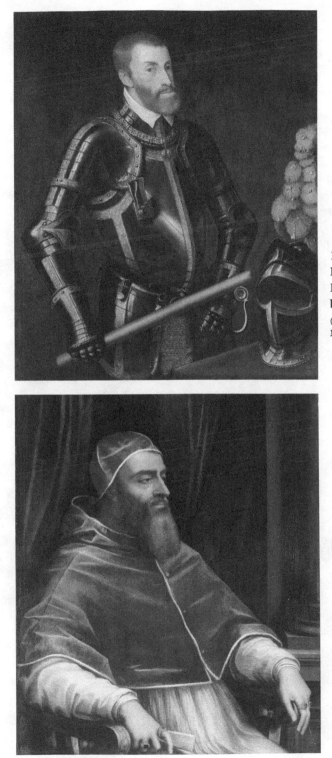

1. Portrait of the
Holy Roman
Emperor Charles V,
by Titian
(Kunsthistorisches
Museum, Vienna)

2. Portrait of Pope
Clement VII, by
Sebastiano del
Piombo
(Getty Museum, Los
Angeles)

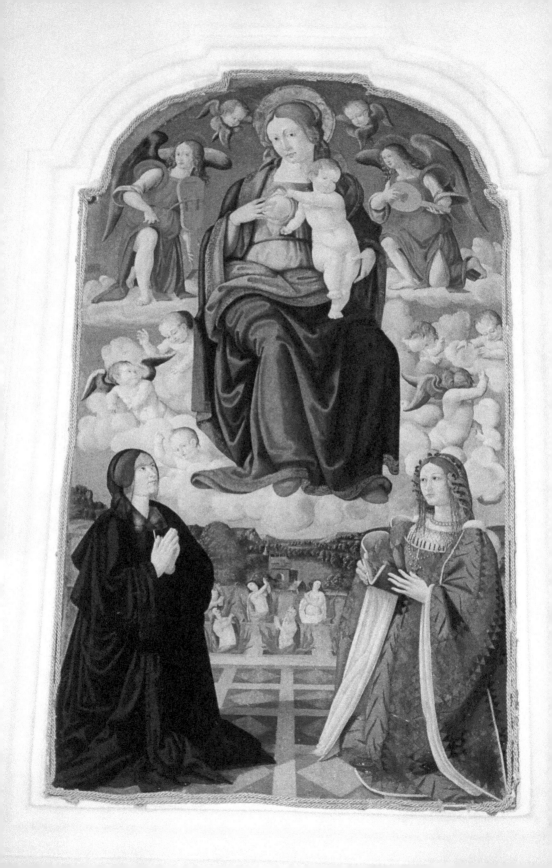

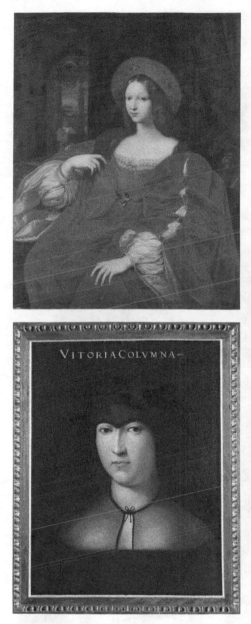

4. Portrait of the beautiful Spanish noblewoman Isabel de Requesens, with whom Ferrante d'Avalos fell in love early in his marriage to Vittoria, by Giulio Romano and Raphael

(Louvre, Paris)

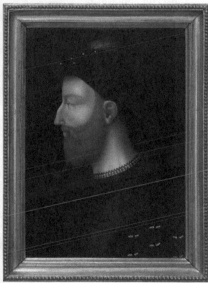

5. Portrait of Ferrante d'Avalos, attributed to Leonardo da Vinci

(Museo Correr, Venice)

6. Portrait of Vittoria Colonna, by Cristofano dell'Altissimo

(Gallerie degli Uffizi, Florence)

FACING PAGE: 3. Unattributed altarpiece from Ischia depicting Vittoria Colonna and Costanza d'Avalos (Sant'Antonio di Padova, Ischia; photo courtesy of John Palcewski)

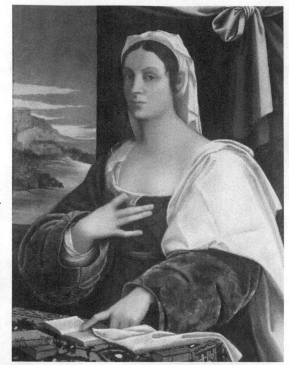

7. Portrait generally believed to be of Vittoria Colonna, pointing to a manuscript containing one of her sonnets, by Sebastiano del Piombo (Museu Nacional d'Art de Catalunya, Barcelona)

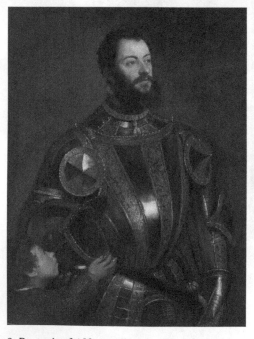

8. Portrait of Alfonso d'Avalos, Marchese del Vasto, Ferrante d'Avalos's cousin and heir, by Titian (Getty Museum, Los Angeles)

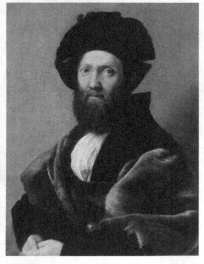

9. Portrait of Baldassare Castiglione, author of *The Courtier* and friend of Vittoria's, by Raphael (Louvre, Paris)

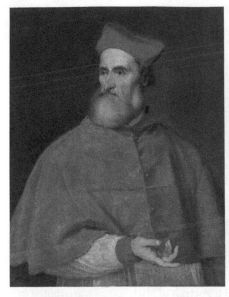

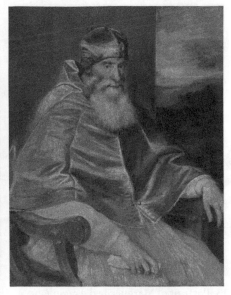

10. Portrait of the great poet and man of letters Pietro Bembo, after he was made a cardinal in 1536, by Titian

(National Gallery of Art, Washington, D.C.)

11. Portrait of Pope Paul III, the enemy of Vittoria's brother Ascanio, by Titian

(Museo di Capodimonte, Naples)

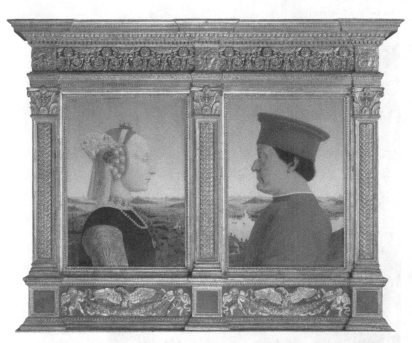

12. Double portrait of Federico da Montefeltro and Battista Sforza, Duke and Duchess of Urbino and grandparents of Vittoria, by Piero della Francesca

(Gallerie degli Uffizi, Florence)

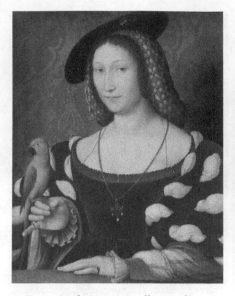

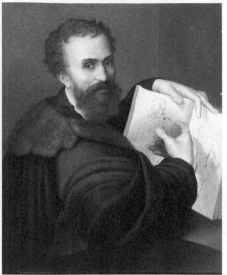

13. Portrait of Marguerite d'Angoulême, queen of Navarre, a fellow poet and reformer whom Vittoria never met in person but corresponded with until her death, by Jean Clouet

(Walker Art Gallery, Liverpool)

14. Portrait of Michelangelo, attributed to his friend Sebastiano del Piombo

(Galerie Hans, Hamburg)

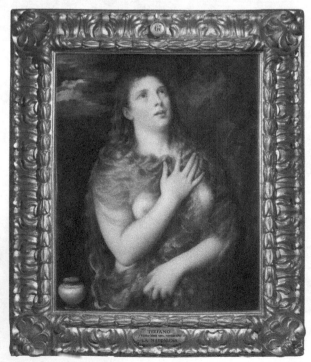

15. *The Penitent Magdalene*, by Titian. This is believed to be the painting of the Magdalene that Vittoria commissioned.

(Palazzo Pitti, Florence)

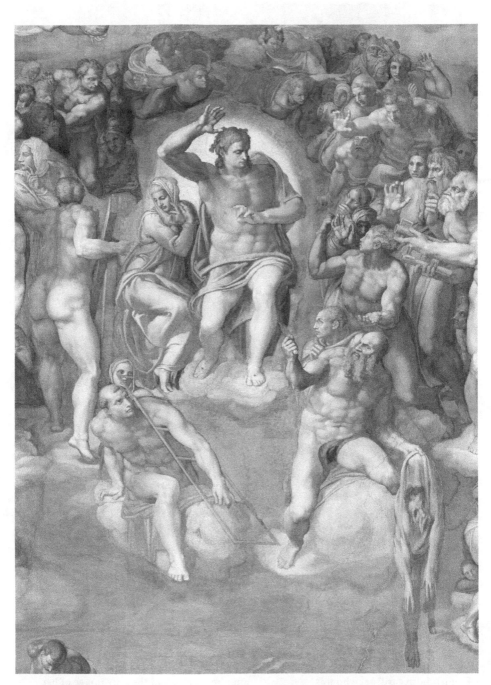

16. Detail of Michelangelo's *Last Judgment*. Some believe the female figure behind Saint Lawrence is a portrait of Vittoria. (Sistine Chapel, Vatican City)

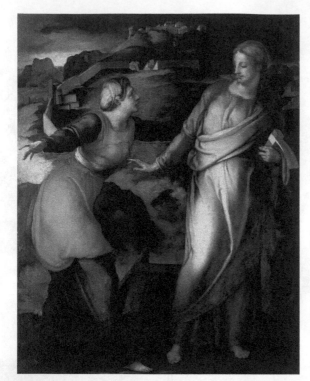

17. *Noli me tangere*, executed as a painting based on the drawing done by Michelangelo following a commission from Vittoria, by Jacopo Pontormo
(Casa Buonarroti, Florence)

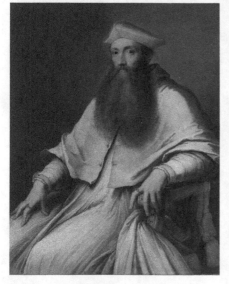

18. Portrait of Reginald Pole, the English-born cardinal who was perhaps the greatest love of Vittoria's life, by Sebastiano del Piombo
(The State Hermitage Museum, St. Petersburg)

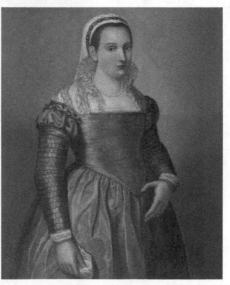

19. Portrait of Vittoria Colonna painted after her death, and the only image of her hanging in the gallery inside the Palazzo Colonna in Rome, by Bartolomeo Cancellieri
(Galleria Colonna, Rome)

dred or so spiritual sonnets offer the strongest proof of her Protestant leanings. Consider, for instance, the sonnet that begins:

> Elect souls, for whom the ample, clear,
> crystalline, secret waves of heaven
> gather every hour to make a greater sea
> of God's bounty, and give you eternal joy.

"Elect souls" ("*anime elette*") is an unambiguous reference to the Protestant idea of predestination—"election" was a buzzword for Protestants—and the sonnet concludes with a further allusion to the chosen few:

> Pray to him that with the same voice
> that it pleased him to call man to heaven
> he may now wake us from our deep inner sleep.*

In the same spirit, in a sonnet that begins with an address to Christ's presence in the Holy Eucharist, Vittoria seems nearly to take for granted her place among the elect:

> Holy food, through whose marvelous effect
> my soul perceives with its clear, inner eye
> your highest cause, and renews my faith
> in you, the true God, and my only object.
> Nourished by your warmth, with my humble breast
> almost certain of its undeserved grace,
> I aspire to make glorious conquests
> there above, armed with your love alone.

The sonnet concludes, however, not in a tone of self-celebration, but rather in a declaration of our general helplessness, if not outright

---

*S2.32: "*Anime elette, in cui da l'ampie e chiare / Cristalline del cielo onde secrete / Ristagna ogni or per farvi sempre liete / De la bontà di Dio più largo mare, / . . . / Pregate lui che con le voci stesse / Con le quai chiamar l'uom al ciel li piacque, / Lo svegli omai dal grave interno sonno.*"

sinfulness. "You give yourself in a gracious pledge," she declares to Christ,

> all this to ensure that we become yours,
> you do this, and even still we employ
> all our skill and power against ourselves.*

The yoking of election and unworthiness that she expresses is the paradox at the very heart of Protestant theology: God's creatures are completely undeserving, and yet they receive God's grace. Christ's sacrifice is so great, in other words, that it can never be compensated—from a Protestant perspective, to think otherwise is the fallacy, as well as the presumption, of Catholic works.

In addition to those poems expressing her belief in the idea of election and the centrality of grace, Vittoria also wrote a number of sonnets in which she emphasizes her close and unmediated relationship to God. This, too, was a belief at the core of reformed theology—we have seen it in both Valdés and Luther—and it resonated powerfully for her. In this sonnet, for example, she stresses her direct access to the divine, without the intervention of a priest or the structure of the church to guide her:

> But when you gather my confused thoughts
> and open with force my stubborn heart
> and extinguish all my earthly passions
> so that my true desire goes to heaven,
> all this can I do through your grace alone.†

The notion that there was nothing she could do herself to win God's

---

* S1.18: "*Cibo, del cui meraviglioso effetto / L'alma con l'occhio interno dentro vede / L'alta cagion divina e acquista fede / Che sei Dio vero e sua verace obietto: / Nudrita del tuo ardor, con umil petto / Quasi del ciel sicura indegna erede, / Vorrei là su far gloriose prede / Per forza d'un sol puro acceso affetto. / . . . / Tutto sol per far noi divenir tuoi / Facesti, e pur da noi s'usa ogni ingegno / Ed ogni poder nostro incontro a noi.*"

† S1.92: "*Ma legar i contrari miei pensieri, / Aprir per forza l'indurato petto, / Far ch'in me sian l'ardenti voglie spente / Onde vadano al ciel i desir veri, / Sol de la tua bontà fie vero effetto.*"

love, and that everything came from his direct intervention in her life—God breaks open her hardened heart; he calms her longing and directs it toward heaven—was a sure sign of her Protestant leanings. "Weak and infirm," she similarly opens another sonnet,

> I run toward salvation . . .
> and however much my soul distrusts itself
> so much the more it trusts in Christ's heavenly gift,
> whose great power can restore its richness
> and health, and make it burn with his loving heat.

"Then no longer," she concludes, "will my deeds and desires / be my own, but I will go with celestial wings / wherever his holy love takes me."*

The idea that Vittoria's spiritual sonnets were filled with expressions of Protestant belief and doctrine was recognized by her contemporaries, and even got her into trouble. Already in 1540 Vittoria's poems were being read by a suspicious Catholic official, Anne de Montmorency, Grand Constable of France. Montmorency, a fierce conservative and enemy of Marguerite de Navarre, had repeatedly warned Francis of his sister's heretical beliefs and was keen to prove that she was in contact with Protestant allies abroad. In this instance, Montmorency intercepted a gift of Vittoria's poems that Marguerite had personally requested. The manuscript was assembled not by Vittoria, but by someone working very closely with her (most likely, her secretary Gualteruzzi, although the letter is not signed). Hence the compiler of the poems explained in his cover letter to the queen:

> It has recently come to our attention in Rome that Your Excellency desired a copy of the spiritual sonnets of the illustrious Marchesa of Pescara, and to that end you have sent word to us that you wish that they should be found and dispatched to you as soon as possible. I find I have collected and kept them all, having copied them out one by one

---

*S1.52: "*Debile e 'nferma a la salute vera / Ricorro . . . / . . . / E quanto in sé disfida, tanto spera / L'alma in quel d'ogni ben vivo tesoro, / Che la può far con largo ampio ristoro / Sana, ricca, al suo caldo arder sincera. / . . . / Non saranno alor mie l'opre e 'l desire, / Ma lieve andrò con le celesti piume / Ove mi spinge e tira il santo ardore.*"

as she dictated them . . . and I have decided that it would be unchristian to [fail to send] the same to you.

This description of the sonnets as needing to be gathered is intriguing: it suggests that Vittoria had not yet collected the poems herself, and that Gualteruzzi (or whoever the letter's author may have been) was forced to compile them. This might simply have been a gesture of courtliness on his part—he may have wanted to play the role of the obliging servant to the French queen—or it might have reflected some resistance on Vittoria's part to sharing her sonnets at this time with Marguerite. Everything about the manuscript, however, which is today at the Laurentian Library in Florence, suggests a gift of state. The title is formal and impersonal: *Sonetti de più et diverse materie della divina Signora Vittoria Colonna, Marchesa di Pescara con somma diligenza revisti et corretti nel anno MDXL* (*Sonnets on various subjects of the Divine Signora Vittoria Colonna, Marchesa of Pescara, revised and corrected with great diligence in the year 1540*). The "S" in "Sonnets" is illuminated in gold, as is the fleur-de-lis below the date. Opposite the title page is an elaborate illumination of Marguerite's coat of arms, in gold, red, and royal blue. The sonnets that follow—one per page—have illuminated letters at the beginning of each group of lines (there are four golden letters per poem). This is not, in short, a manuscript that was prepared in haste, and Gualteruzzi must have commissioned the finest of scribes to prepare it.

Whenever Vittoria learned about Gualteruzzi's manuscript for Marguerite, she certainly would have been upset to know that the poems had fallen into enemy hands. After Montmorency read them, he steadfastly refused to send the gift along to Marguerite, and ultimately complied only under direct orders of the king. He apparently reported to Francis, however, that Vittoria's sonnets contained "many things that ran counter to the faith of Jesus Christ," and that he was shocked to see such ideas linked to the "good name of the Marchesa of Pescara." It is interesting that the Grand Constable of France had a sense of Vittoria's reputation in the first place—a sign of her fame extending far beyond the Italian peninsula. But it is also important to note that her "good name" was already tarnished by its association with Protestantism.

Vittoria could not have predicted any of this as she worked peacefully on her poems in the tranquility of Ferrara's convent of Santa Caterina di Siena, and visited the duke and duchess at the palace. We know the time she spent in Ferrara was immensely satisfying to her from letters she sent both during and after her visit. First, in June 1537, she wrote to Ercole's cousin Cardinal Ercole Gonzaga: "It has pleased God that here in Ferrara I should be very calm and consoled, praised be God, as his Excellence the Duke and all the others respect my great desire for the freedom to attend only to true acts of charity and not to those mixed acts produced by conversation." Her emphasis on the tranquility of her days suggests that the time at the convent may have been more pleasing to her than the visits to the ducal palace. In her correspondence with Ercole after her departure, however, Vittoria stressed the pleasure she took both with the nuns and in the company of his court. She also conjured up an image of Ercole's happy family, which, despite the obvious problems between husband and wife, was nonetheless growing at a fast pace. When Vittoria arrived, there were already three small children; a fourth was born during her visit, and a fifth the following year. "I pray to God," she wrote from Rome in December 1539, "that he will allow me to return to your sweetest Ferrara to be with Your Excellency, my many friends, relatives, and sisters [at the convent], and with your duchess and divine children." Several years later, she signed another letter to Ercole: "From Santa Caterina, but not that most beautiful one in Ferrara, rather this mediocre one in Viterbo."

Ferrara clearly suited Vittoria's soul, but it served her body less well. Her pilgrimage had been canceled almost certainly due to her health, and Ferrara's damp climate had not been conducive to a full recovery. Toward the end of 1537, she wrote to Aretino to say that the air in Ferrara was so harmful to her that she was leaving for the healthier climate of Bologna. The two cities are very close to each other—a mere twenty-three miles separate them—but Ferrara is famously marshy and full of mosquitoes, which regularly brought malaria, literally *mal aria*, or "bad air," whereas Bologna is near the Appenine foothills and much drier.

Ercole marked the occasion of Vittoria's departure by throwing a grand dinner in her honor, which coincided with the festivities for

Carnival. Among the many guests was Ercole's aunt, Isabella d'Este. Vittoria had almost certainly met Isabella before: she had been a guest at the Palazzo Colonna in Rome in 1525, and would also have attended many of the same weddings and festivities as Vittoria over the years. This evening in Ferrara is the only occasion, however, that we know the two women—perhaps the most illustrious women of the period—were together.

Isabella d'Este combined many of the qualities that Vittoria had most admired in two of her earlier role models: her aunts Costanza d'Avalos and Elisabetta Gonzaga, the latter of whom was also Isabella's sister-in-law (Isabella had been married to Francesco II Gonzaga). Like Costanza, Isabella was a very accomplished female ruler, having been the active regent of Mantua following her husband's death in 1519. She was famous for her fine negotiation of foreign treaties, her skillful control over the military, and her successful defense of the city. She was also known for her kindness to her people, who showered her with love. Like Elisabetta, Isabella presided with supreme elegance over her court, and was the patron of some of the most important artists of the period. She commissioned two portraits from Titian—the first, painted when she was fifty-five years old, she regarded as too matronly; the second, done seven years later, represents her as a young woman in her twenties. When she was in truth twenty-five, she commissioned a portrait from Leonardo da Vinci. This never got beyond a preliminary drawing, done in black and red chalk and roughly two feet in length, but even in its unfinished state, the head-and-shoulders portrait has a regal serenity not unlike Leonardo's infinitely more famous work also at the Louvre, the *Mona Lisa*.

At the time of Ercole's dinner for Vittoria, Isabella was sixty-four years old, and nearing the end of her life; she died the following year. A letter written by Benedetto Accolti, cardinal of Ravenna, to one of Isabella's daughters described the pleasures of the evening in some detail:

> This morning, to the great sadness of the Lord Duke's Excellency and myself and this whole city, the Signora Marchesa di Pescara left for Bologna, but his Most Excellent Lordship and I took in some most

divine entertainment and, too, we console ourselves with the promises that her Ladyship made us that she would return soon. Yesterday
evening we enjoyed dinner all together, the Lord Duke's Excellency
and myself, and the most illustrious lady mother to Your Most Illustrious Lordship, with whom we dined and likewise dined the Lady
Marchesa mentioned above. After dinner five sonnets by the abovementioned Lady Marchesa were read aloud, which were so beautiful
that I am certain an angel from Heaven could not create anything
more perfect; after these were read aloud, to everyone's endless delight and applause, the maidens of the Lady your mother, and Signora
Anna played some small pieces on the harpsichord excellently; then
moving into some dances Morgantino leapt out with the lady Delia
and they did great things with their little bodies.

This is a fortunate letter to have survived, for it offers one of the loveli-
est images we have of Vittoria immersed in her world: sharing her poems, listening to the harpsichord, enjoying the dancing performed by
the little people Delia and Morgantino, Isabella's beloved jesters. Here
are the elegant pastimes of the Renaissance nobility just as Castiglione
described them, with Vittoria at their very center.

In February 1538, Vittoria left Ferrara for Bologna. Upon her arrival, she wasted no time in seeking out the best sermons in the city:
she went to hear the young Franciscan monk Cornelio Musso, who was
rising in fame as both a teacher of metaphysics and a preacher, and was
on his way to becoming one of Pope Paul's favorites. A few weeks later,
however, she was once again on the move, following the trail of
Ochino. Perhaps her health had improved, or perhaps she was simply
determined to hear more of Ochino's preaching, and confident that
the spring air in Tuscany would be fine. After attending Ochino's sermons in Pisa and Florence, where she also met her brother Ascanio,
she seems to have settled for a few months to take the thermal baths in
the town known today as Bagni di Lucca. For the first time in her life,
she seems to have devoted herself to taking care of her body.

Bagni di Lucca had been famous for its springs since the time of the
ancient Etruscans—the baths the Romans built there were still largely

intact at the time of Vittoria's visit. In the early nineteenth century, following Napoleon's conquest of northern Italy, his sister Marie Anne Elisa, to whom he had given the principality of Lucca, along with that of Piombino, transformed Bagni di Lucca into one of the most sought-after social destinations for European nobility, and many members of Napoleon's court spent their summers there. Elisa's principal innovation was the introduction of individual tubs, rather than common pools (a genuine revolution in the history of spas), but she also sought to make the town a more lively social destination by building a dance hall and casino. In the sixteenth century, Bagni di Lucca was strictly a spa—a retreat from the demands of court life—and Vittoria's visit there was therapeutic.

If Vittoria adhered to the recommended course of treatment, she would have followed a demanding regimen of drinking the waters and bathing. Another visitor some forty years later, the great French essayist and philosopher Michel de Montaigne, recorded drinking seven glasses of the water in a row just after sunrise, and remarked that this was nothing compared with the sixteen or seventeen glasses drunk by several of his fellow guests. According to the Latin inscription on the marble tablet outside one of the baths, the result of the treatment was to "cure all stomach illnesses, aid digestion, stimulate appetite, restrict vomiting, clean the kidneys, diminish stones, eliminate fevers, restore an optimal complexion, heal the lungs, strengthen the frail, remove all obstructions from the veins completely, and rid the body of all ulcers and sores." No wonder Vittoria stayed so long.

Vittoria might well have chosen to stay even longer had she not been recalled to Rome in September 1538. In the letter to Aretino written from Lucca on September 25 that we looked at earlier, she complained that His Holiness had requested her to return at the urging of Alfonso d'Avalos. There was no account of why Alfonso needed her, but however free she may have felt in her movements, there was no avoiding a summons from the pope. By October, she was back in her familiar quarters in the convent of San Silvestro in Capite, just in time to absorb some astonishing news. Vittoria had become a published poet.

THE POWER OF PRINT

FROM THE TIME OF HER LITERARY SALON on Ischia in the late 1520s through her visit to the ducal palace in Ferrara ten years later, Vittoria had grown accustomed to sharing her sonnets with friends. These poems, as we have seen, were on the whole very personal: she gave voice to her anguish over her husband's death; her frustration with her mourning; her longing to live a religious life; her desire for greater intimacy with God. As she said in the first of the posthumous sonnets to Ferrante, "I write only to vent my inward pain." However comfortable Vittoria was circulating her poems in literary circles, she had no ambition to be a public figure, nor did she ever express a desire for fame. In her poetry, as in her personal life, she cherished her privacy. This was a woman, after all, who had wanted to spend her days in the cloister of the convent.

It is therefore not surprising that the idea of printing her poems— and, in so doing, making her innermost thoughts available to an anonymous and unknown audience of readers—had no appeal to Vittoria. The problem was not that she considered the medium of print to be beneath her, as if publishing were an inherently vulgar thing to do.

Such an attitude, commonly referred to by literary historians as "the stigma of print," was common in Renaissance England: even a great poet such as John Donne described his regret at feeling "under an unescapable necessity" to publish his verse, as if he would do anything to avoid such a fate. (In the end, Donne managed to resist printing more than a small number of occasional poems, with the result that the first edition of his splendid "Songs and Sonnets" appeared in 1633, two years after his death.)

There was no comparable prejudice against publishing in Italy—Bembo and his fellow aristocratic poets printed their poetry with great frequency—and Vittoria was under increasing pressure to do so. The problem for Vittoria was not part of a general resistance among the Italian elite to allowing their works to be printed; it was more particular to her. Part of this no doubt came from the fact that no woman in Italy had ever published a book of poems, and all evidence suggests that Vittoria never imagined herself as a path-breaker. When the poet and humanist Benedetto Varchi came to visit her in Ferrara in 1537 and raised the question of publication to her directly, she responded by saying that she wanted the poems to be left alone.

We can imagine Vittoria's reaction, then, in 1538, when an unknown printing house in the northern city of Parma published a book of her sonnets without her permission. Entitled *Rime de la divina Vittoria Colonna, Marchesa di Pescara*, the book was printed by Antonio Viotti and edited by Filippo Pirogallo—neither of whom had any personal connection to Vittoria—and contained 145 poems. Nine of these were in fact wrongly attributed to Vittoria; of the remaining 136 poems, 17 were spiritual sonnets, and the rest were secular. In his dedicatory letter, Pirogallo described his own labors in obtaining Vittoria's poems; he claimed that he copied out whatever sonnets he could find, and then assembled them himself. This account made clear that he was not part of her inner circle: he had not received a personal manuscript or borrowed one from someone who knew her. He represented the world outside.

Viotti and Pirogallo chose to print the *Rime* in the small format known as *ottavo*, which was one of the cheapest and most portable sizes. The names of book sizes referred to the number of times each large printed sheet of paper was folded over: the largest was the folio, which had one fold in the sheet, producing two pages; the quarto, folded twice to become four pages, was the size of a modern paperback; and the ottavo was a small book made from folding each sheet four times to render eight (*otto*) small pages. The book was austere in its presentation, and other than a clover on the title page, it was entirely without ornamentation.

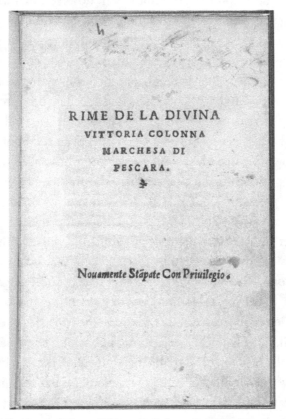

Title page of the first edition of Vittoria Colonna's *Rime* (Parma: Viotti, 1538)
(*IC5 C7191R 1538, Houghton Library, Harvard University)

The fact that Vittoria's *Rime* was printed in a pirated edition was by no means uncommon at the time—it was not even illegal. In 1545, after one too many complaints from authors fed up with their lack of control over their own publications, the authorities in Venice, which was the capital of the Italian publishing industry, ruled that books could no longer be published without the author's consent. According to a decree issued by the powerful governing body known as the Council of Ten: "The audacity and greed for gain of some printers in this city of ours has grown to such an extent that they permit themselves to print what they like and to name the authors of the things they print without their knowledge, indeed completely against their wishes." The new Venetian laws against pirating did not mean, however, that authors necessarily profited from the sales of their books; our modern system of royalties had yet to be invented. In order for authors to make money personally, they needed to have invested directly in the costs of the printing. This was, in fact, a fairly regular occurrence, and legal agreements were signed with printers or publishers that specified how profits, should there be any, were to be distributed. Less financially well-off authors often found the support of a patron who subsidized the publication and had their own arrangement with the printer. But there was no such thing as copyright during this period—the first copyright statute in Europe was passed in England in 1709—and authors had no inherent rights to what we now consider their intellectual property.

However common the practice of publishing works without authorial permission may have been in 1538, it was a very bold move in relation to Vittoria. This was something that Viotti and Pirogallo openly recognized, and even capitalized on in presenting the book. In the dedicatory letter addressed to his friend, "The Most Learned Alessandro Vercelli," Pirogallo boasted about publishing the poems against Vittoria's will: "I present you with the sonnets of the Divine Pescara, which I have personally collected over a long period of time . . . I have had the great desire to publish them, even if it goes against the wishes of so great a lady, for I consider it less of an error to displease one woman (however rare and great) than to deny so many men what they want." "Even if it goes against the wishes of so great a lady": the idea of displeasing one woman in order to give "so many men what they want" sounded a provocative note on grounds of both class and gender. Pirogallo was laying hold of a precious and protected commodity, and sharing it with the masses.

Because Pirogallo did not have access to Vittoria's own manuscripts, he also acknowledged that his edition was almost certainly full of errors:

> Maybe the mistakes that you will find in the poems, I having been unable to take them from their original [texts], will make them seem less beautiful or pleasurable. But your wise judgment will no doubt emend the errors made by the diversity of different pens that have copied them out, since I for one have not felt confident doing so, because of the prospect of not concurring with that most immortal Lady who has produced these miraculous poems.

There had been, he declared, many different "pens," or hands, involved in copying the poems out, which meant that by the time the poems reached him, they had accumulated no end of mistakes. Pirogallo consoled himself, however, by assuming that even in their flawed state, the poems would be "useful" to many young men, who would forever be grateful to him for bringing the book into the world. Even Vittoria, he concluded, adopting a conspicuously male metaphor for the first published female poet, "seeing the fruit that thanks to her seed will mature in the minds of the most talented youth, will in the end be satisfied with it."

The allure of publishing Vittoria's *Rime* depended upon the fact that she had already earned a reputation in Italy as an important poet. Her fame, that is, did not depend on the publication of her poems: on the contrary, the publication of the poems built upon the fact of her celebrity. We will recall that as early as 1519, Vittoria's name appeared in the Neapolitan poet Girolamo Britonio's *La gelosia del Sole*: he called her "this gentle new Phoenix in the world." Gaining her much more attention, she was praised in the 1532 edition of the greatest epic poem of the period, Ariosto's *Orlando furioso*, which told the tale of the Christian knight Orlando (better known in English by his French name, Roland). In the introduction to canto thirty-seven, dedicated to the story of the female warriors Bradamante and Marfisa and their victory over the tyrant Marganorre, Ariosto laments how difficult it is for women to

be recognized in the manner they deserve, and offers his own defense of
their excellence as writers. He singles out one woman in particular—
Vittoria—whom he admires for "a sweetness I have never heard bet-
tered." Apollo, he declares, "gives such power to her lofty words that in
our day he has adorned the heavens with another sun."

Ariosto's praise of Vittoria was not entirely unmotivated. Despite
his terrific talent, he had failed to find a worthy patron to support him;
his long-term relations with both Cardinal Ippolito d'Este and Ippolito's brother Alfonso I d'Este (Ercole II's father) had never produced the
income that he had hoped for. It was only in 1531 that he received a
major pension, from none other than Alfonso d'Avalos, whose relation
to Vittoria was certainly well known. Whatever Ariosto's reasons for
complimenting her so extravagantly, the appearance of her name in
such a prominent place cannot be overstated. Then, three years after
the final edition of Ariosto's epic appeared, Bembo published his sonnet exchange with Vittoria in the new edition of his own poems. By
1535, the two most famous poets in Italy had honored Vittoria in print.

None of this very careful and exquisite praise of Vittoria's gifts had
anything to do, however, with what happened when Pirogallo's colla-
tion of her sonnets arrived in Viotti's shop in Parma. From this moment on, the sonnets were no longer Vittoria's private property, to be
shared and exchanged within her coterie circles. They became com-
modities. Compositors set the text from the two trays, or cases, of type
(hence our use of the terms "uppercase" and "lowercase" letters, to indicate the higher or lower of the two cases). Others laid the galleys in
wooden forms. *Battitori* and *tiratori*, or beaters and pullers, applied the
ink to the press and pulled the bar. The damp pages were hung to dry
overnight (the press worked better when the sheets were wet), and then
folded and cut to the designated size. After the pages were assembled
in the right order, others wrapped them tightly in heavy paper, and
marked on the front the book's title and the number of copies included.
These bundles were then packed in barrels or wooden caskets also
wrapped with waxed cloth, and then sent off to be shipped either by
land or by sea.

The books' travel to their destinations was also complex. Because

Italy was not a unified country, every boundary crossed, from one city or principality to another, had its own tolls and customs to be paid. A bookseller traveling from Bologna to Milan in 1497 described paying fees to cross the Panaro, Secchia, Taro, Enza, Po, and Lambro Rivers, and to pass in and out of the city gates of Parma, Piacenza, Pavia, and Cremona. Once the books arrived in cities throughout the peninsula, there were multiple places where they were sold. The most obvious was the bookshop, which was already a standard feature of Renaissance cities. Larger cities had specific districts known for bookselling, which were usually separate from where the books were being printed. In Rome, bookshops filled the area around the Campo dei Fiori; in Venice, they were clustered along the Mercerie. The booksellers displayed their wares both in their windows and on tables outside their doors, with the hopes of attracting foot traffic. Beyond the designated bookstores, there were also informal stalls in most Italian towns rather like the stands we find today in piazzas or along the banks of rivers; these stalls typically sold whatever volumes happened to have come the owner's way. Books were sold as well in many *cartolerie*, or stationery stores, and from peddlers who traveled through the town with books in baskets or trays. There are even records of peddlers who sold books by attaching them to the ends of long sticks.

"Books," however, is not necessarily the right term for what was being sold, or at least the books did not usually take the form that we imagine today—that is, an object with a front and back cover, with bound pages in between. In the sixteenth century, most books were sold as loose pages, without any binding. There is no record of what the unbound pages of Vittoria's *Rime* sold for, but based on printers' catalogs and inventories from the period, a rough estimate of the cost would be fifteen soldi, the daily wages for a skilled laborer. The binding was an entirely separate cost—it was an accessory, similar to the frame you might choose for a painting. Depending on how much money the buyer wanted to spend, he or she could choose from different qualities of leather for a hardbound book, or from a range of vellum and parchment for a softbound book. Wealthy collectors often preferred to buy their books unbound in order to match the new bindings to the rest of their collection—this is why so many beautiful private libraries look as if all of the books were bound at the same time. Less wealthy readers often bought several different books as loose pages and then bound them together. This helps to explain the miscellaneous materials that often make up a single volume from this period: a cookbook might be combined with a spiritual manual and several political treatises. The Houghton Library at Harvard has a 1539 edition of Vittoria's *Rime*, for example, which was bound with a 1536 Italian translation of the Latin poet Horace. This particular reader must have been interested in keeping his or her preferred poetry together.

Wherever it was purchased and however it was bound, there was nothing remotely personal about the presentation of Vittoria's poems once they became the *Rime de la divina Vittoria Colonna, Marchesa di Pescara*. The world of the sonnets hand-delivered by Giovio to Bembo at the congress in Bologna, or warmly recited by Isabella d'Este's gentlewoman in the elegant rooms of the palace in Ferrara, was far away indeed. There is no record of Vittoria's reaction to seeing her poems in print for the first time, but we know something about her feelings from a letter that Bembo wrote to her secretary Gualteruzzi on November 8, 1538. Bembo, who at this point regarded himself as Vittoria's literary adviser—the two had become increasingly close, and he took a lively interest in her poems—was horrified by the book's appearance, and he minced no words in saying so: "You should know of the injury and villainy done to the Signora Marchesa di Pescara by whoever printed her poetry most incorrectly and with the worst form and paper. About which she has sweetly written to me, not only not regretting it but also saying that she deserved it for worrying about vain things." What exactly Vittoria meant by "vain things" ("*vane cose*") is not clear, but most likely she was referring to the sheer act of writing so many secular poems, a project that she had come to renounce. We will remember how she opened the spiritual sonnets:

> Since my chaste love long kept my soul inflamed
> with hope of fame, and nourished a serpent
> in my breast, so that now I turn in pain

to our Lord, who is my only remedy,
may the holy nails now be my quills,
and may his precious blood now be my ink,
may my paper be his lifeless sacred flesh
so that I may record what he suffered.

The fact that she was not full of regrets about the publication of the poems did not, however, mean she was in favor of it. Instead, Bembo's words suggest that Vittoria allowed her penitential side to take over, so that the printing of the poems seemed to her a just punishment for wasting her time in the first place. The published *Rime* became, in effect, an act of self-flagellation.

For his own part, Bembo was not upset that the poems had been published, but that the edition was so full of errors—and, adding insult to injury, printed on such poor paper. As he reported to Gualteruzzi, he had already written to Vittoria urging her to allow him personally to oversee a new edition:

I replied begging her to be content with sending me a corrected copy of the *Rime*, so that I could have them printed here in a nice manner. I have not had any response from her Ladyship about it, and I fear the letter did not pass into her hands. Thus if you would be content, dear friend, when she passes through Rome as I expect that she will do, to devise that she sends me these *Rime* of hers, so that I can amend the error of that sad thing . . . In any case it would be a great shame if they are not sent out in such a way that they are read exactly as they came out of that pilgrim's genius. She should not say, "I don't care about worldly glory," because these are only words. Glory, which can come from good works, must not be disdained; on the contrary, it should be loved and treasured by all the saintliest souls.

A subsequent letter written to Gualteruzzi on December 7 suggests that Vittoria had agreed to allow a new version to be printed: "Please kiss the hand of the Signora Marchesa di Pescara in my name and thank her for coming around to the idea of giving you a copy of the poems to print there [in Rome]. They should not have been hidden and neglected, but rather adorned with gold and jewels, and left in this way to make themselves known in the world." But Vittoria's mind, it appears, was only fleetingly changed. Four days later, Bembo wrote Gualteruzzi a letter that betrayed signs of real frustration, if not outright anger: "But I will not permit for any reason her failing to give me the copy of her *Rime* to print there. And I beg you above all to get these to come out correctly and nicely." Despite the strength of Bembo's pleas, his demands seem to have gone unanswered, and the poems were never presented either to him or to Gualteruzzi for an authorized publication. The following year, a new unauthorized edition appeared in Parma, with the claim on its title page of being a "corrected" version, although the revisions were minimal, and certainly not initiated by Vittoria. Most egregiously, the title page boasted of a new additional set of poems ("*le sue stanze*"), but the stanzas were written by another poet, Veronica Gambara. This edition was only the first of four new editions issued in 1539: two from Viotti's shop, one whose printer remains unknown, and one from the well-known Nicolò di Aristotile, known as il Zoppino, who usually worked in Venice but printed Vittoria's poems in Florence. In the Zoppino edition, the title page highlighted the inclusion of sixteen spiritual sonnets that were placed at the beginning of the volume (six of these had in fact appeared in the earlier collection), and also boasted that the poems had been reviewed "with the greatest diligence." Although the revisions were not so extensive as Zoppino claimed, the volume does show signs of some genuine editorial work.

The multiple editions of the *Rime* issued in 1539 were followed by yet another edition in 1540, published under the supervision of Zoppino in Venice. This volume included twelve new spiritual sonnets, as well as a poem on the triumph of Christ on the cross. By the time of Vittoria's death in 1547, a total of twelve editions of the *Rime* had been published—twelve editions in the space of nine years—and nine more were issued before the end of the century. There is no record of the print runs for any of them, but in the year 1500, the average print run in Venice was a thousand books, and a small shop such as Viotti's probably published somewhere between four hundred and five hundred copies per edition. Whatever the number of copies sold, the sheer fact of the book's nearly constant reprinting gives us a good sense of its success. Vittoria's *Rime* was a Renaissance bestseller.

The popularity of the *Rime* did nothing, however, to change Vittoria's mind about seeing her poems in print. In the fall of 1546, she complained to Donato Rullo—a friend of Ascanio's and an agent of the Colonna family in Venice, who was involved in editing her poems—about the new book of her spiritual sonnets issued by the famous Venetian printing house of Vincenzo Valgrisi. In a letter to Ascanio, Rullo related that Vittoria had chastised him for not having stopped the press. "Your most illustrious sister, and my patron," he wrote, "has turned against me, because I gave the poems to the press to print, or because I did not prohibit it." It is hard to believe that Vittoria did not have the power in 1546 to prevent her poems from being printed. She was, after all, a formidable person with powerful connections—how many other women were in regular correspondence with both the pope and the Holy Roman Emperor?—and after one or two pirated editions, things surely could have been brought to a halt. Moreover, apart from her self-punishing comment to Bembo about deserving the publication of her "vain things" and the complaint to Rullo some eight years later, there are no traces of her either resisting or resenting the printed *Rime*.

The only possible hint of an intervention against her appearance in print surfaced in a minor collection of poems that was found in the late nineteenth century in the great Biblioteca Estense (the Este family library) in Modena. The title of the book, *Opera nova non più posta in luce nella quale troverai molto bellissimi Sonetti di diversi Eccelentissimi ingegni*, or *New works never before seen in which you will find many of the most beautiful sonnets by a range of most excellent talents*, specified the special addition of certain sonnets of the "*divina Vittoria Colonna*," which, it boasted, were "never before seen by anyone." And yet, inside the volume, Vittoria's poems are nowhere to be found. Perhaps it was simply a marketing ploy to attract buyers, or perhaps the printer had hoped to obtain copies of the new poems but failed to do so. Whatever happened with this peculiar little book, it stands out as Vittoria's single triumph over the medium of print.

At the same time that the *Rime* was being printed in multiple editions, there were still readers coveting manuscript copies of Vittoria's poems. It is hard today fully to grasp the profound difference that existed in Renaissance Italy between the elite, coterie readership of private manuscripts and the public audience of print. Even if someone like Castiglione, for example, complained that Vittoria had shared his manuscript too freely, the number of people reading copies of *The Courtier* within Vittoria's circle of friends in Naples did not remotely compare with the vast and completely uncontrollable readership he acquired once *The Courtier* was published. In the sixteenth century, there were in effect two separate systems operating simultaneously, catering to very different sets of demands. Thus when Vittoria's poems were printed, the desire among her friends to have them in manuscript did not by any means abate. Anyone with money could purchase a printed book, but only those with personal connections could obtain an authorized handwritten copy.

The best example of this double system comes in an exchange between Francesco della Torre, the secretary of Vittoria's friend Giberti, and Gualteruzzi in 1540. At this point, della Torre could have chosen from at least five printed editions of the *Rime*, but he wrote to Gualteruzzi to request a manuscript copy. Della Torre did not even acknowledge the existence of the printed books: in his letter to Gualteruzzi, he mentioned that he had heard about a collection of Vittoria's "many very beautiful sonnets" from his friend the Sienese ambassador Lattanzio Tolomei, as if the poems were a well-kept secret. Gualteruzzi granted della Torre's request, and sent him a manuscript of the poems. In his letter of thanks, della Torre promised not to circulate the poems, "since," he declared, "I would not want such rare compositions to be in any other hands than my own," and promised he would return the manuscript to Gualteruzzi as soon as he had copied it in its entirety. Although the exact contents of della Torre's manuscript are not known— there is debate among scholars as to which manuscript he actually received—one of the likeliest candidates, a manuscript now in Florence, contains one hundred poems, ninety of which had already appeared in the 1538 *Rime*. Thus the idea that the poems were "rare" would only have made sense in a universe that refused to recognize the existence of print.

While della Torre and his circle were still clinging to the notion that Vittoria's poems needed to be copied out by hand, the printed editions of her *Rime* were making literary history. Up to this time, individual poems by women had been included in collections of men's poetry—Vittoria's sonnet appearing in Bembo's 1535 *Rime* is a good example—but there had never before been a single-authored book of poetry written by a woman. This was a watershed moment, and the history of Italian women's writing can be divided between before and after the publication of Vittoria's poems.

In the wake of Vittoria's *Rime*, scores of Italian women poets began to publish their poems. Some of them came from backgrounds similar to Vittoria's, but there was a marked shift in the mid-sixteenth century away from the aristocratic women who were popular in manuscript circles—the most famous of whom, Gambara, saw her poems appear only in collections of other poets'—toward a new group of women from decidedly different worlds. Gaspara Stampa, one of the most celebrated female poets of the mid-sixteenth century, was the daughter of a jeweler in Padua; Laura Terracina, whose *Rime* was issued from the prestigious Giolito house in Venice starting in 1548, was an impoverished gentlewoman; Tullia d'Aragona, whose poems were first published in 1547 also by the Venetian Gabriele Giolito, was by vocation a courtesan, even if she claimed to have noble blood. (D'Aragona was in fact so impressive intellectually that the duke of Florence, Cosimo I de' Medici, excused her from having to wear the yellow veil required of all sex workers due to her "rare knowledge of poetry and philosophy.") The fact that both Terracina's and d'Aragona's publications appeared within a year of Vittoria's death was probably not a coincidence: the market had opened up for a new woman poet to fill Vittoria's place.

Many of these women explicitly modeled themselves as Vittoria's heirs. Already during Vittoria's lifetime, Gambara had written a sonnet to her that began, "O unique glory of our present age." "Our sex," she declared, "should raise to you a noble temple / As in the past to Pallas and to Phoebus, / Built of rich marble and of finest gold."* Many other tributes followed, but perhaps the most interesting was from a much younger writer from Venice, Maddalena Campiglia, who was born six years after Vittoria's death. In Campiglia's 1588 play, *Flori*, the female protagonist, who is filled with dreams of her own literary immortality, exclaims to her friend: "Come set yourself like me on that path on which one sole immortal woman has ventured, the most VICTORIOUS and DIVINE among all those of our sex who have attained fame and glory." *Vittoriosa e Divina:* Divine Vittoria.

The second landmark publication for Italian women writers after Vittoria's *Rime* was an anthology of women's poetry published in 1559 by the famous Venetian editor Lodovico Domenichi. Entitled *Rime diverse d'alcune nobilissime, et virtuosissime donne* (*Assorted poems by some of the most noble and the most virtuous women*), this was the first anthology ever dedicated to women's verse. The volume had a total of 316 poems, including 26 of Vittoria's; there were 54 women represented in all (the volume also included 14 poems by men, but only because they formed parts of dialogues with women authors). Domenichi, who in 1552 had published an anthology of male Neapolitan poets, represented himself here as a champion of women's writing. "I was determined," he wrote in the dedicatory letter, "to find whatever way I could to make them public to the world through the medium of print, to show those who are in doubt of the greatness of female *ingenio* [intellect or talent]."

Thanks in part to the success of Domenichi's anthology, roughly two hundred women in Italy had their poems appear in print by the end of the sixteenth century. To give some sense of how significant this number was: in France, there were thirty published women poets; in Germany, there were twenty. In England—and this was exactly the period of Elizabeth I, who was herself a talented translator and poet—the figure was seventeen. It is hard to believe that Italy was so far ahead of

---

*"O de la nostra etade unica gloria, / . . . / Il sesso nostro un sacro e nobil tempio / Dovría, come già a Palla e a Febo, alzarvi / Di ricchi marmi e di finissim'oro."

its northern European peers, but this was unambiguously the case. And Vittoria had led the way.

One of the keys to the success of Vittoria's *Rime*—and to volumes such as Domenichi's—was the strong presence of Italian women as readers and buyers of books. Female literacy in Italy was, relatively speaking, impressively high. At the end of the fifteenth century, 33 percent of Italian men were literate, and 13 percent of women. We can compare this, for example, with 10 percent of men, and 1 percent of women, in England. Although in his dedicatory letter to Vittoria's first edition, Pirogallo represented her poems as intended for a male audience—"I consider it less of an error to displease one woman (however rare and great) than to deny so many men what they want"—there is good reason to believe that women made up a significant share of Vittoria's readers, as they did of vernacular poetry in general. The fact that the *Rime* was printed in such a small format, and on what Bembo regarded as poor paper, also meant that it was certainly cheaper to buy than many of the more elaborately produced volumes of verse.

The most compelling evidence of Vittoria's strong female readership is the increasingly religious emphasis in the poems' presentation over the course of the 1540s. It is hard to say exactly what books were purchased or read specifically by women within a Renaissance household, as inventories of family libraries generally listed all of the titles together. In the examples that have been passed down of women's personal collections, however, the titles leaned heavily toward religious topics. Most of the books were by men, but Saint Catherine of Siena's mystical dialogue, *The Book of Divine Doctrine*, and her collection of letters frequently appeared, as did the small handful of devotional books also published by women in the early 1500s.

It is therefore not surprising that after the first few editions of the *Rime*, which were composed almost exclusively of the sonnets to Ferrante, Vittoria's success as a poet came to depend upon her spiritual poetry. Indeed, the shift in her representation from aristocratic widow to religious author was clearly a deliberate decision on the part of her publishers. The first sign of this change was the Venice edition of 1540, whose title page included a somewhat primitive woodcut of a veiled religious woman, possibly a nun, praying before a crucifix (see page 5). This image appeared just below the title, giving the very strong impression that it was a portrait of Vittoria herself. On the back of this page, to reinforce the religious message, there was an image of the crucifixion with the Virgin and Saint John at the foot of the cross. (The title pages of the Parma editions, we will recall, had a purely decorative clover.) Along with the conspicuously religious title page and illustrations, the contents of the 1540 volume were arranged, as had already happened in the 1539 Zoppino volume, so that the spiritual sonnets were in the very front, and those to Ferrante relegated to the back.

There is no way to know for sure whether these alterations to the *Rime* were specifically targeted to women. It is certainly the case, however, that whereas reading love sonnets was not necessarily regarded as morally instructive or improving (even when the poems were written by a chaste widow to her deceased husband), reading a book of religious sonnets was deemed spiritually useful. Women were encouraged, moreover, to emulate exceptionally pious women and female saints, so that the poems Vittoria wrote to the Virgin Mary or Mary Magdalene may have been considered especially inspirational for her female audience. Given that the 1540 edition's title page depicted a veiled figure, it is hard not to think Vittoria was being presented as a model for female piety herself.

Adding to this sense of Vittoria's poems as exemplary religious texts for women was the 1543 publication of a book of commentary on thirty-six of her spiritual sonnets, written by a very young scholar from Correggio, Rinaldo Corso (he was only seventeen or eighteen when the book appeared in print). The commentary was commissioned by and dedicated to Gambara, who was also from Correggio. In Corso's preface, he specified that he hoped the commentary would be useful especially for *amorose donne*, or "women in love." Entitled *Dichiaratione fatta sopra la seconda parte delle Rime della Divina Vittoria Collonna* [sic], or *Exposition on the second part of the poetry of the Divine Vittoria Colonna*, this was in fact another milestone in Italian literary history: Vittoria was the first poet, male or female, to have a commentary published on her verse during her lifetime.

Corso's volume was followed by a 1544 edition of the collected *Rime*, two editions in 1546—one exclusively dedicated to the spiritual sonnets (this is the book Vittoria complained about to Rullo), and the other including the poems to Ferrante—and two more editions of the spiritual sonnets in 1548. In the 1546 edition of the spiritual sonnets, there was a dedicatory letter written by the editor Vincenzo Valgrisi, which rehearsed certain features of Pirogallo's letter that served as a preface to the first edition of 1538. Like Pirogallo, Valgrisi declared that he was doing the world a favor by publishing these miraculous poems, hitherto hidden from sight. But this time, the message was pointedly religious:

> It would seem to me too great an injustice to the world to keep such a great treasure hidden, so I am publishing [her poems], begging all of the singular minds who delight in poetry to devote their own language and style to God by imitating this most noble lady, if they want to acquire real immortality, which they cannot acquire, but can only lose, along with their talent and their time, both precious gifts of God, by writing vain fables and fictions.

Valgrisi's praise of Vittoria's poems as sacred verse came one year before her death. However much she resented the publication of the volume, it is hard not to believe this account of the poems would have given her some satisfaction. For the idea that her sonnets might pave the way for others to write sacred verse—the idea that her words, like those of Ochino or Valdés, might inspire her readers to look deeper inside their souls and forge more personal relationships to God—corresponded to her deepest beliefs about the power of spiritual writing. In her own quiet way, and perhaps against her better judgment, she had become the most celebrated religious poet of the era.

MICHELANGELO IN LOVE

O N A SUNDAY AFTERNOON in October 1538—just around the time that the *Rime* first appeared in print—Vittoria sat in the church of San Silvestro al Quirinale in Rome listening to a lesson on the Epistles of Saint Paul. Not far above her family's primary residence in the city, the Palazzo Colonna in Piazza dei Santi Apostoli, where Vittoria was a regular visitor during her Roman sojourns, San Silvestro al Quirinale sat on the highest of the original seven hills of Rome. In ancient days, the Quirinal was the site of a small village where the Sabines erected altars to their god Quirinus; tombs have been found on the site dating to the eighth century BCE. Later the Quirinal Hill was home to a temple dedicated to Semo Sancus, also known as Dius Fidius, the god of oaths and light worshipped by the Romans, the Umbrians, and also possibly the Sabines—the ancient Italic tribe whose women the first Roman men supposedly raped (a more accurate translation of the Latin word, *raptus*, would be "kidnapped") around 750 B.C.E. In the fourth century C.E., the emperor Constantine chose the Quirinal Hill as the site for his elaborate baths, the very last complex of this sort erected in imperial Rome.

Long after it was stripped of its ancient gods and thermal baths, the

Quirinal came to be known for the colossal ancient statues known as the Horse Tamers, which were commonly identified as Castor and Pollux, and their horses. The sculptural group, which stood roughly eighteen feet high, was first brought to the hill by Constantine to grace his baths; in 1589, Pope Sixtus V moved it to the Quirinal's central piazza. It was at this time that the popes began to spend their summers there, in search of cooler air, in a new palazzo originally conceived by Gregory XIII in 1574 and dramatically expanded over the next few centuries. The Palazzo del Quirinale remained the summer residence of the popes until 1870. Today it is the official home of the president of the Italian Republic, the Italian equivalent of the White House.

Vittoria came to San Silvestro al Quirinale from her lodgings at the convent of San Silvestro in Capite, just over a half mile away, to hear the weekly lessons delivered by the Dominican friar Ambrogio Catarino. Several years later, Catarino emerged as one of the most vocal enemies of the Italian reformers, and wrote scathing attacks both on Vittoria's friend Cardinal Contarini and on Ochino (Catarino had, in fact, already published a Latin treatise denouncing Ochino in 1537, which appeared in an Italian translation in 1544). In 1538, however, Catarino was still interested in some of the reformers' ideas, and obviously did not identify Vittoria with Ochino. Indeed, in 1540 he dedicated the first edition of his book on heresy, the *Speculum haereticorum*, to her, and addressed her as a "saintly widow and the grace and glory of the women of our age." (The second edition of the *Speculum*, which appeared the following year, was dedicated to Paul III.)

Vittoria, for her part, was always eager to learn more about Saint Paul's Epistles, one of her favorite biblical texts, and Catarino was known to be a very gifted theologian. She attended his lessons with a group of reform-minded friends, who would then gather afterward, often joined by Catarino himself, in the sacristy of the church or outside in its gardens to talk at leisure about religion, art, and poetry. Among the friends who regularly met, Vittoria treasured above all the company of Michelangelo Buonarroti (see plate 14).

On this particular day in October, Vittoria did not find Michelangelo among those in the pews—the church was small, and it was therefore easy to see who was there—but she joined a mutual friend of theirs, the Sienese ambassador Lattanzio Tolomei. Toward the end of the lesson, a new acquaintance of Tolomei appeared: the Portuguese miniature painter Francisco de Hollanda, who had recently arrived in Rome. In truth, Hollanda had come to the church not to hear Catarino but to meet the great Michelangelo, whom Tolomei had said would be present. It was for this reason, no doubt, that Hollanda arrived so late: he was eager for the conversations that followed the theological lesson, not for the lesson itself.

Or at least this was Vittoria's interpretation of his tardy arrival. As Hollanda related it, "When [Vittoria] had bidden me be seated, and the lesson and praises for it came to an end, she looked at me and at Messer Lattanzio and began to say: 'If I am not mistaken, Francisco de Hollanda would rather listen to Michelangelo discoursing on painting than Fra Ambrogio giving this lesson.'" Hollanda took offense, and asked if she really believed that he was "worthless, or capable of nothing more than painting." "In truth," he declared, "I shall always be delighted to listen to Michelangelo, but when the Epistles of Saint Paul are read, I would rather listen to Fra Ambrogio." Vittoria, he reported, simply smiled. Several minutes later, she quietly sought to fulfill his wish. Summoning one of her servants (she was never without attendants), she bid him to go to Michelangelo's house to ask him "if he wishes to come and squander a bit of the day with us, [so] that we may gain it with him."

Michelangelo lived a short distance away from San Silvestro al Quirinale—a mere five-minute walk—on a street then known as the Macello dei Corvi, across from the ruins of the early second-century forum of Trajan. One of the grandest ancient Roman sites, the forum had so dazzled Constantine two hundred years later that he wanted it reproduced in his new capital of Constantinople. In the Renaissance, the site was best known for the magnificent Column of Trajan. Its marble frieze spiraling round and round roughly 125 feet high told the story, in 155 separate scenes, of the emperor's triumph over the barbarian kingdom of the Dacians, who ruled the territory north of the Danube River in what is now Romania. (One of the most underrated sites in all of modern Rome is the Fascist-era Museo della Civiltà Romana in EUR, the extraordinary district Mussolini built to host the 1942 world's fair. Among the museum's many extravagant models, there is a plaster reproduction of Trajan's column completely unwound, so that it forms several long aisles.) Michelangelo would have passed this symbol of Roman grandeur—one of the great testaments to the sheer power of both the empire and classical art—in his comings and goings every day. Perhaps he also occasionally craned his neck up to the sky to glimpse the bronze statue of Trajan, which crowned the top until 1588, when Pope Sixtus V replaced it with a statue of Saint Peter.

Before enough time had passed for Vittoria's servant even to have reached Michelangelo's house, the artist arrived at the church and climbed the narrow flight of stairs that led from the noisy street below to the quiet of San Silvestro's central nave. He was sixty-three at the time, but outside of the pronounced wrinkles on his face, he seemed a much younger man, with a full head of mostly dark hair, and a body still strong and muscular. Michelangelo explained to Vittoria that he had been walking up the Via Esquilina when he ran into her messenger, and had rushed immediately to meet her. Indeed, he was so delighted by the sight of his beloved friend that he later claimed not even to have noticed the presence of Hollanda.

Michelangelo and Vittoria had one of the most celebrated friendships of the Renaissance. The two were not lovers, or at least not in the usual sense of the word. She seems to have been erotically uninterested in men after the death of her husband, and his erotic interests were never in women. The great romantic love of Michelangelo's life was the young Roman nobleman Tommaso de' Cavalieri, whom he met in 1532, when Tommaso was about twenty-three years old and Michelangelo fifty-seven. The artist's passion for Tommaso produced a great outpouring of art and poetry: within a few years of their first meeting, he wrote a series of sonnets and madrigals dedicated to him, and gave him at least five finished drawings. One of these, *The Rape of Ganymede*, depicted an older man (Zeus, here disguised as an eagle) abducting a beautiful young boy.

Michelangelo's love for Vittoria was of a quieter sort, but no less profound. He did not merely regard Vittoria as his "muse," as she has often been described, although she did play that role for him at times. Nor, for her part, did she simply consider Michelangelo an artistic genius whom she should patronize and adore. Instead, despite the differences in their backgrounds—Michelangelo came from a family of middling status in Florence, where his father held minor government jobs—and the differences in their age (Vittoria was fifteen years his junior), their friendship was one between equals, marked by ease and familiarity on both sides. Although only a small number of the letters they exchanged have survived, we are lucky to have many other traces of their bond, which together create a deeply moving portrait of what was shared between them.

One of the richest of these traces is the book that Hollanda wrote upon his return to Portugal in June 1540, *Da pintura antigua*, or *On Antique Painting*. The first half of this work was an unremarkable treatise on the theory and practice of painting, but in the second half, Hollanda recorded four separate "dialogues" that he had during his time in Rome, including the visits to San Silvestro al Quirinale. In his pages, we sit beside Michelangelo and Vittoria in the small garden behind the church, and hear their voices come alive. The topics they discussed were lofty and serious. How does Flemish art compare to Italian? How does poetry compare to painting? What is the greatest art, and who are the greatest artists? To get Michelangelo even to broach these topics required great tact. He was reluctant to talk about art, especially his own, and Hollanda described Vittoria's skill in luring him into conversation. "I saw her act like one who means to attack an impregnable city through cunning and wiles," he reported, "and likewise we saw the painter on his guard and vigilant as if he were the besieged, placing sentinels here and erecting bridges there, making mines and girding all the walls and towers; but in the end the Marchesa was bound to win."

And win she did. Vittoria warmed Michelangelo up by seeking his advice about a new project of her own. Pope Paul, she reported, had given her permission to build a convent for the Poor Clares on the very slopes of the Quirinal Hill where they were conversing; the exact location was to be the site of the broken portico where legend had it the emperor Nero had watched Rome burn during the great fire of 64 c.e. She commented on how appropriate this was as a way of cleansing the site of its wicked past: "other, more virtuous footsteps of women," she remarked, "may stamp out such evil footprints of a man." Turning then to Michelangelo, Vittoria posed a series of questions about the convent's architectural design: "What form and proportions to give to the house? Where the door might go? And whether it is possible to adapt some part of the old structure to the new?" Michelangelo thought for a minute before responding, "Yes, Signora, the broken portico can serve as a bell tower." He then offered to visit the site with her when they left the church later that day, and to "make a plan of it for you."

Outside this moment in Hollanda's book, there is no further record of Vittoria's plans for the convent, nor do any drawings of Michelangelo's related to it survive (the artist famously burned many of his drawings for unfinished projects, so we will likely never know whether he made Vittoria's plans). In 1536, Pope Paul had given Vittoria permission, as we have already seen, to celebrate Mass in a chapel either already in existence or newly constructed, but he did not specify that she could found a new convent altogether. It is possible that an additional letter giving her this permission has been lost. From Hollanda's perspective, however, the conversation about the plans for the convent was simply a ruse on Vittoria's part to get Michelangelo talking. Soon after this brief exchange, Vittoria asked if she might "put a question to Michelangelo about painting," to which he responded: "Your Excellency has but to ask of me something that I can give, and it shall be yours." The gallantry with which he addressed her was not necessarily Michelangelo's usual manner—he was notoriously grumpy—but with Vittoria, he seems to have been at his most gracious.

At the same time, however, Michelangelo was not courtly at the expense of honesty, and he shared his opinions with her frankly, even when they ran counter to her own. Hence in response to her first question about painting—"I want very much to know what the painting of Flanders is, and whom it pleases, for it seems to me more devout than the Italian manner"—Michelangelo scoffed, declaring that Flemish art may look good at first glance, "but it is in truth executed without reason or art, without symmetry or proportion." "Only works that are done in Italy," he remarked, "can we call in effect true painting." Who knows if Vittoria meant what she said or was merely trying to provoke her friend into a more lively conversation: there is no indication elsewhere that she particularly admired Flemish devotional art, and her own collection seems to have been entirely Italian.

Vittoria pursued her line of questioning about Italian art in their second meeting—when Hollanda once again managed to miss the lesson on Saint Paul's Epistles, arriving only after Catarino had already left the church. On this occasion, Vittoria lavished praise on Michelangelo's art, while also perhaps teasing him for how long he took with some of his commissions. In his ceiling fresco for the Sistine Chapel, she declared, he had portrayed God's creation in "a divine manner": "And what is extraordinary is that, while he has done nothing more than this work, which he still has not completed, having begun it when he was a young man, the work of twenty painters together is contained there on that single ceiling." It is not clear exactly what Vittoria meant: Michelangelo had finished the Sistine ceiling more than twenty years earlier, but he was working at the time on *The Last Judgment*, and perhaps she had this in mind. She may also have been alluding to his multi-decade, endlessly thwarted project of building Pope Julius II's tomb. This was first commissioned in 1505 by Julius himself, and Michelangelo began work on a very grand, three-story monument with more than forty figures, to be sited within Saint Peter's. The tomb was completed in a drastically reduced form thirty years later, and placed in the minor basilica of San Pietro in Vincoli, where it stands today. The central figure of Moses, which dates from 1515, gives some sense of the majesty of the original design.

When the conversations took place in San Silvestro al Quirinale, Vittoria and Michelangelo were very comfortable in their friendship, and spoke to each other without reserve. No one knows for sure when they first met, but it was most likely around 1534, after Michelangelo left Florence to live permanently in Rome, and Vittoria had returned to the city from Ischia. Some historians speculate that they were introduced through Pope Paul, who had named Michelangelo the "supreme architect, sculptor, and painter of the Apostolic Palace" in 1535. Others think it was Tommaso de' Cavalieri, whom Vittoria also knew, who brought them together. However they came to meet, Vittoria already knew about Michelangelo as a celebrated artist. The two of them also had a prior history, albeit indirect, which formed an interesting contrast with the intimate friendship they later enjoyed.

In 1531, when Vittoria was still in Ischia, she desired to obtain several paintings of Mary Magdalene. As a fallen woman, the biblical Magdalene may seem an odd choice for the chaste Vittoria, but there was a well-known apocryphal tradition in which she was presented as an exemplary widow who lived a life of prayer and penitence (Vittoria, we will recall, was living just such a life at the castle). She may also simply have regarded the Magdalene as an inspiring example of unswerving faith, as she described in a long poem on the triumph of the cross, which was first printed in the 1540 edition of the *Rime*:

> At the holy feet of God I saw the woman
> whom the same name [of Mary] also honors,
> burning with love, shining splendidly, with golden hair.
> She was moved by true piety to weep here,
> so that in place of the seeds of sorrow
> God wills her to reap those of glory.*

Vittoria's first move to acquire her paintings was to appeal to Isabella d'Este's son Federico II Gonzaga, Duke of Mantua, who was a great patron of the arts. No record of Vittoria's initial request survived, but in a letter Federico subsequently sent to her he confirmed her wish for a Mary Magdalene as "beautiful and tearful as possible," and informed her that the painting would be done by Titian. He also reassured her

---

* S2.36: "*Ai santi pie' colei che simil nome / onora vidi, ardendo d'amor, lieta / risplender, cinta da l'aurate chiome. / La mosse a pianger qui ben degna pieta, / onde il Ciel vuol che con equal misura / per seme di dolor or gloria mieta.*"

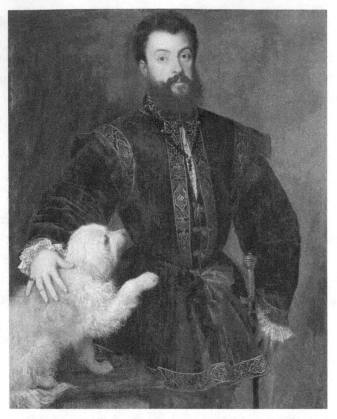

**Portrait of Federico II Gonzaga, first Duke of Mantua
and son of Isabella d'Este, by Titian** (Prado, Madrid)

that it would not take a long time: he had asked Titian to finish it
quickly.

There is no definitive record of which of the many Mary Magdalenes Titian painted in his career was Vittoria's painting: he (and his
workshop) painted the Magdalene more than forty times. But the most
likely candidate is the *The Penitent Magdalene* in Florence's Palazzo
Pitti (see plate 15). This painting, dated to 1531, certainly fits the re-
quirement that Vittoria gave to the artist for the Magdalene to be as
"beautiful and tearful as possible." It is in fact the most erotic version
that Titian painted, despite the claims of the sixteenth-century painter
and historian of art Giorgio Vasari, who insisted that "although she is
very beautiful, [the picture] moves not to lust but to compassion." Un-

like Titian's other Magdalenes, in which she is at least partially dressed, the Pitti Magdalene is naked, her breasts scantily covered by her luxurious golden hair. The Magdalene's nudity was part of the legend that had surrounded her since the Middle Ages. In her long years of repentance in the desert following Christ's ascension, her clothes apparently fell apart.

It is hard to imagine how Vittoria would have responded to the sensuality of Titian's painting. We know only that she thanked Federico warmly: "For the Magdalene," she wrote, "I thank you infinite times." Along with her letter she sent him a lovely, if somewhat odd, gift of several small pillows filled with rose petals, for which he in turn thanked her rather extravagantly in a subsequent letter (the pillow would not have represented Titian's payment for the work, but simply a gesture of gratitude for her friend). Federico also reported having shared her praise of the painting with Titian himself. It is worth noting that Vittoria's letter was dated May 25, 1531, only two and a half months after Federico had written to her promising that the painting would be done as quickly as possible. Given that it would have taken at least ten days to transport the canvas from the northern city of Mantua to the southern island of Ischia, Titian must have taken Federico's instructions to rush very seriously.

The second painting of Mary Magdalene that Vittoria commissioned was from none other than Michelangelo. Once again, the commission did not come directly from her. In a letter sent to Federico from his agent in Florence on May 19, 1531—only six days before Vittoria wrote her letter thanking Federico for the Titian—he related that Michelangelo had received a request from Alfonso d'Avalos for a painting of the Magdalene, to be done for the Marchesa of Pescara. Michelangelo was clearly put off by the request—the name Vittoria Colonna meant nothing to him at the time—and said he would not accept the job unless instructed to do so by Pope Clement himself. Clement had in fact given him strict orders to accept no new projects beyond his papal commissions, but in this case, the pope must have made an exception to satisfy his friend Vittoria. In the summer of 1531, Michelangelo began work on Vittoria's Magdalene.

Unlike Titian, who depicted Mary Magdalene alone in a state of penitential rapture, Michelangelo opted for a more chaste and biblically resonant moment in the Magdalene's life. Without even knowing Vittoria, he seems intuitively to have known her tastes, or, more likely, his tastes were similar to her own. The specific encounter he chose to represent was between the Magdalene and Christ immediately following the Resurrection, a scene that is known as the "Noli me tangere" after Christ's famous utterance as related in the Gospel of John. Jesus said to Mary Magdalene: "Touch me not, for I have not yet ascended to my Father: but go to my brethren, and say unto them, I ascend unto my Father, and your Father and to my God, and your God." Then Mary Magdalene, John continued, "came and told the disciples that she had seen the Lord, and that he had spoken these things unto her."

Michelangelo began with a drawing intended as a preliminary study for the painting, which, according to instructions he had received from one of Clement's advisers, was to be done on either canvas or wood, and should not be too large. He was told the painting was meant "to be in chambers, rather than a hall or church." Vittoria's intentions for this work of art were fundamentally private: she was not planning to hang her painting in one of the public spaces of the Ischia castle, but wanted it for her own devotional purposes. This use of her art resonates as well with something that Hollanda recorded her as having said to Michelangelo. "What virtuous and quiet man is there," she asked the artist, "who (even if he looks down upon it out of piety) does not greatly revere and worship devout and spiritual contemplations of sacred painting? I believe that time is more likely to run out than material or praises for this virtue. In those who are melancholy it inspires happiness; in those who are content and those who are troubled, [it inspires] recognition of human suffering." However beautiful the works of art she possessed may have been, their beauty ultimately served a devotional end. For Vittoria, art was a spiritual tool.

Vittoria did not end up, at least at this point in her life, with a work by Michelangelo to add to her collection. According to letters from the time, he finished the drawing of the "Noli me tangere" in a great hurry and was not happy with the result. Given how little time he had been given to deliver the painting—like Titian, he had been told to finish quickly—he decided to pass the job on to his fellow artist Jacopo Pontormo, who executed the painting based on Michelangelo's drawing. This was not the only time that Michelangelo relied on Pontormo in this way. The following year, in 1532, he gave Pontormo a drawing of Venus and Cupid for a commission from the wealthy Florentine Bartolomeo Bettini, who wanted to decorate a room in his sumptuous palazzo with images celebrating the "poets who have sung of love in Tuscan prose and verse." Michelangelo's original cartoon is lost, but Pontormo's painting, a version of which can be seen today at the Accademia in Florence, was one of the most widely copied images in the period: there are records of thirty-six copies, of which nineteen have survived, including one by Vasari.

Michelangelo's drawing for the Mary Magdalene is also lost, but the Pontormo panel made for Vittoria was discovered in a private collection in Italy in 1956 (see plate 17). Assuming, as scholars have reason to believe, that Pontormo's painting closely adhered to Michelangelo's sketch, what is perhaps most striking is the posture Michelangelo chose for his female subject. In most depictions of the "Noli me tangere," the Magdalene sits passively on her knees before Christ. In Michelangelo's version, she is on her feet with her arms outstretched, while Christ in turn retracts in a quiet gesture of arrest. Michelangelo captured the exact moment that mattered most of all: the moment when Christ uttered his famous words and instructed the Magdalene to leave his side, so that she might share the news of his resurrection with others.

Even if Michelangelo did not execute Vittoria's painting himself, it seems altogether fitting that the first interaction between the two friends involved an image of Christ with a faithful female servant. For what perhaps drew Michelangelo and Vittoria to each other above all was their shared conviction that faith was not something that could be taught by the church: it needed to be experienced personally. Both of them also believed that one of the best ways to enhance such an experience was through works of art. Michelangelo and Vittoria were at heart religious artists, and the art that they exchanged was profoundly influenced by the ideas that shaped the Reformation.

The idea that Michelangelo, the great artist of the popes, had Protestant leanings may come as a shock: How could it be that the painter of the Sistine Chapel was sympathetic to Lutheranism? But there is no question that he was very interested in the Italian reformers, and that he owed his interest in no small degree to his relationship with Vittoria. In the many letters, poems, and drawings that the two friends exchanged over the years, the emphasis always fell, in a manner that Ochino and Valdés would very much have approved, on the personal experience of the divine. Although Michelangelo was for many of these years working on the most crowded and frenetic of biblical scenes—his fresco of the Last Judgment—in the drawings he made for Vittoria, he opted for scenes of exquisite intimacy.

Vittoria received from Michelangelo at least three presentation drawings (finished works rather than preparatory drawings for works in another medium), two of which directly addressed her own interests in female figures and their relationship to Christ. The first of these was of Christ and the Samaritan woman at the well, based on an episode in the Gospel of John in which Christ revealed himself as the Messiah. The drawing is lost, but Vittoria referred to it in a letter she sent Michelangelo in 1542 or 1543 when she was living in Viterbo. "I hope," she wrote, that "upon my return to Rome, I will find you and your true faith with his [the Lord's] image so renewed and alive in your soul, as you have depicted it so well in my Samaritan woman." For Vittoria, Michelangelo's drawing brought to life what the text of Scripture could only suggest: what it felt like to be the Samaritan woman, and to have "true faith in your soul." She also implied that Michelangelo's own faith might have been revived through making the drawing itself.

The second drawing that Michelangelo gave to Vittoria figuring Christ with a woman was his splendid *Pietà*. Ascanio Condivi, a minor painter who worked in Michelangelo's workshop beginning around 1545 and wrote the artist's first biography—some believe Michelangelo more or less dictated the text to him—described Vittoria's having asked for this drawing herself: "At this lady's request, he made a nude figure of Christ when He is taken from the cross, which would fall as an abandoned corpse at the feet of His most holy mother, if it were not supported under the arms by two little angels." Vittoria was focused on the Virgin Mary in her own writing at the time; in addition to composing a number of sonnets to the Virgin, she also wrote a prose meditation on the *Pietà*. This work, which was posthumously published with the title *Pianto della Marchesa di Pescara sopra la passione di Christo* (*The Weeping of the Marchesa of Pescara on the Passion of Christ*), took the form of a letter addressed to Ochino, whose preaching on the topic had been deeply inspiring to Vittoria.

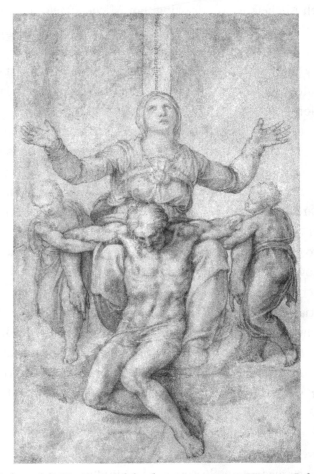

Michelangelo's *Pietà*, one of the drawings given to Vittoria Colonna as a gift (Isabella Stewart Gardner Museum, Boston)

Vittoria's meditation opened with a vision: "The day of Venus [this is the literal translation of *venerdì*, or Friday] and the late hour move me to write of the moving scene of seeing Christ, dead, in the arms of his mother . . . I see the sweet mother whose breast is full of the most ardent compassion, tied so deeply to the love of her son." "The Virgin," she declared several lines later, "has made of her nearly dead body a sepulcher in that hour." To describe Mary as she took Christ in her arms as herself "nearly dead" (*"suo corpo quasi morto"*) and then to imagine her nearly dead body as the tomb for her dead son was a remarkable way to understand the *Pietà*, and it resonated in interesting ways with Michelangelo's drawing. For Michelangelo has the Virgin seated with Christ's body suspended between her legs, his arms draped over her knees (each arm is held by a small angel, but they seem to bear very little of the burden). As Mary supports Christ's weight with whatever strength she has left, she looks up to the heavens for consolation.

Of the three drawings that Vittoria received from Michelangelo, the one for which we have the fullest record of her impressions is the magnificent *Christ on the Cross*. Unlike the *Pietà*, in this drawing Christ looks surprisingly undefeated. Despite his tortured position on the cross, his eyes are wide open, and his body, which has not yet been pierced, seems remarkably strong. He is flanked, moreover, not by the traditional two thieves, but instead by two lamenting angels, whose presence pulls us toward his heavenly future at the very moment of his agony. He is, in effect, already victorious.

Vittoria was deeply moved by the drawing, and shared her feelings with Michelangelo in two different letters. Both are undated, so there is no way to know which came first. In one letter, she explained how the drawing had replaced for her all other images of the Crucifixion. Or rather, she wrote, it performed within her a crucifixion of its own:

> I have seen the crucifix, which certainly has crucified in my memory whatever other pictures I have ever seen, nor could one imagine a design better made, more alive or more beautifully executed. Certainly I could not ever explain how subtly and wonderfully it is made . . . I

have looked at it well in the light, and with a magnifying glass and a mirror, and I never saw anything more perfectly done.

This description of studying the drawing with a magnifying glass was one way for Vittoria to acknowledge the very fine work Michelangelo had done. Through techniques known as stippling and hatching, he created what looks like a three-dimensional image, so that Christ's body seems to be immediately before us, with the cross and then the angels receding into the background. Vittoria's looking at the drawing in a mirror is a less obvious thing to do, but perhaps showed her

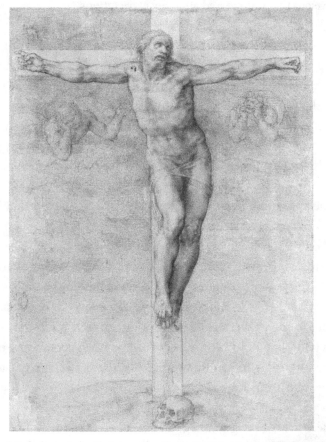

Michelangelo's *Christ on the Cross* (British Museum, London)

appreciation of Michelangelo's work on a more devotional, and less technical, register. To hold the drawing up to the mirror was to free it from its status as an artifact, and render it pure spirit.

In the second letter to Michelangelo on the subject of the *Christ on the Cross*, Vittoria focused precisely on its role in stirring her faith:

> The things you've done necessarily excite the judgment of anyone who looks at them, and after seeing them I can speak with real experience of the possibility of adding goodness to perfect things. And I have seen that *omnia possibilia sunt credenti* [all things are possible for one who believes]. I had the greatest faith in God that He would give you a supernatural grace to make this Christ: then I saw it to be so marvelous that it surpassed all of my expectations.

Vittoria described here a more or less explicitly Protestant understanding of vocation: the drawing proved, as it were, Michelangelo's status among the elect. She concluded with a more traditional account of putting the drawing to devotional use. "In this interim I don't know how else to serve you," she declared, "but by praying to this sweet Christ, whom you have depicted so well and so perfectly, and by praying to you, that you command me as one who is entirely yours [*in tutto e per tutto*]."

Michelangelo's *Christ on the Cross* was not only the gift that Vittoria seems to have most treasured, but it was also the occasion for the friends' only recorded disagreement. Vittoria knew that Michelangelo was making the drawing for her, and she was growing increasingly impatient with his slow progress (from her earlier commissions for the Mary Magdalenes, it seems clear that patience was not her strong suit). She wrote to him, therefore, as always in her own hand—all seven of her surviving letters to him were written by her personally, not by a secretary—to ask him kindly to send her the drawing right away, in whatever state it was in:

> My dearest Michelangelo, I beg you to send me the Crucifix for a little while even if it's not finished, because I want to show it to the gentle-

men who have come from the Most Reverend Cardinal of Mantua [Ercole Gonzaga]; and if you are not busy with work today, you might come to talk to me at your leisure.

Yours to command, The Marchesa of Pescara

There is something comical about her closing, "Yours to command" ("*Al commando vostro*"), given the demanding nature of the letter. There is also something charming about the casual invitation to come visit: Michelangelo presumably dropped by the convent of San Silvestro in Capite to see her on his days off from the Sistine Chapel.

Letter from Vittoria Colonna to Michelangelo, undated but probably written around 1539–40 (Casa Buonarroti, Florence)

Michelangelo, however, was not amused in the slightest by Vittoria's letter, and sent back this angry response:

> Signora Marchesa. Given that I am myself in Rome, there was no need to leave the crucifix with Messer Tommaso, and to make him a messenger between Your Ladyship and me, your servant, especially since I serve you, and have the most desire possible to do more for you, than for any man whom I have ever known in the world; but the demanding work [*occupazione grande*] that I have taken on, and am still involved in, has not permitted me to make this known to Your Ladyship. And because I know that you know that love admits no taskmaster, and that the lover never sleeps, I did not think an intermediary was necessary. And although it may have seemed that I had forgotten, I was doing what I did not talk about in order to deliver a surprise. But my purpose has been spoiled. *Mal fa chi tanta fè*

It's hard not to sympathize with Michelangelo. Busy at the time with nothing less than *The Last Judgment* (his *"occupazione grande"*), he wanted to finish the drawing for Vittoria in his own time and have the pleasure of surprising her with his gift. Her asking for the drawing was to him a sign not only of her impatience, but also of her lack of faith. The detail about leaving the crucifix with Tommaso (almost certainly Tommaso de' Cavalieri) remains opaque. Vittoria may have left a different crucifix with Tommaso to give to Michelangelo in order to jog, as it were, his memory of the promised gift. It is also possible that she had asked Michelangelo in a letter that has not survived to give the crucifix she was waiting for to Tommaso, who would deliver it to her. It is not clear, in other words, who is leaving which crucifix with Tommaso, but it is certainly the case that Vittoria's unnecessary involvement of Tommaso enraged Michelangelo.

Whatever the opening remark may refer to, the conclusion Michelangelo ultimately reached—"my purpose has been spoiled" ("*È stato guasto il mio disegno*")—brilliantly conveyed the depth of his dismay. The Italian is much richer and more nuanced than the English: *guasto* literally means something like "busted"—travelers to Italy will have seen this word on broken toilets or ticket machines—and "*disegno*" can mean both "drawing" and "design," in the sense of "intention." By asking for her present before its time, Vittoria has ruined both the gesture of giving the gift and the gift itself. Michelangelo closed the letter by citing the first half of an unusually bitter line from Petrarch's *Canzoniere*: "*Mal fa chi tanta fè sì tosto oblia*" ("He does ill who forgets such faith so quickly"). She had, in short, disappointed him.

There is no way to know how Vittoria answered this letter, as no response has survived. But given her general sensitivity, it is likely that she took in all too well the pain she had caused her friend. It is universally understood that to demand a gift meant as a surprise ruins its pleasure; this is not specific to any particular culture or period. But in the case of Michelangelo's drawing, Vittoria had also committed an additional offense particular to the reformed theology that both of them to some degree espoused. For Luther and his followers, the idea of the gift was directly linked to Christ's sacrifice. Since there was no way to earn or repay this gift, the true believer needed to receive Christ's love simply with gratitude and faith. Vittoria's tone of entitlement in her letter to Michelangelo—her behaving as if the gift were already hers, as if she had an inherent right to demand it—violated the Protestant principle of our fundamental lack of merit. Michelangelo wanted his gift of the drawing, like the gift of Christ's sacrifice itself, to be a pure act of generosity, and not a means of satisfying a request from his friend. *Guasto* indeed.

The letter that Michelangelo sent to Vittoria has survived only in a drafted version. Paper in the Renaissance was a much more expensive commodity than it is now, and Michelangelo regularly used the same sheet for multiple purposes, so that drafts of letters and poems are mixed together, along with sketches or studies for drawings—his pages were almost always full. In the left corner of the sheet that contains the draft of his letter to Vittoria, which was written horizontally across the top from left to right, there is a draft of a poem, written vertically from the bottom of the page. This poem, a madrigal, was also addressed to Vittoria:

Now on my right foot, and then on my left,
I walk with unease, seeking salvation.
Torn between vice and virtue
my confused heart wearies and exhausts me;
like one who does not see the heavens,
and loses his way on every path.
I give to you a blank page
to fill with your sacred ink, so that
love will mislead me no longer, and truth prevail:
may my soul be liberated from itself
and fall not into further errors
in the short time that remains, may I live less blind.
I ask you, my lady, high and divine,
if the humble sinner has a lower place
in heaven than he who has done only good.*

We might imagine Michelangelo picking up the piece of paper with the letter to Vittoria and turning it ninety degrees to the left to write out the madrigal. Perhaps he even reserved particular pieces of paper for particular people, so that this was a Vittoria page. The two texts that he wrote to his friend were so different in mood and tone, however, that they must have been written on separate occasions. The letter was petulant and self-righteous, the poem humble and self-doubting. The letter conveyed Michelangelo's sense of superiority, the poem his total abjection. The letter highly valued the gift he wanted to give her; the poem asked Vittoria to fill his "blank page" with her sacred ink.

Of all Michelangelo's letters to Vittoria—and there is no way of estimating how many there may have been—only two, both undated,

---

* 162: "*Ora in sul destro, ora in sul manco piede / variando, cerco della mie salute. / Fra 'l vizio e la virtute / il cor confuso mi travaglia e stanca, / come chi 'l ciel non vede, / che per ogni sentier si perde e manca. / Porgo la carta bianca / a' vostri sacri inchiostri, / c'amor mi sganni e pietà 'l ver ne scriva: / che l'alma, da sé franca, / non pieghi agli error nostri / mie breve resto, e che men cieco viva. / Chieggio a voi, alta e diva / donna, saper se 'n ciel men grado tiene / l'umil peccato che 'l superchio bene.*"

Letter from Michelangelo to Vittoria Colonna, with draft of poem
(Biblioteca Apostolica Vaticana, Vatican City)

have survived. The other letter was also on the subject of gifts, although in this case the gift was from Vittoria to Michelangelo. He begins by expressing his initial reluctance to accept what she has given him: "Before taking possession, Signora, of the things which Your Ladyship has several times wished to give to me, I wanted, in order to receive them as little unworthily as possible, to execute something for you by my own hand." There is no mention of what exactly the "things" ("*le cose*") she wanted so often to give him were, but the most likely guess would be her poems. This makes sense as well of his impulse to reciprocate with something made "with my own hand" ("*di mia mano*"), since the poems were made with hers.

It is possible that this letter preceded Michelangelo's giving Vittoria one of his drawings, although it is more likely that he did not in the end respond with a gift of his own, for later in the letter, he made clear that he had changed his mind. Before receiving her gift, he explained, he had thought about sending her something of his own in return. But he ultimately came to a different conclusion, one much more in keeping with the Protestant ideas about gifts and reciprocity that were raised in the letter about his *Christ on the Cross*. Michelangelo realized, that is, that his idea of being unworthy of her gift was an error—a theological error, he might have added—that he needed to correct. This was not because he was worthy: on the contrary. From a Protestant perspective, worth played absolutely no role in receiving God's grace. At this point the letter reads, in fact, like a Protestant catechistical lesson: "Then I came to realize that the grace of God cannot be bought, and that to keep you waiting is a grievous sin. I confess my fault and willingly accept the things in question."

Having spelled out like a good schoolboy what he had come to understand, Michelangelo then shifted gears entirely and closed the letter with a beautiful expression of love for his friend: "And when [the poems] are in my possession, I shall think myself in paradise, not because they are in my house, but because I am in theirs." Coming from just about anyone, this would have been a magnificent compliment. But for the painter of the Sistine ceiling to tell Vittoria that her gift made his home feel like paradise must have given her a special sense of satisfaction.

Michelangelo's letter responding to Vittoria's gift has also survived only in draft, and the sheet of paper on which he wrote it once again also contains a poem addressed to her. In this case, however, the letter and poem seem to have been written at the same time, or at least in the same spirit: they are both concerned with the challenge of accepting Vittoria's gift. The poem, a sonnet, begins by recapitulating the problem Michelangelo faced:

> In order to be less unworthy, high lady,
>   of the gift of your immense kindness,
>   at first I thought my lowly talent
>   might return your gift, fueled by my full heart.

He then reaches more or less the same conclusion that he came to in the letter: that the gift of grace can never be reciprocated. This time, however, he imagines Vittoria herself as the divine figure:

> But once I saw that my own merit
> could never reach so high a point,
> my bold error now begs your pardon,
> and I grow ever wiser from my mistake.
> I see now how he errs, who thinks the heavenly grace
> that pours out from you, divine one,
> might be equaled by my works, so fleeting and frail.
> Genius, art, and memory all give way:
> for your celestial gift cannot be repaid
> with even a thousand earthly gestures.*

The poem is in effect simultaneously Protestant and idolatrous, for it is Vittoria's grace that cannot be equaled or repaid. His "high lady" becomes the equivalent of Christ pouring out her grace upon him. "*Voi divina*," he calls Vittoria, "divine you."

There is no record of how Vittoria responded to the beautiful compliments that Michelangelo showered upon her from the very beginning of their friendship. His central perception of her as "divine"—this is the single term that resonates throughout his poems—came to him in one of the very first poems he wrote to her, a madrigal written sometime between 1536 and 1538:

> If, lady, it is true that you,
> divine in your beauty, can live

---

* 159: "*Per esser manco, alta signora, indegno / del don di vostra immensa cortesia, / prima, all'incontro a quella, usar la mia / con tutto il cor volse 'l mie basso ingegno. / Ma visto poi, c'ascendere a quel segno / propio valor non è c'apra la via, / perdon domanda la mie audacia ria, / e del fallir più saggio ognor divegno. / E veggio ben com'erra s'alcun crede / la grazia, che da voi divina piove, / pareggi l'opra mia caduca e frale. / L'ingegno, l'arte e la memoria cede: / c'un don celeste non con mille pruove / pagar del suo può già chi è mortale.*"

as if a mere mortal,
and eat and sleep and talk here among us,
what punishment would match
the immense sin of not following you,
your grace and goodness having canceled all doubts?
A man wrapped up in his own thoughts,
whose eye does not see before him,
by his nature is slow to fall in love.
Draw inside me from without,
as I do with stone or on a white sheet
that has nothing within it, and becomes what I want.*

Here, too, Vittoria replaces for him the figure of Christ: it is her "grace and goodness" that has "canceled all doubts"; it is she who holds the key to his salvation. She also becomes the artist, working upon his blank slate.

"A man in a woman," Michelangelo declares in another poem,

or rather a god
speaks through her mouth,
so that listening to her
I am so transformed, that I will never be mine own again.
I well believe that since I was taken
by her away from myself,
now being outside myself, I can show myself pity.
So high above vain desire
her beautiful face moves me,
that I see only death in all other beauty.
O lady who takes souls

* 111: "S'egli è, donna, che puoi / come cosa mortal, benché sia diva / di beltà, c'ancor viva / e mangi e dorma e parli qui fra noi, / a non seguirti poi, / cessato il dubbio, tuo grazia e mercede, / qual pena a tal peccato degna fora? / Ché alcun ne' pensier suoi / co' l'occhio che non vede, / per virtù propria tardi s' innamora. / Disegna in me di fuora, / com'io fo in pietra o in candido foglio, / che nulla ha dentro, e èvvi ciò ch'io voglio."

through water and fire to joyous days,
please do unto me so that I never return to myself.*

He was equally dazzled, it seems, by her beauty and her spiritual power. Thanks to her, he imagines himself reborn.

Given how much Michelangelo esteemed Vittoria both spiritually and physically—as he puts it in the poem above, he sees "death in all other beauty"—it is surprising that he never painted her portrait. He writes about preserving her beauty for posterity, however, in one of his sonnets:

How is it, lady, as one can see
from long experience, that images
made in rugged stone outlive their maker,
whom the years reduce to mere ashes?
The cause tilts and yields to the effect,
whereby nature is conquered by art.
This I know, as I see in beautiful sculpture
upon which time and death lose all power.
Thus I can give to us both long life,
in whatever form, either paint or stone,
by picturing us, your face and mine;
so that a thousand years after our deaths
it will be known how beautiful you were,
and how in loving you I, poor wretch, was no fool.†

---

*235: "*Un uomo in una donna, anzi uno dio / per la sua bocca parla, / ond'io per ascoltarla / son fatto tal, che ma' più sarò mio. / I' credo ben, po' ch'io / a me da·llei fu' tolto, / fuor di me stesso aver di me pietate; / sì sopra 'l van desio / mi sprona il suo bel volto, / ch'i' veggio morte in ogni altra beltate. / O donna che passate / per acqua e foco l'alme a' lieti giorni, / deh, fate c'a me stesso più non torni.*"

†239: "*Com'esser, donna, può quel c'alcun vede / per lunga sperienza, che più dura / l'immagin viva in pietra alpestra e dura, / che 'l suo fattor, che gli anni in cener riede? / La causa a l'effetto inclina e cede, / onde dall'arte è vinta la natura. / I' 'l so, che 'l pruovo in la bella scultura, / c'all'opra il tempo e morte non tien fede. / Dunche, posso ambo noi dar lunga vita, / in qual sie modo, o di colore o sasso, / di noi sembrando l'uno e l'altro volto; / sì che mill'anni dopo la partita, / quante voi bella fusti e quant'io lasso / si veggia, e com'amarvi i' non fu' stolto.*"

The modesty he usually expressed in relation to his talent is strikingly absent from this poem—indeed, he embraces the ancient idea that his art would be immortal, or at least endure for a very long time. The great Roman poet Horace famously boasted that his poetry would last as long as the "priest climbs the Capitol with the silent virgin," a ritual associated with the Roman Empire whose end he could not imagine. In a similar spirit, Michelangelo mentions the period of a thousand years. What Michelangelo dreams of in this poem is in fact a portrait of himself and Vittoria together, giving "us both long life / in whatever form, either paint or stone." He wanted, that is, to commemorate them as a couple. This dream may never have been fulfilled. But some believe it is Vittoria lurking behind the figure of Saint Lawrence in *The Last Judgment*, gazing over toward Michelangelo's self-portrait figured on the skin that Saint Bartholomew holds in his hand (see plate 16).

Although Vittoria was by far the more prolific poet of the two, she did not write poems for Michelangelo. By the time they became close, she was already fully immersed in the project of her spiritual sonnets. She did, however, compose a sonnet responding to Michelangelo's madrigal, "Now on my right foot, and then on my left," which begins with an address to Christ, whom she calls her *dolce conforto* ("sweet comfort"):

> I cannot say to you, my sweet comfort,
> that the place or time or hour is not right
> to reveal with works so great a passion,
> which is the desire I carry within.
> But if this or that little diversion
> distracts my senses from honoring you
> always, I have through your grace a firm heart,
> and never direct my sail toward other ports.

In the tercets, she turns away from her holy address and ponders, in the spirit of Michelangelo's poem, the path to salvation:

> I realize now that in this world twigs and thorns
> cannot twist the right foot of the wise man,

from the straight path he foresees the end,
but our great love for ourselves, and our poor faith
in things invisible, high and divine,
slow us down on the path toward salvation.*

The reference to the "right foot" ("*il destro piede*") invokes Michelangelo's opening image of moving hesitantly from one step to the next—his slow pace reflects his uncertainty about the right path to take—but Vittoria otherwise maintains her distance from his poem, and speaks in generalizations. The wise man will choose the right foot, she declares, but she does not reassure her friend that he is among the wise. There is no comfort given.

Vittoria may not have written Michelangelo poems that were either admiring, in the manner of his poems to her, or encouraging in the way he might have hoped. But she did give him what was probably her most precious gift: a manuscript of her spiritual sonnets. This manuscript, now owned by the Vatican Library, is most likely what Michelangelo wrote to her about when he described his feelings of unworthiness—"Before taking possession, Signora, of the things [*le cose*] which Your Ladyship has several times wished to give to me"—and "the things" a reference to the 103 sonnets included in the book's pages.

Compared with the manuscript prepared for Marguerite de Navarre at roughly the same time—both were made about 1540—the gift for Michelangelo was positively plain. Marguerite's book, as we have seen, is filled with illuminated letters, coats of arms, and other decorative flourishes. Michelangelo's, by contrast, has no decorations or illuminations of any kind. Even the title, *Sonetti spirituali della Sigra*

---

*S1.97: "*Non potrò dire, o mio dolce conforto, / Che non sia destro il luogo, e i tempi, e l'ore, / Per far chiaro con l'opre un tale ardore, / Quale è il desio che dentro acceso porto. / Ma se ben questo o quel picciol diporto / Sottrae dal sempre procurarvi onore / I sensi, ho pur per grazia fermo il core / Non mai drizzar la vela ad altro porto. / M'accorgo or che nel mondo e sterpi e spine / Torcer non ponno al saggio il destro piede / Dal sentier dritto s'antivede il fine; / Ma il molto amore a noi, la poca fede / De l'invisibil cose alte e divine, / Ne ritardano il corso a la mercede.*"

Vittoria is surprisingly informal, lacking even Vittoria's family name, and abbreviating the word "Signora."

Not only the relative informality of the manuscript's presentation but also the actual selection of the poems suggests Vittoria's own hand in its preparation. The sonnets are arranged with a meaningful beginning and end, and clustered around certain themes or topics in a manner very different from the Navarre and della Torre manuscripts. The selection was also restricted: by the end of 1540, when the manuscript is likely to have been compiled, only 26 of the manuscript's 103 sonnets had appeared in any of the printed editions, so this meant that Michelangelo was largely receiving poems no one else had seen. The sonnet "I cannot say to you, my sweet comfort," for example, was included in Michelangelo's book—it was, after all, a response to one of his poems—but did not appear in print until the 1546 edition of the spiritual sonnets published in Venice.

Perhaps the most subtle, but also most interesting, hint of Vittoria's personal involvement in making the gift for Michelangelo can be perceived only by holding the book in your hands. Whereas the manuscript for Marguerite was made of ordinary parchment, the pages chosen for Michelangelo's gift were of the finest sheep's vellum. "Vellum" is used nowadays as a term to describe high-quality papers made of different materials, but in the sixteenth century it was treated animal hide, and extraordinarily smooth. The choice of the manuscript's pages did not go unnoticed. In a letter Michelangelo wrote in 1550— three years after Vittoria's death—to a friend who had asked to borrow some of her poetry, he responded that he had "a little book on parchment" ("*un libretto in carta pecora*") with 103 of her poems. He mentioned as well a group of forty additional poems she had sent him from Viterbo, where she lived for roughly three years starting in 1541; those poems, he specified, were "*in carta bambagia*"—a special kind of paper made of cotton wool made famous in Amalfi. It is unlikely that his friend was interested in the quality of the paper on which the sonnets were written—he simply wanted to read the poems—but the fact that Michelangelo specified this in both cases is telling. For Michelangelo, reading Vittoria's poetry was a tactile as well as an intellectual experience. Or rather—as she no doubt well understood—he drew no meaningful distinction between the two.

In his biography of Michelangelo, Condivi summarized the bond between the two friends in this way:

> More particularly he greatly loved the [Marchesa] of Pescara, whose sublime spirit he was in love with, and she returned his love passionately. He still has many of her letters, filled with honest and most sweet love, and these letters sprang from her heart, just as he also wrote many many sonnets to her, full of intelligence and sweet desire. She often traveled to Rome from Viterbo and other places where she had gone for recreation and to spend the summer, prompted by no other reason than to see Michelangelo.

Whether Vittoria ever returned to Rome with the sole purpose of seeing Michelangelo cannot be verified, but there is evidence that Michelangelo came to see her in Viterbo on at least one occasion, and that the two remained in close contact during these years. Two letters Vittoria wrote from Viterbo, one to Michelangelo and one to a mutual friend about the artist, convey their friendship in particularly vivid terms. In the first, Vittoria wrote to Michelangelo to voice her concern, expressed with great humor, that they were exchanging letters too frequently, and thereby distracting each other from what they ought to be doing. "Magnificent Messer Michel Angelo," she begins,

> I have not answered your letter sooner, because it was, one might say, an answer to mine; for thinking that if you and I continue to write to one another so often, according to my obligation and your courtesy, I would need to neglect the Chapel of Santa Caterina here, and not be present at the ordained hours in the company of these sisters, and you would have to leave behind the Chapel of Saint Paul.

Vittoria was living at the time in the convent of Santa Caterina in Viterbo, and although she was a lay resident, she followed as closely as possible the strict rules of the order. Michelangelo, meanwhile, was working on his final frescoes: *The Conversion of Saul* and *The Crucifixion of Saint Peter*. Pope Paul had just completed a new chapel—the aptly named Pauline Chapel—as part of his reconstruction of the ceremonial rooms of his Vatican residence, and he had commissioned Michelangelo to adorn its walls.

As Vittoria seems well aware, the consequences of their losing time in their respective "chapels" were not comparable: she risked missing some of the liturgical hours at the convent, and he risked not finishing two great works of art for the pope. But however much she appreciated the difference in their current activities—and her lighthearted, at times almost comical tone makes clear that she did—she also genuinely understood how important it was to both of them to remain fully engaged in their immediate worlds. "You would be absent," she continued, "without finding yourself from early in the morning through the day in sweet conversation with your painted figures, which speak to you with their natural accents no less than real people [speak] to me when I am around them. Thus I would fail Christ's brides, and you his Vicar [the pope]." Vittoria's idea of Michelangelo's figures speaking to him—of his conversing with Saul about his extraordinary experience when he was struck from his horse while riding to Damascus, or sympathizing with Peter as he was raised by the Roman soldiers onto the cross, head down—suggest her powerful sense of her friend's inhabiting the art that he made. His paintings were alive for him, just as the nuns were for her. "Sweet conversation" ("*dolce colloquio*") was also a good description of what passed between the two friends when they were together, which their letters could only approximate.

Vittoria did not only try to imagine Michelangelo's creative process and to make sure he had the time he needed to devote to the Pauline frescoes. She also worried, like a loving mother or wife, about the toll this commission was taking on his health. The second letter involving the two of them that has survived from this period was written to their mutual friend and fellow reformer Alvise Priuli. She wrote to Priuli to share her concern that Michelangelo, who had just come to Viterbo, was suffering from pain in his eyes due to the strenuous work he was doing in the chapel of Saint Paul. She asked Priuli if he might be able to lend the artist a monocle until the special glass, mounted with gilded silver, that she had ordered from Venice arrived, which she estimated would be sometime in the next fifteen days (we can therefore assume that Michelangelo would have been staying in Viterbo for at least this long). This careful attention to Michelangelo's well-being—her concern that he was struggling with his vision, or complaining of fatigue to his eyes—gives us a rare glimpse of Vittoria's nurturing side.

We will never know if Vittoria got to visit the Pauline Chapel when she returned to Rome in 1544. She was ill at the time, and may not have made even the short trip from the center of the city across the Tiber to the Vatican. If she did, she would no doubt have found Michelangelo working hard on his frescoes, his gilded monocle in hand. We might add this precious object—the only one not made of paper—to the virtual archive of letters and poems and drawings, both lost and found, which made up the fabric of their friendship. But the extraordinary quality of their bond was best captured in their words. "I'm sending you . . . verses I wrote for the Marchesa di Pescara," Michelangelo wrote to a friend after Vittoria's death; she was "devoted to me, and I no less to her." For her part, Vittoria reserved for him the most beautiful of titles. He was, she declared, *mio singularissimo amico,* "my most singular friend."

SALT WAR

O N APRIL 9, 1541, the governor of Orvieto, Brunamonte de' Rossi di Assisi, witnessed something outside the gates of the monastery of San Paolo in his city that he deemed worthy of reporting to the highest authorities in Rome. In a letter to Cardinal Alessandro Farnese, the grandson of Pope Paul III who had been appointed to the curia in 1534 at the age of fourteen, de' Rossi described what he had seen:

> As I was going to the citadel, passing in front of the monastery of San Paolo where the said Signora is staying, I found a gentleman with sword and spurs on, who had just arrived, and who was speaking with the said above-mentioned Signora at the grating. I asked him cleverly, and under pretense of being anxious to pick up any news, who he was and whence he came . . . And I saw when he gave her a packet which he put through the grating, about as high as two little boxes one on top of the other, and sewn up in some sort of linen. What was inside I know not, because one could not see, and he put it through the grating as soon as I arrived there.

The *Signora* in question was Vittoria Colonna; the gentleman, one Berardino de Lassis of Loreto who had been dispatched from Naples with news for Vittoria from Giovanna d'Aragona, Ascanio's estranged wife, who was living in Ischia. Why the governor of Orvieto was interested in the conversation Vittoria was having with this unknown gentleman; why he had sent the news of the meeting to Cardinal Farnese in order, as he put it, "to execute and satisfy your wish"; and why Vittoria was in Orvieto and under surveillance in the first place bring us to a very tense moment in her life.

By 1540, Vittoria seems finally to have created a world for herself that fulfilled her deepest desires. She spent a great deal of time with her beloved Michelangelo; she attended inspiring sermons and became ever more involved with the project of religious reform; she completed the hundred or so spiritual sonnets that would be included in the new editions of her *Rime*; she dwelt with her favorite nuns in the convent of San Silvestro in Capite. With her days full of religion, art, poetry, and friendship, she had finally managed to integrate the pieces of her life in a way that gave her great satisfaction. All of this came to an abrupt halt, however, in the early months of 1541, when a major crisis struck the Colonna family and Vittoria was once again involved in political turmoil.

As in the past, the trouble had to do with relations between Ascanio and the pope. Several years earlier, Pope Paul had introduced new taxes on salt from all of his subjects in the Papal States. It is odd to think that the pope was involved in selling salt, but in addition to running the church, he was in effect the ruler of a small kingdom. Salt had for centuries been one of the most lucrative products to buy and sell throughout all of Europe—everyone, rich or poor, ate food flavored or preserved with salt—and regulating its trade generated an enormous income. In the north, the salt trade was dominated by Venice, which developed an entire administration around this single commodity. The Venetian salt office not only issued licenses to merchants dictating how much salt they could export and the price at which they could sell it, but also maintained Venice's amazingly complex water system and public buildings. In the Papal States, the pope himself enjoyed the monopoly over salt until 1862, when the privilege was given to the newly unified Italian state.

Paul's official reason for raising the taxes on salt was that he needed money to fight against the two central threats menacing the church: the Turks and the Protestants. The less official reason was that, like most of his recent predecessors on the papal throne, he had extravagant tastes and habits and had run into deep debt—it was Paul, we will recall, who had as a cardinal purchased a very grand palazzo for his family residence, and he was still in the midst of transforming it into one of the most splendid homes in Rome.

Whatever Paul's justification for introducing the new tax, it met with immediate and fierce resistance. The first stage of the conflict that came to be known as the Salt War was waged between the pope and the ruling families of Perugia. Perugia was one of the most powerful cities among the Papal States, and had for several centuries managed to operate as if it were independent. But Perugia's freedom came to an absolute end with the events of 1540. When the city's rulers refused to pay what they regarded as the exorbitant new tax, the pope's armies attacked. In the bloody war that followed, the papal troops destroyed much of the city and brought the oligarchic rulers to their knees. According to local legend, the Salt War also had the disastrous culinary consequence of introducing the idea of baking bread without salt. This began as a protest against the new taxes—it was Perugia's equivalent of the Boston Tea Party—but the tasteless habit unfortunately not only stuck with the city, but also spread throughout much of Italy.

Ascanio was certainly familiar with what had happened in Perugia, but he could not be swayed from his determination to fight Paul himself. He asserted his right to a papal exemption from the tax based on an arrangement that his ancestor Oddone Colonna had made on behalf of the family when he assumed the papacy as Martin V in 1417. In truth, Ascanio's anger against the pope was not limited to the new salt tax. He also had a serious personal grievance. This was a complicated domestic drama, but given the importance of everyone involved, it became a matter of real consequence. Indeed, very little that affected families such as the Colonna was contained to their household alone: the stakes were consistently high.

In 1539, Marzio Colonna, the son of the celebrated *condottiere* Ottaviano, who had fought with Ascanio and Vittoria's father, Fabrizio, on behalf of the kings of Naples, asked Ascanio for permission to marry their cousin Livia. Livia was the daughter of the Colonna *condottiere* Marcantonio I; following his death during the Spanish siege of Milan in 1522, she had become Ascanio's ward. Famously stingy and reluctant to provide dowries even for his own three daughters, let alone for Livia, Ascanio refused to give his consent. Frustrated by this refusal and determined to make the marriage, Marzio took matters into his own hands. He obtained the help of Pier Luigi Farnese, the illegitimate son of Paul III and captain general of his army. The idea that the pope had children seems shocking today, but this was a more or less ordinary and accepted occurrence in the Renaissance. The papal offspring, who were referred to by the wonderfully capacious term *nipoti*, which can usefully mean either nieces and nephews or grandchildren, were often treated as if they were legitimate, and enjoyed all of the benefits of their father's power. This is in fact the origin of the English term "nepotism": the favoring of "nephews" or other relatives on the part of the pope.

Marzio and Pier Luigi succeeded in abducting Livia, and entrusted her for safekeeping to Isabella Colonna, princess of Sulmona, with whom Ascanio was on bad terms due to a property dispute a decade earlier. Isabella was the daughter of Ascanio and Vittoria's second cousin Vespasiano, who had married Giulia Gonzaga after the death of Isabella's mother, Beatrice Appiani. As Vespasiano had no male heir, his lands were bequeathed to Isabella, but Ascanio had tried to assert his rights, as head of the Colonna family, over those of his female cousin. Fighting between Ascanio and Pope Clement had ensued, and the fortress of Paliano, which was one of Isabella's valuable holdings, ultimately was given to Ascanio. Shortly after Livia's abduction, she and Marzio Colonna were married. Ascanio rightly perceived that Pope Paul had done nothing to stop the marriage, and hence was already in high dudgeon when the conflict over the salt tax began.

Pope Paul, for his part, was eager to bring the Colonna down. As we have seen, his family was new to the Roman elite, and he was ambitious to expand their power. Paul resented above all the independence of the old noble families within the Papal States, and wanted to reduce feudal lords such as Ascanio to subservient vassals who would render him more profit. Invoking a particularly resonant passage from the Hebrew Bible, he referred to the Colonna as "pricks in my eyes." The phrase comes from the Book of Numbers, when God instructs Moses to "drive out all the inhabitants of the land from before you." "But if ye will not drive out the inhabitants of the land from before you," God warns, "then it shall come to pass, that those which ye let remain of them shall be pricks in your eyes, and thorns in your sides, and shall vex you in the land wherein ye dwell." The Colonna family's extensive lands and armies in such close proximity to Rome were a constant strain on Paul's sense of dominion, and they represented to him precisely those whom his predecessors had foolishly "let remain." Ascanio's refusal to pay the salt tax, in short, gave him the perfect opportunity to pounce.

Things got started on a very small, even petty, scale. Ascanio declared his opposition to the taxes, and blocked the pope's importation of corn seed into Rome. Paul retaliated by incarcerating several of Ascanio's vassals who had, following Ascanio's orders, denied the tax collectors their fees. Ascanio responded by incarcerating some pilgrims, who had passed through his territories on their way to Rome, in the dungeons of the Colonna castles. He also seized thirty of the pope's cows, which had been grazing on his lands. At this point, Paul summoned Ascanio to Rome—he issued a pontifical brief demanding his presence within three days—but Ascanio refused to comply. The pope's next move was to declare war. Vittoria's reaction to this was rather wry. "For many serious things," she wrote to Ascanio, "such as the slaughter of captains, governors, and cardinals, retaliation is taken, but there was no reason to have such a war over thirty cows." She was well aware, of course, that the conflict went beyond the cows, or even the tax. This was a war between two competing powers to control the region.

The war began with Paul's ordering his son Pier Luigi Farnese to besiege the Colonna castle at Genazzano, thirty miles east of Rome. Genazzano, as we have already observed, was built on a narrow slice of volcanic tufa some twelve hundred feet high; like many of the Colonna properties in the region, it was not easy to penetrate. Ascanio was holed up within the walls of the town's fortifications with two thousand soldiers. Pier Luigi's army was much larger: he came with close to ten thousand men, most of whom were mercenaries from Germany and Switzerland. Already in this first encounter between the two sides, the scale of the conflict was alarming, and word of the pope's aggression spread throughout the peninsula. According to a report given to the Venetian senate by Francesco Contarini, a member of Charles V's imperial court who had recently returned from Germany, "It is impossible to put into words how much His Holiness is talked about by everyone because of the war he is waging in Italy. It is generally thought that [the pope] does not care if he ruins the church if he succeeds in aggrandizing his own family . . . The majority [of the princes] said that the Lord Ascanio should come here, and if the emperor does not want to help him, he will be assisted by others."

When the hostilities broke out between Ascanio and Paul, Vittoria was quickly identified on multiple fronts as the person most likely to resolve the conflict. As her friend Gasparo Contarini, a distant relative of Francesco Contarini's and a strong supporter of the pope, wrote to his fellow cardinal Reginald Pole:

> It was greatly troubling to me that Ascanio Colonna acted so rashly and imprudently against the Pontiff; I am indeed exceedingly pained by the partiality of his sister the most Illustrious Marchesa, for whom I will do very much, as you know. The emperor can scarcely bear it and damns that man's actions exceedingly; he is, however, about to move forward with an arrangement between the Pontiff and himself . . . You will please ask the Marchesa as strongly as possible in my name, knowing that she is to be solicited most honorably with a preliminary statement from me, to do all she can to settle this commotion, for which a great loss will be visited upon her brother, if he won't accept it willingly, and is forced to do so all the same.

Letters began to pour into the convent of San Silvestro in Capite, where Vittoria was still residing, begging her to intervene. Within weeks, she had become the de facto negotiator for the Colonna family.

"Ask the Marchesa." It is truly extraordinary that a woman who had no formal role became such a crucial figure in this political battle. Women did not officially serve as diplomats during this period, and Vittoria had little experience handling a matter of this magnitude. But she was gifted at thinking through difficult situations—Ferrante, we will recall, turned to her for advice fifteen years earlier in his struggle with the Italian league—and in the spring of 1541, she devoted herself to finding a solution that might save her family from ruin.

For most of the events in Vittoria's life, there are scores of missing letters and records, and we are left to piece together what must have happened from the sources that remain. In the case of the Salt War, however, we are fortunate to have a rich set of documents. Above all, what has survived, and can be read today in the Colonna archive now in Subiaco, is the original correspondence between Vittoria and Ascanio from the first month of the conflict. Because the letters were between siblings, Vittoria wrote them all in her own rather messy hand—as with her letters to Michelangelo, they are difficult to decipher—and even addressed them herself, suggesting that no secretaries were involved. On the outside fold of one of the letters, which still has Vittoria's (broken) seal, she scribbled, "to the Lord Ascanio, most beloved brother." This combination of formality and intimacy seems to capture the complexity of their relationship. Given his position as head of the family, she needed to treat him with respect, but she also maintained a sisterly affection. The tone of the letters was also markedly different from that of most of Vittoria's other correspondence, revealing qualities in her—humor, irony, even sisterly bossiness—that otherwise surfaced only rarely. Above all, Vittoria's letters to Ascanio show her fantastic versatility. At exactly the moment in which she was so deeply engaged in her own religious and literary life in Rome, she was able to redirect her energy to her family, and concentrate on the serious threat at hand.

What was at stake in this conflict for Vittoria that she allowed it to draw her in so completely? Nothing less, it seemed, than the reputation and fortune of the Colonna. As she said in one of her letters to Ascanio, "the house of Colonna always comes first" ("*Casa Colonna sempre è la prima*"). In the immediate context of the letter, she meant this as an explanation for why Pope Paul had targeted them so ruthlessly: the Colonna were, she reminded her brother, the most powerful family in Rome. But in a broader sense, the comment speaks to what we might regard as her tribalism. However independent Vittoria often seemed, and however occupied with her own interests and concerns, she was at the same time never completely detached from her family. The house of Colonna was perhaps always first.

The letter in which Vittoria made this declaration was written in early March, and it spelled out the path she thought Ascanio should follow in the war. She made clear that she did not think he could succeed on his own, and she urged him not to take action until he secured the support of "His Majesty," the Holy Roman Emperor Charles V. "Your Lordship," she began, adopting a very formal address in an otherwise informal letter, "should wait to make sure that everything you will do once the order from His Majesty has come, will be honored." Vittoria was counting on the fact that Charles still felt indebted to the Colonna from their long-standing loyalty to him and his predecessors in Spain, and that he would rush to join them in battle.

What Vittoria had not fully taken in, however, was how little Charles wanted to disrupt the precarious peace he had recently negotiated with the pope. As was so often the case among the ruling classes, a political solution had depended upon an arranged marriage: Charles had married his illegitimate daughter Margaret of Austria to Paul's grandson Ottavio Farnese. At the time of the marriage, which took place in November 1538, Ottavio was fourteen years old and Margaret two years his senior. Despite her youth, Margaret was already a widow, having been married in 1536 to Alessandro de' Medici, Duke of Florence. That marriage lasted a mere six months before Alessandro was murdered by a distant cousin who had lured him into a sexual encounter with his cousin's sister.

Like so many daughters of powerful men, Margaret was for Charles a valuable pawn: he had arranged her first marriage in order to consolidate his relations with Florence, the second to secure his relations with the pope. The fact that she was illegitimate seemed to make no difference—everyone in this marital story was illegitimate in one way or another. Margaret was the issue of Charles's fling with a Flemish maidservant (the daughter of a carpet-maker) whom he had met during a visit to one of his chamberlains. Ottavio was the legitimate son of Pier Luigi, Pope Paul's illegitimate son. Alessandro was said to be the illegitimate son of Lorenzo II de' Medici, Duke of Urbino and ruler of Florence in the mid-1510s (to whom Machiavelli dedicated *The Prince*), but rumor had it that he was in fact the son of Lorenzo's cousin Giulio di Giuliano de' Medici, who became Clement VII. This means that both of Margaret's husbands may have been the offspring of popes.

Vittoria knew very well that Charles had married his daughter to Paul's grandson—she may even have attended the wedding—and she would have understood that the match presented an obvious obstacle to gaining the emperor's support for Ascanio's new war. But she seems to have counted on the fact that everyone, including Charles, was aware of how catastrophic a marriage it had turned out to be. Margaret had been strongly against marrying Ottavio in the first place, and had made her opposition clear. She had set her eyes, in fact, on Cosimo I de' Medici for her next husband, and apparently arrived at her own wedding to Ottavio, which took place in the splendor of the Sistine Chapel, wearing her widow's black. To violate the ritual in such a way, and in such a place, must have been an extraordinary sight, and there was good reason to think Charles and Paul might not be quite so reconciled as they had hoped.

After the wedding, things looked no more promising. Margaret refused to live with Ottavio, whom she regarded as an immature adolescent, and resided instead in the Medici palace in Rome, which she had inherited with a life tenancy upon the death of her husband Alessandro. This palace, which today houses the Italian Senate, came to be called Palazzo Madama after Margaret herself, due to the number of titles she acquired over the course of her life: she was Margaret of Austria, then duchess of Florence, and finally, through her marriage to Ottavio, duchess of Parma and Piacenza. It became widely known, moreover, that the marriage to Ottavio took almost two full years to be consummated. As we saw with Vittoria's uncle Guidobaldo and his wife, Elisabetta, in Urbino, there was no sense of privacy in relation to the sex lives of the ruling class: the consummation of a marriage was a matter of public interest. In this case, however, and only in this narrow respect, the outcome was ultimately happier than with the ill-fated couple in Urbino. On October 18, 1540, the long-awaited event was publicly announced, to the great satisfaction of both the pope and the Holy Roman Emperor.

The extreme delicacy of Margaret and Ottavio's marriage and its crucial importance to Charles's foreign policy help to explain his resistance to taking Ascanio's side several months later, when the conflict over the salt tax began. Charles was willing, and indeed eager, to help negotiate a peaceful solution, but he had no intention of committing troops to battle. This is where Vittoria got things wrong, in part because she was convinced that she had an additional winning card to play. Once again it involved a high-stakes marriage. Rumor had it that a contract was being drawn up between Pier Luigi Farnese's daughter, Vittoria, and a member of the French royal household, thereby creating a new alliance between Pope Paul and Francis I. News of such a match was in fact disagreeable to Vittoria, who had tried the previous year to arrange a marriage between Vittoria Farnese and Ascanio's son Fabrizio. This match had failed both because of the pope's ambitions for his granddaughter to marry someone aligned with a powerful European court (and not simply someone from an important Roman family), and because Ascanio had been unwilling to give Fabrizio the necessary feudal properties—the male equivalent of a dowry—to make him a sufficiently appealing groom.

Now, however, the failure of the marriage negotiations between the Farnese and Colonna families took on much greater consequence. It seems likely, in fact, that the Salt War would never have begun had the match been made. Vittoria was clearly frustrated by the entire affair, but also saw something to gain from the new engagement: she thought the pope's secret plans for an alliance with France, which remained the emperor's principal enemy, might motivate Charles to come to Ascanio's aid. In the same letter to her brother in which she declared "the house of Colonna always comes first," she wrote that "the marriage negotiations with France are concluded, and I wrote as much to his Majesty, and they say it isn't looking good for anyone." Presumably she wanted to convey that relations between Charles and Pope Paul might now be in jeopardy, but avoided stating it too bluntly. "From now on I won't really be able to write too clearly," she confided, "in the event that it may please God to ensure that our letters are not kept to us alone." Vittoria was being spied on, or so she thought.

What is perhaps most surprising about this communication is the fact that Vittoria might have been responsible for breaking the news of the marriage planned between the pope's granddaughter and the French nobleman to the emperor: "I wrote," she announced, "as much to his Majesty." She was not, that is, an outlier in the unfolding drama, but one of its principal players. In a second letter to Ascanio written a day or two later, she confirmed that the marriage was going forward, and encouraged him once again to trust in Charles:

> I believe that things with France will soon be uncovered, whereupon one will see that his Holiness is not on your side alone, whereupon I'm quite afraid that not conventions but deceptions will result. But it is well [to remember] that you may not come up short if any possible solution can be found. I have not stopped hoping for this. Nevertheless, I would like you to write to his Majesty again . . . It is hard to understand this pope, but make sure that with the grace of God all is done for serving his Majesty.

Nowhere else in her correspondence did Vittoria say anything so critical of church authority as "It is hard to understand this pope," and nowhere else did she plot so openly against the pontiff's interests.

If Vittoria was far from naïve, however, about Paul—her comment that "there was no reason to have such a war over thirty cows," for example, was followed by her reflection that the pope simply "wanted to arm with this excuse"—she did have a blind spot in relation to Charles. Perhaps she felt that Charles still owed her for the extraordinary service of Ferrante at the Battle of Pavia; perhaps she held him in a certain sense responsible for her widowhood, and thus assumed that his sense of guilt or obligation would propel him to the Colonna side. Whatever her reasons, she remained confident of Charles's support long after the signs were abundantly clear that help was not forthcoming.

In the spring of 1541 when the conflict broke out, Charles was in Germany, where he had convened a major conference known as the Diet of Regensburg, with the aim of restoring religious unity to all of his territories in the wake of the Protestant Reformation. Although he remained in occasional contact with Vittoria during these months, he appointed his ambassador to Rome, Don Juan Fernandez Manrique II de Lara, Marquis of Aguilar, to conduct the negotiations in Rome. Aguilar communicated the pope's demands to Vittoria, who then communicated them to Ascanio. The initial proposal that was made at the beginning of March involved the Colonna's surrender of Nemi and Marino, with one of the pope's presumably less valuable properties, Castro or Nepi, given to them in compensation.

Aguilar's proposal to surrender Nemi and Marino, however unattractive to Ascanio, was not enough for the pope, who insisted that Rocca di Papa—the third property in the region, three miles to the east of Marino and fifteen miles from Rome—should also be handed over. Rocca di Papa, a settlement of ancient origins built on the edge of the central crater of the Alban Hills, came into the hands of the church in the late twelfth century, when Pope Lucius III took possession of the town and built its fortress (it was likely at this point that the town acquired its name, which means "the Pope's fortress"). In the early 1400s, Rocca became a property of the Orsini family before being purchased by the Colonna in 1426 for the price of ten thousand ducats. By the 1540s, as Paul well understood, its central location and well-fortified castle made it one of the Colonna's key defensive properties. Charles, meanwhile, promised Vittoria through Aguilar that he would ultimately make sure all of the Colonna lands in discussion (Nemi, Marino, and Rocca di Papa) were returned to her family after the conflict was resolved. The transfer to the pope, he quietly assured her, would be only temporary.

Vittoria wrote to Ascanio with all these details in a series of letters sent between March 6 and 8, 1541—the fact that she signed one of the letters "From Rome, today Sunday, at the 22nd hour" suggests both how frequently they were writing to each other and how much was happening on a daily basis, so that knowing whether the letter was written in the morning or at night made a difference. Throughout these letters, she made clear her opinion about the pope's demands: she thought the handing over of Marino and Nemi was acceptable, but the surrendering of Rocca di Papa, even temporarily, out of the question. She also indicated to Ascanio that his responses to her were not likely to be private—as we saw earlier, she imagined their letters were being read by others—and she concluded one of the letters with the advice to "make sure to respond in a manner that will guarantee that the Marquis sees it."

From the back-and-forth between Vittoria and Ascanio during this negotiation, we learn a few important things. First, that Ascanio was totally dependent upon his sister's guidance and advice. He called her, however jokingly, "*mia imperatrice*" ("my empress"), and declared that he would do whatever "your Ladyship advises." Second, that Vittoria was no man's fool, and was not going to be pushed around, even by the Holy Roman Emperor. In one of her letters to Ascanio, sent on either March 7 or 8, she added this postscript: "To the emperor I write that the agreements were impossible and that it is not his right to give [away] the Rocca, which His Majesty looked at while passing through Marino and said '*esta es la roca de Izo*' ['this is the Rocca of Izo']. In writing this I believe I have done well. Take care of yourself, among other things." Third, and finally, that Vittoria supported Ascanio's desire not to surrender the family lands, and therefore however much she hated the idea of war, she ultimately backed his decision to take up arms.

All of this returns us to the convent of San Paolo in Orvieto, where Vittoria arrived on March 17, accompanied by two maidservants and two male valets, following her failure to reach an agreement over Rocca di Papa. Where to go had in fact been a difficult question. She obviously could not stay in Marino or one of the other Colonna feuds in the Castelli Romani, since this was exactly where the battles were being waged. She had the option of joining her sister-in-law, Giovanna, at the

Ischia castle, but the prospect of being so far away probably did not appeal to her. Orvieto, by contrast, sixty miles from Rome, was close enough that she could return should Ascanio need her, but far enough to feel safely removed. The specific choice was also strategic: the city had long been a papal stronghold—we will recall that Clement fled there after the Sack of Rome, and called it "our city." Orvieto also had close ties to Pope Paul, whose family had been among its ruling class for several centuries. In her decision to stay there during the months of the war, Vittoria sent Paul a clear message that she remained, in effect, his subject. This was a wise decision on her part, given how high the stakes actually were. At the end of the war, Ascanio was excommunicated, but Vittoria remained in the fold of the church.

Vittoria's arrival in Orvieto was unexpected, and she was not at first received with what Shakespeare wonderfully described in *King Lear* as the "ceremonious affection" to which a king—or an illustrious noblewoman—might be accustomed. But the elite of the city quickly made up for their initial lack of pomp. Two days after her arrival, a meeting between the governor and the city's ruling men was held to discuss how they should acknowledge her presence. The minutes from this meeting have been preserved in Orvieto's archive, and they indicate that the group made the unanimous decision that given Vittoria's status and her relations with the pope, an official delegation should visit her at the convent immediately. In addition to offering her their services, they agreed they should bestow upon her elaborate gifts of food worth ten florins. (An ordinary mason in Rome would earn at most thirty florins a year, so this was a significant sum.) The abstemious Vittoria, who had already begun what ultimately became an obsessive regimen of fasting, received four pairs of chickens, thirty pounds of fish, and fourteen and a half pounds of sweetmeats and marzipan. We can imagine the joy of the sisters when these offerings arrived at San Paolo's gates—who knows when they had last received such a bounty.

This outward showing of hospitality belied, however, the governor's secret distrust of his celebrated guest. Indeed, although the convent may in some sense have been the safe haven that Vittoria sought—there is no reason to suspect the nuns—Orvieto was enemy territory. Whether she was fully aware of what was going on is difficult to say: she was certainly already being careful in her letters to Ascanio, and no doubt kept up her guard in all of her correspondence. But the idea that someone was keeping track of whom she talked to, and watching her when she received a package, represented entirely new levels of surveillance. "I have not failed," de' Rossi wrote to Cardinal Farnese, "nor will I fail, to visit the Signora Marchesa di Pescara continually, with the greatest assiduity possible."

De' Rossi's first letter, sent on April 1, described the religious and quiet life Vittoria was living, and had no news to report. In his letter of April 9, however, he presented a few bits of what he regarded as more valuable information, which he boasted to have obtained directly from the local bishop: "I have cautiously found out and heard from the Bishop of Orvieto that, about a week ago, a retainer, secretary or servant of the most reverend Cardinal Fregoso, came here and spoke with the said Marchesa, and stopped and lodged one evening with her servants, and only brought one other horse with him; and the Bishop tells me that he came solely to inform her Excellence about the war." The idea that someone was bringing Vittoria news, and that he had "only brought one other horse with him," hardly seems worthy of attention. But the governor was clearly committed to reporting absolutely anything related to this important noblewoman, and the fact that Federico Fregoso, an old friend of Bembo's who was one of the central figures in the conversations recorded in Castiglione's *Courtier*, was visiting her was the best that he could muster up at the time.

De' Rossi began to make more progress, however, if not with Vittoria, then with the bishop, who shared more concrete news with him at their next meeting. He proudly related to Cardinal Farnese: "I write to inform you that, when I was in conversation with the Bishop of Orvieto a few days ago, I wormed out of him that the aforesaid Signora Marchesa, who seems to repose great confidence in his most reverend Lordship, has shown him two letters: one was from his Caesarian Majesty the Emperor [Charles V], and the other from the Marquis of

Vasto." Neither of the two letters the bishop had managed to intercept revealed much of anything: they both encouraged her to maintain her goodwill ("*buona voglia*"). But the sheer fact that Vittoria was receiving personal letters from the Holy Roman Emperor was certainly worthy of notice.

The attempts on the part of Charles and Alfonso to keep up Vittoria's spirits were ultimately in vain, as the war was going very badly for Ascanio. Within weeks of the fighting having begun, one Colonna castle after another was taken by the papal army. By early April, Rocca di Papa had fallen, leaving only the remote fortress of Paliano, some eighteen miles east of Rocca, in Ascanio's hands. The papal soldiers, meanwhile, had been ruthless in their treatment of both soldiers and civilians. In dispatches sent to Pope Paul from the field, his commissioner Giovanni Guidiccioni reported the terror of the local townspeople. "Fearing our soldiers and not having the protection they need to return to their homes," he wrote, they "are simply taking to the road in desperation." Giovanna, who kept abreast of the events even while in Ischia, sent a desperate letter to the pope:

> I appeal to [Your Holiness] begging you . . . to desist from such an invasion and [such] ruin for the people and poor vassals, for who, Most Holy and Beatified Father, will be pious, who will be merciful if piety and mercy cannot be found in the heir and legitimate possessor of the sacrosanct and divine keys of the early pastor Saint Peter, ever just and good? . . . May it please you to allow that no more blood is shed by the sheep, for whom Your Holiness is the real shepherd.

Vittoria, for her part, did something she had never done before: she put her poetry to use as a political tool. In what was likely to have been an act of desperation, she wrote two sonnets to Paul in which she begged him to show mercy and end the violence being wrought upon her people. One of the two sonnets begins with a vision of bloodshed in the Colonna lands, and then implores Paul to remember the common bonds that tie them together:

I see only armed soldiers light up
my vast, great fields, and I hear all song
turned to weeping, all laughter to tears,
there, where I first touched my homeland . . .
Under a single sky, within one womb,
Born and nurtured together in the sweet shade
of a single city were our people.*

The second sonnet was subtler in its message, and adopted a tone of prayer. Vittoria asked God to fill Paul's heart with "so great a flame of divine fire" that his anger would abate:

Then will you see the sheep leave their flocks
to seek your lap, to be warmed by the torch
that the great fire of Heaven lights on earth.
Then will your sacred and glorious nets
already be full; with the scepter of peace,
not the arms of war, will the world be yours.†

However moving Giovanna's letter or Vittoria's sonnets may have been, they had little effect on Paul, whose army continued its advance upon Paliano. Located at the top of a high hill between two sets of mountains, and well off the main road that leads from Palestrina to Genazzano, this was the most isolated of the Colonna properties in the region, and Ascanio had retreated to the upper town with what remained of his troops. (Even today, visitors need to leave their cars behind after climbing a good distance on a windy road, and then ascend several

---

* E22: "*Veggio rilucer sol di armate squadre / i miei sì larghi campi, ed odo il canto / rivolto in grido, e 'l dolce riso in pianto / là 've io prima toccai l'antica madre. / . . . / sotto un sol cielo, entro un sol grembo nati / sono, e nudriti insieme a la dolce ombra / d'una sola città gli avoli nostri.*"
† E23: "*Prego il Padre divin che tanta fiamma / mandi del foco Suo nel vostro core / . . . / Vedransi alor venir gli armenti lieti / al santo grembo caldo de la face / che 'l gran Lume del Ciel gli accese in terra. / Così le sacre gloriose reti / saran già colme; con la verga in pace / si rese il mondo, e non con l'armi in guerra.*"

very steep ramps and vertical flights of stairs by foot.) Both the soldiers and the townspeople in Paliano were suffering from a nearly complete lack of provisions, and according to one of Guidiccioni's reports to Pope Paul, Ascanio was a desperate man. Although nearly emptied out of supplies, however, he forbade his soldiers to surrender. "He did not willingly allow them to leave the fortress," Guidiccioni wrote, "which is also a sign that he does not have too many people, and he said that in order to get bread, wine and oil, they were bargaining with everything they had—especially shoes, which cost a half a scudo the pair." Having no money to pay the troops, Ascanio's officers began to distribute his personal property—valuable silks and silver vessels— to appease the soldiers' increasing discontent. But the men were discouraged by something greater than their lack of pay: there were fewer than nine hundred of them, and they were facing some eight thousand papal troops. After a long battle that lasted more than a month, the Colonna army finally surrendered on May 9. The pope had decisively won the war.

In the aftermath of the Colonna surrender, Paul began his final round of destruction. Despite fervent pleas from Charles to spare a few of the Colonna's feudal lands, he razed the fortifications of Marino, Rocca di Papa, and Paliano to the ground. Ascanio was declared an enemy of the Papal States, and went into exile in the kingdom of Naples, living in holdings he had inherited from his father at Albe and Tagliacozzo, roughly forty miles to the east of Marino. Charles continued to plead on Ascanio's behalf, asking the pope at least to allow Ascanio's son Marcantonio to have possession of some of the Colonna fiefs, but Paul was not to be dissuaded. Ascanio remained in exile until Paul's death in 1549; the new pope, Julius III (born Giovanni Maria Ciocchi del Monte), offered him pardon and returned his lands. As a gesture of thanks, Ascanio gave Julius an enormous porphyry basin, dug up from the ruins near the Colosseum, which is now in the rotunda of the Pio Clementino Museum in the Vatican. The reconciliation lasted only a few years: in 1556, Julius excommunicated Ascanio again and confiscated all of his goods. But that is another story.

And Vittoria? How did she react to her brother's exile and the loss of so many of the family's properties? In a letter sent to Cardinal Farnese on May 14, de' Rossi described a recent conversation he had with her: "Great satisfaction is universally felt at the taking of Paliano, which I immediately made known and published everywhere . . . Nor did I fail to report the news to the Signora Marchesa, who replied: 'Possessions come and go, so long as people are safe.'" Of all the splendid things Vittoria said in her poems or letters, this comment is among her finest. What a perfect retort to the gloating governor, who was so pleased with the bad news he had to share; what an elegant and sharp and humanly decent response to the loss of Paliano and the destruction of so much of her family's lands.

The only other comment of Vittoria's that has survived comes in a letter she sent to Ercole II d'Este two weeks after de' Rossi's letter to Farnese. "Your Excellence should know," she began, "that I am most consoled in my distress, and I thank God that with the loss of worldly goods, fortune has given me the occasion to acquire goods of the mind." Vittoria hardly needed a reminder of this lesson: When was it not the case that spiritual goods were more important to her than earthly possessions? But she had allowed herself to get involved in this conflict in a way she never had before, and the emotional cost was high. Despite her reassurances to Ercole, Vittoria seems to have struggled to reconcile herself to what had befallen her family, and she made an unusually quick series of moves in search of a new home. First she took leave of Orvieto, which had given her little more than chickens and marzipan, and found her way back to Rome. But Rome did not suit her, it seems, at this time; perhaps she needed to be farther away from everything that had just transpired. Within a few months of her arrival, she set out again in pursuit of a more strictly spiritual community, drawn by the presence of a particular holy man.

LATE LOVE

I N AUGUST 1541, Reginald Pole was preparing to take up his new post as legate of the patrimony of Peter, the area of the Papal States centered in Viterbo. The position of legate was equivalent to that of governor for the provincial cities ruled by Rome, and the cardinals who assumed these roles were in charge of the ecclesiastical administration in each region. Vittoria had come to know Pole in Rome sometime between 1536 and 1538, and found him one of the most compelling people she had ever met. Pole was by birth an English aristocrat of the highest rank. His mother, Margaret Pole (née Plantagenet), Countess of Salisbury, was the daughter of George, Duke of Clarence, the brother of the kings Edward IV and Richard III. Clarence was one of the principal players during the final throes of the War of the Roses, the civil war that divided England in the second half of the fifteenth century. After betraying his brother Edward's interests on several occasions, Clarence was ultimately brought before Parliament on charges of treason and executed in the Tower of London in 1478. (Shakespeare's version of the story in *Richard III* is largely a distortion of the facts.) Pole's father, Sir Richard, was an important nobleman from North Wales, and served as the personal chamberlain to Arthur, Prince of Wales, the eldest son of Henry VII. Arthur was briefly married to Catherine of Aragon before dying at the age of seventeen, leaving his bride, with famously disastrous consequences, to his brother.

Reginald Pole began his own career promisingly enough. He was a favorite of Henry VIII, who granted him a handsome position in the English church—the deanery of Wimborne Minster in Dorset—when he was only eighteen years old. Three years later, in 1521, Pole persuaded Henry's lord chancellor, the (at the time) all-powerful Sir Thomas Wolsey, to send him to Padua to study. In Padua, Pole was introduced to the rich world of Italian humanism by none other than Bembo, who took the young Englishman under his wing. Pole returned to England in 1527, but was soon sent off to Paris to help secure support for Henry's divorce from Catherine. At this point, relations began to sour between Pole and Henry, due to Pole's negative opinion of the divorce. Before long, he ran into opposition from none other than Thomas Cromwell, Henry's chief henchman, who gave him the sinister advice that he should read Machiavelli's *Prince* more carefully.

By 1532, Pole found himself in more trouble due to rumors that a marriage was being arranged for him with Catherine's daughter, Princess Mary, the future Mary I. The idea of such a union, with English royalty on both sides, was threatening to Henry, who was finalizing plans to wed Anne Boleyn and had high hopes of producing a male heir. Whether or not the rumors of the match between Mary and Pole were true, Pole realized he had become a target of Henry's suspicion, and decided to flee England. After some months in France, he returned to Padua, where he once again received a very warm reception. Between the time of his arrival in Padua and his being called to Rome in 1536, he wrote what would become his most famous book, *De unitate*, or *A Defense of the Unity of the Church*, which circulated for several years in manuscript before its publication in 1539. As its title suggests, this was a treatise in favor of holding the church together with the pope at its helm, and hence argued against Henry's claim for royal supremacy. It concluded with a strong warning to the English king to repent.

At the same time that *De unitate* defended the pope's authority, its

doctrinal position was unequivocally in favor of Protestant-minded reform. For Pole used the occasion both to lay out the arguments for
justification by faith, and to stress the importance of personal experience over the sacraments or priestly instruction as the basis for religious belief. This combination of loyalty to the institution of the Catholic
Church and a commitment to core tenets of Protestantism would come
to haunt Pole later in his career—Catholics accused him of being a
Lutheran; Lutherans accused him of being a Catholic. But in the 1530s,
it was still possible to bring these two strands together. Indeed, Pope
Paul rewarded Pole for *De unitate* by making him a cardinal in 1536,
along with Bembo and Contarini. In retrospect, this was the moment
of Paul's greatest interest in reform. Henry, meanwhile, was ever more
incensed by Pole's behavior, and with good reason: in addition to at-
tacking Henry's claims for independence from Rome, Pole was also
responsible for spreading rumors that Henry had burned the bones of
Thomas Becket, the supreme Catholic martyr of the English church.
Henry ultimately blamed Pole for his excommunication from the
Roman church in December 1538, and tried multiple times to arrange
for Pole's assassination. Pole, in turn, called the rulers of England "of-
fensive to the whole human race."

It is likely that Vittoria met Pole around the time of his appointment to the curia—Pope Paul supposedly consulted with her about his
choice of new cardinals, so she would certainly have heard about the
unusual Englishman at this time. Whenever it was that she came to
know him personally, he seems to have made a strong impression upon
her as a deeply spiritual being. In a letter to Marguerite de Navarre
written in February 1540, she described the lofty conversations she
and Pole had together, and declared that he was "always in the heavens,
and only for the needs of others does he look to and bother with the
earth." This account of Pole does not entirely square with a life spent
maneuvering between factions in England and Italy, and surviving
plot after plot against him (in this regard, he had read his Machiavelli
very well). But Vittoria was obviously uninterested in these aspects of
her new friend. What she saw was his manner, which was innocent and
unassuming—he was a man of slender build, with a cheerful face and

an immensely bushy beard (see plate 18)—and his habits, which were especially abstemious for a cardinal of the Roman church. He did not eat large meals, he slept very little, and he had no interest in accumulating wealth. In his modest self-presentation, along with his aristocratic pedigree and his subtle intertwining of Protestant ideas with loyalty to the Catholic Church, Pole may have reminded Vittoria a bit of herself—they were, in many respects, secret-sharers. Whatever the source of the attraction, Vittoria was sufficiently drawn to Pole by the fall of 1541 that she followed him to Viterbo.

Vittoria's decision to move to Viterbo within a month or two of resettling at the convent of San Silvestro in Capite in Rome was in many ways surprising. Viterbo was not a city she knew well, and her only experience there had been traumatic: it was in Viterbo that she had received the news of Ferrante's death in the fall of 1525. Rome, however, may well have felt gloomy to her following the recent devastation visited upon her family; not only was Ascanio in exile and his properties in the Castelli Romani all lost, but the pope had even seized the Palazzo Colonna at the foot of the Quirinal Hill. Despite the many friends she still had in the city, including Michelangelo, Vittoria felt the urge to move, as she had on so many other occasions in her life. It is quite extraordinary, in fact, how frequently she moved from place to place: the idea that she had once wanted to live the rest of her days within the walls of a single convent seems hard to believe.

The choice of Viterbo, as opposed to the many cities in which she had friends and relations, made sense only in terms of her desire to be near Pole and the extraordinary group of people he was assembling around him. In the space of a few months, Viterbo had become the absolute center of the Italian reform movement. Pole was known to be one of the strongest advocates for reform in the Roman church, and from his days in Padua, he had developed close ties with a number of the leading Italian reformers. This group included Giovanni Morone, the bishop of Modena (and, by coincidence, the son of the man whom Ferrante had betrayed behind the arras in 1525); Marcantonio Flaminio, the great humanist and philosopher; and Alvise Priuli, the Venetian nobleman whom Pole met when he first came to Padua in 1521, and who became Pole's lifelong companion. According to Pole's recent biographer, the two men lived more or less as a married couple for thirty years; Priuli accompanied Pole whenever possible on his travels, and Pole retired for long stretches of time to Priuli's beautiful home in the Veneto. There is even evidence that they requested (but were denied) a joint burial.

What made this remarkable assembly in Viterbo possible was not only the arrival of Pole, but also the death of Valdés in the summer of 1541, which resulted in the fracturing of his tight-knit *spirituali* circle in Naples. Certain members of that group had already begun to disperse due to the perceived threat from the office of the Spanish Inquisition, which seemed to be weighing the possibility of expanding its jurisdiction to the Kingdom of Naples (the Roman Inquisition had not yet been reestablished, as we shall discuss shortly, but the Spanish sought to operate through bishops and even secular authorities). These men were in search of a safe haven when Pole moved to Viterbo and established what came to be known as the Ecclesia Viterbiensis, as if it were a church of its own. Among Valdés's followers who came to Viterbo was Pietro Carnesecchi, who had long enjoyed the patronage of the Medici family and was one of the absolute favorites of Clement VII, for whom he had served as papal secretary. Carnesecchi was at the same time deeply involved with the *spirituali* movement, and a close friend of Valdés's great devotee Giulia Gonzaga. This combination of papal privilege and reformist zeal was not unusual for this group, many of whom held major positions in the church.

What took place at Viterbo in the first years of the 1540s was different from anything Vittoria had participated in over the past decade. She was no stranger to reformist circles: she had spent, as we have seen, nearly a year at the ducal palace in Ferrara with Renée and her fellow French Protestants, and she had been around the followers of Ochino and Valdés for several years in Rome. But the atmosphere in Viterbo was much more tense. By the fall of 1541, the problems facing the Roman church had taken on real urgency, and Pole and his friends were desperately trying to hold on to whatever strands of reform they could.

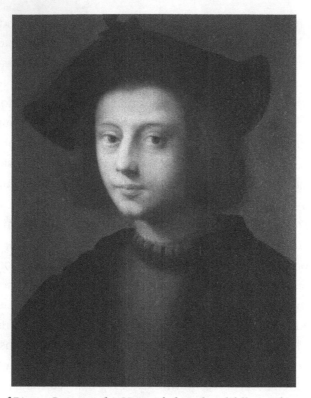

Portrait of Pietro Carnesecchi, Vittoria's friend and fellow reformer, by the
sixteenth-century painter Domenico Puligo (Gallerie degli Uffizi, Florence)

There was, in effect, a bomb ticking under the floors of the Ecclesia Viterbiensis: the bomb of the Counter-Reformation.

The members of Pole's circle were as aware as they could possibly
be, without the benefit of hindsight, that they were living at one of
the most crucial moments of transition in the history of Western
Christianity. The immediate context for the crisis was the collapse of
negotiations between Protestants and Catholics at the Diet of Regensburg, which Charles V had convened in the spring of 1541 in an effort
to calm the ever-growing religious tensions within his realm. This was
not the first time Charles had called such a meeting: there were two
other conferences held in 1534 and 1539 at Leipzig, but neither had
achieved any success, and the emperor had been determined to do
everything possible to reach an agreement at Regensburg. He chose six

theologians to participate in the discussions: three Protestants, including the famous Philip Melanchthon and Martin Bucer, and three Catholics, whose names are less well known. The dialogue lasted approximately
a month before ending on a note of failure in late May 1541.

Contarini had served as the papal representative to Regensburg and
had tried, often against Pope Paul's will, to forge a compromise with
the Protestants on the central issue of justification by faith. He brought
back to Rome the agreement he had proposed in Germany with the
hope that it might be adopted by the papal curia. Pole and others in
Viterbo, meanwhile, were in regular contact with Contarini, with the
aim of finding a solution that might placate the different camps. But
the battle lines had been drawn on both sides. For the committed Italian Lutherans, the proposals put forward by Pole and his allies were nothing short of embarrassing. Thus Francesco Negri, an ex-Benedictine
schoolmaster and Protestant enthusiast, exclaimed:

> I cannot but be amazed at Cardinal Pole of England with his Priuli
> and Flaminio, at Cardinal Morone, at Signor Ascanio Colonna . . .
> who seem to have created a new school of Christianity fashioned to suit
> themselves, where, true, they do not deny that the justification of
> man is accomplished by Jesus Christ but then do not want to admit
> the consequences which necessarily flow from them. Because they
> want just the same to have the pope, they want to have Masses, they
> want to observe a thousand other papist superstitions and impieties,
> all wholly contrary to truly Christian piety.

The whole group at Viterbo was accused of conceding too much to the
papal cause, and compromising the crucial message of the Reformation. (The mention of Ascanio, meanwhile, who was in exile at the time
and could hardly be considered a major player, was perhaps in lieu of
naming his actively involved sister.)

On the other end of the spectrum, Paul was under great pressure
within the papal curia from the increasingly powerful Gian Pietro Carafa, a fiercely conservative cardinal of violent tendencies who wanted
to prevent any contamination of Catholicism by the Lutherans. Carafa,

who came from an aristocratic family in the kingdom of Naples, and later became a truly tyrannical pope as Paul IV, was himself a zealous reformer, but in a direction diametrically opposed to the Protestants. He wanted a much stricter adherence to Catholic doctrine, and a more ascetic approach to clerical life. He was, in effect, a fundamentalist. Carafa especially hated the Jews, whom he punished with one of the most repressive bulls ever issued, restricting them to the Roman ghetto, which was locked up every night, and limiting their ownership of property, their employment, even their right to keep accounting books in Hebrew (they had to be in Italian). In addition to his immensely unpopular religious measures, he also made some grievous political mistakes: swayed by his manipulative and treacherous nephew Carlo

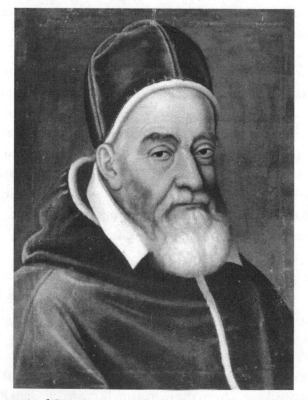

Portrait of Gian Pietro Carafa after he became Pope Paul IV,
by an eighteenth-century artist from the Veneto
(Accademia di Belle Arti Tadini, Lovere)

Carafa, Paul IV forged an alliance with the French and went to war against Spain, resulting in the massive defeat of the papal armies in 1557. So loathed was the Carafa pope by the entire Roman populace that when he died in 1559, the people rioted in the streets and laid waste to his statues, as well as to the palaces he had built for the church.

In the early 1540s, Pope Paul III fell under Cardinal Carafa's sway, and was ultimately persuaded to close all talks with Contarini and the other moderates in the curia. In July 1542, Paul issued his fateful bull known as the *Licet ab initio*, which reconstituted the office of the Inquisition in Rome (the earliest known document of the Roman Inquisition dates from 1266, but it then entered a dormant state for several centuries). In Renaissance Italy, there were inquisitorial courts operating locally—individual cities and states had their own inquisitors, who were dedicated to rooting out heresy in the area—but the church had no real administration dedicated to the cause. In Spain, for example, the most independent of the national churches, the Inquisition was famously active, but it did not coordinate its efforts with Rome. This was why Valdés was able to escape from the Spanish inquisitors to the safe haven of Rome in the early 1530s.

Efforts on the part of the pope to coordinate the various offices of the Inquisition dated back to the thirteenth century, but it was not until after Paul III published the *Licet ab initio* that Rome sought to centralize the persecution of heresy. Paul called for a church council, to be held at the northern city of Trent, in order to consolidate the Catholic faith and tighten the noose around anyone who broke away from its most orthodox positions. In this respect, the Council of Trent had the opposite aim of the Diet of Regensburg, which had been Charles V's attempt to bring Protestants and Catholics together. From the moment the council was invoked, the reformers inside the curia were no longer colleagues. They were potential heretics.

Although Paul began to gather delegates in Trent in 1542, the council officially began in 1545, and ended eighteen years later, in 1563. Over the course of its twenty-five sessions, it shaped the positions of the church for the next four hundred years. The delegates at Trent, who ranged in number, depending on the session, from 34 to more than

250, systematically clarified, and hardened, nearly every position in Catholic theology. The sacraments were given new emphasis; justification by faith was denounced; Lutheran ideas of predestination were roundly condemned. Holy Scripture, the council decreed, could be read only after a license was obtained in writing from the proper church authorities—something that happened in the rarest of cases— and booksellers were prohibited from selling Bibles in any vernacular language. The so-called Index of Forbidden Books was introduced, naming all of the heretical texts that could not be printed or read, under pain of severe punishment. Clerical morals and behavior were more narrowly defined, and the enclosure of nuns much more strenuously enforced. These positions, and seemingly innumerable others, came to define the Catholic Church, so that religious scholars typically divide its history between pre- and post-Trent. The extravagance and laxity that Luther so despised were now strictly reined in, but certainly not in the direction he had hoped.

Let us return, however, to the moment before the door closed on the Italian reformers, the moment when change still seemed within their grasp. In the early 1540s, it was not only an elite group of cardinals and humanists in Viterbo—or Ferrara or Naples—who were drawn to the tenets of Protestantism. Luther's ideas were spreading far and wide, and there were priests throughout the Italian peninsula both preaching against the corruptions of the papacy and advocating for serious changes in the way individuals understood their relationship to God. Italian translations of the Bible were circulating widely, almost all of which had a distinctly Protestant orientation. The most popular of these, a translation by the humanist scholar and reformer Antonio Brucioli, was dedicated to Anna d'Este, the daughter of Renée and Ercole II. Brucioli began his text with a prefatory letter challenging the church's monopoly over access to Holy Scripture:

> Some may indeed exclaim that it is an unworthy thing for a woman, or a shoemaker to speak of Sacred Scriptures and attempt to comprehend it through their own reading. Let us consider, also, who were Christ's listeners, oh, do we not find a varied multitude of blind

men, cripples, mendicants, publicans, centurions, craftsmen, women, and children? Should Christ now be deprived of being read by those by whom he wanted to be heard?

In addition to reading the Bible in their mother tongue, Italians interested in reformist ideas also had access to several very popular books of spirituality. The most successful of these was entitled the *Beneficio di Cristo*. The earliest version of the *Beneficio* was written by a Benedictine monk known as Benedetto of Mantua during his residence in the late 1530s at the monastery of San Nicolò l'Arena in the Sicilian city of Catania; his text was then extensively revised by Flaminio, possibly with the help of others in the Viterbo circle. The *Beneficio* was published in 1543, but circulated in manuscript a few years earlier. In late 1541 or early 1542, a fierce attack on it was written by Catarino, the same friar who had delivered the sermons Vittoria and Michelangelo attended so enthusiastically at San Silvestro in 1537.

Despite Catarino's opposition, the *Beneficio* captured in nearly every way what people like Vittoria and Michelangelo found appealing about reformed theology. At its core, it set out to persuade its readers that all they needed for salvation was the love of Christ. The authors were not interested in institutional problems, nor did they engage very much with matters of ecclesiastical authority. In this respect, the book was above the fray of contemporary debate, its tone more mystical than political. But although its central message—that the most important relationship in Christianity was between the individual believer and Christ—may not sound polemical, it threatened the very core of the church establishment. The problem was a simple one: If each individual, however humble or poor, can receive the "benefit of Christ" directly, what need is there for priests and bishops and popes? The *Beneficio* was not consistently Lutheran, but it openly embraced the doctrine of *sola fide*. "Faith itself justifies," the author concluded, "meaning that God receives as just, all those who truly believe that Jesus Christ has satisfied for their sins."

Condemned by the Council of Trent in 1546, the *Beneficio di Cristo* was placed on the Index of Prohibited Books in 1549. But in the years between its publication in 1543 and its arrival on the Index, it was said to have sold forty thousand copies in Venice alone. The bishop of Modena, Morone, even commissioned a local bookseller to distribute free copies to all interested members of his diocese. This was a rather extravagant gesture of proselytizing, and it shows how openly, and aggressively, the ideas of reform were being pushed. From our perspective, the book gives a tantalizing glimpse of the direction the Catholic Church could have taken if things had gone differently: if the Diet of Regensburg had been successful and a compromise had been reached between Catholics and Protestants; if the pope had been more open-minded and listened to Contarini and Pole; if Carafa had not assumed so much power; the list goes on. The *Beneficio* captured the spirit of optimism and ambition that was still in the air on the eve of Trent.

This was the climate that Vittoria entered when she came to Viterbo in 1541. As always, she eschewed lodgings in the palaces or villas of friends, and took up residence instead in the convent of Santa Caterina, located just inside the formidable city walls on the outskirts of Viterbo's medieval center. The convent itself has not survived, and the original building has been extensively changed over the centuries, but the piazza on which it stood still boasts a beautiful church, San Giovanni Zoccoli, whose origins date to the early eleventh century, and an impressive stone fountain built in 1246, whose lions were therefore spouting their water when Vittoria came and went from her rooms.

It is not clear, however, that Vittoria ventured out very often. Unlike her comings and goings from the convent to the ducal palace in Ferrara, her life in Viterbo seems to have been more sedentary. This was almost certainly due to her state of health, which continued to decline. But her lack of physical mobility did not mean she was in any way removed from the conversations of the Viterbo group. In a letter she sent to Giulia Gonzaga in December 1541 thanking her for sending Valdés's commentary on Saint Paul's Epistle to the Romans, she indicated that she and the others had been discussing the book together. "It was," she wrote, "in great demand, especially by me, who needs it the most." Another indication of her engagement came in a letter Contarini sent to Pole in the summer of 1542 describing in detail his position on penance, in which he specifically solicited Vittoria's opinion: "It is up to you and your *sancta et docta compagnia* [your holy and learned company] including the Marchesa, and to the pilgrims, to examine this carefully and to correct whatever needs correction." Vittoria also referred frequently in her letters to visits that various members of the group made to her rooms at Santa Caterina, including Priuli, Flaminio, Morone, Carnesecchi, and—albeit less regularly than she would have liked—Pole himself.

At the same time that Vittoria was clearly enjoying the stimulating atmosphere at Viterbo, she was also going through a spiritual crisis. The remark she made to Giulia about her having "the most need" of the commentary on Paul was linked to her feeling overwhelmed by her own sinfulness, and unsure of the path to take in order to find some relief. This crisis was likely in part precipitated by her having lost Ochino as her spiritual guide shortly after her arrival in Viterbo. The Capuchin monk had been under the pope's surveillance for many years, but in 1542, he was finally summoned to Rome. Guessing, correctly, that this could only be very bad news—life in prison, torture, burning at the stake were all very real possibilities—Ochino shed his cassock and fled Italy dressed as a layman. According to some contemporary reports, he was helped by Ascanio, who gave him a horse and a servant. Others claimed he went to Ferrara, where Renée furnished him with supplies. Whoever aided him in his journey, Ochino crossed the border to Switzerland and ended up in Calvin's Geneva, where he became preacher to the community of Italian Protestant exiles living in the city. There, he made any future return to Italy extremely unlikely by publishing several virulent works against the pope.

Vittoria almost certainly had nothing to do with Ochino's escape—indeed, she expressed genuine disapproval. She was in her heart very cautious, and would no doubt have preferred Ochino to reach some kind of compromise with Paul rather than disobey him so flagrantly. His disobedience to the pope was also threatening to her personally: given her well-known closeness to Ochino, she was rightly concerned that suspicion could turn to her. With these fears likely in mind, she had already begun to withdraw from her spiritual mentor and friend the year before his flight. Ochino sent her several letters that went unanswered, and even complained that she seemed to have forgotten him. "I would have been more than grateful to speak with you," he wrote to her from Florence just before leaving Italy in August 1542, "or to have ... a letter from you, but it has been more than a month since I have heard from you."

Even receiving a letter from Geneva, the hotbed of Calvinism, was a red flag at the time, and Vittoria quickly passed the next letter that Ochino sent her on to the papal authorities. In her cover letter to the archly conservative Marcello Cervini—the cardinal who presided over the Council of Trent and in 1555 was elected to the papacy as Marcellus II, a position that he held for only twenty-one days before dying of an apoplectic fit—she explained that she was well aware that "if a letter or anything else should come to me from Fra Bernardino [Ochino], I had better send it to your most reverend Lordship without answering it." She also indicated that she was enclosing both Ochino's letter and a small book that he had sent her. "The whole was in one packet," she specified, "without any other writing inside." The only palpable note of distress in her letter came in the postscript, where she scribbled: "It grieves me very much that the more Ochino thinks to excuse himself, the more he accuses himself, and the more he thinks to save others from shipwreck, the more he exposes them to the flood, since he is already outside of the ark that saves and secures." Vittoria clearly felt exposed, if not abandoned, by Ochino, whose behavior by no means protected her interests. However much she may have still cared for him, she had no intention of leaving the ark of the church and finding herself among the drowning.

It was surely no coincidence that Vittoria turned her full attention to Pole at the moment of losing Ochino. However close she was to Michelangelo, she craved the presence of a religious figure who could help with the spiritual crisis she was undergoing. The choice of Pole, meanwhile, was a much safer one than Ochino had ever been: he was a distinguished member of the church elite, and enjoyed, at least at the time, the full protection of the pope. But there was nothing strictly rational or strategic about Vittoria's attachment to Pole, which became like an obsession, and at times seemed to nurse rather than heal what she regarded as her disease.

The first important episode in Vittoria's friendship with Pole came a year before Ochino's flight. At this time, Pole made an extraordinary gesture: he asked Vittoria, who was ten years his senior, to be his new mother. Pole's real mother, Margaret, had met a horrific end earlier that spring at the hands of Henry VIII. Her execution was largely a form of retaliation against Pole, who had become an ever greater enemy of Henry's, and yet continued to escape his grasp. Normally Henry was not known for having trouble killing those in his way, but he somehow could not get his hands on Pole. When Pole was staying at Priuli's house in the Veneto in 1538, an English agent named Harry Phillips made an assassination attempt, but Pole was unscathed, and proceeded to Toledo on a mission to convince Charles V to help depose Henry by ending all trade relations with him. Pole's bid was unsuccessful, but Henry seems to have learned of the meeting, and subsequently outlawed Pole from England. Meanwhile, Pole's two brothers, Henry, Lord Montagu, and Sir Geoffrey, were also working from within England to depose Henry, and were arrested for their involvement in the so-called Exeter Conspiracy, a supposed plot to replace the king with Henry Courtenay, Marquis of Exeter, a close ally of the Pole family. Geoffrey was ultimately pardoned, but Montagu was beheaded along with Exeter himself.

Margaret Pole, too, was arrested at the time, and became Henry's prisoner. The king regarded her as an enemy not only because of her involvement with her sons' various plots against him, but also due to her continued closeness to his own daughter Mary, whom he had denounced as a bastard. Indeed, Henry held Margaret personally responsible for having tried to arrange the marriage between his daughter and her son (Reginald) years earlier. In 1539, there was also rumor of a threatened invasion of England by the French king, Francis I, with the possible involvement of Charles V. Due to Pole's ties to Henry's enemies, his mother's estates on England's south coast were regarded as a potentially dangerous staging ground for the foreign troops crossing

the Channel and, in November 1539, Margaret was taken to the
Tower of London. She remained there for nearly a year and a half, when,
on the morning of May 27, 1541, she was brought to East Smithfield
Green, where a wooden block awaited her. According to one witness,
she was met by "a wretched and blundering youth . . . who literally
hacked her head and shoulders to pieces in the most pitiful manner."
Even her interrogators conceded that she was a heroic figure. "We have
dealt with such a one as men have not dealt with before us," one of
them said, and "may call her rather a strong and constant man than a
woman."

When the news of Margaret's death reached Pole, he was hiding
away in the remote town of Capranica on top of a rocky outcrop in
the north of Lazio. According to his secretary and first biographer,
Ludovico Beccadelli, Pole reacted by withdrawing into his oratory for
an hour, and then emerged in good humor, declaring that he was now
the son of a martyr. A few months later, Pole approached Vittoria to
take Margaret's place. This idea had first been proposed by Vittoria
herself, in a sonnet she sent to Pole sometime after his mother was imprisoned. "My son and my lord," the sonnet began,

> if your first and true
> mother lives in prison, they have not taken
> her wise soul or stripped her fine spirit . . .
> To me, who seem to go about free and light,
> and keep my closed heart buried in a small space,
> may it please you to turn your glance here,
> so that your second mother does not perish.*

Following Margaret's death, Pole warmly embraced the idea. The letter
of condolence Vittoria sent to him is missing, but in Pole's response
from early August 1541, he eagerly affirmed her new role:

* S1.141: "*Figlio e signor, se la tua prima e vera / Madre vive prigion, non l'è già tolto / L'anima saggia o 'l chiaro spirto sciolto / . . . / A me, che sembro andar scarca e leggera / E 'n poca terra ho il cor chiuso e sepolto, / Convien ch'abbi talor l'occhio rivolto / Che la seconda tua madre non pera.*"

It is fitting that your Excellence do so, You whom I have always revered after recognizing in your virtues the highest gifts of God, and
especially now, since Pharaoh's madness has ripped away from me my
own mother, I accept you in her place, not like the woman whose son
Moses later denied being, although she was the daughter of the Pharaoh, but like the woman whom, if you should undertake to care for
me, I will surely always be praising—I who seem no less deserted than
Moses as an infant, exposed not only to the dangers of the river as he
was, but also to those of the land and sea . . . I who will be received by
the daughter of a great king, the same who deserted the Pharaoh and
his army.

In this extraordinary use of the biblical story, Pole casts himself as Moses, the abandoned infant, desperately in need of maternal care. Vittoria, meanwhile, is not the maternal surrogate, Pharaoh's daughter—a
poor substitute for Moses's real mother—but the equivalent of Jo-
chebed herself, who pretended to be a nursemaid in order to suckle her
son. Since Pharaoh is so clearly identified with Henry VIII, it seems
Pole ultimately identifies Vittoria both as his new mother and as the
pope's spiritual daughter: she is "the daughter of a great king," who has
given up the treasonous ruler.

Vittoria's role as Pole's new mother was not a passing fancy that arose
in the immediate aftermath of his loss. On the contrary, he treated it as
an official position. In a letter written in mid-August 1541 to Antonio
Pucci, the governor of Bagnoregio, he referred to Vittoria's new role as
if it were official: "I cannot omit," he concluded, "that the Marchesa of
Pescara, my new mother, whom I saw recently at Bagnoregio, has been
well served by relatives of your Lord and guests in your name." Bagnoregio, a beautiful town not far from Orvieto, was where Pole spent
much of the summer of 1541; Vittoria presumably stopped there on her
way back from Orvieto to Rome. Word of the new arrangement between Vittoria and Pole, meanwhile, circulated among their mutual
friends. In a letter sent to Vittoria that fall, Bembo referred to Pole as
"*vostro figliuolo*," or "your little boy."

At first Vittoria embraced the idea of assuming a maternal relationship to Pole. There was, of course, a real poignancy to this: as a childless woman, she seems to have welcomed the opportunity to occupy the role of mother, however artificial the ties might be. We see her trying out the part, as it were, in her only letter to Pole from the summer of 1541 that has survived. She began by apologizing for bothering him with her "*frascarie*," or "worthless ramblings"—the word literally means "twigs"—and then begged him to accept what she, as his mother, could give him: "If Your Lordship is truly wont to say, in the words of Saint Paul, that it is better to give than to receive, allow me this blessedness, and allow yourself to be deprived of the desire to be more blessed than your mother, given that Saint Paul says it is the parents who should give to their children, not the children to parents."

No sooner, however, did Vittoria declare her desire to be the generous one—to give rather than receive—than she asked him to acknowledge her great indebtedness to him. "And believe," she continued, "that I am extremely obligated to you, both for spiritual things and for worldly things, which in my great need and exile, you of all people have given to me, and consoled me, and helped me, and accommodated me, and I kiss your hands." Vittoria's mention of her "exile" may offer a clue as to what drew her to Pole. Perhaps the devastating losses sustained by her family earlier that year had made her feel homeless; perhaps she felt that Pole, himself in exile from England, understood what it felt like to be unmoored in this way. But even more important than the idea of exile was her feeling of being "extremely obligated" ("*extremamente obligata*"). With this phrase, the pretense of her being in loco parentis fell away, and the desperate emotional dependence she felt in relation to Pole came flooding over her. However much she wanted to be his parent, she inevitably ended up as his child. As she candidly put it in a letter to Morone: "I confess to your Lordship that I was never so obliged to anyone as I am to Pole."

What was it about Pole that made Vittoria feel so dependent? One of the earliest and most revealing explanations came in a letter she sent to Giulia in the fall of 1541—the same letter in which she thanked Giulia for sending Valdés's commentary on Saint Paul to Viterbo. There, she wrote that she owed to Pole "the health of both my soul and my body, whereby the one for superstition, the other for bad governance, were in danger." According to Carnesecchi, who had occasion to give testimony about Vittoria's letter more than twenty years later, under circumstances to which we will return:

> The Lady Marchesa, before she took up a friendship with the cardinal, afflicted herself so much with fasting, hairshirts, and other types of mortifications of the flesh that she was reduced almost to skin and bones; and she did all this perhaps by putting too much faith in such works, imagining that in these lay true piety and religiosity, and, consequently, the salvation of her soul.

Fasts, hairshirts, mortifications of the flesh: these were practices that Giovio had already described Vittoria's partaking in with too much enthusiasm in 1527. It is possible she had never given them up, and also possible that she resumed her strict bodily penitence in times of turmoil or sadness.

Carnesecchi also explained that Vittoria had come to change her ways while she was in Viterbo, thanks to Pole's intervention: "But once she was admonished by the cardinal that by using such austerity and rigor against her body she was actually offending God more than anything else . . . the abovementioned lady began to withdraw from such an austere life, slowly scaling herself down to a reasonable and honest middle ground." We can conjure up the scene before us: Pole visiting the fragile and emaciated Vittoria in her rooms at Santa Caterina, where she was starving herself, and urging her, even commanding her, to treat her body as God's vessel.

Vittoria sent Morone a similar account of Pole's having rescued her from the brink:

> Every word of my Monsignor [Pole] is—I won't say the law that reduces the spirit into servitude, but an infallible rule, which liberates me to go along the straight path . . . If on this truest subject, which is so dear to me, I could have expounded, Your Magnificence would have seen the chaos of ignorance in which I used to dwell, and the labyrinth

of errors where I used to walk in safety, in which I believed that I
walked safely, dressed in that gold of light that flashes without holding
up to the comparison of true faith.

A "chaos of ignorance," a "labyrinth of errors": this is how Vittoria
characterized her life before meeting Pole. "My body," she continued,
"[was] continually moving to find inner tranquility, and my mind in
constant agitation trying to find peace. And God willed that he [Pole]
address me, saying *Fiat lux* [Let there be light], which showed me that
I was nothing and that in Christ I would find all things." Pole had, in
short, saved her from herself.

For Vittoria, the relationship with Pole was so obviously spiritual
that it was above all suspicion of carnal desire. Priuli, however, saw it
otherwise, and was clearly irritated, if not threatened, by Vittoria's attention to his companion. In a letter Vittoria sent to Priuli in the spring
of 1543, she defended herself against his accusation that she was too
physically drawn to Pole:

> As concerns my too famous flesh, that you all speak about, that is, that
> I have too much affection for such a spirit of God [Pole], which ac-
> cording to you can be a temptation . . . in writing about this to others,
> [our most venerable monsignor] has made me understand that it is
> not an error, for if it were error and temptation, his compassion would
> never have permitted him to declare it a sign of good.

Vittoria concluded with a strong affirmation of the spiritual bond between them: "with the monsignor, I further practice my faith by being
as directly receptive to God as he is." Vittoria and Priuli had a prickly
relationship, and she was clearly jealous of his much greater intimacy
with her beloved cardinal. But this letter serves as the strongest example of her conviction that her feelings were proper and chaste.

How exactly Pole produced such strong feelings in Vittoria remains
something of a mystery. He was neither a powerful preacher like Ochino,
nor a brilliant artist like Michelangelo; there were no sermons or paintings to move her. But Vittoria seemed to crave the company of Pole more

than anyone she had ever known (with the possible exception of Ferrante when she was a young bride). In July 1543, a month or two after she defended herself to Priuli, she wrote Pole a long letter in which she tried to explain her devotion to him:

> The Lord knows that I don't desire excessively to speak with you but for the fact that I perceive in [you] an order of spirit, which only the spirit senses, and which pulls me up to that fullness of light [so] that it does not let me wallow too long in my own misery, but rather with such high and substantial ideas it shows me the greatness up there and this baseness and lowness here below.

It is not clear whether Pole himself may have questioned her desire to speak with him, or whether she was still responding to Priuli's accusations. "The closer I, through His grace, walk toward Him," she continued,

> the more I need to speak to you, not out of anxiety or doubts or any worries I might have or fear to have through the goodness of He who assures these things, but because every time Your Lordship speaks of that stupendous sacrifice of eternal election, of being rewarded and of what was hidden being found on those mountains, gates and fountains . . . It makes my soul soar with its wings, sure that it is flying to the desired nest.

In all of Vittoria's correspondence, nothing comes close to the mysticism of this letter. Nowhere else did she describe her sensation of her spirit soaring, her recognition of the smallness of this world compared with the heavens, her perception of the brilliant radiance surrounding the divine. This kind of visionary rapture was what Pole alone unleashed in her. At the end of the letter, she declared: "For me, speaking with you is like speaking with an intimate friend of my groom [Christ], who readies me through this medium, and calls me to him and wills that I engage in discussions to spark and console me." Vittoria may have stared at Michelangelo's drawings of Christ for hours at a time.

But the closest she came to experiencing Christ's presence on earth was in the company of Pole.

Sometime the following year, in early 1544, Vittoria sent a letter to Pole in which she complained about Priuli's treatment of her. Relations between the two of them seem to have deteriorated further, and she claimed Priuli had actually chased her away from visiting Pole at all. "It seemed to [Priuli]," she bitterly remarked, "to take a thousand years before he could get me to leave, in order to protect you from the bother of a woman's visits." She then reassured herself, however, that her bonds to Pole could never be severed by mere physical distance. "I find in every way that this is the greatest truth," she exclaimed, "what you have written to me: namely, that we don't need to have our own place in this life, and in this regard I thank God, who saw fit to use Your Most Reverend Lordship to set for me the happiest place, reached through my faith, at your right hand, like a shoot of that true vine, which alone is sweet-smelling and dear." Vittoria's "we" is ambiguous— and Pole's original letter to which she is responding has not survived— but it could refer either to women, who are not assigned a place in the world in the same way as men, or to human beings more generally, whose life on this earth is inevitably temporary. But whoever else was included in this "we," for Vittoria the sentiment had a special resonance. As someone who had spent the previous two decades moving from place to place without ever fully settling, she finally thought she had found her home on this earth, at Pole's side.

At least this is where she would like to be, she declared, if only Pole would give her some sign of his dedication to her: "If I could truly feel that your only delight is to provide me with justice and wisdom and sanctification and redemption, I would not only be consoled in my wandering, even if the journey were full of thorns, but I would also have such a guarantee of the joy awaiting me at the port, that I would feel as if I were already on the path to peace, and not only on the path of hope." Vittoria may not ever have made her trip to the Holy Land, but she imagined her life as a pilgrimage—the verb she used here for "wandering" is *peregrinare*, the act of being a pilgrim—and Pole as her spiritual leader. For this reason, the letter concluded, she needed him to be near her: "since I cannot smell from far away the sweet smell of Christ borne in Your Most Reverend Lordship's voice, even if the mind has quieted the anxiety of its outer ills, my desires have grown through the nearer hope for my inner wellness." For someone whose language was almost always decorous and restrained, these words stand out as exceptional. It is hard not to think that Vittoria had fallen deeply in love, whatever that might mean, and that, as had happened to her with Ferrante some thirty years earlier, Pole's failure to return her affection was nearly unbearable.

All of this, needless to say, went far beyond anything Pole had bargained for when he asked Vittoria to be his mother. At times, he was clearly overwhelmed by her needs or demands. She sent him lengthy letters, he answered with short replies. "Two letters I've had from you," she wrote in August 1543, adopting the tone of a jilted lover, "which I must say was miraculous, more so to someone who did not know how brief they are, and that they are responses to many [letters] of mine." In letters to Morone, who had accompanied Pole to Trent when the council there was first convened, Vittoria complained about her loneliness in Viterbo, confiding that she felt "alone, cold, and unwell" ("*io sola fredda et inferma*"). Her only comfort, she said, came from "the certainty that [Your Lordship and Pole] pray to God for me and that Your Lordship consider my matters worthy of aiding."

There is one long letter from Pole to Vittoria, however, in which he expressed some of the complexity, if not outright anguish, of his feelings about her love. Written in October 1546, and addressed to "the Most Illustrious Lady and most honored mother," it reads like an apology—and perhaps also a justification—for the ways he had failed her. Pole began by recounting a conversation he had recently had at Bembo's house in Padua, where he had received a visit from an English friend, George Lily. Lily had come from Rome, where he had seen Vittoria, who had talked to him at length about her devotion to Pole (on this subject, it seems she shared her feelings quite freely). "No sooner had our Lily arrived here," Pole reported, "than he tired himself out in his first talk with me in vehemently trying to make me understand how heartily your Excellence wishes me well; and, as if this were something new and not already known to me, I let him go on as long as he liked (which was a long time), awaiting the conclusion he might draw from this."

Although Lily did not reproach Pole directly for his failure to reciprocate Vittoria's love, Pole made this point himself: "If this [conclusion] had been that which it deserved to be, drawing a comparison between my behavior and your great, and more than motherly love in order to condemn me for my ingratitude . . . I certainly would have taken pleasure in such a just reproof delivered with that simplicity which I have always treasured in him." "More than motherly love" ("*più che materno amore*")—the phrase is an intriguing one, and suggests that Pole was well aware that the title of "mother" did not fully accommodate the range of Vittoria's feelings. He continued:

> But, as he did not conclude thus, I will draw this conclusion myself, as so much the more to my embarrassment as I feel myself to have erred greatly in this and not ever to have set myself to correct the error, although I cannot say that I haven't worked hard to do that, which I know I ought to do in this regard, but, finding by experience that I cannot succeed as I would like, I let it go, as if God had deprived me of that grace of being able to satisfy my mind in that thing which I so much desire to do, which, in truth, sometimes gives me much trouble.

For Pole to say that "God had deprived me of that grace" of loving Vittoria, for him to wish that he could have returned her affection: this was the most honest, and no doubt the most painful, confession he ever made to her. He had tried to love her, and he had failed.

At this point in the letter, after having plumbed the depths of his self-reproach, Pole's tone became more pastoral:

> And when I try to console myself, I find no other form of consolation except to persuade myself, as I have said and written to Your Excellence on other occasions, that the divine will is such that it will give you the full reward that it promises to all of those who do not expect

any reward, as our Lord declares in the parable of those who invite the poor to share their feast.

Pole invoked here the Parable of the Guests in the Gospel of Luke, in which Jesus instructed his disciples: "when thou makest a feast, call the poor, the maimed, the lame, the blind / And thou shalt be blessed." It was with this hope of her future reward, Pole continued, that "I console myself, praying to God that he will make you ample restitution with as much affection of the soul as I am found on my part infinitely lacking in it." He ended by asking for her "pardon for my shortcomings." This was the last letter that Pole sent to Vittoria, or at least the last that has survived. Written only four months before her death, it was, in effect, a farewell to his friend.

When Vittoria received Pole's letter in the fall of 1546, the intense circle of reformers in Viterbo had dispersed. Pole had spent much of the previous year at Trent before withdrawing that summer to Priuli's house in the Veneto, and then continuing on to Padua. His official reason for leaving the council was due to his poor health, although some accused him of feigning illness to avoid signing the strict new decree against justification by faith, which was counter to everything he had always believed (under pressure, he later changed his mind). In Rome, meanwhile, the Holy Office of the Inquisition had begun its work, and the mood in the city was decidedly gloomier than it had been since perhaps the Sack of Rome. Vittoria, for her part, had withdrawn to a new convent, and closed the doors on the world.

LAST RITES

S OMETIME TOWARD THE END OF 1544, a rumor reached the ears of
Marguerite de Navarre that Vittoria was dead. Although they had
never met in person, Marguerite considered Vittoria a close friend—
she even imagined them to be related—and she took the news very
hard. After a few days of mourning, however, she was greatly relieved
to receive a letter from Vittoria herself, written sometime after the date
of her supposed death. Marguerite sent back this response:

> My cousin. It seemed to me that, having received your letter, I ought
> to say what Jacob said, who didn't respond to his sons, when they told
> him that Joseph was alive and reigning in Egypt, thinking that they
> were just trying to cheer him up. But when he saw the wagons filled
> with gifts sent from Joseph, then he believed them, and he said: it is
> enough for me, simply that Joseph lives. So, my cousin, having wept
> over your death, not questioning, of course, your happiness [in heaven],
> but considering the unhappiness of those for whom your presence on
> earth is so necessary (among whom I count myself), for several days I
> was unable to believe that you were really recovered; but when I then

not staying at San Silvestro in Capite, but whatever her reasons for switching convents, she was very happy in her new home. In a letter written to Ascanio sometime after she had settled in, she reported: "I get better every day, the place is dry and comfortable, and these most honorable and honest sisters have lived here for a long time."

Vittoria was in certain respects still living a life more suited to an aristocratic lady than a simple nun. She had a set of private rooms, where she was attended by her own maids, including her favorite, Prudenza Palma d'Arpino, who, according to Carnesecchi, shared Vittoria's reformist beliefs. She also kept several secretaries and valets in her employment until her death. But although she did not adhere to the more austere conditions of the sisters, she seems to have organized her days more than ever around the rituals of monastic life. She was also involved in keeping the nuns engaged with religious learning from the larger world. There is a letter, for example, that Vittoria wrote to the famous Spanish priest Ignatius of Loyola, the founder of the Jesuit order, to request that he send one of his preachers to Sant'Anna for the nuns' edification. A later report confirmed that the Jesuit scholar Alfonso Salmerón came to Rome, and obtained from Vittoria "*muçha satisfaçión y contentamiento.*"

At the same time that Vittoria concerned herself with the nuns' "edification," she seems to have valued Sant'Anna less for its intellectual stimulation—she had presumably had enough of this in Viterbo—than for its tranquility and isolation. In May 1545, Vittoria described to Morone how comfortable she was at the new convent: "I am much pleased with the solitude of Rome, and with the company of these pure and sweet spouses of our Lord, who maintain the faith that he has instilled in them both outwardly and inwardly. And at the same time, my Lord, Christ has always shown me that I am not adapted to the affairs of the world, so that so much the more it seems to me that I am doing the best." Nowhere else in her vast corpus of letters did she state her preference for "solitude" ("*la solitudine*") so plainly, or her feeling ill-equipped for the "affairs of the world" ("*negotii del mondo*"). As we know, this was hardly an accurate description of her activities over the past few decades: she was one of the most politically engaged women of

saw your letter, in which I seemed to hear your voice and spirit speak to me, I needed to say: it is enough for me, and praised be to God that my cousin and dear friend lives.

Marguerite's fear that Vittoria might be dead was not entirely unfounded. Vittoria had become very ill in the spring of 1543, and it was not clear she would survive. The cause of her illness was unknown. It was not simply her usual ailment, catarrh, which had been plaguing her for many years, but something more serious. In June 1543, the humanist scholar Claudio Tolomei wrote to Giuseppe Cincio, a well-known physician who was taking care of Vittoria in Viterbo, to inquire after her health:

> I am exceedingly distressed about the illness of the Marchesa of Pescara of which you write to me, as she is one of the women who ought to be revered by all, because having collected within her so much virtue, and goodness, and worth, and above all, because in these corrupt times she has done so many good works in the service of Christ . . . I beg you, Messer Giuseppe, to do everything in your power for the health of so noble a lady.

Less than two weeks later, the situation had improved, and Tolomei wrote to Cincio again to express his relief: "I am delighted to find from your letters that she is gradually recovering from her illness, for let me remind you, Messer Giuseppe, that in her life is bound up that of many others, who are continually sustained by her both in body and soul."

Vittoria was well enough to return to Rome sometime toward the end of that year, and in a letter that Bembo sent to Gualteruzzi in November, he described his great pleasure in hearing that "the Signora Marchesa has had a change of air, and vigorously ridden her horse [from Viterbo] to Rome, which," he added, "I take as a sign that her condition has improved and [that] she has regained her strength." By the summer of 1544, however, she was once again in a perilous state. At this point, one of the most celebrated doctors of the Renaissance,

Girolamo Fracastoro, came from Verona to see her. Fracastoro became famous for proposing a theory of disease based on the spreading of germs—some three hundred years before Louis Pasteur—and for his groundbreaking study of syphilis, a disease that he himself named. When he examined Vittoria, however, he found no trace of contagious disease, or of any physical ailment.

In an unusually frank letter that Fracastoro sent to her secretary Gualteruzzi upon returning to Verona, he declared that Vittoria's problems were not strictly physical. "Concerning the state of the most illustrious Marchesa of Pescara," he wrote,

> This, as you know, is my opinion, that as the body when it tyrannizes over the mind ruins and destroys all its soundness, so in the same way when the mind becomes the tyrant, and not merely the true lord, it wastes and destroys the soundness of the body first, and then their common bond of union . . . I have put forward this little discourse, my Lord, because I fancy that all of the Marchesa's sufferings had their origin in this.

"All of the Marchesa's sufferings had their origin in this": Vittoria's illness, he declared, began in her mind. The circumstances of Vittoria's life thankfully bore little resemblance to those of Shakespeare's Lady Macbeth, but Macbeth's questions to the physician attending on his wife resonate powerfully with Fracastoro's diagnosis:

> Canst thou not minister to a mind diseased,
> Pluck from the memory a rooted sorrow,
> Raze out the written troubles of the brain,
> And with some sweet oblivious antidote
> Cleanse the stuffed bosom of that perilous stuff
> Which weighs upon the heart?

The physician's response to Macbeth was a resounding no. "Therein," he said, "the patient / Must minister to himself."

Fracastoro was more hopeful than the Macbeths' physician about a cure for his patient, and he concluded his letter to Gualteruzzi with this recommendation:

> On which account, Signor Messer Carlo, I should wish for a physician of the mind to be found, who should minutely calculate and justly balance all the Marchesa's actions, giving to the master what is his and to the servant what belongs to him. And this physician must be wise, and of so much authority that her Ladyship would believe and obey him, like the most illustrious and most reverend Cardinal of England.

Whether he learned about her great attachment to the English cardinal from Vittoria directly or from other mutual friends, the time he spent with her had convinced him that Pole was the "physician of the mind" she most needed. Without him, or someone like him, he warned there was little chance of her surviving: "This beginning once put right, I do not doubt that all the rest will follow. Otherwise, I see that the most beautiful light of this world will in some strange way be extinguished and removed from our eyes, which may God avert of His goodness." It is hard to imagine how Fracastoro reached these conclusions, and what his encounter with Vittoria must have been like. Did she sound to him as if she had lost her mind, or convey a lack of desire to live? Whatever the conversation was between them, Fracastoro felt there was little chance of her recovering without what we would today consider psychotherapy.

There are no surviving letters between Pole and Vittoria from the summer or fall of 1544, so we cannot know whether it was he who brought about her recovery. But by the time she wrote to Marguerite, the crisis had passed. Vittoria was living in the Benedictine convent of Sant'Anna dei Funari, also known as Sant'Anna dei Falegnami (the names honor, respectively, the rope-makers and the woodworkers who lived in the neighborhood), not far from the Campo dei Fiori in the very heart of the city. For the first time in nearly twenty years, she was

the period, from her interventions for the Capuchins to her role as family diplomat. But it is striking that at the end of her life, Vittoria wanted to imagine herself only as a woman of the spirit.

Nearly everyone who saw Vittoria in person or communicated with her through letters during this period seems to have shared her perception. Sometime in 1545, Marguerite wrote to Georges d'Armagnac, who had recently been named a cardinal in Rome:

> My cousin, this letter will be only to ask you that you present and read to Madame the Marchesa of Pescara what I'm writing to her now, and since I recommend you to her in this way I pray that you please trust her and obey her as if it were myself . . . The life and conversation of Madame the Marchesa gives example both to you and to me of how to abandon all the transitory things in this world in order to live the life that will last eternally, and to learn to speak in the way they do in that great celestial court, where I believe that many of these great courtiers, who discuss things of the future and are eloquent in words, will find themselves more ignorant than beasts.

To be with Vittoria was to learn "how to abandon all the transitory things in this world"; it was to glimpse the "life that will last eternally." The idea that her language belonged to the "celestial court" was perhaps the greatest compliment that the poet and queen could give: even the finest courtiers, she remarked, were "more ignorant than beasts" compared with her eloquent friend.

Similar themes arose in a letter from June 1546 written to a friend by a nobleman from Brescia, Fortunato Martinengo, who had recently seen Vittoria in Rome:

> Certainly, my Monsignor, she is a rare and singular woman, and, from what I gather, very passionate about her love for Christ, which she speaks about all the time no less with her heart than with her mouth . . . I visited her on multiple occasions, and if I hadn't been afraid to bother her, I would never have agreed to leave her. She has

such a power of speech that it almost seemed as if chains fall from her mouth, which capture the senses of her listeners.

However weak Vittoria may have been physically, her voice had become formidable. Indeed, Martinengo's impression of being entranced by both the intensity of Vittoria's faith and her ability to convey her passion in words suggests she had entered a new phase of religious conviction. The angst she repeatedly described in Viterbo seems to have dissipated, and her focus shifted almost exclusively to the life that awaited her after death.

Signs of this transformation surfaced in Vittoria's letters to her dearest friends. To Marguerite, she wrote in May 1545 that "we never stop desiring divine things until we have reached the fruition of that which is real peace and the true end of every good desire." "In the infirmity of my body," she affirmed, "I feel the health of my inner being to be safe." Later that year, on Christmas Day, Vittoria expressed similar feelings to Pole: "I desire nothing in this world that has to do with this world, and I lack nothing in my assurance of enjoying the world to come." Although even in this context she did not deny her continued attachment to him—"I lack only your reverend," she confessed, "I desire only you"—she explained her desire for his company in terms much less desperate than before: "because you continually helped me (more than I could ever believe) to know myself, to humble myself, to reduce myself to nothing and live only in he who is our every good, consolation, joy, and happiness."

One of the surprising consequences of Vittoria's newly gained spiritual confidence was that she seems to have stopped writing poems. She left behind no explanation for this decision—if, of course, it was a decision, and not simply an accident of the archive. But given her fame as a poet, it is unlikely that a later body of her poems has been lost. Indeed, Vittoria's fame reached new heights in the last few years of her life. Not only were new editions of her sonnets regularly appearing, but a number of public lectures dedicated to individual poems from the *Rime* were also given at the prestigious Florentine Academy. In 1542, one member of the Academy spoke about the sonnet that opens, "*D'ogni sua gloria fu largo al mio sole*" ("God gave to my sun of every grace"); in 1545, another member gave a lecture on her sonnet "*Perché dal tauro l'infiammato corno*" ("When Apollo fills the fiery horn of the bull"). It is striking that both of these came from the early poems to Ferrante: for the literary scholars of the Florentine Academy, the more traditionally Petrarchan sonnets were of greater interest, it seems, than the spiritual sonnets circulating so widely among the public.

At the same time, however, that Vittoria's poetry became more and more celebrated, she herself retreated from the literary world. It is possible that as she became more confident about her spiritual life, even composing religious poems lost its appeal. Poetry had always been a means for her to work through uncertainty and doubt: it was a medium of change and transformation, not conviction. This was already clear in the poems for Ferrante, which helped her through mourning, and ultimately led her to exchange her earthly love for that of the divine. Once she felt more settled in her faith, she may have been less drawn to poetry as a vehicle for speaking to God. This is something she suggests in the last sonnet of the Michelangelo manuscript, which begins with a vocational cri de coeur:

> I fear the knot, which I have used for years
> to bind up my soul, now makes my poems
> through habit alone, and not for that first cause,
> when they were truly turned toward God and inspired.
> I fear that the knots are tied so tightly
> by one who works poorly, with a dull file,
> and fueled with false esteem, I think the days
> well spent, when perhaps they are all in vain.

Poetry has become a habit (the word she uses is *usanza*) and not the sincere and spontaneous expression of her faith that she wants it to be. She is ready, she declares, to put an end to her art:

> I see small reason for my poems' use, but much
> for their harm, whereby I pray the fire

that comes in silence will ignite my heart.
Broken up by cries painful and hoarse
is the true song that God hears from above,
He who looks to my heart, and not to my style.*

This was an extraordinary gesture: to conclude the collection of poems prepared for the great artist with a renunciation of art. Although
there is evidence that she continued to revise the sonnets over the following years—hence the multiple versions we have for many of them—
this sonnet may well have been her farewell to poetry.

If Vittoria gave up on the idea of communicating with God through
her poems, she did not give up on religious writing altogether. In the
final years of her life, she composed what was officially a series of
letters, but was in fact more like a spiritual meditation on the subject of
female piety. The letters were addressed to Costanza d'Avalos Piccolomini, Duchess of Amalfi and the sister of Alfonso, who had also
been raised in Ischia by their aunt Costanza d'Avalos when Vittoria was
living at the castle. The younger Costanza shared with Vittoria a passion for both poetry and religious reform: she was involved in the
spirituali movement in Naples, and became herself an accomplished
writer of devotional verse. Costanza also resembled Vittoria in her desire
to escape from the demands of her social world. Toward the end of her
life, although her husband, Alfonso Piccolomini, was still living, she
withdrew from his company to reside in the convent of Santa Chiara in
Naples.

In the first of the three letters, Vittoria addressed Costanza as
someone who enjoyed a rare and privileged relationship to Christ. She
imagined Costanza's spirit as having traveled to the heavens, where

---

* S1.179: "*Temo che 'l laccio, ov'io molt'anni presi / Tenni li spirti, ordisca or la mia rima / Sol per usanza, e non per quella prima / Cagion d'averli in Dio volti e accesi. / Temo che sian lacciuoli intorno tesi / Di colui ch'opra mal con sorda lima, / E mi faccia parer da falsa stima / Utili i giorni forse indarno spesi. / Di giovar poca, ma di nocer molta / Ragion vi scorgo, ond'io prego 'l mio foco / Ch'entro in silenzio il petto abbracci ed arda. / Interrotto dal duol, dal pianger roco / Esser dee il canto vèr colui ch'ascolta / Dal cielo, e al cor non a lo stil riguarda.*"

she communed with the divine, while Vittoria remained in a passive, vicarious role, awaiting her return to earth. "If you understand yourself," she wrote, "as I believe you do, as being that young beloved, who understands divine secrets in his most holy heart, by that dear delight that ties us into one desire, I pray that upon your expected return you allow me to share, as you always do, in the grace you have received." For the first time in her life, Vittoria was seeking spiritual enlightenment from another woman.

By the second letter, Vittoria dropped Costanza's role as her intermediary and described her own mystical visions of Mary. Upon awaking that morning, she wrote, "my dearest thought saw with my inner eye Our Lady of the heavens embrace her Son with great affection and overabundant joy, and in the purest light I seemed to see a thousand strands, which tied them together with knots of the most burning compassion." Vittoria saw in her "inner eye" Mary's flight above the celestial choir, the archangels, the cherubs, and the seraphim until Mary reached the Holy Trinity. Through this experience, Vittoria related, Christ's mother became a divine teacher herself: "Think . . . what wise words flowed from her saintly mouth, what pious and clear rays shone from those divine lights, what most righteous advice gave law to those who heard her without ever deviating from the laws, like a real master made by the first master of all."

After seeing Mary's heavenly journey, Vittoria turned her inner gaze in her third letter to two other female figures in heaven: Mary Magdalene and Catherine of Alexandria. "I see the converted woman who passionately loved [Christ]," she declared, "every day more on fire with new and humble affection following him to the cross . . . I see the bold and intrepid virgin with her most solid and wise faith expose herself to every torment, desiring with pure and strong affection to give her life to her redeemer." Vittoria had long admired Mary Magdalene—we will remember the beautiful paintings she commissioned from Titian and Michelangelo—but Catherine of Alexandria was perhaps an even more important role model for her at this stage in her life. Indeed, the story of the fourth-century Egyptian girl of noble birth and great learning who refused to abandon her Christian faith despite the personal efforts of the emperor Maxentius to win her back to paganism was a powerful example of resilient faith in the face of adversity. Catherine famously broke the spiked wheel that was supposed to be the instrument of her death, and was subsequently beheaded. But what Vittoria wanted to celebrate was the fate of Catherine's soul: after her martyrdom, she was joined to Christ in a mystical marriage.

At the end of the third letter, Vittoria reflected on the wisdom of these two female figures, Mary Magdalene and Catherine of Alexandria, and then applied the lessons to be learned from their examples: "Now let us take as our own mirror the works of their most beautiful bodies, and imitating the thoughts of their holy and pure minds, may we truly worship in the manner most appropriate to our Lord, at the divine feet of which the one [Magdalene], I believe, rests in eternal peace and joy, and the other [Catherine], stands on his side, to the right of Christ's heavenly spouse." Although she was putatively writing to Costanza, the conclusions she reached seemed aimed at a much wider audience. Under the guise of writing to her friend, Vittoria had composed a mystical text of her own.

This fact did not escape the attention of the publishing world, which was quick to capitalize on Vittoria's fame and print the letters as a small book. In 1544, the Venetian printer Alessandro Viani published a volume with the title *Litere della divina Vetoria Colonna Marchesana di Pescara a la Duchessa de Amalfi sopra la vita contemplativa di santa Caterina e sopra de la attiva santa Maddalena non più viste in luce* (*Letters of the Divine Vittoria Colonna Marchesana di Pescara to the Duchess of Amalfi, on the contemplative life of Saint Catherine, and on the active Saint Magdalene, never before seen in print*). Although there was no discussion of this publication in any of Vittoria's surviving correspondence, the letters could never have been printed so quickly without either her cooperation or Costanza's—one of the two women must have agreed to give the printer the text. These were Vittoria's last new writings to appear during her lifetime, and they consolidated her status as one of the most prominent religious authors in the period. The fact that the letters were written from one woman to another on the topic of heavenly women also specifically strengthened Vittoria's role as a leader in the world of female spirituality.

By the mid-1540s, Vittoria seems both to have found the spiritual peace she had so long craved, and to have cultivated a voice that enabled her to share her wisdom with others. Her physical health, however, enjoyed no comparable moment of triumph. By early 1547, it was clear to all that she was dying. Sometime in late January or early February, she moved out of the convent of Sant'Anna to be in the home of her cousin Giulia Colonna Cesarini. The Cesarini palace was presumably chosen for its proximity to the convent: it was located just a few minutes away on Largo di Torre Argentina, which once housed the Theater of Pompey, where Julius Caesar was long believed to have been assassinated (most historians now think he died in the Curia of Pompey, a meeting hall some six hundred feet away). It is not clear if Vittoria chose to leave Sant'Anna or if she left at her relatives' insistence, but the pattern of being forced out of a convent to return to her family was certainly familiar.

Before leaving Sant'Anna, Vittoria drew up her last will and testament. The papers were signed by a notary on January 27, but lacked Vittoria's signature. On February 15, at Palazzo de' Cesarini, she drew up a second will almost identical to the first, but now including instructions about her wishes for her burial. This document ended with the Latin phrase "*Ita testavi ego Vittoria Colonna*," "I, Vittoria Colonna, have hereby exercised my will." Scribbled in her own hand, these were probably the final words she wrote.

Vittoria died at her cousin's palace on February 25, 1547. Her death was recorded as having occurred at the "hour of None," the liturgical service held in the middle of the afternoon. Depending on her exact birthday, she was either fifty-six or fifty-seven years old. Her personal confessor, Don Tomasso Maggio, was with her when she died, and sent a letter describing the circumstances to Ascanio. "I will not duplicate the information you already have received," Maggio wrote, "so as not to open the wound once again." But he wanted to make sure Ascanio knew how peaceful Vittoria's death had been:

You should rest assured that she went quickly to embrace her creator whom she desired so much to meet, and it was a sure sign of this that the night before the day she died, at the hour of None, she said to me: "Tomorrow morning at Mass I would like to confess and take Communion." I responded to her, "and extreme unction," to which she replied, "Yes, please." And thus it was that she received the Holy Sacraments each with great devotion, attention, and reverence, not missing one word, and having finished, she breathed her last breath.

As Maggio related it, on the morning of Vittoria's death, both Priuli and Flaminio came to see her. They spoke, he reported, "with great meaning about the matters of God, the Evangelist, and Saint Paul." Vittoria was completely engaged in the conversation, even, he claimed, "explaining certain passages herself in a way that seemed she did not have any infirmity nor would have led one to think she would die so soon." And yet, the fact that she requested her last rites suggests she knew very well she was dying. Maggio concluded by reassuring Ascanio: "Now that it has pleased Our God to free her from such long suffering, it cannot but be great consolation on this count and for the strong hope that we all have that she has gone exactly where she so much desired to go."

Pole was not mentioned among those present on the day of Vittoria's death, and there is no record of when their last meeting may have been. We know only that he returned to Rome from Padua in November 1546, and, based on his correspondence from the following months, he was almost certainly in the city when she died. His only explicit mention of her death came in a letter dated March 6 to Cardinal Cristoforo Madruzzo, who had just lost his brother. Pole confided in Madruzzo that he was "already oppressed by pain from the death of the Most Illustrious Lady Vittoria Colonna, whom I worshipped as a mother, and was barely holding myself together when a letter arrived from the Reverend from Rano, which told me of the death of your brother Aliprando." Given everything that had passed between them, it seems hard to believe he was still holding on to the idea of Vittoria as his mother. But for someone who claimed to have recovered from his real mother's death within a space of a few hours, the idea that he was "barely holding [himself] together" following Vittoria's death suggests an unusually intense emotional response.

The most touching report of Vittoria's death came from Michelangelo. According to his biographer Condivi, Michelangelo was at Vittoria's bedside as she was dying (it is not clear whether she was still alive when he arrived), and was seized by an unusual bout of resistance or fear in the face of death. As Condivi related it, "I remembered him saying that his only regret was that, when he went to see her as she was departing this life, he did not kiss her forehead or her face as he kissed her hand." We can imagine the scene before us: Vittoria lay either dying or newly dead in her chamber in the Palazzo de' Cesarini while the greatest living artist of the human form stood beside her, somehow made timid by the lifelessness of her body. He leaned over to kiss her face—the face he said he loved more than any other face in the world—but at the last second pulled away, instead kissing only her hand. The experience of seeing the woman with whom he had shared so much passing from one state to the next was so unsettling that "he remained a long time in despair and as if out of his mind." In a letter Michelangelo wrote several weeks later to his friend Giovan Francesco Fattucci, the priest of Santa Maria in Florence, he declared himself "overwhelmed with grief." Looking back at his loss even three years later, he wrote to Fattucci: "Death deprived me of a very great friend." (In keeping with his poem that complimented Vittoria as a "man within a woman," Michelangelo used the masculine *amico* to describe her here.)

In the immediate aftermath of Vittoria's death, there was great confusion about both her burial and her estate. Ascanio was designated her "universal heir," which meant that he was to inherit all property that was not otherwise assigned, and was authorized to make whatever decisions had to be made. But Ascanio was in exile far from Rome, and thus unable to take care of things personally. He therefore delegated to his agent Lorenzo Bonorio, who was also one of Vittoria's executors, the responsibility of gathering her personal property and arranging for her tomb.

Neither of these tasks went smoothly. Of her personal property, Bonorio sent a letter to Ascanio on February 27 complaining that he had trouble making sense of anything in Vittoria's rooms at Sant'Anna due to the interference of the mourners he found there. "Yesterday Messer Bartolomeo and I had the notary come by to do the inventory," he wrote, but "there happened to be so much weeping among the ladies that we were forced to let it be." It is not clear if he was referring to some of the nuns, or to friends and maidservants of Vittoria's, but he was so overwhelmed by the sheer volume of tears that he could not conduct his business.

The next day, Bonorio gathered his strength and returned to Sant'Anna. This time he was able to compile an itemized list of what he found:

> A few tables
> Dishes
> Several mattresses of extremely little value
> A water jug and washbasin
> A pair of candlesticks
> Six silver spoons
> Four silver forks
> One gold spoon
> A box with all of her papers, that is, contracts, agreements, and
>   privileges

In addition, Vittoria had left behind at Sant'Anna two *ronzini* (small horses) of little value: one large, and one very small. The small one, Bonorio proposed, should be left behind for one of the servants, "the little Giovan Nello" (possibly a little person); he made no suggestions for the other.

This is a very modest inventory for a woman of Vittoria's grandeur, and it leaves many questions unanswered. Where were the jewels and precious gifts she had been given over the years? Where were her personal letters, and the manuscripts of her poems? Where were the Titian and Pontormo paintings, and the Michelangelo drawings? Presumably some of these things she had taken with her to the Palazzo de' Cesarini, or had otherwise disposed of in the preceding weeks. On February 24, for example, the day before she died, Maggio reported that Vittoria had given him a good number of books to be brought directly to Pole; this gift was later confirmed in one of the letters from Bonorio to Ascanio, in which he wrote that he had not seen her books but knew that there were many, and noted that all of them had been put in the house of the "English cardinal."

The paucity of valuable items on the inventory—only the golden spoon perhaps had any real worth—was a very minor blow for Ascanio compared with the other news that Bonorio had to share. This had to do with the terms of Vittoria's will. For the most part, Vittoria's bequests were small enough as to make little difference to Ascanio's inheritance. She gave three hundred scudi to three of the convents where she had lived for long stretches—Santa Caterina in Viterbo, and San Silvestro al Quirinale and Sant'Anna in Rome—and one hundred scudi to San Paolo in Orvieto, where she had stayed for several months (the convent of Santa Caterina in Ferrara, which she spoke about so warmly, was somehow overlooked). She gave gifts ranging between fifty and five hundred scudi to individual servants who had worked for her over the years: three hundred fifty scudi went to her maid Prudenza. To one Margherita Rucellai, she gave a velvet cloak "in gratitude for her affection and her kindness."

The shocking part of the will, however, involved its largest gift. This was a bequest of nine thousand scudi—an enormous sum of money, and much larger than the total of all of the other bequests. Vittoria was obviously well aware of the controversy that this large bequest might produce, and hence chose not to reveal in the will itself where the money was to go. Instead, she indicated that instructions had been given in a separate document. In Vittoria's first will, this document was to be entrusted to Priuli—however much she may have disliked him personally, she must have trusted him enough to name him for this job. She obviously had second thoughts, however: in her revised will, she replaced Priuli with Vettor Soranzo, bishop of Bergamo and a fellow reformer. Vittoria and Soranzo's friendship dated back to the early 1530s, when he was the go-between for her exchange of sonnets with Bembo (it was to Soranzo, as we saw earlier, that Bembo had written in 1531 to praise Vittoria's poems as "more than one would expect from a woman"). During her stay in Viterbo, she seems to have spent time with Soranzo, something we learn about in a letter from Bembo. "I am very envious of my friend Vettor Soranzo," he wrote to Vittoria in November 1541, "who is able to be with you so frequently, something I am not able to do."

Vittoria specified that Soranzo was to give the nine thousand scudi to the trustee named in the separate document in order that he or she would in turn distribute the money to be used in "*pio opere,*" or pious works. Neither Soranzo nor her heirs, she added, were to impede or disturb this gift in any way. Moreover, since she wanted the gift to remain secret, she also strictly prohibited Soranzo from showing the document that named the trustee to anyone. In case all of this was not protection enough—and never before have we seen Vittoria act with such paranoia—she concluded by saying that her heir (she used the singular noun) could not "pressure or force" Soranzo to show him the secret writ. She was, in short, determined to keep the information regarding the gift from Ascanio.

These precautions, it turned out, were well founded. Anyone who read Vittoria's will perceived immediately that her brother had been terribly slighted. In Bonorio's letter to Ascanio dated February 27—two days after Vittoria's death—he included a copy of the will, and expressed his own dismay about its terms:

> Included here is the testament of [Vittoria]. Because I know that you will not be able to read the details of the 9,000 scudi without being upset, as I myself could not, God knows how much it grieved me to think that that blessed soul in her last will could be accused by God of such ingratitude toward her most illustrious house [the Colonna], toward which she was always so courteous, and also toward the world, which having praised all of her actions in her life and in death, now sees the product of such an enlightened and Catholic spirit be so ungracious.

How could Vittoria, who always seemed to love her family so dearly, have neglected them in this way? Did she not, he asked, feel loyalty toward her "illustrious house"? What happened to the person who had remarked only six years earlier that the *"Casa Colonna sempre è la prima"*?

Bonorio made haste to reassure Ascanio that he had known nothing about Vittoria's decision until that day, and that he would make sure the will was corrected—in other words, altered—in Ascanio's favor. "Soon," he promised, "you will see the Colonna house be consoled, and not left defrauded of that which it so reasonably expected to receive." What happened next is hard to say, but however much Vittoria had tried to ensure that her money would be protected and the terms of the gift kept secret, word soon got out that the trustee—the person to whom the nine thousand scudi were to be given—was none other than Pole. This was, no doubt, confirmation of Ascanio's worst suspicions. There are no traces of exactly what went on in the next few months—moments from *The Godfather* come readily to mind—but on May 29, a special meeting was convened at Pole's residence in Bagnoregio. Present at the meeting were Priuli and Maggio (Pole's inner circle) as well as several unnamed witnesses. The purpose of the gathering was, as Bonorio had promised, to amend Vittoria's will.

The document drawn up by the notary at this meeting is held today in the Secret Archive of the Vatican, and its contents, to my knowledge, have never before been examined. After finding an obscure reference to it, I got permission from the Vatican archivist to have the document photographed—it was a several-page, handwritten manuscript in Latin—and then arranged to have someone translate it from Latin into Italian before I translated it into English. Given that there was not even a printed copy of the letter available, it is not surprising that none of Vittoria's earlier biographers seem to have known about this meeting; they report simply that she gave the money to Pole. But at Bagnoregio in May 1547, Pole legally declared that he would redirect the nine thousand scudi Vittoria had given him for charitable deeds to be used as payment for Ascanio's daughter's wedding dowry. Pole declared that he made this decision willingly—the pressure Ascanio and his allies must have put on him was no doubt immense—and that he did so in order to honor the illustrious Colonna family. The circumstances of the meeting were sufficiently suspicious that the notary himself made sure to rehearse his credentials at great length, and to confirm that he, too, was acting of his own free will.

It is hard to imagine how Vittoria would have felt had she been present at this meeting. To be sure, she was fond of her niece, who was named after her; she had even helped to raise the young Vittoria during the years following the Sack of Rome when she lived in Ischia with her mother, Giovanna d'Aragona. But Vittoria did not die suddenly, nor had she lost her wits—according to Maggio, she was completely clearheaded even on her deathbed. Vittoria's last will and testament, that is, reflected her actual will: had she wanted to give the nine thousand scudi to Ascanio to pay for his daughter's dowry, there was absolutely nothing stopping her from doing so. Thus what happened at Bagnoregio, no doubt following a series of unrecorded conversations and exchanges in the intervening months, was a complete overturning of Vittoria's authority. In the end, the men decided they knew better.

In late 1551 or early 1552, the young Vittoria Colonna was married to Don García de Toledo, the son of Don Pedro Álvarez, viceroy of Naples. In a letter dated January 6 (the year is not given, but is most likely 1552), Pole wrote to Ascanio:

> I have gathered from the letters from Your most Illustrious Lordship and from your Majordomo who has written on your behalf that you wish the nine thousand scudi, which I had always intended to give to the signora Vittoria your daughter at her marriage, now be signed over to the most Illustrious Lord Viceroy of Naples along with the dowry promised to the Lord Don Garcia, his son . . . I am firm in that conviction I have always had, however little [Your Lordship] knew of it, that the most Illustrious Marchesa, your sister, was moved to leave these moneys in my hands so that I could aid the poor people of my country, who repair to me continuously, just as the abovementioned lady said with her own mouth to trustworthy people who can relate as much to Your most Illustrious Lordship. Despite all this, I resolved to

do what I would have exhorted [Your Lordship's] lady to do when she informed me of her intention, namely, to use those funds to help you marry off your daughter lady Vittoria . . .

If she has no children, the money is to be returned and used for pious causes in Rome, which I will arrange according to the plan that I always had in such an event, and with this assuring and making certain every promise [made] to the Lord Viceroy and to Lord Don Garcia and to you, such that I will have never failed my promises, I send you my greetings.

Much more than the document from Bagnoregio, which was drawn up by a notary and lacked in mood and tone, this letter captured Pole's regret about the whole affair. This was not a letter sent between friends: it was strictly a business transaction. Pole may have promised to keep his word, but he made clear that he resented doing so. The only remaining piece of evidence concerning this ill-fated gift is a notarial record from May 4, 1552, confirming the transfer of the nine thousand scudi to Ascanio's lawyer. Vittoria's money for the poor became a dowry for the rich, or rather for the impoverished nobility.

If Vittoria's nine thousand scudi found a fate far from what she had intended, at least her corpse ultimately ended up where she wanted it to be. In the revised will that she drew up on February 15, she indicated her desire to be buried at Sant'Anna "in a manner to be chosen by the Mother Superior," and added that her burial was to be treated "in the usual style and manner of that monastery." This was yet another slight to the Colonna family, in keeping with the decision to leave her money to charity. Vittoria did not, in other words, want to lie in one of the exquisite Colonna chapels in the churches of Santi Apostoli or San Giovanni Laterano in Rome, nor did she want to lie near Ferrante in San Domenico Maggiore in Naples. Instead, she sought in death what had been denied her in life: a permanent home with the nuns.

Bonorio reported to Ascanio that on the evening of Vittoria's death, her body had been moved from Palazzo de' Cesarini to Sant'Anna following her request, but added that he awaited word as to "what your Excellence wishes may be done with it." He did not imagine, in other

words, that Vittoria's will would necessarily be honored, and anticipated that Ascanio might have other plans for her burial. Two days
later, in the letter of February 27 in which Bonorio shared the unpleasant details about the money, he also reminded Ascanio about Vittoria's
corpse: "The body is still here in a pitched coffin; it would be well if
your Excellence would give your orders whether you wish it to remain
here, and whether you wish to have a velvet cover made for it, as is
usual." Coffins were "pitched," or sealed with tar, to keep water out and
smells in—this was a practice dating back to the Egyptians. The velvet
cover, by contrast, was simply ornamental.

The very next day, on February 28, Bonorio wrote to Ascanio again
to say that in the absence of any response, he had consulted Pole, who
had advised that the coffin "be covered with velvet, as is usual, and
placed where they shall think fit in the Church of Sant'Anna, so that it
can be removed when it is desired to do so." No doubt irking Ascanio
even further, Bonorio mentioned that the seventy scudi for the velvet
was to be paid out of Ascanio's account, as was the sum of one hundred
scudi owed to Vittoria's doctors. Nearly three weeks later, Bonorio finally received a response from Ascanio. There is no explanation for
why it took so long for him to answer. Perhaps he was so irate about the
nine thousand scudi that he could not be bothered with worrying about
the coffin. Ascanio's letter has not survived, but Bonorio's response
made clear what Ascanio told him to do: "Your orders about the body
have been carried out; it is in a pitched coffin; in three days' time, it will
be placed in the velvet case and deposited above ground, and, if your
Excellence decides that it will be better to leave the body where it is, it
will be left here." This letter, which was sent on March 15, was the last
word on the matter between them.

The confirmation of Vittoria's burial in Sant'Anna came only a
century later, in Sant'Anna's church annals for 1651. At that time, it was
recorded that the body of the blessed Santuccia Carabotti—the late
thirteenth-century nun who founded the convent—was moved from the
high altar to the church's burial ground. In passing, it was mentioned
that Vittoria's corpse was buried there as well. This small detail tells us
that in 1547 her coffin was almost certainly placed "above ground" ("*in*

alto"), as Ascanio had requested—it would have been in one of the walls of the church, as was common at the time for persons of great distinction—until new burial policies introduced by the church in the seventeenth century mandated that all corpses needed to be interred (literally, *in* + *terra*, put into the earth). More than a hundred years after her death, Vittoria was finally laid to rest among the nuns.

There is, unfortunately, no way to visit Vittoria's tomb today. In 1887, the church and convent of Sant'Anna were destroyed, along with much of the old neighborhood, to make way for the modern Viale Arenula, where a busy tram shuttles Romans crossing the Tiber from Trastevere. No one knows exactly what happened to Vitttoria's coffin. One late nineteenth-century scholar, Bruto Amante, developed an elaborate theory that her remains were moved to Naples and lie next to Ferrante's in a misidentified tomb, but this idea has been roundly dismissed, and it is likely that Vittoria's coffin was left behind at the convent in the general debris. The only visible trace of her that remains in the warren of cobblestone streets surrounding the former convent is on the Via dell'Arco del Monte, where, sandwiched between an excellent Sicilian bakery and a reasonably good shoe store stands a *scuola secondaria di secondo grado*—a high school—proudly bearing her name.

CONCLUSION: IN THE ARCHIVE
OF THE INQUISITION

A SHORT DISTANCE FROM SAINT PETER'S BASILICA is the Palazzo del Sant'Uffizio, headquarters for the Congregation for the Doctrine of the Faith. The Congregation for the Doctrine of the Faith, which was known as the Holy Office until the Second Vatican Council changed its name in the 1960s, is the branch of the Roman Church dedicated to the Inquisition. Of the three Inquisitions—Spanish, Portuguese, and Roman—only the Roman office has survived into the modern era, although its mandate has obviously changed since the prosecutorial frenzy of the sixteenth century. Originally founded in 1542 by Paul III to root out heresy, its mission now is to promote and defend Catholic doctrine. The Palazzo del Sant'Uffizio was admitted into the Holy See as an extraterritorial property in 1929, which means that although it physically lies in the city of Rome, it belongs to the Vatican.

Visitors approaching the palace today have no way to know what lies within its massive wooden doors; even the buzzers alongside the entrance keep the building's secrets. But if you ring for the doorman and ask for the Congregation's archive, he will point you to the rear left corner of a grand internal courtyard. There, through a small door—also lacking a proper sign, but with a taped-over label on it that reads in a tiny font, *Archivio Congregazione per la dottrina della fede*—you will find the records of the Inquisition.

In 1983, an Italian priest and scholar named Sergio Pagano was working in this archive when he came upon a mysterious file. Pagano had recently been appointed to the position of "Writer of the Secret Archives," and was given permission to prepare a new publication of the documents related to the 1633 trial of Galileo. Galileo had been tried as a heretic in part due to his belief in heliocentrism, or Copernicanism—the idea that the earth moves around the sun, and not the other way around—which he famously supported with findings from his telescope. (Contrary to common opinion, Galileo did not invent the telescope: it was first patented in 1608 by a German-born Dutchman, Hans Lippershey, who was a maker of eyeglasses. Galileo was the first, however, to use it for purposes of astronomy.) In 1616, the church had issued an injunction forbidding Galileo to "hold, teach, or defend" his Copernican beliefs; according to the theologians appointed to investigate the matter, the idea that the sun was stationary was "foolish and absurd in philosophy, and formally heretical since it explicitly contradicts in many places the sense of Holy Scripture." At the end of his trial, Galileo agreed to recant—the alternatives were not attractive—and he publicly declared that he "held, as most true and indisputable, the opinion of Ptolemy, that is to say, the stability of the Earth and the motion of the Sun." In exchange, he was given a relatively light sentence: he was to live under house arrest for the rest of his life, and was required to recite the seven Penitential Psalms once a week for three years. His book *The Dialogue of Galileo Galilei* was placed on the Index of Forbidden Books, where it remained until 1835.

In the early 1980s, Pagano was among a tiny number of scholars who had been given permission to use the inquisitorial archive. The lack of any public access to these materials changed shortly thereafter: in 1998, Pope John Paul II officially opened the archive to qualified readers as a gesture of goodwill in anticipation of the Jubilee in 2000. John Paul was responding to decades of requests and complaints from historians, whose scholarship of the Roman Inquisition was severely impaired by the Congregation's refusal to allow its files to be seen. Surprisingly, the change in policy was thanks in part to a letter sent by the eminent Italian scholar Carlo Ginzburg, which reportedly began with his announcing himself as a Jewish historian and an atheist who had been working for many years on inquisitorial papers. Joseph Ratzinger, the future Pope Benedict XVI, was the head of the Congregation at the time, and later credited Ginzburg as having played a crucial role in the decision to let the barbarians, as it were, through the doors. There are still serious obstacles to using the archive: in addition to the sheer difficulty of finding the right building and ringing the appropriate bell, there is no clear set of instructions anywhere as to how to gain admission, the reading room seats only twelve scholars at a time, and the opening hours are hard to predict. But this is all a great improvement from the situation before 1998.

Even before the archive was opened to the public, scholars knew that what they found within would be far from complete, as the files chronicling centuries of persecution had themselves been subjected to several episodes of violence and upheaval. First, following the death in 1559 of the loathed Paul IV, an unruly Roman mob had ransacked the Holy Office's palace and set fire to whatever books and files they could get their hands on. Some two hundred fifty years later, a victorious Napoleon ordered the transfer of the surviving archive to Paris following his occupation of Rome, and the files were duly packed up and shipped to France. The archive's time in France was short-lived, however: after Napoleon's defeat at the Battle of Waterloo in 1815, the Vatican was given permission to reclaim the precious archive, with the one stipulation that the delivery to Rome was to be at its own expense. The priest in charge of making the arrangements claimed the costs were so high that he needed either to sell or destroy a good share of the files in order to raise the necessary funds for shipping. He supposedly sold many original documents as scrap paper.

The files that survived these various assaults were then put back in the Palazzo del Sant'Uffizio, although certain volumes consisting of more miscellaneous materials were stored in the attic of a neighboring palace, where they remained until early in the twentieth century. At this point, they were moved to the so-called Stanza Storica, or Historic Room, of the Holy Office's headquarters. Finally, during World War II, the entire archive was transported into the rooms of the palace's ground floor and mezzanine. It was in one of these rooms in 1983 that Pagano's hand fell upon an odd volume from the former Stanza Storica collection.

There was nothing particularly impressive about the book that caught Pagano's eye: it looked like many other old volumes that had been neglected over the centuries. Bound in ordinary parchment, and held together with two cloth ties, it bore on its spine the vague title *Miscelanea Abusus contra Ritus Ecclesiae Altamurae. Diver. Proced. contra Episcopos, Prelatos et Abbat. Diversa Neg. Pisarum*, or *Miscellaneous Abuses against the Church of Altamura, Various Proceedings against Bishops, Prelates, and Abbots; Various Proceedings against Pescara.* Something about it piqued his interest, however, and he looked inside.

Among the odd collection of documents the book contained—it was, as the title promised, truly miscellaneous—Pagano found a file of papers grouped together that still bore the marks of having been folded, as if to fit into a packet or envelope for delivery. The nearly blank page preceding the documents bore the title, written in a sixteenth-century hand, "*Quinternus literrarum quondam Illustrissimae Dominae Marchionissae Piscariae et aliarum*," or "Five-sheet quire of former letters of the Most Illustrious Marchesa of Pescara, and others." Pagano had stumbled upon an inquisitorial file for Vittoria.

To discover a collection of documents that has been overlooked for centuries, filled with evidence of a historical event that otherwise left no traces, is one of the most thrilling experiences a scholar can have. But Vittoria was not Pagano's subject—he was busy at work on the Galileo trial, and also became more interested in another file in the *Miscelanea* volume, involving a fascinating episode of heresy in the northern city of Brescia. He therefore put the Vittoria discovery aside. He might never, in fact, have returned to it had he not had a conversation several months later with a professor of Italian literature named Concetta Ranieri who was working on an edition of Vittoria's letters. The two scholars were discussing some of the challenges they were each facing in conducting their research in the Vatican's Secret Archive when Pagano realized some of the letters Ranieri was looking for were in the *Quinternus* file. After further discussion, the two scholars submitted a formal request to the Congregation to study the documents together. In October 1984, the secretary of the Congregation granted the necessary permissions, and Pagano and Ranieri began the research that would result in their publication of the entire *Quinternus* with the Vatican Archive press in 1989.

The original materials in the *Quinternus* cover fifty-two pages of writing—there are also ten blank pages between documents, for a total of sixty-two pages—and consist of the following:

- Six letters from Vittoria to Pole (1541 to 1546)
- The letter from Vittoria to Marguerite de Navarre, in which she describes her spiritual well-being (and also talks about Pole's delegation to Trent) (1545)
- The letter from Marguerite de Navarre to Georges d'Armagnac in which she recommends that d'Armagnac visit Vittoria (1545)
- The letter from Marguerite to Vittoria in which she expresses her joy in learning that contrary to rumor, Vittoria has not died (1545)
- A prose meditation on Christ's crucifixion, mistakenly attributed to Vittoria
- A letter from Ferrante d'Avalos, Vittoria's husband, to the Holy Roman Emperor, written on the day of the Battle of Pavia in 1525 (this letter had no bearing on the rest of the file, and must have been included only due to its relationship to Vittoria)
- Several pages of notes from an inquisitorial censor detailing the heretical beliefs found within these documents, including page and line references

There is no indication of when the file was assembled. Although the date "1547" was scribbled just below the title of the collection, this was almost certainly not when the documents were compiled, but referred instead, as Pagano has argued, to the year of Vittoria's death. It is also clear that the materials were not all collected at the same time: the letters and the meditation were gathered first, and the censor's notes were added at a later date, inserted between the last letter to Pole and the first of Marguerite's. These notes were written on smaller-sized paper than the other letters, and in a heavy ink that bled through to both sides of each sheet, making them almost impossible to decipher.

There had long been rumors that Vittoria was put on trial by the Inquisition after her death. But until Pagano opened the *Miscelanea* volume in 1983, no evidence of such an event, either realized or merely planned, had ever surfaced. The rumors had largely arisen in connection to Vittoria's close relationship to Pole, who had become a very problematic figure in the Roman church in the years following Vittoria's death, and was ultimately regarded as one of the most dangerous heretics inside the papal curia. Before Pole fell permanently out of favor in Rome, however, he came close to enjoying his greatest success. In the papal conclave that elected Giovanni Maria Ciocchi del Monte (Julius III) in February 1550, Pole was actually considered the favored candidate: the odds set by bankers for his election were at 95 percent, and his pontifical garments had already been made when he lost the election by a mere two votes. Happily for Pole, Julius did not hold a grudge, or at least he saw how useful the English cardinal could be: in 1553, he appointed Pole legate for England's reconciliation to the church after Henry VIII's fervently Catholic daughter Mary Tudor became queen.

Before Julius allowed Pole to return to England, he made two demands: first, that he negotiate a full restoration of the Church of England's obedience to Rome; and second, that he ensure all of the monastic properties Henry had seized when he dissolved the monasteries were returned to the mother church. Pole was also under great pressure from Rome to support Mary's so-called Spanish match—her marriage in 1554 to Philip of Spain, the son of Charles V—which he had opposed for reasons never specified, but most likely because of the widespread fear on the part of the English that the Spanish would take over their country (however alienated Pole may have seemed at times from his country, he was at heart an English patriot).

In 1554, Pole publicly expressed his approval of Mary's marriage, and also settled the final terms of English "obedience" to the pope. (The restoration of the monasteries was never fully resolved to the pope's satisfaction, although Mary did return several of them at her own expense.) With this behind him, Pole set out for England, and crossed from Calais to Dover on November 20. Ten days later, he was led by six knights of the Garter from Lambeth to Westminster Palace in order officially to reconcile England to the papacy. From this point on, he emerged as the de facto religious leader in the renewed Catholic nation, and in December 1555, he was appointed Archbishop of Canterbury.

Despite this sudden rise to great prominence in England, Pole's relations with Rome took a very bad turn in 1557, during the papacy of his longtime enemy Carafa, who became Paul IV in 1555. Paul began his pursuit of Pole by arresting key members of the Viterbo circle, all of whom were questioned specifically about Pole's beliefs; he then ordered the inquisitors to draw up formal charges against the English cardinal, which consisted of eighteen separate counts of heresy. Pole spent the next few years trying to defend himself on multiple fronts, and somehow managed to ward off arrest or deportation to Rome, when he became very ill. He died at Lambeth Castle in the company of Priuli on November 17, 1558—the very same day, as fate would have it, that Queen Mary herself passed away. With the crowning of Elizabeth I in 1559, the Roman church saw England resume its status as a nation of Protestants.

Given Pole's position as one of the most sought-after heretics in Rome, the simplest explanation for Vittoria's file in the Holy Office is that the inquisitors were investigating her as a way of gathering information about him. Evidence supporting this account can be found in the trial records of two members of Pole's inner circle in Viterbo— Morone and Carnesecchi—who were also, as we have seen, close to Vittoria. The prosecution of Morone, who had been named a cardinal in 1542, lasted from 1557 to 1559. There were twenty-one charges of heresy leveled against him, and he was formally questioned in ten separate sessions while detained as a prisoner in Castel Sant'Angelo. The inquisitors were interested not only in Morone's heretical beliefs, but also in those of the others around him, including Vittoria. The evidence they had compiled against her came from letters she and Morone had exchanged, twelve of which were appended to the trial documents.

Here is a summary of the key charges, as outlined in the *Compendium* of Morone's interrogations written up after the proceedings had ended:

- The Marchesa of Pescara, spiritual daughter and disciple of Cardinal Pole, accomplice of him and other heretics, [was] drenched in false doctrine through the works of the Cardinal and for this reason very attached to him.
- She has declared that she adhered to the opinion expressed in the text of Contarini according to which justification is by means of faith alone, which she learned from Pole.
- The Marchesa was to a very great degree influenced by false doctrines and close to Cardinal Pole . . . She was possibly also influenced by the ideas of Fra Bernardino Ochino.
- The nuns of the convents in which she has stayed in Rome, Florence, and Viterbo can testify against her.

In addition to pursuing Vittoria's role as a conduit to Pole—she was accused of being his "spiritual daughter" (not, in this case, his mother)—the inquisitors were also concerned that she had specifically corrupted the nuns in Viterbo. This accusation was based on a comment she made in the letter to Morone from 1543 in which she reassured him that the nuns were praying for Pole's and Morone's success at Trent. Although the *Compendium* suggested that the nuns might be called upon to testify against her, there is no evidence this was ever pursued.

Following Paul IV's death in 1559, Morone was set free. He went on to resume his very distinguished career in the church, and in 1563 became president of the Council of Trent, where he brought the last session to a successful end. But his trial by no means settled the record of either Pole or Vittoria. Seven years later, Carnesecchi was brought to trial, for the third time. He was first prosecuted in 1546 but released thanks to the intervention of both Paul III and Cosimo I de' Medici, Duke of Florence, who was Carnesecchi's lifelong friend and patron. He was tried for a second time in 1559, which resulted in his being condemned to death, but with the help once again of Cosimo I, he

managed to escape to Venice. Carnesecchi stayed in Venice under protection until Paul IV's death, after which his sentence was suspended.
At this point he enjoyed some years of reprieve.

What led to Carnesecchi's final arrest was the death in 1566 of
Giulia Gonzaga. Giulia, who, as we have seen, was Valdés's devotee and
an engaged member of the Italian reform movement, had been a close
friend of Carnesecchi's for decades; in the extensive correspondence
between the two of them confiscated by the Holy Office, the inquisitors
found substantial evidence to be used against him. Over a period of
thirteen months, Carnesecchi was interrogated in 119 sessions, twice
under torture. The outcome in this case was as horrible as could be. In
September 1567 at the church of Santa Maria Sopra Minerva, where
his enemy Paul IV lay buried in the ornate Carafa chapel surrounded
by frescoes of Filippino Lippi, Carnesecchi was sentenced to death. Ten
days later, he was beheaded and burned at the stake in Piazza di Ponte
next to Castel Sant'Angelo; the bridge in front of the castle, now famous
for its magnificent angels sculpted by Bernini in the late seventeenth
century, was used to display the bodies executed in the piazza. According to the letter sent to Cosimo I from one of his agents who was present
at the execution, Carnesecchi walked up to the block with great decorum and dignity, wearing a tight-fitting white tunic and a pair of new
gloves; he carried a white handkerchief in his hand.

During Carnesecchi's interrogations, which took place on and off
from July 1566 to August 1567, he was asked about Vittoria on several
occasions. The inquisitors wanted to know how the two of them had
met; whether he knew what she and Pole discussed; whether she ever
affirmed her beliefs in justification by faith and predestination; what
she meant when she wrote to Giulia Gonzaga that Pole had saved her
from her "superstition"; whether she was reading the works of Luther,
Bucer, Melancthon, or Calvin; and why she counseled Pole to leave Trent
before the final discussions on justification.

At first, Carnesecchi avoided answering the questions directly.
He had not heard Vittoria's conversations with Pole—they always met
alone. He did not know what books she was reading, but Pole always
discouraged her from being too curious, and advised her to remain

within the boundaries "appropriate to her sex and to her humility and modesty." He knew she overdid her fasting, but had no idea what she meant by her "superstition." A month or so after giving this testimony, however, he seems to have changed his mind on two different fronts. Perhaps he decided it was not worth protecting Vittoria to this degree, given the torture he was enduring—she was, after all, long dead—and that his treatment might improve if he offered at least a little evidence against her.

The first incriminating testimony Carnesecchi provided was related to the question of Vittoria's familiarity with Protestant texts. He claimed to have suddenly recalled a conversation in which she told him how much she admired a particular commentary on the Psalms. The commentary turned out to be Luther's. Vittoria did not know, he hastened to add, who the author was when she praised the text. But the sheer fact that Luther's words resonated so powerfully with her—Carnesecchi reported her having said that she had never taken such delight in a contemporary piece of writing—confirmed the inquisitors' worst suspicions.

The second piece of evidence Carnesecchi gave against Vittoria involved her theological beliefs. After initially denying that he knew anything about her Protestant leanings, Carnesecchi recommended that the inquisitors read her spiritual sonnets. There, he offered, they would find clear evidence of her belief in the Lutheran idea of predestination. Outside of the French constable Anne de Montmorency's report to Francis I some twenty-five years earlier that Vittoria's poems contained "many things that ran counter to the faith of Jesus Christ," this was the only moment on record in which her poetry was categorized as heretical. Indeed, the many printed volumes of the *Rime* circulated freely throughout the period of the Council of Trent: not only were they never placed on the Index of Forbidden Books, but two further editions of the collected poems also appeared in 1559 and 1560, respectively. It is possible that Carnesecchi thought it unlikely that the Holy Office would embark on a literary analysis of more than one hundred spiritual sonnets, or maybe he imagined such an endeavor would be useful in slowing down his own prosecution. Whatever his reasons for raising the issue, it is fascinating that Carnesecchi, who almost certainly knew

Vittoria's poems well, imagined them to contain the most damning evidence of her Protestantism.

When it came time to investigate Vittoria directly, however, the sonnets played no role in the file drawn up against her. Whether the censor who prepared the *Quinternus* was familiar with Carnesecchi's testimony is unclear, but Pagano speculated that the notes were in fact compiled some years following Carnesecchi's execution—he suggested a date after the papacy of Pope Pius V, who died in 1572. Pagano's reasons for so late a date turned on the nature of the censor's interests. Unlike the inquisitors during the Morone and Carnesecchi trials, who were largely asking about Vittoria as a means of gathering evidence against Pole and the others in the Viterbo circle, the inquisitor combing through Vittoria's letters was focused strictly on the theological errors she herself had committed.

What interested the censor above all was Vittoria's confidence in her salvation. From his perspective, only someone who believed she was among the elect—and thus believed in predestination—could be so entirely unconcerned about her heavenly prospects. Even a confident Catholic would continue to perform good works until the bitter end, and provide for prayers or Masses to be said on behalf of her soul after death. And yet, according to the inquisitor's assessment, Vittoria revealed no such plans in any of her letters, nor did she reveal any anxiety. When she wrote to Pole about her gratitude to God for placing her "at your right hand, like a shoot of that true vine, which alone is sweet-smelling and dear," the inquisitor commented: "it seems that here Vittoria affirms the confirmation and certainty of grace." Or when she affirmed to Pole that she would "go to Christ completely assured and consoled, and I seem to see Your Most Reverend Lordship together with that divine goodness, entirely one with his most righteous will," he remarked: "Here it seems that Vittoria errs, mistaking that we can get close to God simply through faith . . . It seems that she advances the same argument as before, regarding the confirmation and certainty of grace."

Other objections the inquisitor raised similarly fit the Lutheran pattern. Vittoria declared, for example, that she was an infinite sinner, and deserved very little from Christ: "Whatever bitterness Christ might give me," she wrote to Pole, "such bitterness nonetheless seems alto-gether sweet, given my infinite lack of worth and his infinite merit." To this, the censor demurred: "It seems that here [Vittoria] denies her own merits and affirms only her own errors" (in other words, the cen-sor believed she completely ignored the value of human works). Or in the letter to Marguerite of Navarre in which she declared that when she spoke with Pole and his company in Viterbo, she felt the true health of her spirit despite the infirmity of her flesh, the censor found fault with her "conviction of the rightness of her spiritual path."

There is no discussion in the *Quinternus* of what the Holy Office in-tended to do with the evidence amassed against Vittoria. Given that she had been dead for several decades, the most likely answer is that the in-quisitors were considering a *damnatio memoriae*, the damning of Vit-toria's name. *Damnatio memoriae* was a traditional practice in ancient Rome, where it usually took the form of defacing stone or wax inscrip-tions that bore the name of the condemned, and thereby effectively erasing the visible traces of his or her life. Given the enormous change in attitudes about the afterlife between the ancient world and the Renaissance—ancient Romans did not generally believe in a meaningful afterlife, and therefore the reputation they left behind on earth was what mattered—it is puzzling that the tradition of *damnatio memoriae* per-sisted in a Christian world focused on heavenly judgment. But the Cath-olic Church did not limit its jurisdiction to the living. Just as charitable gifts or Masses sung on behalf of the dead were considered to shorten the deceased's term in purgatory, so the damning of someone's memory was considered to influence where he or she ended up for eternity.

Whatever the rationale behind the persistence of *damnatio memo-riae*, the Holy Office in Rome routinely conducted such trials: in the same miscellaneous volume in which Vittoria's file was found, there were documents from a *damnatio memoriae* against a noblewoman from Naples, Isabella Brisegna, who was put on trial for heresy in 1570. There is no comparable evidence for any such proceedings against Vittoria, and based on the materials in the *Quinternus*, it seems quite certain that the trial against her never took place. But the fact that the *Quinternus* exists at all—the fact, that is, that the Holy Office took the time not only to collect some of Vittoria's letters, but also to appoint a censor to read through them and write up a formal report—confirms that they were pursuing some kind of further action.

At roughly the same time that the censor was poring over Vittoria's letters for signs of heresy, the Colonna family was enjoying a restoration to its former glory. This reversal in fortunes was largely thanks to the triumphant military service of Ascanio's son Marcantonio at the Battle of Lepanto on October 7, 1571. During this naval contest fought in the waters off the southwest coast of Greece, Marcantonio, who was the admiral of the papal fleet, helped to lead the Holy League—a union made up of Spain, Venice, and a number of smaller Italian states—to a stunning defeat of the Turks. Lepanto was widely regarded as the most important victory of Christian Europe over the Ottomans of the entire period, and it successfully curtailed the Turks' expansion over the Mediterranean.

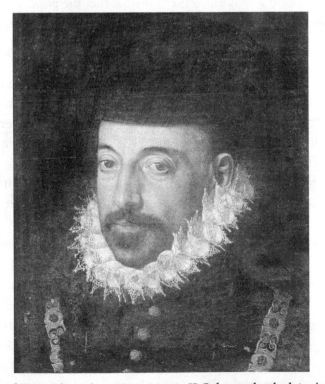

Portrait of Vittoria's nephew Marcantonio II Colonna, by the late sixteenth-century painter Scipione Pulzone (Galleria Colonna, Rome)

In Rome, the victory was celebrated extravagantly. There were triumphs and processions reminiscent of the glory days of the Roman Empire, and Turkish slaves were dragged through the streets in chains. Pius V named October 7 a new holiday in the liturgical calendar: the feast of Our Lady of Victory (the name was subsequently changed to Our Lady of the Rosary). He also commissioned Giorgio Vasari to paint frescoes of the naval battle on the walls of the Sala Regia outside the Pauline Chapel in the Vatican Palace. The historical accuracy of Vasari's depiction of the battle formation—he supposedly consulted with Marcantonio himself—is oddly juxtaposed with its heavily allegorical program: the frescoes include divine spirits that crown figures representing the Christian forces, a personification of the church wearing a papal tiara, and villainous images of the Turks. There is no way to know for certain the impact of the victory at Lepanto on Vittoria's posthumous fate. But it seems altogether possible that the pope decided not to pursue charges against the beloved aunt of his great military hero. Whatever the reasons, Vittoria's file was all but forgotten until Pagano's discovery more than four hundred years later.

Today Vittoria's distant relatives still celebrate the Battle of Lepanto in the central hall of the Palazzo Colonna, where above the vault of the Room of the Battle Column that leads down to the main gallery, there is a magnificent fresco painted in 1700 by Giuseppe Bartolomeo Chiari, depicting the apotheosis of Marcantonio, who is presented to the Virgin Mary in heaven. This space, familiar to many of us as the site where Audrey Hepburn's character, Princess Ann, greets the press at the end of *Roman Holiday*, was created as part of Cardinal Girolamo I Colonna's ambitious renovations to the palazzo in the mid-seventeenth century. As you descend the stairs—one of which still bears an actual cannonball shot by the French army in 1849 from the top of the Janiculum Hill, more than a mile away—you may be too overwhelmed by the baroque splendor of the marble columns, the sumptuous painted mirrors, the golden statues supporting the tables, the magnificent paintings separated by decorative stucco, and the many chandeliers to notice a very modest portrait of a Renaissance lady on your right (see plate 19). She is dressed in a rich green velvet gown with a high lace collar, her hair discreetly covered by a long white veil; she wears no jewelry out-side of a simple string of pearls, and holds a handkerchief in her right hand. This is the Vittoria that the Colonna family has chosen to re-member: a young, aristocratic woman of serious disposition, who had not yet made her name. How much more there was to her—how rich and complex a life she led—would take most visitors by surprise.

It is hard to say what exactly made Vittoria the remarkable person she was, or what single feature was most responsible for her fame. From the perspective of Italian literary history, she has the obvious distinction of being the first woman ever to see a book of her own po-ems in print. But the simple designation she is given on the card next to her portrait—"poetess and friend to Michelangelo"—does not begin, as I hope this book has shown, to capture her. Who was Vittoria Co-lonna? A religious pioneer who embraced Protestant ideas at the very moment when the Catholic Church came closest to a reformation of its own; a canny and strategic diplomat who negotiated on behalf of her family with emperors and popes; an important critic and friend of the greatest writers and artists of her time; a spiritual inspiration to many of those around her, who regarded both her sonnets and her company as uplifting to their souls; a role model for women through-out Italy and the continent, whose example emboldened endless numbers of women both to write and to publish their own works. Vittoria was, in short, at the very heart of what we celebrate when we think about sixteenth-century Italy. Once her story has been told, it is impossible to imagine the Renaissance without her.

NOTES AND BIBLIOGRAPHY

For the Italian texts of Vittoria Colonna's sonnets addressed to Ferrante and all miscellaneous poems by her, see the edition of the *Rime* by Alan Bullock (Rome/ Bari: Laterza, 1982), unless otherwise specified. For the Italian texts of the spiritual sonnets, labeled with the letter "S" in footnotes, see Vittoria Colonna, *Sonnets for Michelangelo: A Bilingual Edition*, trans. and ed. Abigail Brundin (Chicago: University of Chicago Press, 2005).

For letters to and from Vittoria, see the *Carteggio di Vittoria Colonna, Marchesa di Pescara*, ed. Ermanno Ferrero and Giuseppe Müller (Turin: Loescher, 1892), unless otherwise noted.

All translations of Vittoria's poems and letters, as well as all other translations from Italian sources, are my own, unless otherwise noted. My translations of the letters have been edited and slightly emended by Troy Tower.

INTRODUCTION: IN SEARCH OF VITTORIA COLONNA

For a history of the monastery and early printing activities at Subiaco, see *St. Scholastica's Abbey—Subiaco: An Historical and Artistic Guide* (Subiaco, Italy: Edizioni S. Scolastica, 1986). On the Colonna archive in Subiaco, see Prudence Renée Baernstein, "'In My Own Hand': Costanza Colonna and the Art of the Letter in Sixteenth-Century Italy," *Renaissance Quarterly* 66.1 (2013).

For an extensive genealogy of the Colonna family, see George Williams, *Papal Genealogy: The Families and Descendants of the Popes* (Jefferson, NC: MacFarland, 1998). Further genealogy of the Colonna and other Roman families is in Francesco Sansovino, *Cronologia del mondo* (Venice: Luna, 1580).

On the birthdate of Vittoria, the majority of scholars accept 1490, the year proposed by Giambattista Rota in his 1760 edition of Colonna's *Rime* (Bergamo: Lancilotti). Domenico Tordi argues for 1492 in his "Luogo ed anno della nascita di Vittoria Colonna," *Giornale storico della letteratura italiana* 19 (1892).

On the question of Vittoria's siblings, Ascanio is the only brother who figures in her correspondence, but there are references in a number of sources to a second brother, Federico, who died in 1516. Beyond these two brothers, historians have argued for a range of other siblings who remain completely missing from the documents Vittoria left behind. For the most recent account of her family, see Christine Shaw, *The Political Role of the Orsini Family from Sixtus IV to Clement VII: Barons and Factions in the Papal States* (Rome: Istituto Storico italiano per il Medio Evo, 2007).

For Burckhardt's description, see *The Civilization of the Renaissance in Italy: An Essay*, trans. Samuel Middlemore (London: Phaidon, 1960); for the German text, see *Die Kultur der Renaissance in Italien*, ed. Horst Günther (Frankfurt: Deutscher Klassiker, 1989).

General Reference and Further Bibliography

Stanislao Benito Andreotti, "L'Archivio e la Biblioteca," in Claudio Giumelli, ed., *I monasteri benedettini di Subiaco* (Cinisello Balsamo, Italy: Silvana, 1982).

Agostino Attanasio, "La documentazione delle famiglie gentilizie romane negli studi storici: il caso dell'Archivio Colonna," in Lucio Lume, ed., *Archivi ed archivistica a Roma dopo l'Unità. Genesi storica, ordinamenti, interrelazioni. Atti del convegno, Roma, 12–14 marzo 1990* (Rome: Ministero per i Beni Culturali e Ambientali, 1994).

I. THE VIEW FROM THE CLIFF

For the role of Costanza d'Avalos in Spanish military affairs, see Suzanne Thérault, *Un cénacle humaniste de la Renaissance autour de Vittoria Colonna, châtelaine d'Ischia* (Florence: Sansoni, 1968).

On the various occupations of Naples and Ischia, see Luca Cerchiai, Lorena Janelli, and Fausto Longo, eds., *The Greek Cities of Magna Graecia and Sicily* (Los Angeles: Getty Museum, 2004); see also Ronald Musto, *Medieval Naples: A Documentary History, 400–1400* (New York: Italica, 2013).

The authoritative history of the relationships between the papacy and the Colonna and other noble families is Christine Shaw, *The Political Role of the Orsini Family from Sixtus IV to Clement VII: Barons and Factions in the Papal States* (Rome: Istituto Storico Italiano per il Medio Evo, 2007), which prints the Italian text of Ferdinand's remarks about the Roman barons. For documentation of the Colonna family's finances and acquisitions, see Antonio Coppi, ed., *Memorie colonnesi* (Rome: Salviucci, 1855).

For the history of the Palazzo Colonna in Marino, see Gilbert Bagnani, *The Roman Campagna and Its Treasures* (London: Methuen, 1929); for the claim that Vittoria was born in the Marino castle, primarily based on a Latin poem by the sixteenth-century poet Marcantonio Flaminio celebrating her association with the castle, see Domenico Tordi, "Luogo ed anno della nascita di Vittoria Colonna," *Giornale storico della letteratura italiana* 19 (1892).

On the interiors of early modern castles and *palazzi*, see Marta Ajmar-Wollheim and Flora Dennis, *At Home in Renaissance Italy* (London: Victoria & Albert Museum, 2006).

On travel, epistolary culture, and other everyday practices in early modern Europe, see Fernand Braudel, *Civilization and Capitalism, 15th–18th Century*, trans. and ed. Siân Reynolds (New York: Harper & Row, 1982). On the epistolary practices of Vittoria and other early modern women, see James Daybell, ed., *Early Modern Women's Letter Writing, 1450–1700* (Basingstoke, UK: Palgrave, 2001); Virginia Cox, *Women's Writing in Italy, 1400–1650* (Baltimore: Johns Hopkins University Press, 2008); and Gabriella Del Lungo Camiciotti, "Letters and Letter Writing in Early Modern Culture: An Introduction," *Journal of Early Modern Studies* 3 (2014).

The brief from Leo X to Agnese da Montefeltro is cited in Shaw, *The Political Role of the Orsini*; the translation from Latin to Italian was done by Francesco Caruso; the English translation is my own.

For a more detailed description of the complex political situation of the Italian peninsula in these decades, including accounts of the financial and military relationships with other European states, see Michael Edward Mallett and Christine Shaw, *The Italian Wars 1494–1559: War, State and Society in Early Modern Europe* (Hoboken, NJ: Taylor & Francis, 2014).

For an account of the Battle of Ravenna, see Frederick Lewis Taylor, *The Art of War in Italy: 1494–1529*, rev. ed. (London: Greenhill, 1993).

On the commission for *The Last Supper*, see Ross King, *Leonardo and the Last Supper* (New York: Walker, 2012). For a full history of Leonardo's patronage, see Massimiliano Capati, *Leonardo: A Life Through Paintings*, trans. Catherine Bolton (Florence: Mandragora, 2009).

Machiavelli's account of the Sforza family's machinations is found in chapter 7 of *The Prince*.

Paolo Giovio's Latin biography of Ferrante was translated into Italian by Ludovico Domenichi in 1551; for a modern printing of Domenichi, whose text I have cited and translated into English here, see Giovio, *Le vite del Gran Capitano e del marchese di*

Pescara, trans. Ludovico Domenichi, ed. Constantino Panigada (Bari, Italy: Laterza, 1931).

For Guicciardini's *Storia d'Italia*, see Silvana Seidel Menchi's Italian edition (Turin: Einaudi, 1971). The English translation is from *The History of Italy*, trans. Austin Parke Goddard (London: John Towers, 1755).

General Reference and Further Bibliography

Scipione Ammirato, *Delle famiglie nobili napoletane* (Florence: Marscotti, 1580).

The Biographical Dictionary of the Society for the Diffusion of Useful Knowledge (London: Longman, Brown, Green and Longmans, 1842–1844).

Kenneth Clark, *Leonardo da Vinci*, ed. Martin Kemp (London: Penguin, 1988).

Alberto Maria Ghisalberti, gen. ed., *Dizionario biografico degli italiani* (Rome: Istituto della Enciclopedia italiana, 1960–).

Lisa Kaborycha, *A Short History of Renaissance Italy* (Upper Saddle River, NJ: Prentice Hall, 2011).

Martin Kemp, "'Your Humble Servant and Painter': Towards a History of Leonardo da Vinci in His Contexts of Employment," *Gazette des Beaux-Arts* 140 (2002).

Pompeo Litta Biumi, *I Colonna di Roma* (Milan: Ferrario, 1836), volume 3 of *Celebri famiglie italiane*, ed. Luigi Passerini, Federico Odorici, Federico Stefani, and Francesco di Mauro (various Italian imprints, 1819–1885).

Niccolò Machiavelli, *The Prince: With Related Documents*, trans. and ed. William Connell (Boston: Bedford/St. Martin's, 2005).

Filadelfo Muñoz, *Historia della augustissima famiglia Colonna* (Venice: Turrini, 1658).

Charles William Chadwick Oman, *A History of the Art of War in the Sixteenth Century* (London: Methuen, 1937).

Meredith Ray, *Writing Gender in Women's Letter Collections of the Italian Renaissance* (Toronto: University of Toronto Press, 2009).

Jean Paul Richter, ed., *The Literary Works of Leonardo da Vinci*, trans. R. C. Bell (London: Low, Marston, Searle & Rivington, 1883).

Diana Robin, Anne Larsen, and Carole Levin, eds., *Encyclopedia of Women in the Renaissance: Italy, France, and England* (Santa Barbara, CA: ABC-CLIO, 2007).

Giuseppe Tomassetti, *La campagna romana antica, medioevale e moderna*, rev. ed., eds. Luisa Chiumenti and Fernando Bilancia (Florence: Olschki, 1979–1980).

2. DONNING WIDOW'S WEEDS

On early modern Viterbo, see Simonetta Valtieri and Enzo Bentivoglio, *Viterbo nel Rinascimento* (Rome: Ginevra Bentivoglio, 2012). For a history of carriage travel, see John Hunt, "Carriages, Violence, and Masculinity in Early Modern Rome," *I Tatti Studies in the Italian Renaissance* 17.1 (2014).

For the extensive correspondence of Isabella d'Este translated into English, see Deanna Shemek, trans. and ed., *Isabella d'Este: Selected Letters* (Toronto/Tempe, AZ: Iter Press/ACMRS, 2017).

Ferrante's letters to Mario Equicola discussing Delia—or *Delya*, in his spelling—are published in Alessandro Luzio, "Vittoria Colonna," *Rivista storica mantovana* 1 (1884). They are treated in English in Jerrold, *Vittoria Colonna*. Luzio also transcribes a letter from Francesco Gonzaga, the Mantuan ambassador in Rome, written one week after Ferrante's death, which described Vittoria's reaction to the news of Ferrante's death (the letter is kept in the Archivio Gonzaga in Mantua).

The identification of Isabel de Requesens as the figure in the Louvre portrait, which was executed by Giulio Romano with the collaboration of his mentor Raphael, is Michael Fritz's; see *Giulio Romano et Raphaël: la vice-reine de Naples, ou, La Renaissance d'une beauté mythique*, trans. Claire Nydegger (Paris: Réunion des Musées Nationaux, 1997).

For details on the daily life and personal effects of Vittoria and Ferrante, see Alfred von Reumont, *Vittoria Colonna, marchesa di Pescara: vita, fede e poesia nel secolo decimosesto*, trans. Ermanno Ferrero and Giuseppe Müller (Turin: Loescher, 1892); Maud Jerrold, *Vittoria Colonna, with Some Account of Her Friends and Her Times* (London: Dent, 1906); Amalia Giordano, *La dimora di Vittoria Colonna a Napoli* (Naples: Melfi & Joele, 1906); and Amy Bernardy, *La vita e l'opera di Vittoria Colonna* (Florence: Le Monnier, 1928). These modern biographers each draw from two sixteenth-century chroniclers still lacking critical editions, Giuliano Passero (or Passaro) and Filonico Alicarnasso, pseudonym of Costantino Castriota. The manuscript of Alicarnasso's *Vita di Vittoria Colonna*, ms. XB67 at the Biblioteca Nazionale in Naples, is compiled alongside a biography of Ferrante; it is published as an appendix to Ferrero and Müller's *Carteggio*. The manuscript copy of Passero was published by Vincenzo Maria Altobelli under the title *Storie in forma di giornali* (Naples: Orsini, 1785).

Giovio's description of Ferrante is at the end of the second chapter of volume 1 of his biography; see *Le vite del Gran Capitano e del marchese di Pescara*. Vittoria is described as lacking "gran beltà" by Alicarnasso in Ferrero and Müller's *Carteggio*.

Figures pertaining to Vittoria's dowry can be found in the original marriage contract between Fabrizio Colonna and Ferrante d'Avalos in the Colonna archive in Subiaco. The wedding gifts specified in the wedding contract are printed as an appendix to Pier Ercole Visconti's 1840 edition of Vittoria's *Rime* (Rome: Salviucci).

On Roman dowry caps, see Irene Fosi and Maria Antonietta Visceglia, "Marriage and Politics at the Papal Court in the Sixteenth and Seventeenth Centuries," in Trevor Dean and Kate Lowe, eds., *Marriage in Italy, 1300–1650* (Cambridge: Cambridge University Press, 1998). On the Florentine dowry market, see Julius Kirshner and Anthony Molho, "The Dowry Fund and the Marriage Market in Early *Quattrocento*

Florence," *Journal of Modern History* 50.3 (1978). On the intersection of marriage practices and the Catholic Church before and after the Council of Trent, see Merry Wiesner-Hanks, *Christianity and Sexuality in the Early Modern World: Regulating Desire, Reforming Practice* (London: Routledge, 2000). Vittoria's wedding celebration is described in Reumont, *Vittoria Colonna*; her guests' description is given in Bernardy, *La vita e l'opera di Vittoria Colonna*.

For details on the luxurious wedding celebrations typical of early modern Italy, see Jane Bridgeman and Alan Griffiths, eds., *A Renaissance Wedding: The Celebrations at Pesaro for the Marriage of Costanzo Sforza & Camilla Marzano d'Aragona, 26–30 May 1475* (London: Harvey Miller, 2013); the wedding song and menu are translated by Bridgeman, with my slight emendations. On dowry limits and marriage ceremonies in Italy, see Dean and Lowe, eds., *Marriage in Italy, 1300–1650*, and Anthony Mohlo, *Marriage Alliance in Late Medieval Florence* (Cambridge, MA: Harvard University Press, 1994). See also Anthony D'Elia, *The Renaissance of Marriage in Fifteenth-Century Italy* (Cambridge, MA: Harvard University Press, 2004), who translates Bruni's complaint about the expense of his wedding.

Passero's description of Bona Sforza's party and its menu is given in Giordano, *La dimora di Vittoria Colonna a Napoli*; Vittoria's Hungarian dance is described by Giovio in the third dialogue of his *Notable Men and Women of Our Time*, trans. Kenneth Gouwens (Cambridge, MA: Harvard University Press, 2013).

Among the many biographies of Lucrezia Borgia, see in particular Sarah Bradford's *Lucrezia Borgia: Life, Love and Death in Renaissance Italy* (New York: Penguin, 2005), published in Italian as *Lucrezia Borgia: la vera storia* (Mondadori, 2005). Also noteworthy is *La figlia del papa* (Milan: Chiarelettere, 2014), the only historical novel by the late playwright Dario Fo, which was translated into English as *The Pope's Daughter* (New York: Europa, 2015). The death of Alfonso d'Aragona is discussed in Bradford, *Lucrezia Borgia*.

The exchange between Beatrice and her uncle Leonato is in Shakespeare's *Much Ado About Nothing*, act 2, scene 1, lines 48–49; see *The Norton Shakespeare*, 3rd ed., gen. ed. Stephen Greenblatt (New York: W. W. Norton, 2016). All references to Shakespeare are from this edition.

For Pascal's wager, see Blaise Pascal, *Pensées*, trans. John Warrington (London: Dent, 1932).

For the life and death of Margherita Colonna, see Giulia Barone, "Margherita Colonna: A Portrait," trans. Larry Field, *Magistra* 21.2 (2015). For a recent biography of Clare of Assisi, see Joan Mueller, *The Privilege of Poverty: Clare of Assisi, Agnes of Prague, and the Struggle for a Franciscan Rule for Women* (University Park: Pennsylvania State University Press, 2006). Vittoria's plans to join a convent cannot definitively be established, but the documentary evidence (both Clement's letter to the nuns and his subsequent permissions to Vittoria) overwhelmingly suggests this to be the case. For a treatment of these materials, see Veronica Copello, "«La signora marchesa a casa»: tre aspetti della biografia di Vittoria Colonna con una tavola cronologica," *Testo* 73 (2017).

General Reference and Further Bibliography

María Teresa Cacho, "Fuentes impresas de poesía española en cancionerillos musicales italianos del siglo XVI," in Pedro Cátedra, ed., *La literatura popular impresa en España y en la América colonial. Formas & temas, géneros, funciones, difusión, historia e teoría* (Salamanca, Spain: SEMYR, 2006).

Stanley Chojnacki, *Women and Men in Renaissance Venice: Twelve Essays on Patrician Society* (Baltimore: Johns Hopkins University Press, 2000).

Gerardo Cioffardi, *Bona Sforza. Donna del Rinascimento tra Italia e Polonia* (Bari, Italy: Levante, 2000).

Carlo Cipolla, *Before the Industrial Revolution: European Society and Economy, 1000–1700*, trans. Christopher Woodall, 3rd ed. (London: Routledge, 1993).

Benedetto Croce, *La Spagna nella vita italiana durante la Rinascenza* (Bari, Italy: Laterza, 1917).

Victoria Finlay, *Color: A History of the Palette* (New York: Random House, 2002).

Katie Fiorentino, *La chiesa di Sant'Erasmo a Castel Sant'Elmo. Un patrimonio ritrovato* (Naples: Artem, 2013).

Juan-Santos Gaynor and Ilaria Toesca, *S. Silvestro in Capite* (Rome: Marietti, 1963).

David Herlihy and Christiane Klapisch-Zuber, *Tuscans and Their Families: A Study of the Florentine Catasto of 1427* (New Haven, CT: Yale University Press, 1985).

David Jenkins, ed., *The Cambridge History of Western Textiles* (Cambridge: Cambridge University Press, 2003).

Anthony Molho, *Marriage Alliance in Late Medieval Florence* (Cambridge, MA: Harvard University Press, 1994).

3. LONGING FOR THE NUNNERY

On the economic and social motivations for monastic life in early modern Italy and on the financial practices of Italian convents, see Helen Hills, *Invisible City: The Architecture of Devotion in Seventeenth-Century Neapolitan Convents* (Oxford: Oxford University Press, 2004); see also Sharon Strocchia, *Nuns and Nunneries in Renaissance Florence* (Baltimore: Johns Hopkins University Press, 2009).

On Arcangela Tarabotti, see Letizia Panizza's introduction to her translation of *Tirannia paterna*, *Paternal Tyranny* (Chicago: University of Chicago Press, 2004), which is quoted here. All citations of the Christian Bible follow the King James Version; see the 2000 edition published by the American Bible Society.

On the Divine Offices and daily life in an Italian convent, see Strocchia, *Nuns and Nunneries*; see also Kate Lowe, *Nuns' Chronicles and Convent Culture: Women and*

History-Writing in Renaissance and Counter-Reformation Italy (Cambridge: Cambridge University Press, 2003). On the relative comforts of certain conventual orders, see Hills, *Invisible City*; see also Jutta Gisela Sperling, *Convents and the Body Politic in Late Renaissance Venice* (Chicago: University of Chicago Press, 1999). On monastic dietary practices and Jaques de Vitry's comments on the nuns, see Carolyn Walker Bynum, *Holy Feast and Holy Fast: The Religious Significance of Food to Medieval Women* (Berkeley: University of California Press, 1987), and Rudolph Bell, *Holy Anorexia* (Chicago: University of Chicago Press, 1985).

A history of Clare's life and the establishment of the Poor Clares is in Hills, *Invisible City*. For an early history of the Friars Minor, see John Moorman, *A History of the Franciscan Order: From Its Origins to the Year 1517* (Chicago: Franciscan Herald, 1988).

Pope Clement's brief to the nuns at San Silvestro in Capite is printed in an appendix to Pietro Ercole Visconti's edition of Vittoria Colonna's *Rime* (Rome: Salviucci, 1840). The letter was translated from Latin to Italian by Francesco Caruso; the translation from Italian to English is my own.

Giovio's description of Ferrante's funeral is in book 7, chapter 4, of his *Vita*. The funeral procession is described by Passero and recorded in Amalia Giordano, *La dimora di Vittoria Colonna a Napoli* (Naples: Melfi & Joele, 1906), which also includes Ariosto's Latin epitaph. For further details on the Aragonese mausoleum, see Bruto Amante, *La tomba di Vittoria Colonna e i testamenti finora inediti della poetessa* (Bologna: Zanichelli, 1896).

On regulating women's grief in early modern Italy, see Sharon T. Strocchia, *Death and Ritual in Renaissance Florence* (Baltimore: Johns Hopkins University Press, 1992). For a statistically informed survey of legislation concerning funeral attendance and behavior in early modern Italy, see Catherine Kovesi Killerby, *Sumptuary Law in Italy 1200–1500* (Oxford: Oxford University Press, 2002).

Clement's letter to Vittoria was first published by Bartolommeo Fontana in "Nuovi documenti vaticani intorno a Vittoria Colonna," *Archivio della [Reale] Società Romana di Storia Patria* 10.4 (1887). The translation of this letter from Latin to English was done by Dr. Thomas Hendrickson and emended by Dr. Robert W. Ulery.

On ecclesiastical anxieties concerning the host, see, among others, Stephen Greenblatt, "The Mousetrap," in Catherine Gallagher and Stephen Greenblatt, *Practicing New Historicism* (Chicago: University of Chicago Press, 2000); Peter Paludanus is cited here.

General Reference and Further Bibliography

Gino Fornaciari, "Le mummie aragonesi in San Domenico Maggiore di Napoli," *Medicina nei secoli* 18.3 (2006).

Christopher Hibbert, *The House of Medici: Its Rise and Fall* (New York: Morrow, 1974).

Lawrence Landini, *The Causes of the Clericalization of the Order of Friars Minor, 1209–1260, in the Light of Early Franciscan Sources*, dissertation, Pontificia Università Gregoriana, 1968.

Allison Mary Levy, *Re-membering Masculinity in Early Modern Florence: Widowed Bodies, Mourning and Portraiture* (Aldershot, UK: Ashgate, 2006).

Gaetano Pieraccini, *La stirpe de' Medici di Cafaggiolo. Saggio di ricerche sulla trasmissione ereditaria dei caratteri biologici* (Florence: Nardini, 1986).

Paul Strathern, *The Medici: Power, Money, and Ambition in the Italian Renaissance* (New York: Pegasus, 2016).

Ottavio Mazzoni Toselli, *Racconti storici estratti dall'archivio criminale di Bologna* (Bologna: Chierici, 1870).

4. BECOMING A POET

Paolo Giovio's description of Vittoria's grief is in *Notable Men and Women of Our Time*, trans. Kenneth Gouwens (Cambridge, MA: Harvard University Press, 2013). On the regulations on women's behavior and attire in mourning in early modern Italy, see Catherine Kovesi Killerby, *Sumptuary Law in Italy 1200–1500* (Oxford: Oxford University Press, 2002).

Cesare Vecellio's description is from his 1590 encyclopedia *Degli habiti antichi, et moderni di diverse parti del mondo*, published in Venice by Damian Zenaro, in the section of the first book entitled "Habiti delle nobili venetiane, & altre qualità della Città"; the English translation, by Ann Rosalind Jones and Margaret Rosenthal, *The Clothing of the Renaissance World: Europe, Asia, Africa, The Americas: Cesare Vecellio's Habiti Antichi et Moderni* (London/New York: Thames & Hudson, 2008), is of the second 1598 edition, which also includes examples from the Americas.

For the Italian texts of Petrarch, see Marco Santagata's updated edition of the *Canzoniere* (Milan: Mondadori, 2004). On the historical relationship between Petrarch and Laura de Noves, the woman traditionally believed to be the subject of his poetry, see Frederic Jones, "Further Evidence of the Identity of Petrarch's Laura," *Italian Studies* 39.1 (1984). Other scholars insist on a largely symbolic construction where Laura represents poetic glory, based on the likeness of her name to the laurel tree (*lauro*, in Italian) that crowns poetic genius; see John Freccero, "The Fig Tree and the Laurel: Petrarch's Poetics," *Diacritics* 5 (1973).

The bibliography on Petrarchism is vast, but see, among others, Gordon Braden, *Petrarchan Love and the Continental Renaissance* (New Haven: Yale University Press, 1999). On the responses to Petrarchism by early modern Italian women writers besides Vittoria, see Ann Rosalind Jones, *The Currency of Eros: Women's Love Lyric in Europe, 1540–1620* (Bloomington: Indiana University Press, 1990); see also Virginia Cox, *Women's Writing in Italy, 1400–1650* (Baltimore: Johns Hopkins University Press, 2008). For a history of the sonnet before and after Petrarch, see Michael Spiller, *The Development of the Sonnet: An Introduction* (London: Routledge, 1992).

Britonio and Capanio's elegies of Vittoria are translated in Diana Robin, *Publishing Women: Salons, the Presses, and the Counter-Reformation in Sixteenth-Century Italy* (Chicago: University of Chicago Press, 2007).

On the medal of Vittoria and its possible echoes of Raphael's Sappho, see Marjorie Och, "Portrait Medals of Vittoria Colonna: Representing the Learned Woman," in Susan Shifrin, ed., *Women as Sites of Culture: Women's Roles in Cultural Formation from the Renaissance to the Twentieth Century* (Aldershot, UK: Ashgate, 2002); see also Walter Cupperi, "«Il nome fatale di Vittoria»: note su due medaglie della marchesa di Pescara," in Francesco De Angelis, ed., *Lo sguardo archeologico: i normalisti per Paul Zanker* (Pisa: Edizioni della Normale, 2007).

For Plutarch's account of Portia, see his *Lives of the Noble Grecians and Romans*, trans. John Dryden, ed. and revised by Arthur Hugh Clough (New York: The Modern Library, 1992), 2:609. Catullus's description of the "eternal sleep" is from his fifth ode; see *Catullus*, trans. and ed. Francis Warre Cornish, in *Catullus · Tibullus · Pervigilium Veneris*, 2nd ed., ed. George Patrick Goold (Cambridge, MA: Harvard University Press, 1966).

The translation of Plato's *Symposium* is Margaret Howatson's in the edition of Margaret Howatson and Frisbee Sheffield (Cambridge: Cambridge University Press, 2008). For a synthesis of Neoplatonic thought from antiquity onward, see Dominic O'Meara, ed., *Neoplatonism and Christian Thought* (Albany: State University of New York Press, 1982). On the repopularization of Platonic ideas in early modern Italy, especially by Marsilio Ficino, see James Hankins, *Plato in the Italian Renaissance* (Leiden, Netherlands: Brill, 1990); see also Nesca Robb, *Neoplatonism of the Italian Renaissance* (London: Allen & Unwin, 1935).

The standard English translation of *The Courtier* is Charles Singleton's *The Book of the Courtier: The Singleton Translation, An Authoritative Text Criticism*, ed. Daniel Javitch (New York: W. W. Norton, 2002). All citations of Castiglione follow this edition.

Bernardo Tasso's fourth ode is dedicated to Vittoria Colonna; see Vercingetorige Martignone's edition of Tasso's *Rime* (Turin: RES, 1995).

General Reference and Further Bibliography

Virgilio Costa, "Sulle prime traduzioni italiane a stampa delle opere di Plutarco (secc. XV–XVI)," in Maria Accame, *Volgarizzare e tradurre dall'Umanesimo all'Età contemporanea. Atti della Giornata di Studi, 7 dicembre 2011, Università di Roma «Sapienza»* (Rome: Tivoli, 2012).

Eugenio Garin, "From Petrarch to Salutati," in *History of Italian Philosophy*, trans. and ed. Giorgio Pinton (Amsterdam: Rodopi, 2008).

Vojtěch Hladký, *The Philosophy of Gemistos Plethon: Platonism in Late Byzantium, Between Hellenism and Orthodoxy* (Aldershot, UK: Ashgate, 2014).

Teodoro Katinis, *Medicina e filosofia in Marsilio Ficino: il Consilio contro la pestilenza* (Rome: Edizioni di Storia e Letteratura, 2007).

Gianvito Resta, *Le epitomi di Plutarco nel Quattrocento* (Padua: Antenore, 1962).

Brian Richardson, *Print Culture in Renaissance Italy: The Editor and the Vernacular Text, 1470–1600* (Cambridge: Cambridge University Press, 1994).

John Trappes-Lomax, *Catullus: A Textual Reappraisal* (Swansea: Classical Press of Wales, 2007).

Edward Zalta, gen. ed., *Stanford Encyclopedia of Philosophy* (Stanford, CA: Center for the Study of Language and Information, 1997–), http://www.plato.stanford.edu.

5. THE SACK OF ROME

For a history of relations between the Colonna family and the papacy, see Christine Shaw, *The Political Role of the Orsini Family from Sixtus IV to Clement VII: Barons and Factions in the Papal States* (Rome: Istituto Storico Italiano per il Medio Evo, 2007).

For further detail on the Sack of Rome, see Michael Edward Mallett and Christine Shaw, *The Italian Wars 1494–1559: War, State and Society in Early Modern Europe* (Hoboken, NJ: Taylor & Francis, 2014); see also Judith Hook, *The Sack of Rome, 1527* (London: MacMillan, 1972). For the cultural legacy of the siege, see André Chastel, *The Sack of Rome, 1527: The A. W. Mellon Lectures in the Fine Arts, 1977, The National Gallery of Art, Washington, D.C.*, trans. Beth Archer (Princeton, NJ: Princeton University Press, 1983). On the involvement of Charles III of Bourbon, see Vincent Pitts, *The Man Who Sacked Rome: Charles de Bourbon, Constable of France (1490–1527)* (New York: Lang, 1993); see also Luigi Guicciardini, *The Sack of Rome*, trans. James McGregor (New York: Italica, 1993), the second book of which gives Bourbon's speech on the fateful day of May 6, 1527.

Falstaff's description of the soldiers is from *1 Henry IV*, act 4, scene 2, lines 59–60.

On the patronage of the Medici popes, see Loren Partridge, *The Art of Renaissance Rome, 1400–1600* (Upper Saddle River, NJ: Abrams/Prentice Hall, 1996).

Pietro Corsi's account is found in Kenneth Gouwens, *Remembering the Renaissance: Humanist Narratives of the Sack of Rome* (Leiden, Netherlands: Brill, 1998). The critical edition of Corsi's original Latin poem, the *Romae Urbis excidium*, is in Léon Dorez, "Le poème de Pietro Corsi sur le sac de Rome," *Mélanges d'Archéologie et d'Histoire de l'Ecole Française de Rome* 16 (1896). Alcionio's Latin orations are in Gouwens, *Remembering the Renaissance*.

On the relations between the papacy and Orvieto, see Daniel Waley, *Mediaeval Orvieto: The Political History of an Italian City-State, 1157–1334* (Cambridge: Cambridge University Press, 1952).

For Clement's time in Orvieto and his reference to it as "our city," see Anne Reynolds, "The Papal Court in Exile: Clement VII in Orvieto, 1527–28," in Kenneth Gouwens and Sheryl Reiss, eds., *The Pontificate of Clement VII: History, Politics, Culture* (Aldershot, UK: Ashgate, 2005). The comment comes from a 1525 letter addressed to the "*hominibus Civitatis n[ost]r[ae]*." Lippomano's comments on the papal court in exile are in Reynolds, as is Gardiner's letter.

For Erasmus's letter, see *The Correspondence of Erasmus: Letters 1926 to 2081 (1528)*, trans. Charles Fantazzi, ed. James Estes (Toronto: University of Toronto Press, 2011).

General Reference and Further Bibliography

Liliana Barroero, *S. Maria dell'Orto* (Rome: Istituto di Studi Romani, 1976).

John Sherren Brewer, ed., *Letters and Papers, Foreign and Domestic, of the Reign of Henry VIII* (London: Longman, 1862–1920).

Franco Cardini, "Giovanni gentiluomo," in Mario Scalini, ed., *Giovanni delle Bande Nere* (Florence: Banca Toscana, 2001).

Pierluigi De Vecchi, *Raphael* (New York: Abbeville, 2002).

John Edwards, *Archbishop Pole* (Farnham, UK: Ashgate, 2014).

Encyclopaedia Brittanica, 15th ed. (Chicago: Benton Foundation/Encyclopedia Brittanica), http://www.brittanica.com.

Sonia Gallico, *Vaticano* (ATS Italia, 2004).

Giancarlo Malacarne, *I Gonzaga di Mantova. Una stirpe per una capitale europea* (Modena: Bulino, 2004–2008).

Carlo Milanesi, ed., *Il sacco di Roma del MDXXVII. Narrazioni di contemporanei* (Florence: Barbèra, 1867).

Angelo Nicosia, *Museo della città e del territorio: Aquino* (Rome: Istituto Poligrafico e Zecca dello Stato, 2006).

Konrad Oberhuber, *Raphael: The Paintings* (Munich: Prestel, 1999).

Ugo Onorati, *La basilica collegiata di San Barnaba Apostolo. Il patrono di Marino nella storia e nella tradizione popolare locale* (Marino: Associazione Senza Frontiere O.n.l.u.s./Biblioteca di Interesse Locale "Girolamo Torquati," 2010).

Nicola Ratti, *Storia di Genzano, con note e documenti* (Rome: Salomoni, 1797).

Ingrid Rowland, "The Vatican Stanze," in Marcia Hall, *The Cambridge Companion to Raphael* (Cambridge: Cambridge University Press, 2005).

Paolo Sarpi, *Istoria del concilio tridentino* (Florence: Barbèra, Bianchi & Co., 1858).

André Thevet, *Portraits from the French Renaissance and the Wars of Religion*, trans. and ed. Roger Schlesinger (Kirksville, MO: Truman State University Press, 2010).

Giuseppe Tomassetti and Francesco Tomassetti, *La compagna romana antica, medio-evale e moderna* (Rome: Maglione & Strinsi, 1926).

6. LIFE AT COURT

For a history of Urbino under Federico da Montefeltro, see June Osborne, *Urbino: Story of a Renaissance City* (Chicago: University of Chicago Press, 2003).

For the life and works of Castiglione, see John Robert Woodhouse, *Baldesar Castiglione: A Reassessment of* The Courtier (Edinburgh: Edinburgh University Press, 1978). The characteristics of the courtier are discussed throughout the second book of *The Courtier*, while *sprezzatura* is presented in section 1.26. On the popularity of the *Cortegiano* in sixteenth-century Europe, see Amadeo Quondam, *«Questo povero Cortegiano». Castiglione, il Libro, la Storia* (Rome: Bulzoni, 2000); see also Peter Burke, *The Fortunes of the* Courtier: *The European Reception of Castiglione's* Cortegiano (Cambridge: Polity, 1995).

William Butler Yeats's poem "The People," from the 1919 collection *The Wild Swans at Coole*, is republished in *The Poems*, rev. ed., ed. Richard Finneran (New York: Macmillan, 1989).

For Roger Ascham's description of the dialogue, see *The Schoolmaster (1570)*, ed. Lawrence Ryan (Ithaca, NY: Cornell University Press, 1967).

Citations of Paolo Giovio's *Dialogus de viris et feminis aetate nostra florentibus* follow the first English translation, *Notable Men and Women of Our Time*, trans. Kenneth Gouwens (Cambridge, MA: Harvard University Press, 2013); Gouwens's introduction has further detail about Giovio's career and the composition of the dialogues.

On Bembo and the debates over the proper literary language, known as the *questione della lingua*, see Peter Hainsworth, ed., *The Languages of Literature in Renaissance Italy* (Oxford/New York: Clarendon/Oxford University Press, 1988). On Bembo's influence on sixteenth-century Italian literature, see Carol Kidwell, *Pietro Bembo: Lover, Linguist, Cardinal* (Montreal/Kingston: McGill-Queen's University Press, 2004); see also Ted Danforth, *Pietro Bembo: "Foster Father" of the Modern Book* (New York: Typophiles, 2003). Bembo's letter to Giovio was translated by Troy Tower; for the Italian text, see Pietro Bembo, *Lettere*, ed. Ernesto Travi (Bologna: Commissione per i Testi di Lingua, 1992).

Vittoria's sonnet is included in an appendix to the 1535 edition of Pietro Bembo's *Delle rime* printed by Giovan Antonio Nicolini da Sabbio in Venice. The Italian text of their exchange included here follows the edition in Virginia Cox's *Lyric Poetry by Women of the Italian Renaissance* (Baltimore: Johns Hopkins University Press, 2015).

General Reference and Further Bibliography

Luciano Berti, gen. ed., *Gli Uffizi. Catalogo generale* (Florence: Centro Di, 1979).

Caterina Caneva, Alessandro Cecchi, and Antonio Natali, eds., *The Uffizi: Guide to the Collections and Catalogue of All Paintings*, trans. Thekla Clark (Boston: Sandak, 1992).

Vittorio Cian, *Un illustre nunzio pontifio del Rinascimento: Baldessar Castiglione* (Vatican City: Biblioteca Apostolica Vaticana, 1951).

Virginia Cox, *The Renaissance Dialogue: Literary Dialogue in Its Social and Political Contexts, Castiglione to Galileo* (Cambridge: Cambridge University Press, 1992).

Salvatore di Costanzo, *Ischia. Itinerario storico e fotografico dalle origini ai nostri giorni* (Naples: Edizioni Scientifiche Italiane, 1995).

Carlo Dionisotti, "Appunti sul Bembo e su Vittoria Colonna," in *Miscellanea Augusto Campana*, ed. Enzo Cecchini, Adriano Gattucci, Piergiorgio Parroni, and Piergiorgio Peruzzi (Padua: Antenore, 1981).

Joanna Pitman, *The Dragon's Trail: The Biography of Raphael's Masterpiece* (New York: Touchstone, 2007).

Guido Rebecchini, *Private Collectors in Mantua, 1500–1630* (Rome: Edizioni di Storia e Letteratura, 2002).

Bernhard Schimmelpfennig, "The Two Coronations of Charles V at Bologna, 1530," in James Ronald Mulryne and Elizabeth Goldring, eds., *Court Festivals of the European Renaissance: Art, Politics and Performance* (Aldershot, UK: Ashgate, 2002).

Ileana Tozzi, "I Varano. I tempi, i luoghi, la storia: parte III," *Storiadelmondo* 24 (2004).

7. AMONG PREACHERS AND PILGRIMS

A letter addressed to Isabella d'Este confirms that Vittoria was in the audience at Ochino's Lenten sermon in 1535; see Deanna Shemek, trans. and ed., *Isabella d'Este: Selected Letters* (Toronto/Tempe, AZ: Iter Press/ACMRS, 2017). It is likely that Vittoria met Ochino soon after his arrival in Rome in 1534; see Emidio Campi, "Vittoria Colonna and Bernardino Ochino," in Abigail Brundin, Tatiana Crivelli, and Maria Sapegno, eds., *A Companion to Vittoria Colonna* (Leiden, Netherlands: Brill, 2016).

On reform movements within the Franciscan community, see Duncan Nimmo, *Reform and Division in the Medieval Franciscan Order: From Saint Francis to the Foundation of the Capuchins* (Rome: Capuchin Historical Institute, 1987).

On reform movements in sixteenth-century Italy, see Salvatore Caponetto, *The Protestant Reformation in Sixteenth-Century Italy*, trans. Anne Tedeschi and John Tedeschi (Kirksville, MO: Thomas Jefferson University Press, 1999); see also Thomas M'Crie, *History of the Progress and Suppression of the Reformation in Italy in the Sixteenth Century, Including a Sketch of the History of the Reformation in the Grisons,*

2nd ed., ed. Thomas M'Crie, Jr. (Edinburgh: William Blackwood, 1856; reissued, New York: AMS, 1974).

For further detail on the life of Ochino, see Benrath, *Bernardino Ochino of Siena: A Contribution Towards the History of the Reformation*, trans. Helen Zimmern (London: Nisbet, 1876); the translations of his sermon are from this book. On the career and execution of Savonarola, see Lauro Martines, *Fire in the City: Savonarola and the Struggle for Renaissance Florence* (Oxford: Oxford University Press, 2005).

For further biography on Valdés and for further history of the *alumbrados*, see Daniel Crews, *Twilight of the Renaissance: The Life of Juan de Valdés* (Toronto: University of Toronto Press, 2008), which also translates Valdés's letter about Giulia Gonzaga. On Valdés's *Christian Alphabet*, which survives only in sixteenth-century Italian translations of the Spanish manuscript, see Benjamin Wiffen, ed., *Alfabeto Christiano by Juan de Valdés: A Faithful Reprint of the Italian of 1546 with Two Modern Translations, in Spanish and in English* (London: s.n., 1861).

For the debate between Harding and John Jewel, bishop of Salisbury, see the "Reply to M. Harding's Answer," in *The Works of John Jewel*, ed. John Ayre (Cambridge: Cambridge University Press, 1845–1850).

For Longfellow's incomplete *Michael Angelo*, see volume 6 of *The Poetical Works of Henry Wadsworth Longfellow*, ed. Samuel Longfellow (Boston: Houghton, Mifflin, 1886–1891).

Charles's reaction to Ochino's oratory is described in Pietro Giannone, *Istoria civile del Regno di Napoli* (Naples: Niccolò Naso, 1723); see the translation by James Ogilvie, *The Civil History of the Kingdom of Naples* (London: Innys et al., 1729–1731).

Clement's letter summoning the Capuchins and his subsequent decree banning them are described in Zacharias Bovarius, ed., *Annalium seu sacrarum historiarum Ordinis minorum S. Francisci qui Capucini nuncupantur [tomi]* (Lyon: Claudius Landry, 1632); they are treated in Benrath, *Bernardino Ochino of Siena*, and the tenth volume of Ludwig Pastor, *The History of the Popes*, trans. and ed. Ralph Francis Kerr (London: Kegan Paul, Trench, Trübner, 1910).

The hermit's chant upon the Capuchins' expulsion is in Benrath, *Bernardino Ochino of Siena*.

On the life and lifestyle of Alessandro Farnese, later Paul III, see Rodolfo Lanciani, *The Golden Days of the Renaissance in Rome from the Pontificate of Julius II to That of Paul III* (Boston: Houghton, Mifflin, 1906). The translations of Pope Paul's Latin letters to Vittoria are slightly modified from those by Elizabeth Klaassen in the appendix to Och, "Vittoria Colonna: Art Patronage and Religious Reform."

On the career of Gasparo Contarini, see Elisabeth Gleason, *Gasparo Contarini: Venice, Rome and Reform* (Berkeley: University of California Press, 1993).

On the foundation of the Capuchin order and Vittoria's role as "second protectoress" to the order, see Elisabeth Gleason, "The Capuchin Order in the Sixteenth

Century," in Richard DeMolen, ed., *Religious Orders of the Catholic Reformation: In Honor of John C. Olin on His Seventy-Fifth Birthday* (New York: Fordham University Press, 1994). Documents testifying to Vittoria's negotiations over Capuchin property are found in Marjorie Och's 1993 dissertation from Bryn Mawr College, "Vittoria Colonna: Art Patronage and Religious Reform in Sixteenth-Century Rome."

On the industry and culture of Holy Land pilgrimage, see Wes Williams, *Pilgrimage and Narrative in the French Renaissance: 'The Undiscovered Country'* (Oxford: Clarendon, 1998), which summarizes Regnaut's recommendations for pilgrims. On the establishment of Compostela as a pilgrimage site, see Catherine Gasquoine Hartley Gallichan, *The Story of Santiago de Compostela* (London/New York: Dent/Dutton, 1912).

Ludovico Ariosto's description of Pietro Aretino is in the last canto of his *Orlando furioso*, stanza 14. Guido Waldman's prose translation, *Orlando Furioso* (Oxford: Oxford University Press, 1983) is cited throughout.

General Reference and Further Bibliography

Marian Andrews, *A Princess of the Italian Reformation, Giulia Gonzaga, 1513–1566, Her Family and Her Friends* (New York: Scribner's, 1912).

Costanza Barbieri, *Sebastiano del Piombo, i ritratti. Committenti, artisti e letterati nella Roma del Cinquecento*, ed. Paul Joannides (Isola del Gran Sasso, Italy: Staurós, 2012).

Giovanni Bardazzi, "Le rime spirituali di Vittoria Colonna e Bernardino Ochino," *Italique* 4 (2001).

Monica Bianco, "Per la datazione di un sonetto di Vittoria Colonna (e di un probabile ritratto della poetessa ad opera di Sebastiano del Piombo)," *Italique* 11 (2008).

Josephie Brefeld, *A Guidebook for the Jerusalem Pilgrimate in the Late Middle Ages: A Case for Computer-Aided Textual Criticism* (Hilversum, Netherlands: Verloren, 1994).

Costanzo Cargnoni, ed., *I frati cappuccini. Documenti e testimonianze del primo secolo* (Perugia: Edizioni Frate Indovino, 1988).

Lawrence Anthony Hess Cuthbert, *The Capuchins: A Contribution to the History of the Counter-Reformation* (Toronto: Longmans, Green, 1929).

William Eamon, *Science and the Secrets of Nature: Books of Secrets in Medieval and Early Modern Culture* (Princeton, NJ: Princeton University Press, 1994).

Henry Outram Evennett, "The New Orders," in Geoffrey Rudolph Elton, ed., *The New Cambridge Modern History* (Cambridge: Cambridge University Press, 1957–1979).

Bernardino Feliciangeli, *Notizie e documenti sulla vita di Caterina Cibo-Varano, duchessa di Camerino* (Camerino, Italy: Favorino, 1891).

Giulio Firpo, "L'Italia romana nell'*Istoria civile del Regno di Napoli* di Pietro Giannone," *Rivista storica italiana* 118.2 (2005).

Alexandra Gajewski, "The Abbey Church at Vézelay and the Cult of Mary Magdalene: Invitation to a Journey of Discovery," in Zoë Opačić and Achim Timmermann, eds., *Architecture, Liturgy and Identity: Liber Amicorum Paul Grossley* (Turnhout, Belgium: Brepols, 2011).

Mary Giles, "Francisca Hernández and the Sexuality of Religious Dissent," in Mary Giles, ed., *Women in the Inquisition: Spain and the New World* (Baltimore: Johns Hopkins University Press, 1999).

Michael Hirst, *Sebastiano del Piombo* (Oxford: Clarendon, 1981).

Lu Ann Homza, "How to Harass an Inquisitor-General: The Polyphonic Law of Friar Francisco Ortíz," in John Marino and Thomas Kuehn, eds., *A Renaissance of Conflicts: Visions and Revisions of Law and Society in Italy and Spain* (Toronto: Center for Medieval and Renaissance Studies, 2004).

Romeo De Maio, *Riforme e miti nella Chiesa del Cinquecento*, 2nd ed. (Naples: Guida, 1992).

Jose C. Nieto, *Juan de Valdés and the Origins of the Spanish and Italian Reformation* (Geneva: Droz, 1970).

Kenneth Setton, *The Papacy and the Levant (1204–1571)* (Philadelphia: American Philosophical Society, 1984).

Ramie Targoff, *Common Prayer: The Language of Public Devotion in Early Modern England* (Chicago: University of Chicago Press, 2001).

Katharina Wilson, ed., *Women Writers of the Renaissance and Reformation* (Athens: University of Georgia Press, 1987).

8. HIDDEN HERETICS

On the Este rule in Ferrara, see Edmund Gardner, *Dukes & Poets in Ferrara: A Study in the Poetry, Religion and Politics of the Fifteenth and Early Sixteenth Centuries* (London: Constable, 1904). On the ducal palace, see Thomas Tuohy, *Herculean Ferrara: Ercole d'Este, 1471–1505, and the Invention of a Ducal Capital* (Cambridge: Cambridge University Press, 1996); see also Marco Borella, *The Castello Estense in Ferrara*, trans. Christopher Huw Evans (Milan: Electa, 1991).

On the vast cultural production of ducal Ferrara, see Gardner, *Dukes & Poets in Ferrara*; Dennis Looney and Deanna Shemek, eds., *Phaethon's Children: The Este Court and Its Culture in Early Modern Ferrara* (Tempe, AZ: ACMRS, 2005); and Patrick Matthiesen, *From Borso to Cesare d'Este: The School of Ferrara 1450–1628; An Exhibition in Aid of the Courtauld Institute of Art Trust Appeal, June 1st–August 14th 1984* (London/New York: Matthiesen Fine Art/Stair Sainty Matthiesen, 1984). On the development of secular Italian-language theater in Ferrara, see Douglas Radcliff-Umstead, *The Birth of Modern Comedy in Renaissance Italy* (Chicago: University of Chicago Press, 1969).

For more on Lucrezia Borgia, see the notes to chapter 2 above; see also *The Life and Times of Lucrezia Borgia* (London: Phoenix, 2000), Bernard Wall and Barbara Wall's abridged English translation of Maria Bellonci's 1939 *Lucrezia Borgia. La sua vita e i suoi tempi*. For a history of the Borgia family, see Michael Mallett, *The Borgias: The Rise and Fall of a Renaissance Dynasty* (London: Bodley Head, 1969). On Lucrezia Borgia's renovation of her apartments at the palace, see Allyson Burgess Williams, "Silk-Clad Walls and Sleeping Cupids: A Documentary Reconstruction of the Living Quarters of Lucrezia Borgia, Duchess of Ferrara," in Erin Campbell, Stephanie Miller, and Elizabeth Carroll Consavari, eds., *The Early Modern Italian Domestic Interior, 1400–1700: Objects, Spaces, Domesticities* (Farnham, UK: Ashgate, 2013).

On the rediscovery of Nero's palace, see Elisabetta Segala and Ida Sciortino, *Domus Aurea*, trans. Colin Swift (Rome: Electa, 1999). Suetonius's description of the complex is in chapter 31 of his biography of Nero; see John Carew Rolfe's translation, *Lives of the Caesars*, ed. Donna Hurley, in *Suetonius*, 3rd ed., gen. ed. George Patrick Goold (Cambridge, MA: Harvard University Press, 1997–1998).

On the Schifanoia palace, see Tuohy; for its frescoes, see Paolo d'Ancona, *The Schifanoia Months at Ferrara*, trans. Lucia Krasnik (Milan: Milione, 1954).

For further biography on Anne Boleyn, see Eric William Ives, *The Life and Death of Anne Boleyn: 'The Most Happy'* (Malden, MA: Blackwell, 2004). On her relationship with Renée, see Retha Warnicke, *The Rise and Fall of Anne Boleyn: Family Politics at the Court of Henry VIII* (Cambridge: Cambridge University Press, 1989).

Details about Renée and her reformist court are found in Alessandro Roveri, *Renata di Francia* (Turin: Claudiana, 2012), which includes the Italian text of the two letters to Ercole translated here. On Marot's reformist and literary career, see Ehsan Ahmed, *Clément Marot: The Mirror of the Prince* (Charlottesville, VA: Rookwood, 2005).

For further biography on Calvin, see William Bouwsma, *John Calvin: A Sixteenth-Century Life* (New York: Oxford University Press, 1988), from which translations of Calvin's letters are taken.

Lyndal Roper's biography of Luther is *Martin Luther: Renegade and Prophet* (London: Bodley Head, 2016). His remark about a "layman armed with Scripture" is quoted by many sources, among them Roland Bainton, *Here I Stand: A Life of Martin Luther* (Nashville: Abingdon, 2013).

Citations of Calvin's *Institutes* follow John McNeill's edition, translated by Ford Lewis Battles (Louisville: Westminster John Knox, 1960). See also Michael Mullett, *John Calvin* (London: Routledge, 2011).

Weber's claim is found in *The Protestant Ethic and the Spirit of Capitalism*, first translated into English by Talcott Parsons in 1930.

Carnesecchi describes Vittoria's uncertainty about works versus faith in his later inquisition; see the transcription in Massimo Firpo and Dario Marcatto, eds., *I pro-*

cessi inquisitoriali di Pietro Carnesecchi (1557–1567) (Vatican City: Archivio Segreto Vaticano, 1998–2000).

For Rabelais's letter, see *The Complete Works of François Rabelais*, trans. Donald Frame (Berkeley: University of California Press, 1991).

For more on the life and writings of Catherine of Siena, see, among others, Jane Tylus, *Reclaiming Catherine of Siena: Literacy, Literature, and the Signs of Others* (Chicago: University of Chicago Press, 2009).

For further biography on Marguerite, see Patricia Cholakian and Rouben Cholakian, *Marguerite de Navarre: Mother of the Renaissance* (New York: Columbia University Press, 2006).

Accounts of Elizabeth's translations are found in Elizabeth I, *Translations, 1544–1589,* eds. Janel Mueller and Joshua Scodel (Chicago: University of Chicago Press, 2009). On the movements toward and against vernacular Bibles in Europe, see volume 3 of Euan Cameron, ed., *The New Cambridge History of the Bible* (New York: Cambridge University Press, 2016).

Gualteruzzi's letter to Gheri about Vittoria's ambitions is reproduced as entry 31 in Pina Ragionieri, ed., *Vittoria Colonna e Michelangelo* (Florence: Mandragora, 2005).

Montmorency's remarks to King Francis are recounted in a 1540 letter to Ercole II from his ambassador Alberto Sacrati, which is printed in Domenico Tordi, *Il codice delle rime di Vittoria Colonna, marchesa di Pescara, appartenuto a Margherita d'Angoulème, regina di Navarra* (Pistoia, Italy: Flori, 1900).

The letter accompanying the manuscript for Marguerite, identified as Ashburnham 1153 at the Laurentian Library in Florence, is reproduced and translated in Abigail Brundin, *Vittoria Colonna and the Spiritual Poetics of the Italian Reformation* (Aldershot, UK: Ashgate, 2008). For details about the manuscript, see Brundin, *Spiritual Poetics*, and Brundin, "Vittoria Colonna in Manuscript," in Abigail Brundin, Tatiana Crivelli, and Maria Sapegno, eds., *A Companion to Vittoria Colonna* (Leiden, Netherlands: Brill, 2016); see also the appendix to Alan Bullock's edition of the *Rime*.

On Isabella d'Este, see Lorenzo Bonoldi, *Isabella d'Este: A Renaissance Woman*, trans. Clark Anthony Lawrence (Rimini, Italy: Guaraldi, 2015); and Sarah Cockram, *Isabella d'Este and Francesco Gonzaga: Power Sharing at the Italian Renaissance Court* (Farnham, UK: Ashgate, 2013). On Isabella's patronage, see Sally Anne Hickson, *Women, Art and Architectural Patronage in Renaissance Mantua: Matrons, Mystics and Monasteries* (Farnham, UK: Ashgate, 2012); see also Francis Ames-Lewis, *Isabella and Leonardo: The Artistic Relationship Between Isabella d'Este and Leonardo da Vinci, 1500–1506.* On her servants, including the little people Morgantino and Delia, see Julia Mary Cartwright Ady, *Isabella d'Este, Marchioness of Mantua, 1474–1539: A Study of the Renaissance* (New York: Dutton, 1903–1907).

The account of the dinner party where Vittoria's poetry was recited is printed in Alessandro Luzio, "Vittoria Colonna," *Rivista storica mantovana*, vol. 1 (1884), which has the letter signed by one "Rinchinos." It is now understood, however, that "il Rinchinos" was a pseudonym for Benedetto Accolti, cardinal of Ravenna, who adopted "Nasocane" as another pen name.

On Bagni di Lucca and changes made to the baths in the nineteenth century, see Marcello Cherubini and Massimo Betti, *Bagni di Lucca: il fascino di un'antica stazione termale* (Bagni di Lucca, Italy: Bagni di Lucca Terme J.V. & Hotel, 2008).

Montaigne describes the Bagni di Lucca in the journal of his voyage into Italy; see the entries for May 9, 1581, in his *Travel Journal*, trans. and ed. Donald Frame (San Francisco: North Frame, 1983).

General Reference and Further Bibliography

Eleonora Belligni, *Renata di Francia (1510–1575). Un'eresia di corte* (Turin: UTET, 2011).

Gian Biacio Conte, *Latin Literature: A History*, trans. Joseph Solodow, ed. Don Fowler and Glenn Most (Baltimore: Johns Hopkins University Press, 1999).

Rosanna Gorris, "«D'un château l'autre»: la corte di Renata di Francia a Ferrara (1528–1560)," in Loredana Olivato, *Il Palazzo di Renata di Francia* (Ferrara, Italy: Corbo, 1997).

Guido Achille Mansuelli with Ermanno Arslan and Daniela Scagliarini, *Urbanistica e architettura della Cisalpina romana fino al III sec. e.n.* (Brussels: Latomus, 1971).

Clément Marot, *Oeuvres complètes*, ed. François Rigolot (Paris: Flammarion, 2009).

Douglas Radcliff-Umstead, *The Birth of Modern Comedy in Renaissance Italy* (Chicago: University of Chicago Press, 1969).

Emmanuel Rodocanachi, *Renée de France, duchesse de Ferrare. Une protectrice de la réforme en Italie et en France* (Paris: Ollendorf, 1896).

Cecil Roth, *The History of the Jews of Italy* (Philadelphia: Jewish Publication Society of America, 1946).

G. F. Taddei, "Un epigramma mistico di Vittoria Colonna," *Il Vasari* 12.1-2 (1933).

9. THE POWER OF PRINT

For Donne's remark, see his 1614 letter to Sir Henry Goodyer in *Selected Letters*, ed. Paul Oliver (Manchester, UK: Carcanet, 2002).

For further details on the production and distribution of early printed books, see, among others, Angela Nuovo, *The Book Trade in the Italian Renaissance*, trans. Lydia Cochrane (Leiden, Netherlands: Brill, 2013). On piracy in early modern print, see Adrian Johns, *The Nature of the Book: Print and Knowledge in the Making* (Chicago: University of Chicago Press, 1998). On the various attitudes surrounding the early printing press, see Elizabeth Eisenstein, *Divine Art, Infernal Machine: The Reception of Printing in the West from First Impressions to the Sense of an Ending* (Philadelphia: University of Pennsylvania Press, 2011); David McKitterick, *Print, Manuscript and the Search for Order, 1450–1830* (Cambridge: Cambridge University Press, 2003); and Johns, *The Nature of the Book*. On the relationship between the print industry and women writers, see Diana Robin, *Publishing Women: Salons, the Presses, and the Counter-Reformation in Sixteenth-Century Italy* (Chicago: University of Chicago Press, 2007).

On the emergence of the ottavo book format, see Martin Davies's study on Aldus Manutius, the printer who popularized it: *Aldus Manutius: Printer and Publisher of Renaissance Venice* (London: British Library, 1995).

The Venetian Council's decree is found in Brian Richardson, *Printing, Writers and Readers in Renaissance Italy* (Cambridge: Cambridge University Press, 1999).

Fillippo Pirogallo's dedication is in his edition of the *Rime* (Parma: Viotti, 1538).

The best English-language biography of Ariosto remains Edmund Gardner's 1906 *The King of Court Poets: A Study of the Work, Life, and Times of Lodovico Ariosto*, reprinted by Haskell House in 1968. Citations of the *Orlando furioso* are from Guido Waldman's prose translation (Oxford: Oxford University Press, 1983).

Bembo's letters to Gualteruzzi are in his *Lettere*, ed. Ernesto Travi (Bologna: Commissione per i Testi di Lingua, 1992).

For details on the earliest editions of Vittoria's poetry, see the appendix to Alan Bullock's edition of the *Rime*; for a synthesized editorial history, see Tatiana Crivelli, "The Print Tradition of Vittoria Colonna's *Rime*," in Abigail Brundin, Tatiana Crivelli, and Maria Sapegno, eds., *A Companion to Vittoria Colonna* (Leiden, Netherlands: Brill, 2016). For the archival sources reflecting Vittoria's relationship to the print industry, see Tordi, *Codice delle rime*.

On Donato Rullo, see Carlo de Frede, "Un pugliese familiare del Cardinale Pole: Donato Rullo," *Rivista di letteratura e di storia ecclesiastica* 12.1-2 (1980). Rullo's role in publishing Vittoria's poetry is discussed in Crivelli, "The Print Tradition." His letter to Ascanio is printed in Tordi, *Codice delle rime*.

The Italian texts of the exchange between Gualteruzzi and della Torre are found in Abigail Brundin, "Vittoria Colonna in Manuscript," in Brundin, Crivelli, and Sapegno, eds., *A Companion to Vittoria Colonna*; the translations here are my own. See also Alan Bullock, "A Hitherto Unexplored Manuscript of 100 Poems by Vittoria Colonna in the Biblioteca Nazionale Centrale, Florence," *Italian Studies* 21 (1966); and Rossella Lalli, "Una 'maniera diversa dalla prima': Francesco Della Torre, Carlo Gualteruzzi e le 'Rime' di Vittoria Colonna," *Giornale storico della letteratura italiana* 192.639 (2015).

For Veronica Gambara's sonnet, see the translation by Laura Anna Stortoni and Mary Prentice Lillie in Stortoni, ed., *Women Poets of the Italian Renaissance: Courtly Ladies and Courtesans* (New York: Italica, 1997). On the poetry of Gaspara Stampa, see Jane Tylus's introduction to her translation, *The Complete Poems: The 1554 Edition of the Rime, a Bilingual Edition*, eds. Jane Tylus and Troy Tower (Chicago: University of Chicago Press, 2010); and Unn Falkeid and Aileen Astorga Feng, eds., *Rethinking Gaspara Stampa in the Canon of Renaissance Poetry* (Aldershot, UK: Ashgate, 2015). For more on Tullia d'Aragona, see the introduction to Julia Hairston's edition of Tullia's poetry, *The Poems and Letters of Tullia d'Aragona and Others* (Toronto: Center for Reformation and Renaissance Studies, 2014). The privileges granted her by Cosimo are translated by Diana Robin, "The Lyric Voices of Vittoria Colonna and the Women of the Giolito Anthologies, 1545–1559," in Brundin et al., eds., *A Companion to Vittoria Colonna.*

For the Italian text of Maddalena Campiglia's *Flori*, see *Flori, a Pastoral Drama*, eds. Virginia Cox and Lisa Sampson, trans. Virginia Cox (Chicago: University of Chicago Press, 2004).

The Italian text of Domenichi's preface is in Deanna Shemek, "The Collector's Cabinet: Lodovico Domenichi's Gallery of Women," in Pamela Joseph Benson and Victoria Kirkham, eds., *Strong Voices, Weak History: Early Women Writers & Canons in England, France, & Italy* (Ann Arbor: University of Michigan Press, 2005).

Figures on publications by women in early modern Europe are available in Virginia Cox, *Lyric Poetry by Women of the Italian Renaissance* (Baltimore: Johns Hopkins University Press, 2015). On female literacy in early modern Italy, see Peter Burke, *The Historical Anthropology of Early Modern Italy: Essays on Perception and Communication* (Cambridge: Cambridge University Press, 1987).

Valgrisi's preface is printed in his 1546 edition (*Le rime spirituali della illustrissima Signora Vittoria Colonna marchesana di Pescara, non piu stampate da pochissime infuori, le quali altrove corrotte, et qui corrette si leggono*) and in the 1548 reprint from the Venetian press of Comin da Trino.

On Rinaldo Corso, see Sarah Faggioli's 2014 dissertation from the University of Chicago, "A Sixteenth-Century Reader and Critic of Vittoria Colonna: Rinaldo Corso's Commentary on Her Spiritual *Rime*," elaborated in a forthcoming publication.

General Reference and Further Bibliography

Vittoria Colonna, *Sonetti in morte di Francesco Ferrante d'Avalos Marchese di Pescara*, ed. Tobia Toscano (Milan: Mondadori, 1988).

Virginia Cox, "Women Writers and the Canon in Sixteenth-Century Italy: The Case of Vittoria Colonna," in Pamela Joseph Benson and Victoria Kirkham, eds., *Strong Voices, Weak History: Early Women Writers & Canons in England, France, & Italy* (Ann Arbor: University of Michigan Press, 2005).

Jill Kraye, ed., *Cambridge Companion to Renaissance Humanism* (Cambridge: Cambridge University Press, 1996).

Rosa Salzberg, "From Printshop to Piazza: The Dissemination of Cheap Print in Sixteenth-Century Venice," dissertation, Queen Mary College/University of London, 2008.

10. MICHELANGELO IN LOVE

For the life and works of Ambrogio Catarino, born Lancilotto Politi, see *Beyond the Inquisition: Ambrogio Catarino Politi and the Origins of the Counter-Reformation* (Notre Dame: University of Notre Dame Press, 2017), and Don Weinstein's translation of Giorgio Caravale's *Sulle tracce dell'eresia: Ambrogio Catarino Politi (1484–1553)* (Florence: Olschki, 2007). Catarino's dedication to Vittoria is in the first edition of the *Speculum haereticorum fratris Ambrosii Catarini Politi senensis ordinis praedicatorum* (Kraków: Johannes Helicz, 1540).

For further biography on Francisco de Hollanda, see Joaquim Oliviera Caetano, "Francisco de Hollanda (1517–1584): The Fascination of Rome and the Times in Portugal," in Alice Sedgwick Wohl's translation of Francisco de Hollanda, *On Antique Painting* (University Park: Pennsylvania State University Press, 2013), from which citations of Hollanda are taken.

For the two biographies of Michelangelo written by his contemporaries Giorgio Vasari and Ascanio Condivi, see Vasari, *The Lives of the Most Excellent Painters, Sculptors, and Architects*, trans. Gaston du Chene de Vere, ed. Philip Jacks (New York: Modern Library, 2006), and Condivi, *Life of Michelangelo*, 2nd ed., trans. Alice Sedgwick Wohl, ed. Hellmut Wohl (University Park: Pennsylvania State University Press, 1999). Later biographies that treat Michelangelo's attraction to men include John Addington Symonds's 1893 *Life of Michelangelo Buonarroti*, republished in 2002 by University of Pennsylvania Press (Philadelphia), and the first volume of Michael Hirst's *Michelangelo* (New Haven, CT: Yale University Press, 2011–). For a travel guide through Michelangelo's career in Rome, see Angela Nickerson, *A Journey into Michelangelo's Rome* (Berkeley, CA: Roaring Forties Press, 2008).

On Michelangelo's spirituality, see Sarah Rolfe Prodan, *Michelangelo's Christian Mysticism: Spirituality, Poetry and Art in Sixteenth-Century Italy* (Cambridge: Cambridge University Press, 2014). For Michelangelo's idiosyncratic use of paper, see Leonard Barkan, *Michelangelo: A Life on Paper* (Princeton, NJ: Princeton University Press, 2011).

For Vittoria's involvement with the Poor Clares convent, see Och, "Art Patronage."

On Vittoria's cultural patronage, see Marjorie Och, "Vittoria Colonna: Art Patronage and Religious Reform in Sixteenth-Century Rome," dissertation, Bryn Mawr College, 1993. For the Titian commission, see Marjorie Och, "Vittoria Colonna and the Commission for a *Mary Magdalene* by Titian," in Sheryl Reiss and David Wilkins, eds., *Beyond Isabella: Secular Women Patrons of Art in Renaissance Italy* (Kirksville, MO: Truman State University Press, 2001).

For Vittoria's request for Michelangelo's now lost *Noli me tangere*, see Lisa Rafanelli, "Michelangelo's *Noli me tangere* for Vittoria Colonna, and the Changing Status of Women in Renaissance Italy," in Michelle Erhardt and Amy Mooris, eds., *Mary*

Magdalene, Iconographic Studies from the Middle Ages to the Baroque (Leiden, Netherlands: Brill, 2012), which has the Italian text of the specifications Michelangelo received for the drawing. This commission was first hypothesized by Johannes Wilde, *Italian Drawings in the Department of Prints and Drawings in the British Museum: Michelangelo and His Studio* (London: British Museum, 1953), on the basis of a 1531 letter from Giovanni Borromeo, reprinted in Alessandro Luzio, *La galleria dei Gonzaga venduta all'Inghilterra nel 1627–28. Documenti degli archivi di Mantova e Londra*, 2nd ed. (Rome: Bardi, 1974). On the haste with which Michelangelo completed the drawing, see Barbara Agosti, "Vittoria Colonna e il culto della Maddalena (tra Tiziano e Michelangelo)," in Ragionieri, ed., *Vittoria Colonna e Michelangelo.* Jesus orders Mary Magdelene, "Noli mi tangere," in John 20.17 in the Latin Vulgate; the English here follows the King James Version.

For full bibliography on the drawings Michelangelo prepared as gifts for Vittoria, see Monica Bianco and Vittoria Romani, "Vittoria Colonna e Michelangelo," along with the catalog entries that follow it, in Pina Ragionieri, ed., *Vittoria Colonna e Michelangelo* (Florence: Mandragora, 2005); see also Alexander Nagel, "Gifts for Michelangelo and Vittoria Colonna," *Art Bulletin* 79.4 (1997).

For Michelangelo's letters, see the translation of E. Hartley Ramsden, *The Letters of Michelangelo* (Stanford, CA: Stanford University Press, 1963); for the Italian texts, see Michelangelo, *Carteggio*, eds. Giovanni Poggi, Paola Barocchi, and Renzo Ristori (Florence: Sansoni, 1965–1983). All citations of Michelangelo's poetry follow Michelangelo Buonarroti, *Rime*, ed. Matteo Residori (Milan: Mondadori, 1998).

The theory that Vittoria is represented in *The Last Judgment* is Charles de Tolnay's; see "Le jugement dernier de Michel Ange. Essai d'intepretation," *Art Quarterly* 3 (1940). See also volume 5 of de Tolnay's *Michelangelo* (Princeton, NJ: Princeton University Press, 1960).

Horace's vision of his legacy is found in *Ode* 3.30; see *Odes and Epodes*, trans. Niall Rudd (Cambridge, MA: Harvard University Press, 2004).

My translations of Vittoria's letter to Priuli follow the transcription in Sergio Pagano and Concetta Ranieri, *Nuovi documenti su Vittoria Colonna e Reginald Pole* (Vatican City: Archivio Vaticano, 1989), letter 2.6.

General Reference and Further Bibliography

Costanza Barbieri, "'Chompare e amicho karissimo': A Portrait of Michelangelo by His Friend Sebastiano," *Artibus et historiae* 28.56 (2007).

George Bull, *Michelangelo: A Biography* (New York: St. Martin's, 1995).

Michelangelo Buonarotti, *Love Sonnets and Madrigals to Tommaso de' Cavalieri*, trans. and ed. Michael Sullivan (London: Peter Owen, 1997).

Michelangelo Buonarroti, *Rime*, ed. Cesare Guasti (Firenze: Le Monnier, 1863).

Emidio Campi, *Michelangelo e Vittoria Colonna. Un dialogo artistico-teologico ispirato da Bernardino Ochino e altri saggi di storia della Riforma* (Turin: Claudiana, 1994).

Robert Clements, "The Authenticity of de Hollanda's *Dialogos em Roma*," *PMLA* 61.4 (1946).

Stephen Dando-Collins, *The Great Fire of Rome: The Fall of the Emperor Nero and His City* (Cambridge, MA: Da Capo, 2010).

Nancy Thomson de Grummond, ed., *An Encyclopedia of the History of Classical Archaeology* (London: Dearborn, 1996).

Serena De Leonardis and Stefano Masi, *Art and History: Rome and the Vatican*, trans. Paula Boomsliter (Sesto Fiorentino, Italy: Bonechi, 1999).

Franca Falletti and Jonathan Katz Nelson, eds., *Venere e Amore. Michelangelo e la nuova bellezza ideale / Venus and Love: Michelangelo and the New Ideal of Beauty* (Florence: Giunti, 2002).

Sylvia Ferino-Pagden, ed. *Vittoria Colonna: Dichterin und Muse Michelangelos* (Vienna/Milan: Kunsthistorisches Museum/Skira, 1997).

Herman Friedrich Grimm, *Life of Michael Angelo*, trans. Fanny Elizabeth Bunnett (Boston: Little, Brown, 1890–1891).

Susan Haskins, trans. and ed., *Who Is Mary? Three Early Modern Women on the Idea of the Virgin Mary* (Chicago: University of Chicago Press, 2008).

Michael Hirst, *Tre saggi su Michelangelo*, trans. Barbara Agosti (Florence: Mandragora, 2004).

Tyler Lansford, *The Latin Inscriptions of Rome: A Walking Guide* (Baltimore: Johns Hopkins University Press, 2009).

Maria Ruvoldt, "Michelangelo's Dream," *Art Bulletin* 85.1 (2003).

Donald Emrys Strong, *Roman Art*, 2nd ed., ed. Jocelyn Toynbee, revised by Roger Ling (London: Penguin, 1988).

Tommaso Tovaglieri, "Francesco Arcangeli—Alfredo Costa. Attorno al *Noli me tangere* del Pontormo," *Concorso* 6 (2012–2014).

II. SALT WAR

Brunamonte de' Rossi's letters are published in Domenico Tordi, "Vittoria Colonna in Orvieto durante la guerra del sale," *Bollettino della Società Umbra di Storia Patria* 1.3 (1895); the translations are from Maud Jerrold, *Vittoria Colonna, with Some Account of Her Friends and Her Times* (London: Dent, 1906), with some small emendations.

On the salt trade in early modern Italy, see Mark Kurlansky, *Salt: A World History* (New York: Walker, 2002). For the events following Paul III's salt tax in Italy, see Diana Robin, *Publishing Women: Salons, the Presses, and the Counter-Reformation in*

Sixteenth-Century Italy (Chicago: University of Chicago Press, 2007). The biblical passage to which Paul alludes is from Numbers 33.52–55.

Accounts of the abduction of Livia Colonna are found in Roberto Zapperi, "Alessandro Farnese, Giovanni della Casa and Titian's Danae in Naples," *Journal of the Warburg and Courtauld Institutes* 54 (1991).

On the norms surrounding the illegitimate children of popes, see Gerard Noel, *The Renaissance Popes: Culture, Power, and the Making of the Borgia Myth* (London: Constable, 2006).

Francesco Contarini's account to the Venetian senate is translated in Elisabeth Gleason, *Gasparo Contarini: Venice, Rome and Reform* (Berkeley: University of California Press, 1993).

For the Latin text of letters to and from Reginald Pole in this chapter, see the *Epistolarum Reginaldi Poli S. R. E. cardinalis et aliorum ad ipsum collectio,* ed. Angelo Maria Querini (Brescia, Italy: Rizzardi, 1744–1757). The letters are summarized in Thomas Mayer, ed., *The Correspondence of Reginald Pole* (Aldershot, UK: Ashgate, 2002), and were translated by Troy Tower.

On the failed marriages of Margaret of Austria, also known as Margaret of Parma, see Charles Steen, *Margaret of Parma: A Life* (Leiden, Netherlands: Brill, 2013). Details of the Colonna-Farnese proposal are found in Jerrold, *Vittoria Colonna.*

Vittoria's letter to Ascanio in which she declares that "it is hard to understand this pope" and her letter that ends with the postscript "To the emperor I write that the agreements were impossible" were translated by Troy Tower, with my occasional emendations.

For the reception thrown for Vittoria by Orvieto city officials, see Damon Di-Mauro, "Vittoria Colonna in Orvieto," a three-part article published in 2009 by the Studio for Art, Faith and History at Gordon College, Wenham, MA, http://www .gordon.edu/lettersfromeurope/dimauro.

Guidiccioni's letters are translated in Robin, *Publishing Women,* and printed in Tordi, "Vittoria Colonna in Orvieto."

Giovanna d'Aragona's letter to the pope was translated by Troy Tower; the Italian text is in Robin, *Publishing Women.*

General Reference and Further Bibliography
Mark Hudson, *Titian: The Last Days* (New York: Walker, 2010).

Wolfgang Lotz, *Architecture in Italy, 1500–1600,* trans. Mary Hottinger (New Haven, CT: Yale University Press, 1995).

Peter Partner, *The Lands of St Peter: The Papal State in the Middle Ages and the Early Renaissance* (Berkeley: University of California Press, 1972).

Maria Grazia Picozzi, *Palazzo Colonna. Appartamenti: Sculture antiche e dall'antico* (Rome: De Luca, 2010).

Samuel Ball Platner, *A Topographical Dictionary of Ancient Rome*, ed. Thomas Ashby (London: Oxford University Press, 1929).

Clare Robertson, *'Il gran cardinale': Alessandro Farnese, Patron of the Arts* (New Haven, CT: Yale University Press, 1992).

Luis de Salazar y Castro, *Historia genealogica de la casa de Lara justificada con instrumentos y escritores de inviolable fe* (Madrid: Mateo de Llanos y Gozman, 1694–1697).

12. LATE LOVE

For details on when Vittoria and Reginald Pole may have met, see Maria Forcellino, "Vittoria Colonna and Michelangelo: Drawings and Paintings," in Abigail Brundin, Tatiana Crivelli, and Maria Sapegno, eds., *A Companion to Vittoria Colonna* (Leiden, Netherlands: Brill, 2016). For more on the life and career of Pole, see Thomas Mayer, *Reginald Pole: Prince & Prophet* (Cambridge: Cambridge University Press, 2000). For Cromwell's suggestion that Pole read Machiavelli, see Thomas Mayer, "Pole, Reginald (1500–1558)," *Oxford Dictionary of National Biography*, online ed., ed. David Cannadine (Oxford: Oxford University Press, 2004). For the composition of Pole's *De unitate*, see Thomas Dunn, "The Development of the Text of Pole's *De Unitate Ecclesiae*," *Papers of the Bibliographical Society of America* 70.4 (1976).

For Pole's comments about Henry VIII as an enemy of the human race, see the *Epistolarum Reginaldi Poli S. R. E. cardinalis et aliorum ad ipsum collectio*, ed. Angelo Maria Querini (Brescia, Italy: Rizzardi, 1744–1757), 2:36.

On Viterbo and Italian reformist activity, see Salvatore Caponetto, *The Protestant Reformation in Sixteenth-Century Italy*, trans. Anne Tedeschi and John Tedeschi (Kirksville, MO: Thomas Jefferson University Press, 1999), which also includes English translations of Francesco Negri's and Antonio Brucioli's prefaces.

Pole's relationship with Priuli, culminating in their request for a joint burial (confirmed by an epitaph in Morone's papers in the Vatican Secret Archive) is discussed in Mayer, *Reginald Pole*, which also cites Ludovico Beccadelli's biography.

On the life and reign of Paul IV, see Miles Pattenden, *Pius IV and the Fall of the Carafa: Nepotism and Papal Authority in Counter-Reformation Rome* (Oxford: Oxford University Press, 2013).

For details on the history of the Inquisition, see Thomas Mayer, *The Roman Inquisition on the Stage of Italy, c. 1590–1640* (Philadelphia: University of Pennsylvania Press, 2014). On the cooperation between the Spanish Inquisition and Neapolitan officials, see Gigliola Fragnito, "The Central and Peripheral Organization of Censorship," in Gigliola Fragnito, ed., *Church, Censorship and Culture in Early Modern Italy*, trans. Adrian Belton (Cambridge: Cambridge University Press, 2001), which is in response to Massimo Firpo, "Valdésianesimo ed evangelismo: alle origini dell'*ecclesia Viterbiensis* (1541)," *Schifanoia* 5.1 (1985).

For further details on the Council of Trent, see, among others, John W. O'Malley, *Trent: What Happened at the Council* (Cambridge, MA: Belknap, 2013).

On the popularity and prohibition of the *Beneficio*, see Ruth Prelowski, trans. and ed., "The «Beneficio di Cristo»," in John Tedeschi, ed., *Italian Reformation Studies in Honor of Laelius Socinus* (Florence: Le Monnier, 1965), which is the translation used here. See also Adriano Prosperi and Carlo Ginzburg, *Giochi di pazienza: un seminario sul «Beneficio di Cristo»* (Turin: Einaudi, 1975); and Robert Pierce, *Pier Paolo Vergerio the Propagandist* (Rome: Edizioni di Storia e Letteratura, 2003). The free copies Morone arranged for Modena are treated in Prelowski, trans. and ed., "The «Beneficio di Cristo»."

Contarini's letter to Pole, translated by Troy Tower with my emendations, is in Thomas Mayer, ed., *The Correspondence of Reginald Pole* (Aldershot, UK: Ashgate, 2002).

Ochino's flight out of Italy is reported in Karl Benrath, *Bernardino Ochino of Siena: A Contribution Towards the History of the Reformation*, trans. Helen Zimmern (London: Nisbet, 1876).

For further biography on Margaret Pole, see Hazel Pierce, *Margaret Pole, Countess of Salisbury, 1473–1541: Loyalty, Lineage and Leadership* (Cardiff: University of Wales Press, 2003). The description of her execution is from Eustace Chapuys's letter to the queen of Hungary dated June 10, 1541; it is summarized from the French in Pascual de Gayangos, ed., *Calendar of State Papers, Spain,* volume 6, part 1, *1538–1542* (London, 1890). On the Pole family's involvement in the Exeter Conspiracy, see Mayer, "Pole, Reginald."

The remark of Margaret Pole's inquisitor William Fitzwilliam, Earl of Southampton, is printed in Hazel Pierce, "Pole, Margaret, suo jure countess of Salisbury (1473–1541)," *Oxford Dictionary of National Biography,* online ed. The spelling has been modernized here.

Pole's letter to Vittoria proposing that she become his new mother is letter 139 in Ferrero and Müller's *Carteggio di Vittoria Colonna*; it was translated by Troy Tower, as was Pole's letter to Pucci, letter 3:44 in Querini's *Epistolarum.*

Carnesecchi describes Vittoria's spiritual practices in his later interrogation by the Roman Inquisition. See the transcriptions in Massimo Firpo and Dario Marcatto, eds., *I processi inquisitoriali di Pietro Carnesecchi (1557–1567)* (Vatican City: Archivio Segreto Vaticano, 1998–2000); English translations are by Troy Tower.

Vittoria's letter to Priuli is dated according to Mayer's chronology and features his translation; see Mayer, ed., *Correspondence,* entry 407. All of Vittoria's other letters adhere to the chronology established in Ferrero and Müller's *Carteggio di Vittoria Colonna.*

The translation of Pole's last letter to Vittoria is based on Jerrold, with my emendations. The Parable of the Guests is in Luke 14.

General Reference and Further Bibliography

Félix Bungener, *History of the Council of Trent*, 2nd ed., trans. and ed. John McClintock (New York: Harper, 1855).

Giorgio Caravale, *The Italian Reformation Outside Italy: Francesco Pucci's Heresy in Sixteenth-Century Europe* (Leiden, Netherlands: Brill, 2015).

Charles Cocquelines, ed., *Bullarum romanorum, privilegiorum ac diplomatum romanorum pontificum amplissima collection* (Rome: Girolamo Mainardi, 1739–1762).

Roland Connelly, *The Women of the Catholic Resistance: In England 1540–1680* (Edinburgh: Pentland, 1997).

Aaron C. Denlinger, *Omnes in Adam ex pacto Dei: Ambrogio Catarino's Doctrine of Covenantal Solidarity and Its Influence on Post-Reformation Reformed Theologians* (Göttingen, Germany: Vandenhoeck & Ruprecht, 2010).

Massimo Firpo, *Juan de Valdés and the Italian Reformation*, trans. Richard Bates (London: Routledge, 2016).

Carlo Ginzburg and Adriana Prosperi, "Le due redazioni del 'Beneficio di Cristo,'" in Albano Biondi, ed., *Eresia e riforma nell'Italia del Cinquecento* (Florence/Chicago: Sansoni/Newberry Library, 1974).

Ferdinand Gregorovius, *History of the City of Rome in the Middle Ages*, trans. Annie Hamilton (London: Bell, 1900–1906).

Denys Hay and John Easton Law, *Italy in the Age of the Renaissance, 1380–1530* (London: Longman, 1989).

Peter Marshall, *Religious Identities in Henry VIII's England* (Aldershot, UK: Ashgate, 2006).

Hazel Pierce, "The King's Cousin: The Life, Career and Welsh Connection of Sir Richard Pole, 1458–1504," *Welsh History Review/Cylchgrawn Hanes Cymru* 19.2 (1998).

Antonio Santosuosso, "An Account of the Election of Paul IV to the Pontificate," *Renaissance Quarterly* 31.4 (1978).

John Shearman, "Three Portraits by Andrea del Sarto and His Circle," *Burlington Magazine* 102.683 (1960).

13. LAST RITES

Claudio Tolomei's letters to Giuseppe Cincio are printed in *Delle lettere di M. Claudio Tolomei libri sette*, ed. Vincenzo Cioffi (Naples: Albergo de' Poveri, 1829); the translations here are adapted from Maud Jerrold, *Vittoria Colonna, with Some Account of Her Friends and Her Times* (London: Dent, 1906). Bembo's letter is in Ernesto Travi's edition of the *Lettere* (Bologna: Commissione per i Testi di Lingua, 1992).

Fracastoro's letter is printed in a 1574 anthology edited in Venice by Bernardino

Pino (or Pini), *Della nuova scelta di lettere di diversi nobilissimi;* the translation here is from Jerrold, *Vittoria Colonna,* with my emendations. Lady Macbeth's physician suggests mental disturbance in *Macbeth* 5:3.

Vittoria's attendant Prudenza, listed in her will as "D[omina] Prudentia de Palma d[e] arpino," appears in several documents treated by Reumont, *Vittoria Colonna.*

For Vittoria's letter to Saint Ignatius and her meeting with Salmerón, see Hugo Rahner, *Saint Ignatius Loyola: Letters to Women,* trans. Kathleen Pond and S.A.H. Weetman (Freiburg/Edinburgh: Herder/Nelson, 1960); for the Spanish texts, see *Sancti Ignatii de Loyola Societatis Jesu fundatoris epistolae et instructiones* (Madrid: Lopez del Horno, 1903), the first volume of the *Monumenta Ignatiana* in the Monumenta Historica Societatis Iesu series.

The translation of Vittoria's letter to Giovanni Morone is adapted from Jerrold's, in *Vittoria Colonna.*

The Italian text of Marguerite's letter to Georges d'Armagnac is printed in Sergio Pagano and Concetta Ranieri, *Nuovi documenti su Vittoria Colonna e Reginald Pole* (Vatican City: Archivio Vaticano, 1989).

Martinengo's letter is printed in Alfred von Reumont, *Vittoria Colonna, marchesa di Pescara: vita, fede e poesia nel secolo decimosesto,* trans. Ermanno Ferrero and Giuseppe Müller (Turin: Loescher, 1892).

On the public lectures based on Vittoria's poetry, see Abigail Brundin, *Vittoria Colonna and the Spiritual Poetics of the Italian Reformation* (Aldershot, UK: Ashgate, 2008).

On the literary cultivation of Costanza d'Avalos Piccolomini, see Diana Robin, *Publishing Women: Salons, the Presses, and the Counter-Reformation in Sixteenth-Century Italy* (Chicago: University of Chicago Press, 2007); see also Suzanne Thérault, *Un cénacle humaniste de la Renaissance autour de Vittoria Colonna, châtelaine d'Ischia* (Florence: Sansoni, 1968).

For details about Vittoria's death and burial, see Fabrizio Colonna, *Sulla tomba di Vittoria Colonna* (Rome: Stabilito Tipografico dell'Opinione, 1887); and Bruto Amante, *La tomba di Vittoria Colonna e i testamenti finora inediti della poetessa* (Bologna: Zanichelli, 1896).

Vittoria's will is kept in the Archivio Notarile Distrettuale in Rome; copies are in the Archivio Colonna and a transcription is in Amante, *La tomba di Vittoria Colonna.* For the letter of Don Maggio, kept in the Colonna archive, see Colonna, *Sulla tomba di Vittoria Colonna.* Transcriptions and translations of Bonorio's letters to Ascanio are my own; the originals are in the Colonna archive and passages are printed in Amante, *La tomba di Vittoria Colonna,* and Fabrizio Colonna, *Sulla tomba di Vittoria Colonna.* The translation of Condivi's account is Alice Sedgwick Wohl's, in *Life of Michelangelo,* 2nd ed., ed. Hellmut Wohl (University Park: Pennsylvania State University Press, 1999).

Michelangelo's letters are translated in E. Hartley Ramsden, trans. and ed., *The Letters of Michelangelo* (Stanford, CA: Stanford University Press, 1963).

Pole's letters are printed in the *Epistolarum Reginaldi Poli S. R. E. cardinalis et aliorum ad ipsum collectio*, ed. Angelo Maria Querini (Brescia, Italy: Rizzardi, 1744–1757), and summarized in Thomas Mayer, ed., *The Correspondence of Reginald Pole* (Aldershot, UK: Ashgate, 2002). A sixteenth-century copy of Pole's letter to Ascanio, summarized from Italian manuscripts in Mayer, ed., *Correspondence*, was consulted at the British Library; the translation is mine.

On the poet's niece, Vittoria Colonna, see Tobia Toscano, "Galeazzo di Tarsia: indizi per la riapertura di una pratica archiviata," in Renzo Cremante, ed., *La lirica del Cinquecento. Seminario di studi in memoria di Cesare Bozzetti* (Alessandria, Italy: Edizioni dell'Orso, 2004).

General Reference and Further Bibliography

Ann Astell, *Eating Beauty: The Eucharist and the Spiritual Arts of the Middle Ages* (Ithaca, NY: Cornell University Press, 2016).

William Bangert, *Claude Jay and Alfonso Salmerón: Two Early Jesuits* (Chicago: Loyola University Press, 1985).

Massimo Firpo, *Vittore Soranzo vescovo ed eretico. Riforma della Chiesa e Inquisizione nell'Italia del Cinquecento* (Rome/Bari: Laterza, 2006).

Alberto Galieti, "La tomba di Prosperetto Colonna in Città Latina," *Archivio della Società Romana di Storia Patria* 31.1 (1908).

Michael Lovano, *All Things Julius Caesar: An Encyclopedia of Caesar's World and Legacy* (Santa Barbara, CA: ABC-CLIO, 2015).

Deborah Parker, *Michelangelo and the Art of Letter Writing* (Cambridge: Cambridge University Press, 2010).

Rosa Salzberg, "In the Mouths of Charlatans: Street Performers and the Dissemination of Pamphlets in Renaissance Italy," *Renaissance Studies* 24.5 (2010).

Carlos José Hernando Sánchez, *Castilla y Nápoles en el siglo XVI. El virrey Pedro de Toledo: linaje, estado y cultura (1532–1553)* (Valladolid: Junta de Castilla y León, 1994.

Johann Wyss, *Vittoria Colonna und ihr Kanzoniere*, dissertation, Universität Zürich, 1916.

CONCLUSION: IN THE ARCHIVE OF THE INQUISITION

For a general account of the activities of the Roman Inquisition, see Thomas Mayer, *The Roman Inquisition on the Stage of Italy, c. 1590–1640* (Philadelphia: University of Pennsylvania Press, 2014); Jane Wickersham, *Rituals of Prosecution: The Roman Inquisition and the Prosecution of Philo-Protestants in Sixteenth-Century Italy*

(Toronto: University of Toronto Press, 2012); Dermot Fenlon, *Heresy and Obedi-ence in Tridentine Italy: Cardinal Pole and the Counter Reformation* (Cambridge: Cambridge University Press, 1972); Andrea del Col and Giovanna Paolin, eds., *L'Inquisizione Romana in Italia nell'età moderna. Archivi, problemi di metodo e nuove ricerche. Atti del seminario internazionale Trieste 18–20 maggio 1988* (Rome: Minis-tero per i Beni Culturali e Ambientali, 1991); and Adam Patrick Robinson, *The Career of Cardinal Giovanni Morone (1509–1580): Between Council and Inquisition* (Abing-don, UK: Routledge, 2016).

For further biography on Galileo, see, among others, William Shea and Mariano Artigas, *Galileo in Rome: The Rise and Fall of a Troublesome Genius* (Oxford: Oxford University Press, 2003). On the inquisitorial trials of Galileo and their impact, see Maurice Finocchiaro, *Retrying Galileo, 1633–1992* (Berkeley: University of California Press, 2005). For the translated text of the church's injunction against Galileo, see Maurice Finocchiaro, ed., *The Galileo Affair: A Documentary History* (Berkeley: University of California Press, 1989).

On the Vatican Secret Archives, see Terzo Natalini, *The Vatican Secret Archives*, trans. Dieter Schlenker, ed. Sergio Pagano (Vatican City: Archivio Segreto Vaticano, 2000).

For a history of the Vatican's inquisition archive, see William Monter, "The Inquisition," in Ronnie Po-chia Hsia, ed., *A Companion to the Reformation World* (Malden, MA: Blackwell, 2004); Thomas Mayer, *The Roman Inquisition: A Papal Bu-reaucracy and Its Laws in the Age of Galileo* (Philadelphia: University of Pennsylvania Press, 2013); and Ann Jacobson Schutte, "Palazzo del Sant'Uffizio: The Opening of the Roman Inquisition's Central Archive," *Perspectives on History* 37.5 (1999). On Carlo Ginzburg's appeal to the archive, see among others Cullen Murphy, *God's Jury: The Inquisition and the Making of the Modern World* (Boston: Houghton Mifflin, 2012), which reconstructs the opening of Ginzburg's otherwise unpublished and pos-sibly lost letter.

The fruits of Sergio Pagano and Concetta Ranieri's collaboration are in *Nuovi documenti su Vittoria Colonna e Reginald Pole* (Vatican City: Archivio Vaticano, 1989).

On Pole's candidacy for pope, see Thomas Mayer, *Reginald Pole: Prince & Prophet* (Cambridge: Cambridge University Press, 2000).

Carnesecchi's execution is described in Delio Cantimori, "Italy and the Papacy," in Geoffrey Rudolf Elton, ed., *The Reformation: 1520–1559*, 2nd ed., vol. 2 of *The New Cambridge Modern History* (Cambridge: Cambridge University Press, 1957–1979). The inquisition transcriptions are printed in Massimo Firpo and Dario Marcatto, eds., *I processi inquisitoriali di Pietro Carnesecchi (1557–1567)* (Vatican City: Archivio Segreto Vaticano, 1998–2000). For the transcriptions of Morone's interrogations, see Massimo Firpo and Dario Marcatto, *Il processo inquisitoriale del cardinal Giovanni*

Morone (Rome: Instituto Storico Italiano per l'Età Moderna e Contemporanea, 1981–1995).

On Marcantonio Colonna at the Battle of Lepanto, see Hugh Bicheno, *Crescent and Cross: The Battle of Lepanto 1571* (London: Cassell, 2003); see also Nicoletta Bazzano, *Marco Antonio Colonna* (Rome: Salerno, 2003). For depictions of Marcantonio in the literature produced in the wake of the victory at Lepanto, see Elizabeth Wright, Sarah Spence, and Andrew Lemons, eds., *The Battle of Lepanto* (Cambridge, MA: Harvard University, 2014).

General Reference and Further Bibliography

Dermot Fenlon, *Heresy and Obedience in Tridentine Italy: Cardinal Pole and the Counter Reformation* (Cambridge: Cambridge University Press, 1972).

Bernhard Kerber, "Giuseppe Bartolomeo Chiari," trans. Renate Franciscono, *Art Bulletin* 50.1 (1968).

Adriano Prosperi, *L'Inquisizione romana: letture e ricerche* (Rome: Edizioni di storia e letteratura, 2003).

Michael Roberts and Ebenezer Rees Thomas, *Newton and the Origin of Colours: A Study of One of the Earliest Examples of Scientific Method* (London: Bell, 1934).

Christina Strunck, "The Barbarous and Noble Enemy: Pictorial Representations of the Battle of Lepanto," in James Harper, ed., *The Turk and Islam in the Western Eye, 1450–1750: Visual Imagery Before Orientalism* (Farnham, UK: Ashgate, 2011).

Jane Wickersham, *Rituals of Prosecution: The Roman Inquisition and the Prosecution of Philo-Protestants in Sixteenth-Century Italy* (Toronto: University of Toronto Press, 2012).

ACKNOWLEDGMENTS

This book could never have been written without the incredible generosity of friends, colleagues, students, and even strangers; what follows is an inevitably incomplete list of the many people to whom I am grateful.

I owe my introduction to Vittoria Colonna to Gerhard Regn at the University of Munich, who first suggested I read her poems when I was finishing my book *Posthumous Love* (I had never heard of her before). My agent, Jill Kneerim, encouraged me to write Vittoria's biography, and guided me with terrific devotion through the early steps of imagining and launching the book. Jonathan Galassi has been the finest editor I could have, and has made the book infinitely better. I owe thanks to Carolina Baizan at Farrar, Straus and Giroux for making the editorial process run smoothly, and to Judy Kiviat and Karen Ninnis for their outstanding work proofreading the book.

This book represented a new field for my own writing, and I am indebted to Abigail Brundin, Virginia Cox, Julia Hairston, Serena Sapegno, and Deanna Shemek for welcoming me so warmly into the scholarly world of Renaissance women's writing; Julia was especially kind in sharing her library with me during my sabbatical in Rome. Kenneth Gouwens has been remarkably generous in helping me navigate the complex world of sixteenth-century Italian history; on the rare occasions when he has not had answers to my questions, he has tracked them down for me himself. Albert Ascoli, P. Renée Baernstein, Leonard Barkan, Shaul Bassi, Ann Blair, Patrizia Cavazzini, Gigliola Fragnito, Marjorie Och, Jonathan Unglaub, Nick Wilding, and the late John Marino have all answered specific questions that I could never have resolved without their help.

Angelo de Gennaro has been my devoted Italian tutor for the past five years, working patiently with me in weekly sessions to decipher Vittoria's complex letters and poems. Francesco Caruso was an excellent translator of the most obscure Latin letters and documents. Troy Tower has been the finest research assistant imaginable, locating the most difficult texts, reviewing all of my translations and doing additional translations of his own, fact-checking every possible date, name, and event in this book, and working tirelessly over the past year to help bring this project to completion (any mistakes that remain, needless to say, are my own). I also owe thanks to the staff of the Eisenhower and Peabody Libraries at Johns Hopkins for helping Troy in his extensive research.

I am grateful to the directors of the American Academy in Rome, Christopher Celenza and Kimberly Bowes, for sponsoring the conference I organized with Serena Sapegno in the fall of 2014 on Vittoria and her world, and to Andrea Fossà for putting together a magical concert for the opening of that conference at the Palazzo Colonna. I want to thank Jeffrey Knapp at the University of California, Berkeley; Alina Payne at Villa I Tatti in Florence; Yoav Rinon at the Hebrew University of Jerusalem; Shadi Bartsch-Zimmer at the University of Chicago; and Christina Nielsen at the Isabella Stewart Gardner Museum in Boston, for inviting me to present parts of this book as lectures.

Most of the research for this book was done in Italy, and I am indebted to the librarians and archivists at the manuscript room of the Vatican Apostolic Library; the Secret Archive of the Vatican; the Archive of the Congregation of the Doctrine of the Faith; the American Academy in Rome; the Biblioteca Laurenziana in Florence; and, above all, the Colonna archive in Subiaco, where I have worked in the most peaceful conditions, interrupted only by the espresso personally delivered to me by one of the monks sometime in the midafternoon. I want to thank the Trappist nuns in Vitorchiano who opened their convent to me for a visit of a few days in the summer of 2015, and especially Suora Gabriella, who made time to have two private conversations with me about monastic life, and Suora Fiat and Suora Maria Panagia, who kindly arranged for my visit. I am also grateful to Brandeis University for supporting my research.

One of the great pleasures of writing this book has been discovering the thick circle of friends that sustained Vittoria throughout her life; this has made me appreciate all the more the wonderful friends who enrich my own. I want to thank Sara Antonelli, Mary Bing, Jeffrey Blanchard, Glenda Carpio, Judith Clark, Sarah Cole, Ophelia Dahl, Barry Fifield, Carmela Vircilio Franklin, Deborah Greenman, Stefanie Heraeus, Bernhard Jussen, Joseph Koerner, Meg Koerner, Jhumpa Lahiri, Blyth Lord, Louis Menand, Paul Morrison, Ashley Pettus, Adam Philips, Rick Rambuss, Kellie

Robertson, Catherine Robson, Michal Safdie, Moshe Safdie, Alison Simmons, and Sara St. Antoine, for their precious gift of friendship. I also want to thank my siblings, Hannah Saujet, Jason Targoff, and Joshua Targoff, and my father, Michael Targoff, for their abiding love and support.

My last and greatest debt is to my immediate family. My husband, Stephen Greenblatt, has shown me what it means to speak to the larger world about the past, and to make that past matter. He has been my best interlocutor, and my most loving companion. My son, Harry, keeps me engaged in the present, and fills my daily life with joy. I am deeply grateful to them both (along with our beloved dog, Marcus) for making our home such a happy one.

I dedicate this book to my mother, Cheri Kamen Targoff, who is my real-life example of an extraordinary woman. She has been by my side from the very beginning, and has inspired me in ways far too numerous to list here.

INDEX

Page numbers in *italics* refer to illustrations.

ILLUSTRATION CREDITS

Illustrations in the Text

p. 5: © The British Library Board, 09/05/2017, General Reference Collection DRT Digital Store 11426.aa.18

p. 7: Reproduction courtesy of Archivio Colonna, Biblioteca del Monastero di Santa Scolastica, Subiaco

p. 12: Image courtesy of Libreria Imagaenaria, Ischia

p. 19: Image courtesy of Lisa Kaborycha. © 2011. Reprinted by permission of Pearson Education, Inc., New York, NY

p. 27: Image and reproduction courtesy of KHM-Museumsverband, Vienna

p. 38: Photo © Städel Museum–U. Edelmann–ARTOTHEK

p. 62: Image and reproduction courtesy of KHM-Museumsverband, Vienna

p. 79: Image and reproduction courtesy of the Gabinetto Fotografico delle Gallerie degli Uffizi, Florence

p. 93, left and right: Image and reproduction courtesy of the Gabinetto Fotografico delle Gallerie degli Uffizi, Florence

p. 118: Image and reproduction courtesy of the Gabinetto Fotografico delle Gallerie degli Uffizi, Florence

p. 124: Image and reproduction courtesy of Bridgeman Images

p. 137: © RMN-Grand Palais / Art Resource, NY

p. 161: *IC5 C7191R 1538, Houghton Library, Harvard University

p. 184: © Madrid, Museo Nacional del Prado

p. 189: Image and reproduction courtesy of the Isabella Stewart Gardner Museum, Boston

p. 191: © Trustees of the British Museum

p. 193: Photo © Associazione Metamorfosi, Rome

p. 197: 2017 © Biblioteca Apostolica Vaticana

p. 232: Image and reproduction courtesy of the Gabinetto Fotografico delle Gallerie degli Uffizi, Florence

p. 234: © Accademia di Belle Arti Tadini, Lovere, Archivio Fotografico

p. 287: Image and reproduction courtesy of the Galleria Colonna, Rome

Illustrations in the Plate Section (following page 150)

1. Image and reproduction courtesy of KHM-Museumsverband, Vienna

2. Digital image courtesy of the Getty's Open Content Program

3. Photo courtesy of John Palcewski

4. © RMN-Grand Palais / Art Resource, NY

5. 2017 © Photo Archive–Fondazione Musei Civici di Venezia

6. Image and reproduction courtesy of the Gabinetto Fotografico delle Gallerie degli Uffizi, Florence

7. Image and reproduction courtesy of the Museu Nacional d'Art de Catalunya, Barcelona

8. Digital image courtesy of the Getty's Open Content Program

9. Photo: Scala / Art Resource, NY

10. Courtesy National Gallery of Art, Washington, D.C.

11. Image and reproduction courtesy Museo e Real Bosco di Capodimonte - Ministero dei Beni e delle Attività Culturali e del Turismo, Naples

12. Image and reproduction courtesy of the Gabinetto Fotografico delle Gallerie degli Uffizi, Florence

13. Courtesy National Museums Liverpool, Walker Art Gallery

14. Copyright © Galerie Hans, Hamburg

15. Image and reproduction courtesy of the Gabinetto Fotografico delle Gallerie degli Uffizi, Florence

16. Foto © Musei Vaticani

17. Image and reproduction courtesy of the Gabinetto Fotografico delle Gallerie degli Uffizi, Florence

18. Photo © The State Hermitage Museum / photo by Vladimir Terebenin

19. Image and reproduction courtesy of the Galleria Colonna, Rome

Printed in the USA
CPSIA information can be obtained
at www.ICGtesting.com
LVHW090800150724
785511LV00004B/318

9 780374 538224

Girolamo Fracastoro, came from Verona to see her. Fracastoro became famous for proposing a theory of disease based on the spreading of germs—some three hundred years before Louis Pasteur—and for his groundbreaking study of syphilis, a disease that he himself named. When he examined Vittoria, however, he found no trace of contagious disease, or of any physical ailment.

In an unusually frank letter that Fracastoro sent to her secretary Gualteruzzi upon returning to Verona, he declared that Vittoria's problems were not strictly physical. "Concerning the state of the most illustrious Marchesa of Pescara," he wrote,

> This, as you know, is my opinion, that as the body when it tyrannizes over the mind ruins and destroys all its soundness, so in the same way when the mind becomes the tyrant, and not merely the true lord, it wastes and destroys the soundness of the body first, and then their common bond of union . . . I have put forward this little discourse, my Lord, because I fancy that all of the Marchesa's sufferings had their origin in this.

"All of the Marchesa's sufferings had their origin in this": Vittoria's illness, he declared, began in her mind. The circumstances of Vittoria's life thankfully bore little resemblance to those of Shakespeare's Lady Macbeth, but Macbeth's questions to the physician attending on his wife resonate powerfully with Fracastoro's diagnosis:

> Canst thou not minister to a mind diseased,
> Pluck from the memory a rooted sorrow,
> Raze out the written troubles of the brain,
> And with some sweet oblivious antidote
> Cleanse the stuffed bosom of that perilous stuff
> Which weighs upon the heart?

The physician's response to Macbeth was a resounding no. "Therein," he said, "the patient / Must minister to himself."

saw your letter, in which I seemed to hear your voice and spirit speak to me, I needed to say: it is enough for me, and praised be to God that my cousin and dear friend lives.

Marguerite's fear that Vittoria might be dead was not entirely unfounded. Vittoria had become very ill in the spring of 1543, and it was not clear she would survive. The cause of her illness was unknown. It was not simply her usual ailment, catarrh, which had been plaguing her for many years, but something more serious. In June 1543, the humanist scholar Claudio Tolomei wrote to Giuseppe Cincio, a well-known physician who was taking care of Vittoria in Viterbo, to inquire after her health:

I am exceedingly distressed about the illness of the Marchesa of Pescara of which you write to me, as she is one of the women who ought to be revered by all, because having collected within her so much virtue, and goodness, and worth, and above all, because in these corrupt times she has done so many good works in the service of Christ . . . I beg you, Messer Giuseppe, to do everything in your power for the health of so noble a lady.

Less than two weeks later, the situation had improved, and Tolomei wrote to Cincio again to express his relief: "I am delighted to find from your letters that she is gradually recovering from her illness, for let me remind you, Messer Giuseppe, that in her life is bound up that of many others, who are continually sustained by her both in body and soul."

Vittoria was well enough to return to Rome sometime toward the end of that year, and in a letter that Bembo sent to Gualteruzzi in November, he described his great pleasure in hearing that "the Signora Marchesa has had a change of air, and vigorously ridden her horse [from Viterbo] to Rome, which," he added, "I take as a sign that her condition has improved and [that] she has regained her strength." By the summer of 1544, however, she was once again in a perilous state. At this point, one of the most celebrated doctors of the Renaissance,